First Peter

by

D. Edmond Hiebert

MOODY PRESS

CHICAGO

Library of Congress Cataloging in Publication Data

Wiebert, D. Edmond (David Edmond), 1910-
  First Peter.

  Bibliography: p. 313
  Includes indexes.
  1. Bible. N.T. Peter, 1st—Commentaries. I. Bible.
N.T. Peter, 1st. English. American Standard. 1984.
II. Title. III. Title: 1 Peter.
BS2795.3.H54 1984   227'.9207   83-24947
ISBN: 0-8024-0275-5

        1 2 3 4 5 6 7 Printing/EB/Year 89 88 87 86 85 84

Printed in the United States of America

Contents

Preface

Throughout the ages, the first epistle of Peter has challenged the hearts and molded the lives of God's people. Its profound message of hope amid Christian suffering is as timely now as it was in Peter's day.

This interpretation seeks to bring out Peter's message for the diligent student who wishes to delve into the riches of the inspired Word of God. The English text quoted is the *American Standard Version* (1901). That translation, deliberately chosen because of its close adherence to the Greek, offers the best bridge back to the original. Though the commentary is based on a study of the Greek text of 1 Peter, it is intended for students who may not be proficient in that language. Therefore, all Greek words and phrases have been transliterated and, generally, placed in parentheses, with the translation appearing in the immediate context.

A detailed outline of 1 Peter appears at the beginning and has been inserted into the exposition throughout. That outline will aid the student in tracing the rich message of Peter's letter.

My interest in and personal study of 1 Peter goes back many years. It first gripped my heart as a teenaged Christian. It has been the center of repeated personal study since then. My indebtedness to many sources will be readily evident from the footnotes and the bibliography. In the footnotes I have endeavored to give full recognition to the many sources that have contributed to my understanding of this epistle that contains "some things hard to be understood" (2 Pet. 3:16).

Special thanks are due to *Bibliotheca Sacra* for permission to use material in five expository articles prepared for that esteemed quarterly. Thanks are also due to *Studia Missionalia* for use of material in a study prepared for their 1980 annual volume.

1

An Introduction to 1 Peter

First Peter has called forth numerous warm expressions of admiration and praise. E. F. Scott called it "one of the most beautiful writings in the New Testament,"[1] and William Barclay characterized it as "one of the easiest letters in the New Testament to read, for it has never lost its winsome appeal to the human heart."[2] Selwyn called it "a microcosm of Christian faith and duty, the model of a pastoral charge,"[3] and Von Soden stamped "this short, impressive letter [as] one of the most precious monuments of primitive Christianity, a jewel of the New Testament worthy to be inscribed with the name of the great Apostle."[4]

First Peter is preeminently an epistle of triumphant faith amid suffering. It exultantly proclaims the Christ-centered hope of the believer in the midst of an unbelieving and antagonistic world. It contains "some of the most vivid expressions of Christian hope, ennobling ethical admonitions and challenges to courage in suffering to be found in the New Testament."[5] As such, 1 Peter may appropriately be designated "the Epistle of the living hope," for it "breathes a spirit of undaunted courage and exhibits as noble a type of piety as can be found in any writing of the New Testament outside the gospels."[6] Down

1. Ernest Findlay Scott, *The Literature of the New Testament*, p. 217.
2. William Barclay, *The Letters of James and Peter*, p. 164.
3. Edward Gordon Selwyn, *The First Epistle of St. Peter*, p. 1.
4. Quoted in Homer Kinsley Ebright, *The Petrine Epistles, A Critical Study of Authorship*, p. 38.
5. Donald J. Selby, *Introduction to the New Testament*, p. 435.
6. J. W. C. Wand, *The General Epistles of St. Peter and St. Jude*, p. 164.

through the ages, the persecuted church has always treasured it as a priceless possession.

THE AUTHORSHIP OF 1 PETER

TRADITIONAL ACCEPTANCE

There is no evidence that the early church had any doubts concerning the Petrine authorship of 1 Peter. In his famous *Ecclesiastical History* (published in A.D. 325), Eusebius of Caesarea placed it among the homologoumena (III. 25), the books accepted by the whole church. There is no indication that he knew any other view. He explicitly says it "was anciently used by the ancient fathers in their writings, as an undoubted work of the apostle" (III.3).[7] Lumby remarks, "Heretics, no less than the faithful, regarded it as a portion of authoritative Christian literature."[8]

Apparently, the first known quotations from 1 Peter are found in *The Epistle of Clement of Rome to the Corinthians* (written c. A.D. 96). Clement's language reflects the vocabulary of 1 Peter, but his quotations are made indirectly with no indication of source. Though some of his language may well have been derived from the common teaching of the church, other parts seem clearly to indicate that he was drawing from 1 Peter.

According to Eusebius, Papias (c. A.D. 60-130),[9] Bishop of Hierapolis in Phrygia, in his *Exposition of Dominical Oracles* (five volumes, c. A.D. 110), "made use of testimonies from the First Epistle of John, and likewise from that of Peter."[10] But Eusebius does not inform us whether Papias quoted Peter by name or used quotations from 1 Peter without naming his source. Unfortunately, the writings of Papias have been lost.

In his *Epistle to the Philippians*, Polycarp (martyred c. A.D. 155-60) made numerous quotations from 1 Peter. Though his letter is steeped in the language of the Petrine epistle, he did not cite Peter by name. As a rule, Polycarp did not make it a practice to name his authorities (he mentioned Paul in the epistle because Paul had also written to the Philippian church).

Irenaeus, Bishop of Lyons in Gaul, in his famous work *Against the Heresies* (c. A.D. 180), is the first known patristic writer to specify Peter as the author of the epistle. His younger contemporary, Tertullian, likewise identified the author as Peter (*De Oratione*, c. A.D. 200-206). According to Eusebius (*Eccl. Hist.* VI.14), Clement of Alexandria (c. A.D. 150-220) wrote a commentary on 1 Peter.

The rather scanty patristic evidence establishes that 1 Peter was known and used as an authoritative work before the close of the first century, though we

---

7. *The Ecclesiastical History of Eusebius Pamphilus.*
8. J. Rawson Lumby, *The Epistles of St. Peter*, p. 671.
9. The dates used are those given in *The New International Dictionary of the Christian Church* (*NIDCC*), ed. J. D. Douglas.
10. Eusebius, *Ecclesiastical History*, 3:39.

possess no specific identification of its Petrine authorship before the last quarter of the second century. The very fact that the epistle was used so early as an authoritative work without naming its author may well indicate that its Petrine authorship was accepted as self-evident. The language of 1 Peter is reflected in the writings of the early Christians, and the church used it in the battle against false teachings.

INTERNAL DATA

What the epistle itself says about the writer is limited but precise. The opening salutation explicitly identifies him as "Peter, an apostle of Jesus Christ" (1:1). In 5:1 he calls himself "a fellow-elder, and witness of the sufferings of Christ." Selwyn remarked, "This impression of eyewitness runs through the Epistle, and gives it a distinctive character."[11] In 5:13 the writer referred to Mark as "my son," a reference that is consistent with the ancient tradition that identifies Mark as Peter's "interpreter."[12]

The claim of Petrine authorship agrees remarkably with two observations: (1) The epistle contains a number of analogies with the discourses of Peter in Acts,[13] and (2) beneath the surface, the epistle reveals clear connections with the gospels.[14] First Peter does not verbally reproduce the words of Jesus, but it does contain clear echoes of His sayings. It also seems to reflect gospel events in which Peter had a prominent part. The appeal to the readers to "gird yourselves with humility" (5:5) naturally relates to the writer's vivid memory of the scene in the Upper Room (John 13:3-11). And the appeal to the elders to "shepherd the beloved flock of God" (5:2)[15] relates to the scene in John 21:15-17. It is unmistakably clear that the passion and resurrection of Christ made a deep impression on the writer (1:3; 3:18; 4:1; 5:1).

CRITICAL ATTACKS

Attacks on Petrine authorship commenced with F. C. Baur (1762-1860), leader of the "Tübingen School" of German radical biblical criticism. Doubts concerning the traditional view are based almost entirely on internal grounds and relate to several areas.

Its good Greek. Petrine authorship is rejected on the ground that "the Epistle is written in excellent Greek, of which Peter, the Galilean, who for

---

11. Selwyn, p. 28.
12. Eusebius, 3:39.
13. Compare 1 Pet. 1:10-12 with Acts 3:18; 1:20 with 2:23; 2:4 with 4:11; 3:22 with 2:33-34; the use of the distinctive term *xulon* ("wood") in 2:24 with Acts 5:30 and 10:39. Selwyn, pp. 33-36.
14. Compare 1 Pet. 3:9, 14, 17; 4:14 with Matt. 5:10-12 and Luke 6:22; 1:13 with Luke 12:35; 2:12 with Matt. 5:16; 4:10 with Luke 12:42. See further R. H. Gundry, "'Verba Christi' in I Peter: Their Implications Concerning the Authorship of I Peter and the Authenticity of the Gospel Tradition," pp. 336-50.
15. Joseph Bryant Rotherham, *The Emphasized New Testament.*

most of his life had never been outside of Palestine, would not have been capable."[16] Guthrie replies that such an argument gives more weight to Peter's background as a fisherman than is really justified and goes on to say, "At the most conservative dating of this Epistle an interval of more than thirty years separated Peter the writer from Peter the fisherman, and who can measure what facility he might have achieved over so long a period?"[17]

Any suggestion that Greek was a foreign language to Peter, a Galilean, and that he still needed an interpreter in Rome to translate his Aramaic is unwarranted. Zahn remarked, "The idea that Mark performed the office of an interpreter, translating Peter's Aramaic discourses into Greek, or what is still more impossible, his Greek sermons into Latin, cannot be held by anyone having any knowledge at all of language conditions in the apostolic age."[18]

As a fisherman, Peter doubtless could speak Greek. Galilee was a bilingual country, and Peter must have known enough Greek to carry on his business activities. The quality of Greek used by the Galilean Jews would depend on their education. Other New Testament writers who were natives of Galilee knew Greek. Matthew had a good command of that language, and James, who as far as we know never left Palestine, wrote effective Greek. Moulton asserted that they "would write as men who had used that language from boyhood, not as foreigners painfully expressing themselves in an imperfectly known idiom."[19] Even to the strict Jews of Jerusalem, the stronghold of Aramaic, the use of Greek was not forbidden. In fact, there were Hellenistic Jews in Jerusalem who were unfamiliar with Aramaic. Thus, during the early years of his work there, in dealing with the Hellenistic element in the early church, Peter would have needed to use Greek. And when he began work in the Greek Diaspora, Peter must have cultivated its use more intensively.

The excellence of the Greek in 1 Peter must not be exaggerated. It cannot be compared with the Greek of the literary masters. The constructions used in 1 Peter are quite simple. The writer's limitations are evident from his meager use of particles and prepositions and an excessive use of relative clauses. But the language of the epistle is grammatically correct and idiomatic.

Guthrie concludes that "it cannot be asserted that Peter *could* not have written this Epistle on the grounds of language and style."[20] But many scholars, even among those favorable to Petrine authorship, believe that the language of the book is better Greek than we might have expected from the apostle. Kelly, who leans toward Petrine authorship, remarks that "the writer does deploy a limited range of rhetorical conventions, and has evidently had a technical training which we could not plausibly attribute to Peter."[21] The fact that the optative mood, which was scarcely used in the vernacular, is employed

16. Scott, p. 220.
17. Donald Guthrie, *New Testament Introduction*, p. 778.
18. Theodor Zahn, *Introduction to the New Testament*, 2:443.
19. James Hope Moulton, *A Grammar of New Testament Greek*, 1:8.
20. Ibid., p. 778.
21. J. N. D. Kelly, *A Commentary on the Epistles of Peter and of Jude*, p. 31.

three times (1:2; 3:14, 17) suggests that the author had some acquaintance with literary Greek. Indeed, there are some traces of classical Greek vocabulary in the epistle.[22]

That anomaly is commonly explained by recognizing that Silvanus (5:12) was more than a mere amanuensis; he had a share in the formulation of the language itself. The statement "By Silvanus, our faithful brother, as I account *him*, I have written unto you," has often been understood to denote the bearer of the letter.[23] But it is generally held that Peter's remark relates to the *composition*, not the transmission of the letter. However, the two viewpoints need not be mutually exclusive. Selwyn maintained both.[24] Zahn thought it improbable that Peter would have referred to Silvanus as "our faithful brother, as I account *him*," if he was employed simply to take Peter's dictation. He insisted that Peter's commendation of Silvanus could only be explained on the assumption "that Silvanus' part in the composition was so important and so large that its performance required a considerable degree of trustworthiness."[25] Selwyn saw a close connection between 1 Peter and 2 Thessalonians and concluded that Silvanus was associated with both letters.[26] Our knowledge of Silvanus indicates that he was a man who would have been able to give such stylistic touches to the epistle. He was a Jew, an esteemed member of the Jerusalem church (Acts 15:22), and a Roman citizen (Acts 16:37). He was one of the two men chosen for the delicate task of conveying and explaining the decree of the Jerusalem Conference to the Gentile Christians (Acts 15: 22, 32). Paul recognized him as a fit co-worker for his mission among the Gentiles (Acts 15:40). Thus, at an early date, he was associated with that mission.

Frequently, ancient scribes were allowed considerable freedom in composing the message entrusted to them.[27] Silvanus's relation to 1 Peter may account for the stylistic features that cannot be attributed to Peter. Though that hypothesis has not been incontestably established, Guthrie concludes that it "cannot be ruled out, and forms a reasonable alternative for those whose main objection to Petrine authorship is linguistic."[28] But such an hypothesis should not be overstated so that Silvanus appears as the real author of the epistle.

Its quotations from the Septuagint. Petrine authorship is rejected on the grounds that "the OT quotations and allusions originate without exception

22. A. H. McNeile, *An Introduction to the Study of the New Testament*, p. 220, n. 1; W. C. van Unnik, "A Classical Parallel to 1 Peter ii. 14 and 20," pp. 198-202.

23. John Calvin, *The First and Second Epistle of Peter*, p. 322; Henry Alford, *The New Testament for English Readers*, p. 1668; A. F. Mitchell, *Hebrews and the General Epistles*, p. 284; J. Merle Rife, *The Nature and Origin of the New Testament*, p. 121.

24. Selwyn, p. 241.

25. Zahn, 2:150.

26. Selwyn, pp. 9-17, 369-84.

27. But J. N. Sevenster, *Do You Know Greek?*, insists that did not often happen and asserts that "not one single irrefutably clear example of such is to be found in the New Testament. Tertius (Rom. 16:22) is definitely not one and Silvanus is, to say the least of it, doubtful" (p. 12).

28. Guthrie, p. 780.

from the LXX," and that is thought to be "inconceivable" for "a Galilean fisherman, Peter."[29] But such a criticism places too much emphasis on Peter's Galilean background and gives inadequate recognition to the fact that the Septuagint was used regularly in mission work with Gentiles. It must certainly have been used by the Greek-speaking members of the Jerusalem church. At the Jerusalem Conference James, the Lord's brother (who was certainly as Galilean as Peter), quoted from the Septuagint to reinforce his point (Acts 15:15-18). Justin Martyr, who grew up in Samaria in the early days of the second century, depended entirely upon the Septuagint in his writings.

Its strong "Paulinism". Petrine authorship is rejected because "the thought of the Epistle . . . is saturated with Pauline influence."[30] Supposedly, a leading spirit like Peter could not have been as dependent on Pauline thought as the writer reveals himself to be. He seems so imbued with Pauline words and phrases that he uses them unconsciously,[31] borrowing especially from Romans and Ephesians.[32]

But such traces of Pauline influence do not necessarily invalidate Petrine authorship. If 1 Peter was written from Rome, it would be natural to assume that Peter would have read Paul's letter to the Romans, "already a treasured possession of the Roman church at the time of the writing of 1 Peter."[33] And Ephesians, whose recipients were certainly included in the circle of churches addressed in 1 Peter, would also have been readily available to Peter. If Peter had recently read those letters, the use of similar thoughts and expressions in his own letter is quite understandable. According to Bigg,

> There can be little doubt that St. Peter had read several of St. Paul's Epistles. In the Second Epistle (iii. 16) he tells us so; and even if the Second Epistle is regarded as a forgery, it lies in the nature of things that each apostle would desire to know what the other was doing, and would take pains to keep himself informed.[34]

The view that Peter's letter would reflect the impression that Paul's had made upon him is consistent with Peter's impressionable nature. Characteristically, Peter was a man of action, rather than a deep thinker like Paul. The incident in Galatians 2:11-22, for example, reveals him to be a man readily susceptible to outside influences. And the strong personality and fertile mind of Paul would have left positive impressions on Peter.

But the alleged dependence of 1 Peter on the Pauline epistles should not be

29. Werner Georg Kümmel, *Introduction to the New Testament*, p. 423.

30. Scott, p. 220.

31. Francis Wright Beare, *The First Epistle of Peter*, p. 44.

32. For a list of parallels see Charles Bigg, *A Critical and Exegetical Commentary on the Epistles of St. Peter and St. Jude*, pp. 16-20.

33. Robert W. Crapps, Edgar V. McKnight, David A. Smith, *Introduction to the New Testament*, p. 420.

34. Bigg, p. 15.

overdrawn. Bigg's examination of the parallels led him to conclude, "In the case of Romans as in that of Ephesians the resemblances to 1 Peter are quite superficial, attaching only to current commonplaces."[35] Recent scholarship insists that Petrine affinities with Pauline epistles do not demand literary dependence. Kelly maintains, "It seems easier and more natural to conclude that the agreements of Ephesians and 1 Peter are evidence of a shared tradition working independently on the two writers."[36] According to Martin, recent studies indicate that the common matter "relates mainly to liturgical interest (e.g., 1 Pet. 1:3ff.; Eph. 1:3ff.) and that the closeness of the parallels may best be accounted for by the access of both writers to a common fund of liturgical and catechetical material."[37]

On the other hand, it is unwarranted to charge Peter with being unoriginal. He was no mere copyist. He was a man with a mind of his own, quite capable of presenting his thoughts in his own way. Indeed, the differences between Paul and Peter are more striking than the resemblances. Hunter maintains that "there are such decided differences between 1 Peter and the Pauline epistles as to make any case for dependence extremely precarious."[38] Whatever material may have been borrowed has passed through the author's own mind, and he has made it his very own. Thus, the alleged "Paulinism" of the epistle is not convincing evidence against its Petrine origin.

Its meager references to the Spirit. According to Beare, "the meagreness of the references to the doctrine of the Spirit" is a fatal objection to Petrine authorship. He argues that "it is impossible to believe that any important leader of that early period could have written about the moral life of Christians without paying any attention at all to the transforming power of the Spirit."[39]

But the basic assumption of that argument cannot be sustained from the actual evidence in the writings of Paul himself. In Colossians, which has much to say about the moral life of believers, there is only one passing reference to the Holy Spirit (1:8). Second Thessalonians, which makes a strong appeal for conduct becoming a Christian, has only one reference to the work of the Holy Spirit in believers (2:13). Yet, there are four references to the Holy Spirit in 1 Peter. First Peter 1:2 refers to the Spirit's work as basic to the salvation described in verses 3-12. In 1:11 the Spirit is said to have indwelt the Old Testament prophets. And in 1:12 His coming from heaven is connected with the transforming preaching of the gospel. Finally, in 4:14 the Spirit is said to rest on the readers in their suffering. Such strategic references to the Spirit in 1 Peter suggest that Beare's claim is a strained attempt to support his own presuppositions.

35. Ibid., p. 20.

36. Kelly, p. 14.

37. Ralph P. Martin, *New Testament Foundations: A Guide for Christian Students*, 2:332.

38. Archibald M. Hunter and Elmer G. Homrighausen, *The First Epistle of Peter*, p. 79.

39. Beare, p. 42.

Its lack of personal reminiscences. Objection to Petrine authorship is also based on the ground that the epistle lacks personal reminiscences of Jesus. Kümmel asserts that 1 Peter "contains no evidence at all of familiarity with the earthly Jesus, his life, his teaching, and his death, but makes reference only in a general way to the 'sufferings' of Christ."[40] According to Kümmel, that is "scarcely conceivable" for the apostle Peter.

Hunter replies that such a claim "is simply not true," and, furthermore, that the main purpose of 1 Peter was "not to reveal the writer's knowledge of Jesus, but to fortify a suffering church."[41] Ebright, in fact, cites thirty-two passages in 1 Peter that find equivalents in the teachings of Jesus and concludes that they definitely prove the writer's acquaintance with Him.[42] Contrary to Kümmel, it is amazing that the writer managed to reflect so much of the life and teaching of Jesus in such a brief hortatory letter!

Its picture of the persecution. Opponents of Petrine authorship maintain that the letter reflects official Roman persecution of Christians such as did not develop until far beyond the lifetime of Peter. Beare, a leading advocate of the position, argues that the situation in 4:12-16 reflects a time when being a Christian was a crime. Thus, he identifies the persecution in 1 Peter with that revealed in the letter of Pliny the Younger to the Emperor Trajan (A.D. 98-117).[43]

But that identification seems to read too much into the reference to suffering "as a Christian" (4:16). Suffering "for the Name" (4:14) was known to Christ's followers from the very beginning (Acts 5:41). Pliny's letter itself indicates that sporadic persecutions had caused some people to renounce their faith as much as a quarter of a century earlier. Persecution is mentioned four times in 1 Peter (1:6-7; 3:13-17; 4:12-19; 5:9), but there is no hint that martyrdom or even torture (both of which are clearly mentioned in Pliny's letter) had yet been inflicted on the readers. Nor is there any indication that the persecution of Christians described by Pliny was worldwide. Yet, 1 Peter 5:9 clearly shows that the sufferings the readers were called on to endure were liable to befall believers everywhere. The "fiery trial" (4:12) and the possibility of suffering "as a Christian" (4:16) need not imply a persecution essentially different in kind from those experienced by Paul and Barnabas on their first missionary journey (Acts 13:44—14:20) or by Paul and Silas on the second (Acts 16:19—17:15).

It is more likely that the persecution in view in 1 Peter was privately and locally inspired, rather than due to official governmental policy. In 1:6-7 the readers were called upon to rejoice amid the trials they were experiencing, and 3:13-17 reminded them that if they had to suffer for righteousness's sake, they should endure such suffering with humility and be ready to explain their faith

40. Kümmel, p. 424.
41. Hunter, p. 79.
42. Ebright, pp. 50-55.
43. Beare, pp. 26-27, 32-35.

to their persecutors. Kelly believes that the language in 4:12-19 "is at least equally compatible with petty persecutions before civic magistrates."[44] The suffering can be explained as the result of spasmodic outbursts of ill will and pagan fanaticism against Christians, for widespread popular prejudice and false charges made them odious in the eyes of their pagan neighbors. The common suspicion of Christians and the brutal way they were treated by the local population enabled Nero to use them as scapegoats for the incendiarism in Rome (A.D. 64). Thus, it appears that the persecution in 1 Peter has no special connection with an official Roman policy against Christians but is consistent with the type of persecution Christians experienced in Peter's lifetime.

CRITICAL ALTERNATIVES

As we have seen, external evidence supports Petrine authorship of the epistle. The letter claims such authorship, and its contents are consistent with that claim. Critical arguments opposed to it are insufficient to compel its abandonment. Nevertheless, we should note alternative theories to Petrine authorship.

A pseudonymous letter. Kümmel (who rejects Petrine authorship) asserts that "1 Peter is undoubtedly a pseudonymous writing."[45] That hypothesis is a natural alternative for those who reject the epistle's own claim. But since tradition has not associated another name with the authorship of the book, the matter is purely conjectural. And the various guesses that have been made have received scant support.

Beare categorically states that the name *Peter* is a pseudonym but maintains that no fraudulent purpose was involved in the production of such a pseudonymous letter.[46] "The Christians of Asia Minor," he says, "must have known that Peter was long since dead. . . . They would recognize the pseudonym for what it was—an accepted and harmless literary device, employed by a teacher who is more concerned for the Christian content of his message than for the assertion of his own claims to authority."[47]

But it is not at all certain that the original readers would knowingly accept such a pseudepigraph as a valid work. Guthrie notes, "F. Torm has demonstrated that early Christian epistolary pseudepigrapha were so rare that this cannot possibly be regarded as a conventional form, and, if it was not, the main basis of this type of theory collapses."[48]

That the Asian Christian leaders, Polycarp and Papias, would regard it as a harmless device and accept the epistle as authoritative (if they knew that it

44. Kelly, p. 29.
45. Kümmel, p. 424.
46. Beare, pp. 44, 48.
47. Ibid., p. 48.
48. Guthrie, p. 788. See also pp. 671-84, "Appendix C, Epistolary Pseudepigraphy."

was written long after Peter's death) seems highly doubtful. Those men were keenly conscious of the unbridgeable difference between the original apostles and themselves. What would have led them to accept as authoritative a later work that spuriously claimed to speak for one of the original twelve?

The hypothetical pseudonymous writer would have to have been a man closely related to his readers. But since his purpose was to encourage his fellow Christians, why did he not appeal to them on the basis of his *own* concern, rather than hide under a fictitious apostolic claim? Since the letter was not written to denounce any threatening heresy or to sanction any peculiar doctrine, there was no need to claim apostolic authority. Furthermore, why would a pseudo-Peter introduce the unnecessary difficulty of making Mark and Silvanus Peter's special companions, when elsewhere they are associated with Paul?

The difficulty of establishing 1 Peter as pseudonymous has resulted in a compromise view.

An anonymous letter later ascribed to Peter. Some argue that 1 Peter was originally an anonymous homily beginning with "Blessed be the God and Father of our Lord Jesus Christ" (1:3), that it circulated as an anonymous treatise during the second century, and that late in the second century, when the canon was forming, Peter's name was attached to guarantee its apostolicity.[49] A later editor added the opening salutation (1:1-2) and the conclusion (5:12-14), thus giving it the sanction of an apostolic letter. Supposedly, that explains why 1 Peter was known to the early patristic writers but was not quoted by them as Petrine.

Beare well remarks, "This hypothesis . . . has no positive evidence to support it, and very little to commend it."[50] Scott accepted the theory but admitted, "The attribution to Peter must have been due to some misunderstanding, but how it arose we cannot now discover."[51] We must agree with Walls when he remarks, "Such suggestions smack of despair."[52]

If Peter was not the original author, it would have been more probable, due to its Pauline flavor, to have ascribed the epistle to Paul. If the epilogue (5:12-14) was not an original part of the writing, why would a second century editor create the difficulty of bringing Silvanus and Mark into the picture? If those verses are merely an editor's effort to give the homily an epistolary framework, would it not have been more natural for him to name Mark rather than Silvanus as the intermediary? Kümmel asserts, "The supposition that the epistolary framework (1:1f; 5:12-14) has been added subsequently to 1:3—5:11 is contradicted by the evidence that this framework manifests clear points of

49. So A. Harnack, *Die Chronologie der altchristlichen Literatur bis Eusebius*, 1:451-65. See Beare, p. 24; Andrew F. Walls, "Introduction," in Alan M. Stibbs, *The First Epistle General of Peter*, p. 21, n. 3.

50. Beare, p. 43.

51. Scott, p. 221.

52. Walls and Stibbs, p. 21.

connection with the letter corpus itself (cf. 1:1 with 1:17; 2:11 and 5:12 with 4:12)."[53]

The supposition that someone would later dare to add the salutation and conclusion to an already well-known anonymous work is highly questionable. No one dared to add an opening salutation to the anonymous epistle to the Hebrews, though various conjectures were made concerning its authorship. The fact that Clement of Rome and Polycarp did not specify Peter by name in their quotations from 1 Peter does not prove that they only knew it as an anonymous work. Clement quoted or alluded to some twenty-two books of the New Testament without naming his authority. Though he quoted Paul without naming him, he certainly knew that Paul was the author of the letters he quoted. We may confidently accept that he also knew the identity of the writer when he quoted from 1 Peter. Apparently, the Petrine authorship of the epistle was accepted as self-evident.

Guthrie concludes his careful survey of the various theories concerning the authorship of 1 Peter with the restrained remark, "The result of this survey of various theories leaves us in no doubt that the traditional view which accepts the claims of the Epistle to be apostolic is more reasonable than any alternative hypothesis."[54] We fully agree.

THE UNITY AND FORM OF 1 PETER

UNITY

The unity of 1 Peter is denied by those who regard it as an anonymous homily and postulate that 1:1-2 and 5:12-14 were later added to give it the appearance of a letter. Such an attempt to strip off the "epistolary framework" is unwarranted and has gained little support. And such a truncation of the epistle does not eliminate the clear, personal, apostolic reference to the writer in 5:1.

Others propose to divide the document into two independent parts, ending the first part at 4:11.[55] They point out that there are two doxologies (4:11; 5:11), each of which would provide an appropriate ending to its own division, and that 4:12 readily marks a new beginning. They also appeal to the view of suffering in the two parts as evidence against the unity of the epistle. Allegedly, the first part speaks only of the possibility of suffering, but the second describes suffering as a present, serious reality.

But 4:11 does not disprove the unity of 1 Peter. Similar doxologies occur in Romans 11:33-36 and Ephesians 3:20-21. It is understandable that to conclude a train of thought that has deeply stirred him, an author would attach an ascription of praise.

53. Kümmel, pp. 420-21.

54. Guthrie, p. 790.

55. Burnett Hillman Streeter, *The Primitive Church*, pp. 122-24, 128. See the summary of the arguments in Martin, p. 339.

The two parts of the epistle do not necessarily present different pictures of suffering. Beare's assertion that the suffering spoken of in the first part is an "ever-present possibility" and that the last section speaks "in specific terms of a persecution which is actually raging"[56] overstates the evidence. The picture of suffering in both parts is essentially the same. In 1:6 it is more akin to that in 4:12 than to that in 3:17. Though it is possible that the more intense picture of suffering in the latter part of the letter reflects new and disturbing information about the situation of the readers, that assumption seems unnecessary in the light of 1:6.

Kelly maintains that the picture of suffering is actually one clue to the unity of the epistle. He notes that suffering "is hinted at as early as i. 5 ('kept safe by God's power'), is explicitly mentioned in such passages as i. 6; ii. 20f.; iii. 14-17; iv. 4, as well as iv. 12-19; v. 6-10, and throughout is the motive prompting all the writer's exhortations, appeals for exemplary conduct, and glowing delineations of Christ's victory over evil powers and the baptized Christian's share in it."[57] Its picture of suffering, therefore, provides no solid ground for denying the unity of the epistle.

Kelly points to further evidence in support of the unity of 1 Peter.

> The themes in the several parts are exactly the same (it is better to suffer for doing right than the reverse: iii. 17; iv. 15f.; brief tribulation to be succeeded by glory: i. 6f; v. 10; rejoicing in suffering: i. 6, 8; iv. 13f.); and the same strongly eschatological note is present everywhere (i. 20; iv. 5; 7; 17, etc.), the same threatening talk about those "who disobey the gospel."[58]

We conclude that the attempt to divide 1 Peter into two independent parts is improbable.

FORM

First Peter is a letter of exhortation addressed to a specific circle of churches. In his conclusion the writer expressly reminds his readers that he has been "exhorting and testifying" (5:12). We hear the earnest preacher clearly in 1 Peter. Though Peter undoubtedly incorporated previously used sermonic material, that does not militate against 1 Peter having the form and purpose of a letter.

Recent studies have paid special attention to certain features of the sermonic material. Reicke argues that those features can best be understood in the light of a public church service. He says, "On closer examination it is evident that First Peter is really a baptismal sermon in the form of an epistle,

---

56. Beare, p. 25.
57. Kelly, p. 20.
58. Ibid. See further William Joseph Dalton, *Christ's Proclamation to the Spirits*, pp. 62-71, for a defense of the unity of 1 Peter.

first directed to newly baptized people, i 1-iv 6, and after that to the congregation as a whole, iv 7-v 14."[59] A variant form of the liturgical hypothesis understands the book as the president's part for an Easter Baptism Eucharist.[60]

Though the liturgical hypothesis has evoked much recent discussion, Cranfield notes that it "has by no means met with general assent."[61] Arguments used to support the hypothesis have not been generally accepted as convincing.[62] Walls rightly points out that "baptism is less prominent in the Epistle than the discussions of recent years suggest."[63] In fact, it is directly mentioned only once (3:21), and then parenthetically. Other alleged allusions to baptism (1:3, 12, 23; 2:2, 10, 25) are questionable and may more naturally be explained without recourse to that hypothesis. Even granting the allusions to baptism, Klijn feels that it is "more plausible to assume that in his argument the author makes use of various notions that were usually mentioned on the occasion of baptism"[64] than to understand the letter liturgically as a record of a public baptismal ceremony.

Goodspeed granted that some parts of the epistle fit the liturgical theory but noted that "the address to servants, wives, and husbands and especially to preachers and deacons, 4:11, combined with the call to hospitality, 4:9, hardly suits a group of new converts."[65] The epistle witnesses to the radical break with the old life that conversion produced in Peter's readers. But baptism is not made prominent. In fact, we do not need to assume a baptismal setting to make sense of Peter's purpose of offering reassurance to readers who faced persecution. Dalton points out a further difficulty with the baptismal liturgy-homily theory, "We have no criteria for distinguishing such a literary genre at the end of the first century, much less in apostolic times. It is invalid to read back into this period the scattered references to Baptism found in later patristic writings."[66]

Dalton appropriately concludes his discussion of the literary genre of 1 Peter with the following note of warning.

Even if 1 Peter does incorporate a baptismal liturgy, one would never be justified in forgetting the intention and interests of the final author. Taken as a literary unit, a form which it reached through the work of the Holy Spirit in the process of inspiration, it is not actually a baptismal homily, but a letter. There is a danger that this important theological aspect of interpretation should be forgotten by the mod-

59. Bo Reicke, *The Epistles of James, Peter, and Jude,* p. 74.
60. F. L. Cross, *I Peter, A Pascal Liturgy.*
61. C. E. B. Cranfield, *I & II Peter and Jude,* p. 13.
62. Walls and Stibbs, pp. 58-63; C. F. D. Moule, "The Nature and Purpose of I Peter," p. 1-11.
63. A. F. Walls, "Peter, First Epistle of," *The New Bible Dictionary (NBD)*, ed. J. D. Douglas, p. 977a.
64. A. F. J. Klijn, *An Introduction to the New Testament,* p. 155.
65. Edgar J. Goodspeed, *An Introduction to the New Testament,* p. 285.
66. Dalton, p. 70.

ern scholar. In his legitimate zeal to discern the prehistory of a text, he may end up in a sort of exegetical fragmentation, forgetting the final and decisive value of the text as it stands.[67]

THE READERS OF 1 PETER

LOCATION

First Peter is a circular letter addressed to Christians residing in "Pontus, Galatia, Cappadocia, Asia, and Bithynia" (1:1). The concluding benediction, "Peace be unto you all that are in Christ" (5:14), shows that all Christians in those areas were addressed. Their organization as churches is clear from the fact that they were under the care of elders. Peter recognized his various readers as the flocks of Christ (5:1-3).

Whether the five place designations are to be taken in a political or geographical sense is not certain. If the terms are used as political designations, the area included would be considerably larger, since the Roman province of Galatia extended considerably farther south than the old geographical area of Galatia in central Asia Minor. The fact that Pontus and Bithynia had formed an administrative Roman province since 65 B.C. supports the geographical interpretation, though Peter mentioned them separately. On the other hand, Zahn pointed out that all the old geographical names were also used as Roman provinces; under that view Pontus might stand for Pontus Polemoniacus, the eastern section of the area of Pontus that remained under a Greek dynasty until A.D. 63.[68] Under either view Cilicia is clearly excluded; the churches in that area stood closely related to Syria and would have been under the watch-care of Antioch.

ORIGIN

Only the churches in the *provinces* of Galatia and Asia owed their origin, directly or indirectly, to the work of Paul (Acts 13:14—14:13; 19:8-10). According to the South Galatian theory, Paul did not found churches in the northern part of the *province* of Galatia. If Peter used *Galatia* in the old geographical sense, then the Galatian churches he addressed were not founded by Paul. That, then, limits the Pauline churches addressed by Peter to those in Asia, and then only indirectly, except for Ephesus. Therefore, broadly speaking, the churches Peter addressed were not founded by Paul. We have no certain information about their origin. That churches were early established in those regions is certain. The glowing missionary zeal of the early Christians caused the good news to spread rapidly and widely. Wand remarks, "In days when every Christian, whatever his trade or occupation, was necessarily a

---

67. Ibid., p. 71.
68. Zahn, 2:134, 151.

missionary many territories must have been evangelized without the aid of any outstanding leader."[69]

It is improbable that those churches owed their origin to the work of Peter. Peter's reference to those who "preached the gospel unto you" (1:12) seems to exclude the writer himself. Origen's comment that Peter had visited the churches[70] seems to be an inference drawn from the epistle itself. Some church members may have known Peter personally, and certainly they all knew about Peter. Whatever the origin of the churches, Peter would have seen no cause for any hesitancy in writing to them in their hour of need, for he would have considered it part of his commission to shepherd the flock of Christ (John 21:15-17).

BACKGROUND

In the first century A.D. the population of Asia Minor was highly heterogeneous. Though there were various cultural backgrounds, Greek was the *lingua franca*. Generally, the area was economically prosperous, though there was a wide disparity in the distribution of wealth between the landowners and merchants on the one hand and the working classes on the other. Since the epistle contains instructions for slaves (2:18-21) but no corresponding instructions for masters, it may reflect a membership largely drawn from the working classes. But the emphasis on the duties of citizenship (2:13-17), which would apply mainly to free men (cf. 2:16), points to members who were not slaves. Socially, those churches, like most New Testament churches, consisted of a mixed membership.

There are several ways to understand the racial background of the members. Origen[71] and many others[72] saw them as Jewish Christians. The description of the readers as "sojourners of the Dispersion" (1:1) has a strong Jewish coloring. The fact that the readers are described entirely in Old Testament terminology (2:9) seems to be further evidence. And Weiss insisted that the exclusive use of the Septuagint in the Old Testament quotations, as well as the very nature of the entire argument, would make the letter quite unintelligible to non-Jewish readers.[73] Finally, that identification of the recipients is consistent with Peter's position as minister to the circumcision (Gal. 2:10).

Though it is clear that the epistle was written from a Jewish point of view (a fact wholly consistent with its Petrine authorship), that does not prove the readers were Jewish Christians. The term *Dispersion* (used without an article)

69. Wand, p. 33.
70. According to Eusebius, 3:1.
71. Ibid.
72. Calvin, p. 230; John Albert Bengel, *New Testament Word Studies*, 2:727; Bernard Weiss, *A Manual of Introduction to the New Testament*, 2:137-44; Alford, p. 1628; E. Schuyler English, *The Life and Letters of Saint Peter*, pp. 152, 154-56; Kenneth S. Wuest, *First Peter. The Greek New Testament for the English Reader*, p. 14.
73. Weiss, 2:138-39.

and the designation *the twelve tribes* seem to be used figuratively to denote the minority position of his Christian readers as strangers scattered in alien lands. Peter's description of his readers in Old Testament language indicates that he understood such terms to be spiritually fulfilled in the church. Since all Christians in the first century used the Septuagint, they would easily have understood the letter's Old Testament terminology. The division of labor to which Paul, Barnabas, James, Peter, and John agreed (Gal. 2:9) was general in scope and should not be taken too strictly. It did not preclude Paul from preaching in the Jewish synagogues. And so, in addressing churches in need, it is doubtful that Peter would purposefully exclude Gentile Christians (cf. *all* in 5:14b).

Some statements in the epistle seem irreconcilable with the view that the readers were exclusively Jewish Christians. The recipients are described as those who had been called "out of darkness into his marvelous light" (2:9), who once "were no people, but now are the people of God" (2:10). Their life before their conversion was described as "the time of your ignorance" (1:14), but as believers they had been redeemed from their "vain manner of life handed down from your fathers" (1:18). They were warned against heathen practices from which they had been delivered (4:3-4). If they had been Jews, their pagan neighbors would not have thought it "strange" that they no longer indulged in those pagan sins (4:4). The women are spoken of as having *become* daughters of Sarah (3:6) through conversion. Such statements clearly refer to Gentile Christians whom Peter considered strangers in an alien environment.

Peter's readers came from mixed religious and racial backgrounds. As in many of Paul's churches, there was a nucleus of Jewish believers, drawn from the synagogues, around which the churches formed. However, the majority of the members were probably non-Jewish. In writing to those churches, Peter thought of his readers not as Jews or Gentiles but as members of the Body of Christ. As Selwyn remarks, "The abounding grace and salvation of which the Apostle speaks have already flowed over any Judaeo-Gentile controversies that may have existed; and there is something in the Epistle for each and for all, whatever their spiritual past had been."[74]

THE PLACE AND DATE OF 1 PETER

PLACE

First Peter was written from "Babylon" (5:13), but the meaning of that designation is disputed. There are three different interpretations: (1) the city by that name in Egypt, (2) the well-known Babylon on the Euphrates, and (3) a cryptic designation for Rome. The view that "Babylon" refers to Babylon in Egypt (located near the present Cairo) is the least probable of the three. In Peter's day it was a military fortress with a considerable population around it. The Coptic church has preserved a tradition, dating back to ancient times, that

74. Selwyn, p. 44.

it was the place from which Peter wrote. And according to Eusebius, Mark brought Christianity to Alexandria and established churches there.[75] But it seems highly improbable that we should find Peter, Mark, and Silvanus all at that military fortress in Egypt at the same time. If Peter wrote from Babylon in Egypt, it seems most likely that he would have distinguished it from the more famous Babylon on the Euphrates. The "Egyptian hypothesis" has few adherents today.[76]

Various Protestant scholars have supported the position that *Babylon* refers to the Mesopotamian Babylon. Alford argued that that is the natural meaning of *Babylon* as a proper place designation. He insisted, "We are not to find an allegorical meaning in a proper name thus simply used in the midst of simple and matter-of-fact sayings."[77] Babylon was the chief center of the Jews of the eastern Dispersion, and it would have been natural for Peter, the apostle to the circumcision, to work in that region. Though misfortunes had earlier befallen the Jewish colony in Babylon, the Jews may have returned in considerable numbers by the time Peter wrote (when the Jews were expelled from Rome under Claudius, they soon returned in large numbers).

But to understand *Babylon* to refer to Babylon in Mesopotamia is problematic. Early church tradition exclusively associates Peter with the West, not the East. Tradition locates him in Rome, where, supposedly, he lived and was martyred. During the Reformation the Roman origin of 1 Peter was attacked since it seemed to favor the papal claims. Calvin rejected the traditional view. His party spirit is reflected in his tart remarks on 5:13, "The Papists gladly lay hold on this comment, so that Peter seems to have been head of the Church of Rome. The infamy of the name does not deter them, provided they can pretend to the title, nor do they care greatly about Christ, provided Peter is left to them."[78] Luther adhered to the old view, lest it give his enemies a vantage point in the conflict.

Those who oppose understanding *Babylon* literally point out that early church history makes no mention of any church there. Furthermore, there were probably not enough Jews in Babylon to enable Peter to establish a church. According to Josephus, in the fifth decade severe misfortune befell the large and influential Babylonian Jewish colony. Pestilence and persecution caused them to go to Seleucia; later hostilities drove them from there.[79]

Attempts to locate the place of origin of the epistle by examining the order of the five districts named in 1:1 are inconclusive. Beare's conjecture that "Pontus and Bithynia are put at the beginning and the end of the list in order to give them prominence" (since that was where the persecution was raging)[80] is significant only if his view of the time and setting of the persecution in 1 Peter

75. Eusebius, 2:16.
76. Klijn, p. 157-58. Kümmel (p. 422, n. 27) also cites the name of de Zwaan.
77. Henry Alford, *The Greek New Testament*, vol. 4 (part 1, Prolegomena), p. 128.
78. Calvin, pp. 322-23.
79. Flavius Josephus, *The Antiquities of the Jews*, XVIII. 9. 8-9.
80. Beare, pp. 42-43.

is accepted. If the order does suggest the messenger's route of travel, and if Peter wrote from Babylon, it is difficult to see why Pontus should be named first. But if Peter wrote from Rome, the messenger could take a ship to some Pontic port and begin his overland journey from there. And if he came from Rome, Ephesus would be the most natural place to land. The order of the names, therefore, affords no sure clue to the place of writing.

Those who understand *Babylon* to mean Rome must explain the reason for such a cryptic use of the term. Though opponents of the Roman view believe that *Babylon* refers to Rome in Revelation (chaps. 17-18)—for reasons of security—they insist that the use of *Babylon* in the conclusion of 1 Peter demands a literal interpretation. However, Peter's entire concluding sentence has a figurative tone. Certainly, the mention of Mark as "my son" is not literal. The expression "she that is in Babylon, elect together with you," when occurring in a greeting to a series of churches, seems best interpreted as a mystic designation of the Christian church in Babylon. Thus, a figurative meaning would be consistent with the rest of Peter's statement.

Such a cryptic usage of *Babylon* for Rome would be readily understood by Peter's readers, for Babylon was Rome's successor as the world center of power and vice. Van Der Heeren thinks that "no other metaphor could so well describe the city of Rome, rich and luxurious as it was, and given over to the worship of false gods and every species of immorality."[81] Cullmann notes that ancient Christian literature shows that such a "typological use of geographical names" was popular and cites Galatians 4:24 and Hebrews 12:22 as New Testament examples.[82] *Babylon* is also used metaphorically in Jewish pseudepigraphical literature of the New Testament era.[83] Therefore, it is quite possible that such a metaphorical designation for Rome was already known to Peter and his readers. Zahn asserted, "The name did not originate either with Peter or John, both of whom assumed rather that their contemporaries and fellow-believers were familiar with the Babylon of the present."[84] According to that view, if Peter had possessed the modern literary convenience of quotation marks, he would have written "Babylon." Perhaps he tried to indicate that by his figurative terminology in the sentence. Moule says that in view of Peter's exhortation to good citizenship in 2:13-17, his use of the term *Babylon* was not for the sake of security but for the sake of homiletics; "Rome is called Babylon as the place of exile; for the Christian, in the metropolis of the civilized world, is a 'sojourner' and 'pilgrim.'"[85]

That view has ancient support. As far back as the beginning of the second century, *Babylon* was a way to refer to Rome. Eusebius indicated that was the view of Papias (c. A.D. 80-155) and Clement of Alexandria (c. A.D. 155-215).[86] If

81. A. Van Der Heeren, "Peter, Epistles of Saint," *The Catholic Encyclopedia*, 11:753b.
82. Oscar Cullmann, *Peter, Disciple Apostle Martyr*, p. 84.
83. Cullmann, p. 85.
84. Zahn, 2:178.
85. Moule, pp. 8-9.
86. Eusebius, 2:15.

the epistle was actually written from Babylon on the Euphrates, it is difficult to account for the origin of the other view and its acceptance by the early church Fathers. At that time, there were no exaggerated claims for the Roman church.

Though admittedly not free from difficulty, the Roman origin of 1 Peter seems the most probable theory. It was the earliest view and is favored by the majority of scholars today.

DATE

Those who reject Petrine authorship advocate a date either during the time of Domitian (A.D. 81-96) or the reign of Trajan (A.D. 98-117), probably A.D. 111-112.

Acceptance of Petrine authorship requires dating the epistle before A.D. 68, the year of Nero's death; for, according to tradition, Peter was martyred under Nero. Undoubtedly, the letter was written near the close of Peter's life. Dating the letter exactly depends on dating the situation it addresses. Suggestions vary between A.D. 62 and 67. Generally, it is dated either shortly before or shortly after the outbreak of the Neronian persecution during the fall of A.D. 64.[87]

Some interpret Peter's remark about suffering "as a Christian" (4:16) to refer to a time shortly *after* the Neronian massacre. That view assumes that Roman officials in the Asian provinces would readily have followed the action of the emperor in the capital. However, there is no firm evidence that the Neronian edict resulted in systematic persecution of Christians outside of Rome.

More probable is the view that 1 Peter was written shortly *before* the outbreak of the Neronian persecution. Then a date in the summer or early fall of A.D. 64 is likely.

The epistle contains no evidence of martyrdom. The suffering of Peter's readers was that common to believers everywhere (5:9). Peter's advocacy of a loyal and conciliatory attitude toward the government (2:13-17) suggests a time before official action against Christians had been taken. But the trend of events made it clear to discerning Christian leaders that more ominous things lay ahead for the church (4:17-18). Cranfield thinks the church's perception of a gathering storm was based on the recognition that in the eyes of the Roman government "Church and Synagogue were two distinct things."[88] As more and more Gentiles entered the Christian church without accepting Jewish rites and practices, the dichotomy became increasingly clear. Perhaps the case of Paul (Acts 28) further helped to establish that distinction. Previously, the governmental leaders had been prone to regard Christianity as a Jewish sect and had

---

87. Bo Reicke, *The New Testament Era* (p. 249), dates it "around the beginning of 65." John A. T. Robinson, *Redating the New Testament* (p. 146), dates "this initial assault upon the church in the spring of 65."

88. Cranfield, p. 17.

viewed the conflicts between Jews and Christians as intra-Jewish controversies
(cf. Acts 18:12-17). Prevailing suspicions and malicious charges would have
alerted Christians to impending trouble. Since adversaries were railing
against them (3:9), reviling them (3:16), and speaking evil of them (4:4), a wave
of hate-inspired mob actions and even locally-inspired official action was a
growing possibility for the Christians of Asia Minor.

THE PURPOSE 1 PETER

Peter clearly stated the purpose of his letter in the closing paragraph, "I
have written unto you briefly, exhorting, and testifying that this is the true
grace of God: stand ye fast therein" (5:12). His pastoral purpose was designed
to sustain and encourage his Christian readers, whose "troubles are the
ever-felt background of every paragraph."[89] He sought to achieve his goal in
two ways.

EXHORTATION

The hortatory character of 1 Peter is one of its prominent features. It was
not written to expound momentous doctrinal truths; rather it is a practical
appeal to courage, purity, and faithfulness to Christ in the midst of suffering
for His name's sake. It is full of that "comfort which only a true Christian, rich
in faith and rich in love, can give to the suffering."[90]

The opening paragraph (1:3-12), setting forth the glories of our salvation in
Christ, provided a solid foundation for Peter's series of exhortations that were
intended to strengthen and stimulate the suffering readers. The first cycle of
exhortations is grounded in the readers' personal experience of salvation
(1:13—2:10); the second appealed to them on the basis of their position in the
world (2:11—3:12). The remainder of the epistle is devoted to exhortations
dealing with the crucial theme of Christian suffering (3:13—5:11).

TESTIMONY

Peter's fervent appeals, earnestly urging his readers to stand fast in the
midst of suffering, constitute his ringing testimony that "this is the true grace
of God" (5:12). He sought to assure his readers that they were fundamentally
right in spite of the opposition and hatred that they had encountered for the
sake of the gospel. Peter reminded them that Jesus Christ is the touchstone,
the one who inevitably reveals men's characters and determines their ultimate
destinies (2:4-8). Faithful adherence to Christ, the Living Stone, is crucial for
time and eternity.

89. Kelly, p. 25.
90. B. C. Caffin, *The First Epistle General of Peter*, p. xi.

2

The Title of the Epistle

As is true of all the general epistles, the traditional title of 1 Peter identifies it by the name of its author, not its readers. By virtue of their number, the thirteen Pauline epistles were identified by their recipients. But due to their diverse authorship and (in some cases) questions concerning their intended readers, the general epistles were more conveniently identified by author. The uniform association of Peter's name with 1 Peter bears witness to the universal acceptance of Petrine authorship in the church.

The titles, added by unknown hands before A.D. 300, were an obvious convenience; they enabled ready identification of the individual books when they were brought together as a collection. Though not part of the original documents, the titles reflect the traditional views of the early church.

In the earliest known Greek manuscripts, the titles were brief and to the point. This book was simply entitled "First Peter" (*Petrou ā*)[1] or "First Epistle of Peter" (*Petrou epistolē ā*).[2] Later scribes expanded those simple titles to read "The First Catholic (or General) Epistle of Peter," or, "the apostle Peter." In the ninth century the scribe of Codex *L* wrote the pompous title "The First Epistle Catholic of the holy and all-praiseworthy (*paneuphēmou*) Apostle Peter." The numeral indicates the acceptance of a second epistle ascribed to Peter.

The designation of 1 Peter as an "epistle" indicates that the scribes accepted the opening epistolary formula at face value and regarded the document as a true epistolary communication from the apostle. The Greek word *epistolē*,

1. Codex *B*, 4th century.
2. Codex *Aleph*, 4th century; Codex *A* and Codex *C*, 5th century.

from which we derive our English word *epistle*, meant something sent by a messenger—a message whether oral or written. It came to be the common term for a written message from one individual or group to another, whether private or general. Such communications were inspired by different occasions; they arose from a definite life situation and were intended to address specific needs. Aside from its appearance in titles, the word *epistle* (singular or plural) occurs twenty-four times in the text of the New Testament, always of a written communication (except in 2 Cor. 3:2-3 where the sense is metaphorical).

The text issued by Robert Stephanus in the middle of the sixteenth century employed the designation, *Epistolē Katholikē*, "Catholic" or "General Epistle." That became the standard designation for those seven letters.[3] It was not intended to denote general or joint authorship but a general readership. The term *katholikē*, meaning general or universal, carries no modern ecclesiastical implications; it simply indicates that the epistle is general or encyclical.[4] However, in those epistles the term does not refer to the church universal but to a group of churches. As is evident from the opening salutation, the term is entirely appropriate for 1 Peter. Nevertheless, we prefer to use the earliest and simplest form of the title, "First Peter."

3. In the *Textus Stephanici A. D. 1550*, ed. F. H. Scrivener, the designation appears in the title of all seven of the general epistles; other editors omit the designation for 2 and 3 John.

4. The term does not apply in the case of 2 and 3 John, which are both local in destination.

3

An Outline of 1 Peter

PART 1: DOCTRINAL FOUNDATION

1. The Opening Salutation (1:1-2)
   A. The Writer (1a)
   B. The Readers (1b-2a)
      1. True character of the readers (1b)
      2. Geographical location of the readers (1c)
      3. Spiritual supports for the readers (2a)
   C. The Greeting (2b)
2. The Thanksgiving for Our Salvation (1:3-12)
   A. The Description of Salvation (3-5)
      1. The author of salvation (3a-b)
         a) His relation to the Savior (3a)
         b) His act of mercy to the saved (3b)
      2. The nature of salvation (3c-4a)
         a) The living hope grounded in Christ's resurrection (3c)
         b) The glorious inheritance awaiting believers (4a)
      3. The certainty of salvation (4b-5)
         a) The safekeeping of the inheritance (4b)
         b) The preservation of the heirs (5)
   B. The Experiences Relating to Salvation (6-9)
      1. The paradoxical nature of the experiences (6-7)
         a) The experience of exultation (6a)
         b) The experience of distress (6b-7)
            (1) The nature of the distress (6b)
            (2) The purpose behind the trials (7)

(a) The testing of faith (7*a*)
(b) The outcome of the testing (7*b*)
2. The sustaining relations of believers (8-9)
  a) Their dual relation to Jesus Christ (8)
  b) Their experiential relation to their salvation (9)
C. The Magnification of Salvation (10-12)
  1. The magnification through prophetic search (10-12*a*)
    a) Their intensive search (10*a*)
    b) Their prophetic function (10*b*)
    c) Their personal perplexity (11)
      (1) The time and circumstances (11*a*)
      (2) The sufferings and the glories (11*b*)
    d) Their restricted ministry (12*a*)
  2. The magnification through Christian proclamation (12*b*)
  3. The magnification through angelic inquiry (12*c*)

PART 2: PRACTICAL EXHORTATION

1. Exhortations in View of Our Salvation (1:13—2:10)
  A. The Life Arising from Salvation (1:13—2:3)
    1. The Christian life in relation to God (1:13-21)
      a) A life of steadfast hope (13)
        (1) The supports of hope (13*a*)
        (2) The call to hope (13*b*)
      b) A life of personal holiness (14-16)
        (1) The foundation of personal holiness (14*a*)
        (2) The call to personal holiness (14*b*-15)
          (a) The negative demand of holiness (14*b*)
          (b) The positive call to holiness (15)
        (3) The justification of the call to holiness (16)
      c) A life of motivated reverence (17-21)
        (1) The basis for reverent living (17*a*)
        (2) The call for reverent living (17*b*)
        (3) The knowledge that motivates reverence (18-21)
          (a) The means of our redemption (18-19)
          (b) The nature of the Redeemer (20)
          (c) The characteristics of the redeemed (21)
    2. The Christian life in relation to the brethren (1:22-25)
      a) The experience of inner purification (22*a*)
      b) The duty of mutual love (22*b*)
      c) The foundation in personal regeneration (23-25)
        (1) The fact of their regeneration (23*a*)
        (2) The nature of their regeneration (23*b*-25*a*)
        (3) The evangelization leading to their regeneration (25*b*)
    3. The Christian life in relation to personal growth (2:1-3)
      a) The removal of hindering vices (1)

    b) The call to spiritual growth (2-3)
       (1) The duty to promote growth (2*a*)
       (2) The goal of spiritual growth (2*b*)
       (3) The incentive to spiritual growth (3)
B. The Life of the Saved as a Corporate Unity (2:4-10)
   1. The divine work through Christ with believers (4-8)
    a) The living relation of believers to Christ (4)
    b) The corporate character and function of believers (5)
    c) The human responses to Christ the Cornerstone (6-8)
       (1) The divine laying of the Stone (6*a*)
       (2) The human reactions to the Stone (6*b*-8)
          (a) The experience of believers (6*b*-7*a*)
          (b) The frustration of unbelievers (7*b*-8)
   2. The corporate nature and function of believers (9-10)
    a) Their corporate identity (9*a*)
    b) Their God-centered function (9*b*)
    c) Their changed condition (10)
2. Exhortations in View of Our Position in the World (2:11—3:12)
  A. The Appeal for Appropriate Personal Conduct (2:11-12)
   1. The tone of the appeal (11*a*)
   2. The content of the appeal (11*b*-12*a*)
    a) The inner self-discipline called for (11*b*)
    b) The outward winsome conduct needed (12*a*)
   3. The aim of the appeal (12*b*)
  B. The Duty of Submission to the State (2:13-17)
   1. The duty of Christian submission (13*a*)
   2. The characterization of the civil powers (13*b*-14)
    a) The supreme ruler (13*b*)
    b) The subordinate rulers (14)
   3. The elaboration of the believers' submission (15-16)
    a) The intended impact upon foolish men (15)
    b) The true character of those submitting (16)
   4. The scope of Christian well-doing (17)
  C. The Duty of Submission in Household Relations (2:18-25)
   1. The duty of submission by house-servants (18)
   2. The approval by God of submissive suffering (19-20)
    a) The assured acceptableness of such suffering (19)
    b) The true identity of acceptable suffering (20)
   3. The motivation from the example of Christ (21-25)
    a) The call to suffer confirmed by Christ's example (21)
    b) The portrayal of Christ's sufferings (22-25)
       (1) The exemplary sufferings of Christ (22-23)
          (a) What He did *not* do (22-23*a*)
          (b) What He *did* do (23*b*)
       (2) The redemptive sufferings of Christ (24-25)

     (a)   The nature of His redemptive sufferings (24*a*)

     (b)   The purpose of His redemptive sufferings (24*b*)

     (c)   The result of His redemptive sufferings (24*c*-25)

  D.   The Duty of Submission in Marital Relations (3:1-7)

    1.   The submission of the wives (1-6)

      a)   The accepted duty of the wife's submission (1*a*)

      b)   The saving impact of the wife's submission (1*b*-2)

      c)   The true adornment of the submissive wife (3-4)

        (1)   Not mere external adornment (3)

        (2)   Inner spiritual character (4)

      d)   The past examples of godly submission (5-6*a*)

      e)   The personal significance of godly conduct (6*b*)

    2.   The obligations of the husbands (7)

  E.   An Appeal for Becoming Corporate Conduct (3:8-12)

    1.   The portrayal of the desired conduct (8-9)

      a)   The characteristics of believers (8)

      b)   The response to hostility (9)

    2.   The confirmation from Old Testament scripture (10-12)

      a)   The dominating desire (10*a*)

      b)   The necessary activities (10*b*-11)

      c)   The divine response (12)

3.   Exhortations in View of Christian Suffering (3:13—5:11)

  A.   The Experience of Suffering for Righteousness (3:13-17)

    1.   The unnaturalness of suffering for righteousness (13)

    2.   The blessedness of suffering for righteousness (14*a*)

    3.   The directives to those suffering for righteousness (14*b*-16)

      a)   The human response prohibited (14*b*)

      b)   The Christian reactions enjoined (15-16)

        (1)   The personal enthronement of Christ as Lord (15*a*)

        (2)   The ready witness to all concerning their Christian hope (15*b*-16)

          (a)   The necessary readiness to defend their Christian hope (15*b*)

          (b)   The personal factors for an effective witness (15*c*-16*a*)

          (c)   The contemplated impact upon vicious opponents (16*b*)

    4.   The assurance amid suffering for righteousness (17)

  B.   The Experience of Christ Suffering for Righteousness (3:18-22)

    1.   The character of His suffering (18*a-b*)

      a)   The portrayal of His suffering (18*a*)

      b)   The aim of His suffering (18*b*)

    2.   The consequences of His suffering (18*c*-21)

      a)   The death and resurrection of the Sufferer (18*c*)

      b)   The preaching to "the spirits in prison" (19-20*b*)

        (1) The activity in relation to "the spirits" (19)

        (2) The characterization of the "spirits" (20a-b)

     c) The salvation through water typifying baptism (20c-21)

        (1) The statement of the event (20c)

        (2) The typology in the event (21)

  3.) The culmination of His suffering (22)

C. The Equipment for Suffering for Righteousness (4:1-11)

  1. The needed equipment in view of present suffering (1-6)

     a) The call to be armed with the proper attitude (1-2)

        (1) The example of Christ's suffering (1a)

        (2) The call to be armed with the same mind (1b)

        (3) The character of the victorious sufferer (1c)

        (4) The goal in appropriating the equipment (2)

     b) The motivation to effectively endure suffering (3-6)

        (1) The motivation from a sinful past (3)

        (2) The motivation from present opposition (4)

        (3) The motivation from future judgment (5-6)

            (a) The judgment of the blasphemers (5)

            (b) The judgment of the dead (6)

  2. The necessary life in view of the end (7-11)

     a) The apostolic assertion concerning the end (7a)

     b) The urgent duties in view of the end (7b-11a)

        (1) The duties concerning their personal life (7b)

        (2) The activities in their community relations (8-11a)

            (a) The duty of mutual love (8-9)

              i) The nature of mutual love (8a)

              ii) The action of brotherly love (8b)

              iii) The example of loving hospitality (9)

            (b) The duty of mutual service (10-11a)

              i) The nature of Christian service (10)

              ii) The forms of Christian service (11a)

     c) The goal in Christian living (11b)

D. The Need for Steadfastness in Suffering as Christians (4:12-19)

  1. The attitude enjoined when suffering as Christians (12-13)

     a) The attitude prohibited amid the fiery trial (12)

     b) The attitude enjoined in suffering for Christ (13)

  2. The instructions concerning the ordeal of suffering (14-16)

     a) The evaluation of suffering for Christ (14)

     b) The exclusion of unworthy causes of suffering (15)

     c) The reaction when suffering "as a Christian" (16)

  3. The exercise of God's judgment in suffering (17-18)

     a) The explanation of the present ordeal (17a)

     b) The inferences drawn from the experience (17b-18)

  4. The summary exhortation to Christian sufferers (19)

E. The Concluding Appeals to the Suffering Churches (5:1-11)

  1. The appeal to the elders (1-4)

Part 1
Doctrinal Foundation
(1:1-12)

The first epistle of Peter should be viewed in the light of the author's stated purpose. In 5:12 Peter declares, "I have written unto you briefly, exhorting and testifying that this is the true grace of God: stand ye fast therein." His fundamental purpose was to establish his suffering Christian readers in their faith. The entire letter is an earnest appeal for them to staunchly maintain their stand in the true grace of God that they have experienced. That hortatory approach is the basic feature of the epistle.

But Peter well knew that Christian exhortation, to be vital and transforming, must be grounded in Christian doctrine. Therefore, he skillfully laid such a foundation in the first twelve verses of the epistle. The opening salutation, rich in doctrinal content (1:1-2), indicates the need for a firm grasp of the realities underlying the Christian life. Peter's grand doxology of praise to God for the marvelous salvation He has provided in Christ Jesus (1:3-12) forms a solid foundation for the urgent exhortations that constitute the body of the letter (1:13—5:11).

4

1. The Opening Salutation
(1:1-2)

(1) Peter, an apostle of Jesus Christ, to the elect who are sojourners of the Dispersion in Pontus, Galatia, Cappadocia, Asia, and Bithynia, (2) according to the foreknowledge of God the Father, in sanctification of the Spirit, unto obedience and sprinkling of the blood of Jesus Christ: Grace to you and peace be multiplied.

The salutation conforms to the conventional three-point opening employed in first-century correspondence: writer, readers, greeting. But it differs from the familiar Pauline salutation by employing a finite verb with the third member, thus making the first two members an independent construction. Paul followed the terse Greek formula and did not use a verb with *grace and peace*; Peter followed the pattern used in the letters in Daniel 4:1 and 6:25, "Peace be multiplied unto you."

Each of the three parts of the salutation might be expanded according to the situation confronted and the author's purpose. Peter expanded each and gave them a distinctive Christian content. But his main expansion concerned the identification of his readers, and that indicates his central concern in writing.

A. THE WRITER (V. 1a)

The writer's name, *Peter*, would at once establish his identity for his Christian readers.[1] He was the only man in the New Testament with that name. *Peter* (*Petros*) is the Greek form of the Aramaic name Cephas, both of which mean "stone" or "rock." It was given to him by Jesus as a prophetically

---

1. For a summary of the NT account of Peter, see D. E. Hiebert, "Peter," pp. 640-42.

descriptive title when Peter first met Christ (John 1:42). It was reaffirmed by
Jesus after Peter's great confession (Matt. 16:18) when the prophecy was
beginning to be fulfilled. Farrar suggests that if Peter had been writing
exclusively to Jewish Christians, he would probably have used the Aramaic
rather than the Greek form of his new name.[2]

He was originally known by the common Jewish name *Simon* (Matt. 4:18;
Mark 3:16; John 1:41) or *Symeon* (Acts 15:14). The numerous references to him
in the gospels indicate a gradual shift from *Simon* to *Simon Peter* or *Peter*.
Apparently, however, his original name continued to be used sporadically
(Acts 15:14; 2 Pet. 1:1). In non-Jewish Christian circles the name *Peter* was
commonly used. Perhaps Peter prized that Christ-given name as a constant
challenge to maintain the steadfastness of character it implied.

The appositional expansion "an apostle of Jesus Christ" is not defensive;
Peter's apostolic status was never questioned. The phrase briefly indicates
Peter's authority. No further explanation of the source or nature of his
apostleship was needed. The indefinite article in the English translation "an
apostle" (Greek has no indefinite article) does not mean that Peter was only one
of a group of apostles. Nor did he write *the* apostle, as though claiming
superiority among the apostles. The noun without an article is qualitative.[3]
Peter identified himself as "apostle of Jesus Christ." The possessive genitive
defined whose apostle he was, "Jesus Christ's apostle." He was acting as His
agent, having been commissioned by Christ to tend His sheep (John 21:15-17).

The noun *apostle* is a compound derived from the verb *stellō*, "to make
ready, send," and the preposition *apo*, "off, away from;" it has the basic
meaning of one sent forth by another on a mission. In a general sense it might
be used of an individual who for a limited time was commissioned to act as the
authorized representative of another for a specific assignment. Paul applied
the term to Epaphras, who had been sent to minister to him as the
representative of the Philippian church (Phil. 2:25; cf. 2 Cor. 8:23). In Acts
14:14 it is used of Paul and Barnabas as the missionaries sent out by the church
at Antioch.

But Peter used the term in the restricted sense of an official apostle of the
church, one chosen and commissioned by Christ Himself.[4] In Acts 1:21-22 he
mentioned the basic qualifications for the office (cf. John 15:27; 1 Cor. 9:1;
15:8-9; Paul used *apostle* to refer to himself as one chosen and commissioned by
the risen Christ and so as one who had equal authority with the twelve).

By designating himself an "apostle of Jesus Christ," Peter called attention
not to himself but to the One who commissioned him. The double designation
Jesus Christ indicates His true nature. *Jesus (Iēsous)* is the Greek form of the

---

2. F. W. Farrar, *The Early Days of Christianity*, p. 84.

3. "The articular construction emphasizes *identity*; the anarthrous construction emphasizes
   character," H. E. Dana and Julius R. Mantey, *A Manual Grammar of the Greek New
   Testament*, p. 140.

4. For a survey of scholarly views and a full bibliography, see "Apostle," *NIDNTT*, 1:126-37.

Hebrew name Joshua. Both mean "salvation of Jehovah" (Matt. 1:21). It is the name of His humanity, denoting the Jesus whom Peter first met along the shores of the Jordan River (John 1:40-42), the One recognized by His followers as the promised Messiah. *Christ* is the Greek translation of the Hebrew term *Messiah* (transliterated *Messias* in John 1:41 and 4:25) and means "anointed." For Peter and the early church, the name *Jesus Christ* embodied their basic conviction that the human Jesus was the anointed Messiah, the bringer of messianic redemption. "Jesus is the Christ" thus became the earliest Christian confession (Acts 2:36; 3:20; 5:42; cf. John 20:30-31). Early in the gospels *the Christ* is a designation of the expected Messiah (Matt. 2:4; John 1:20; etc.), not a personal name. But because Christian faith inseparably identified the Christ with Jesus, *Christ* came to be used as a personal name; but it never lost its messianic connotations (cf. 1 Pet. 2:21-24).

B. The Readers (vv. 1b-2a)

The recipients of the epistle are identified at considerable length (1:1b-2a). In the original there is no definite article in the lengthy designation. That suggests that Peter was not merely concerned with their identity but with their spiritual character. In view of the difficult situation they faced, Peter's "concern is to emphasize, in the most solemn manner, the supernatural vocation of his correspondents, which should be their sheet-anchor in their trials."[5] The entire designation is best viewed as a unit. Peter delineated the true character (v. 1b), geographic location (v. 1c), and spiritual supports of the readers (v. 2a).

1) TRUE CHARACTER OF THE READERS (v. 1b)

"To the elect who are sojourners of the Dispersion" translates three words in the original (*eklektois parepidēmois diasporas*). The added place names make it obvious that specific groups of believers are in view, yet the absence of an article imparts a qualitative character, "to such as are . . ." It appears that the terms are used figuratively.

It is unclear whether the first word (*eklektois*, "elect") is to be taken as a separate noun or as an adjective modifying the following noun. A strictly literal translation of the first possibility would be "to (such as are) elect ones, sojourners of (the) Dispersion," and the second would be "to (such as are) elect sojourners of (the) Dispersion." The first view identifies the readers under two separate and distinct concepts; they are elect and also sojourners. The second view fuses the two thoughts into one two-sided designation of the readers; they are "elect sojourners." The first view makes it possible to separate the two concepts and even to transfer *elect* to v. 2, as is done, for example, in the KJV.

The word *eklektos* is a verbal adjective, but it may also function as a noun.

5. J. N. D. Kelly, *A Commentary on the Epistles of Peter and of Jude*, p. 39.

When used alone with the article, it naturally serves as a noun (Matt. 24:22, 24; 2 Tim. 2:10; etc.). But it can also be a noun without an article (Matt. 22:14; Rom. 8:33; Titus 1:1; etc.). Peter may have intended it as a noun, but the grammatical structure does not suggest it. It is more natural to accept *parepidēmois* ("sojourners") as the governing noun of the expression, modified by a preceding adjective and a succeeding noun in the genitive. That is in keeping with Peter's use of *eklektos* as an adjective in 2:6, 9, though in both of those instances the adjective follows the noun. We prefer to accept it as an adjective and to translate "to (such as are) elect sojourners of the Dispersion." So understood, Peter's designation fused heavenward and earthward relationships. That two-sided characterization of the readers underlies the material that follows in the epistle.

The verbal adjective *elect* is passive, marking the readers as the objects of the electing action of God, who is the unnamed agent. They were chosen by God to be His own in order that they might be partakers of the heavenly inheritance being reserved for them (1:4). United by faith with Christ, the "corner stone, elect, precious" (2:6), they constituted "an elect race" (2:9). As God's elect people, they formed a group separate and distinct from the world and subject to its hatred and persecution. In themselves they were just ordinary people, not superior to their unsaved neighbors; but the initiative of God made them what they were.

The opening characterization of the readers as elect was meant to strengthen and encourage them in their affliction. The doctrine of election is a "family truth" intended to foster the welfare of believers. Unfortunately, that doctrine, which the human mind cannot wholly comprehend, has been the occasion of much controversy among the saints. The sacred writers do not explain all the problems that cluster around the doctrine, nor do they attempt to harmonize it with "that other great truth, taught in Scripture and revealed in conscience—the freedom of the human will; their statements of the two apparently conflicting doctrines balance, but do not explain, one another; . . . they teach us by their silence that the proper attitude of the Christian, when brought face to face with mystery, is rest in the Lord, humble child-like confidence in his love and wisdom."[6]

Peter was also keenly aware of the earthly status of his readers as "sojourners of the Dispersion." The noun translated *sojourners* (*parepidēmois*) occurs in the New Testament only in 1 Peter 1:1; 2:11, and Hebrews 11:13. That compound term pictures the readers living as resident aliens beside a people to whom they did not belong. They did not expect to be regarded as natives of the places where they resided. Hebrews 11:13 uses the term of the Old Testament saints, and Peter used it metaphorically to refer to Christians. Called to be God's people, they recognize themselves as temporary residents in the world. They are on their way to a heavenly home, one to which they eagerly expect to be removed by the summons of their Lord.

6. B. C. Caffin, *The First Epistle General of Peter*, p. 2.

Peter's understanding of the Christian life is beautifully illustrated in the *Epistle to Diognetus*, an anonymous work dating from the second century.

> Christians are not distinguished from the rest of mankind by either country, speech, or customs. . . . They reside in their respective countries, but only as aliens. They take part in everything as citizens and put up with everything as foreigners. Every foreign land is their home, and every home a foreign land. . . . They find themselves in the flesh, but do not live according to the flesh. They spend their days on earth, but hold citizenship in heaven.[7]

The earthly status of the readers is further described by the added genitive, *of the Dispersion* (*diasporas*). The term supplements the thought of their alien status. It is a compound noun, made up of the preposition *dia*, basically meaning "through," and the noun *spora*, "a sowing." That indicates that Peter's readers were scattered minority groups. *The Dispersion* was a standard Jewish way to refer to Jews living among the Gentiles outside of their Palestinian homeland (cf. John 7:35). In James 1:1 the expression "to the twelve tribes which are of the Dispersion" most likely refers to Jewish Christians outside of Palestine.[8] Those who believe that Peter, too, was writing to Jewish Christians understand the term to confirm their position. But the lack of a definite article and the failure to mention the twelve tribes detract from the alleged parallel with James 1:1. It seems more natural to understand Peter's use of the term metaphorically, as a picture of Christians scattered in various areas as minority groups in a non-Christian world.[9] But that designation does not mean that Peter's readers were individual or unorganized local groups; 1 Peter 5 reveals the addressees as members of organized churches.

The use of the terms *sojourners* and *Dispersion* describes the earthly status of the readers from two different points of view. The former views them in relation to the land in which they were then living as aliens; the latter portrays them in terms of their true homeland from which they were absent.[10] As God's "elect," the readers were living as "sojourners" in an alien land, dispersed and far removed from their homeland. However, they were assured of their future ingathering to their heavenly home.

2) GEOGRAPHICAL LOCATION OF THE READERS (v. 1c)

The nouns *Pontus, Galatia, Cappadocia, Asia,* and *Bithynia* specify the geographical location of the readers and mark 1 Peter as an encyclical letter. How widely the readers were dispersed in each of those regions is not known. Pontus was the rugged region south of the Black Sea, extending east from

---

7. David Otis Fuller, ed., *Valiant for the Truth. A Treasury of Evangelical Writings*, pp. 9-10.

8. D. Edmond Hiebert, *The Epistle of James, Tests of a Living Faith*, pp. 36-38, 63-65.

9. See the Introduction.

10. See Karl Ludwig Schmidt, *diaspora*, *TDNT*, 2:104, n. 21.

Bithynia into the highlands of Armenia. After the overthrow of the kingdom of Mithradates by Pompey in 65 B.C., the area was divided. The western part was united with Bithynia under one administration; the eastern portion continued under the rule of a Greek dynasty. Important Greek cities were located along the shores of the Black Sea, and the Jews in Jerusalem on the Day of Pentecost (Acts 2:9) probably came from those coastal cities. We do not know when Christianity was first introduced into the region.

Galatia was formerly a district in central Asia Minor ruled by the Celtic Galatians. But in 25 B.C. the area was made a Roman province and parts of Phrygia, Lyconia, and Pisidia were added to it, so that the province extended considerably farther to the south than the old ethnic Galatia. Acts 2 makes no reference to Galatian Jews. Apparently, none were in Jerusalem on that Day of Pentecost. On his first missionary journey, Paul established churches in the southern part of the Roman province (Acts 13:13—14:23). According to the North Galatian theory, Paul also established churches in the northern part of the province during the second missionary journey (Acts 16:6). But the South Galatian theory, the more generally accepted of the two, rejects the view that Paul conducted a missionary campaign in the northern part of the province. So according to that view, we have no information about how the gospel was brought to that part of the province.

Cappadocia was a mountainous inland area in eastern Asia Minor. In A.D. 17 the Roman Emperor Tiberius incorporated it as a province into the Roman Empire as a bulwark for its eastern borders. Jews from Cappadocia were present in Jerusalem during the Day of Pentecost (Acts 2:9). But apart from that reference and the one in 1 Peter, the area is not mentioned elsewhere in the New Testament. When and by whom the gospel was first brought to the area is unknown.

Asia, as in all twenty-one occurrences of that term in the New Testament, denotes the Roman province occupying the western regions of Asia Minor. It included the whole western shore of Asia Minor, which was dotted with important Greek cities, and extended east to the borders of Galatia. It was constituted a Roman province in 133 B.C., and in New Testament times the area was strongly pro-Roman. It was the most developed and prosperous region of Asia Minor. Jewish representatives from Asia were in Jerusalem on the Day of Pentecost (Acts 2:9), and certain Jews from Asia later caused Paul's arrest in that city (Acts 21:27-30). The province was effectively evangelized during Paul's ministry at Ephesus on his third missionary journey (Acts 19:10). The church at Ephesus was the mother church of the area and played a prominent part in early church history.

Bithynia lay along the southern shore of the Black Sea west of Pontus. In 74 B.C. the last king of Bithynia bequeathed his kingdom to the Romans; in 64 B.C. Pompey united it with the western portion of Pontus as a single province. Bithynia is not mentioned in Acts 2:9-10. According to Acts 16:7 Paul, on his second missionary journey, for some unstated reason was divinely restrained from working in Bithynia. We do not know when Christianity first entered the province. The well-known letter of the imperial legate Pliny the Younger to the Roman Emperor Trajan in A.D. 112 indicates that Christianity had already been entrenched in the area for many years, with the result that the pagan temples were almost deserted.[11]

If, as seems probable, Peter intended those five names to denote Roman provinces, then the area included all of Asia Minor north of the Taurus Mountains. Bennett observes, "In New Testament times there was no general name in use corresponding to Asia Minor; hence this list is the natural way of describing that area."[12] The existence of Christian churches in those provinces bears witness to much unrecorded missionary work during the first thirty years of the Christian church.

The order of the five names used by Peter has evoked considerable discussion.[13] The most probable suggestion is that the order indicates the anticipated route of travel by the bearer of the letter. But if so, the exact route taken must have been determined by some considerations no longer available to us. We have no information concerning the number of churches or their distribution in those areas.

3) SPIRITUAL SUPPORTS FOR THE READERS (v. 2a)

The three prepositional phrases in v. 2 are best understood to refer directly to the readers for the purpose of giving them spiritual support. The phrases emphasize the fact that as "elect sojourners of the Dispersion" they have a special relationship to God. Peter undergirded their faith by portraying the entire Godhead as active in their Christian experience. Peter's primary purpose was not to teach Christian doctrine but to strengthen Christian faith.

The precise connection of those three phrases has been understood in different ways. Many translations[14] and commentaries[15] directly unite the phrases with the term *elect*. Doctrinal considerations may be found to support that connection, but it is not obvious from Peter's word order. If that was correct, then the word *elect* should properly stand after *Bithynia*. But since seven nouns intervene, that understanding is improbable.

Even more improbable is the view that relates those three phrases with *apostle*, as suggested by various ancient commentators and supported by Cook.[16] An even larger amount of material intervenes between *apostle* and those phrases. Nor is it likely that Peter would have returned to a defense of his apostleship after identifying his readers (cf. Gal. 1:1-2). Cook found support

---

11. Betty Radice, trans., *Pliny, Letters and Panegyricus in Two Volumes*, Book X, XCVI (II. 284-91).

12. W. H. Bennett, *The General Epistles, James, Peter, John, and Jude*, p. 185.

13. See the Introduction.

14. So KJV, 20th Cent., NASB, NEB, JB, NIV, Darby, Weymouth, Williams, Kleist and Lilly.

15. For example, Calvin, Alford, Bennett, Moffatt, Hunter, and others.

16. F. C. Cook, *The First Epistle General of Peter*, 4:173-74, 186.

for his position in the resemblance of the passage with the opening of Romans,[17] but Bigg felt that it was unjustified to seek such support from "the supposed analogy of the Pauline addresses."[18]

More probable is the view that those three phrases modify all of v. 1 and refer both to Peter and his readers.[19] Nevertheless, it seems most natural to take the phrases as part of the entire dative construction that identifies the readers. The three phrases are not merely a closer definition of their election but relate to their total position as "elect sojourners of the Dispersion." The phrases clearly relate to the Godward aspect of their character, but certainly the outworking of that fact should find application to their earthly status. "It is because they are 'chosen' by God that they are now exiles of the dispersion in the world."[20]

"According to the foreknowledge of God the Father" correlates their status as elect sojourners of the Dispersion with God's foreknowledge. *According to* (*kata* and the accusative) indicates a standard or norm; their circumstances as elect sojourners were in full accord with the divine foreknowledge (*prognōsin*). The noun *foreknowledge* occurs twice (Acts 2:23; 1 Pet. 1:2) and the verb five times (Acts 26:5; Rom. 8:29; 11:2; 1 Pet. 1:20; 2 Pet. 3:17) in the New Testament. "In Acts 26:5 and II Peter 3:17 we have the purely classical meaning of the verb, namely, 'previous knowledge.' "[21] But in the remainder of its New Testament occurrences, it "is to be understood less as a passive 'knowing in advance' than an active 'taking note of', an eternal intention to bless."[22] Divine foreknowledge involves God's favorable regard for people as part of His deliberate plans and purposes. His affectionate regard for them is not due to what they are in themselves but can only be understood as the manifestation of His gracious character as God the Father. That double designation declares His infinite power to realize His beneficient purposes, and His character as Father assures them of His loving concern for their well-being amid trying circumstances. "Peter sets aside all doubts and misgivings, and opens new interpretive horizons for those who have become bogged down in the pressures of the moment. God knows about everything; indeed, He has always known. There are no surprises in all of this; it is a part of His purposes."[23]

"In sanctification of the Spirit" indicates the means used to further the Father's loving purposes. The noun *sanctification* (*hagiasmos*) points to the act or process of sanctifying rather than to the resultant state of holiness (*hagiōsunē*). There is a moral dimension to the term; it includes the idea of

---

17. Cook, p. 186.

18. Charles Bigg, *A Critical and Exegetical Commentary on the Epistles of St. Peter and St. Jude*, p. 91.

19. So Hort, Selwyn, Beare, Best.

20. Ernest Best, *I Peter*, p. 70.

21. Kenneth S. Wuest, *First Peter in the Greek New Testament for the English Reader*, p. 15.

22. G. J. Polkinghorne, *The First Letter of Peter*, p. 586.

23. Jay E. Adams, *Trust and Obey. A Practical Commentary on First Peter*, p. 7.

consecration as well as cleansing. But the first concept is more prominent here. The word refers to the Spirit's work of setting Christians apart from the world as God's chosen people by keeping them conscious of their distinctiveness and so making them more and more inwardly holy.

The genitive "of the Spirit" (*pneumatos*) may be interpreted two ways. It may be an objective genitive,[24] making the human spirit the object of the sanctifying work. That seems to be the intended meaning of the Montgomery translation, "in the sanctification of the spirit."[25] More probably the genitive is subjective, meaning that the Spirit is the agent of the sanctifying. The context favors that view because it preserves the trinitarian reference. But Cook suggested that the ambiguity of the expression may be intentional; it "may represent the certain truth that sanctification is the result of a complex work wrought by the Spirit on the consenting will."[26] If the genitive is objective, sanctification of the human spirit is portrayed as the work of the Holy Spirit; if it is subjective, that theological point is not made.

⌐ "Unto obedience and sprinkling of the blood of Jesus Christ" expresses the intended outcome of the work of God with His people. Simply connected by the conjunction, *obedience and sprinkling* indicate a blending of human and divine activity in achieving the intended result.

Interpreters disagree on whether both *obedience* and *sprinkling* are modified by the genitive *of Jesus Christ*. The NIV's "for obedience to Jesus Christ and sprinkling by his blood"[27] has Jesus Christ modifying both obedience and sprinkling. That is possible, but it involves the difficulty of simultaneously giving the genitive *of Jesus Christ* an objective meaning with the first noun ("obedience to Jesus Christ") and a subjective meaning with *blood* ("by his blood"). Any effort to avoid the difficulty by severing the two nouns, connecting *unto obedience* closely with the preceding phrase—*in sanctification of the Spirit unto obedience*—destroys the structural sequence of the three prepositional phrases. William Kelly connected the genitive *of Jesus Christ* (understood subjectively) with both nouns—"to obey as Christ obeyed and to be sprinkled with His precious blood."[28] But such an introduction of the personal example of Jesus is not obvious. It seems better, therefore, to accept *obedience* as standing alone, as also in verse 14. It is a plain reference to the human side in salvation.

As a compound noun, *obedience* (*hupakoēn*) conveys the picture of listening and submitting to that which is heard. It involves a change of attitude in the believer, reversing the characteristic unsaved attitude of rebellion and self-will. Rees remarks, "The sign and proof of being among the 'elect' is not an empty prating of how secure we are once we have believed, but rather how

---

24. Objective genitive—"when the noun in the genitive *receives* the action;" subjective genitive —"when the noun in the genitive *produces* the action," Dana and Mantey, p. 78.

25. Helen Barrett Montgomery, *The New Testament in Modern English*.

26. Cook, p. 174.

27. Similarly, RSV, Berkeley, NASB, Moffatt, Goodspeed, Williams.

28. William Kelly, *The Epistles of Peter*, p. 10.

sensitive we are to the principle and practice of obedience to the Saviour we have trusted."[29]

If the term is used absolutely, then Peter does not indicate to what or to whom our obedience is given. But the primary idea seems to be "obedience to the truth," the saving truth of the gospel as Peter defines it in 1:22 (cf. "the obedience of faith" in Rom. 1:5; 15:18; 16:26). "Obedience is the first act, as well as the permanent characteristic of true faith."[30]

"And sprinkling of the blood of Jesus Christ" closely links the human response with the divine provision. The double statement about obedience and sprinkling of the blood is apparently derived from the scene in Exodus 24:3-8. At Mt. Sinai, after the Israelites heard God's word to them through Moses and said, "All the words which Jehovah hath spoken will we do" (v. 3), Moses sprinkled the altar and the people with blood, thereby bringing them into and sealing the covenant between them and God.

The New Covenant into which Peter's readers had been brought was sealed by the blood of Jesus Christ, the mediator of a better covenant (Heb. 8:6; also 12:24). They were sprinkled by His blood and were the recipients of its blessings (Heb. 9:11-15). The reference to the sprinkled blood is figurative. It "necessarily carries a reference to the death of Jesus, but the emphasis lies not on the violent nature of his death but on its redemptive nature (cf. Heb. 9:22)."[31] Huther noted that by the mention of the blood of Jesus Christ the readers were "here for the first time characterized directly as Christians, all the previous designations having been equally applicable to the children of Israel."[32]

"Unto obedience and sprinkling of the blood of Jesus Christ" seems primarily to refer to the believer's admission into the New Covenant, though the efficacy of His blood certainly extends to their entire subsequent life as Christians. They should constantly be eager to obey the revealed will of God and continuously avail themselves of the blood's cleansing power (1 John 1:7). According to Stibbs, that extension of the picture is suggested by the order of the two nouns in the phrase. He says, "Our calling is to obey; but when we fail the atoning blood can still be sprinkled."[33]

C. THE GREETING (V. 2b)

Peter's greeting is a prayerful request for his readers to experience the distinctive Christian blessings of grace and peace. The greeting embodies the characteristic content of the New Testament epistolary greetings. The formula *grace and peace* soon displaced the colorless *chairein* ("to rejoice, greetings"),

---

29. Paul S. Rees, *Triumphant in Trouble. Studies in I Peter*, p. 25.

30. Cook, p. 174.

31. Best, p. 72.

32. Joh. Ed. Huther, *Critical and Exegetical Handbook to the General Epistles of Peter and Jude*, pp. 52-53.

33. Alan M. Stibbs, *The First Epistle General of Peter*, p. 73.

the commonly employed greeting (Acts 15:23; 23:26; James 1:1; cf. 2 John 10-11).

Grace and peace aptly summarize the basic Christian message. Grace is the free and unmerited favor of God bestowed upon guilty man in and through Jesus Christ. Always named first in such epistolary greetings, it bears witness to man's need, for "a being morally endowed who has never sinned, needs no grace."[34] It involves God's provision for the believer's sinful past and includes enabling grace for daily Christian living. Peace is the result of receiving the grace of God; it denotes the state of well-being that flows from the experience of being reconciled and forgiven.

To you, placed between *grace* and *peace*, emphasizes Peter's concern for his readers in their difficult situation. Thus, he indicated his desire that a growing experience of those gifts would be a vital, personal reality for them.

Be multiplied (*plēthuntheiē*) is the optative of wish, "may it be multiplied, may it be conferred abundantly on you." The verb is singular. Unless the singular is simply regarded as part of a set formula, it may imply that grace and peace are aspects of *one* experience. Though the passive voice does not specify the giver of those gifts, they must come from without. The prayer for their multiplication implies that the readers were already recipients of God's grace and peace. "They that have tasted the sweetness of this grace and peace, call incessantly for more."[35] The effective impartation of grace and peace will assure the completion of God's purposes with them. Hart suggested that the multiplication of grace and peace is needed "to match the growth of hostility with which the Christians addressed are confronted."[36]

Such a verb in the opening greeting occurs only in the Petrine epistles and in Jude. Masterman thought that Peter's use of the verb was "probably a reminiscence of the old high-priestly benediction of Numb. vi. 24-26."[37] But it is more likely that Peter, like the rabbis before him, drew the verb directly from the Septuagint translation of Daniel 4:1 (3:31 LXX) and 6:25.

34. Nathaniel Marshman Williams, *Commentary of the Epistles of Peter*, p. 11.

35. Robert Leighton, *A Practical Commentary Upon the First General Epistle of Saint Peter*, 1:51.

36. J. H. A. Hart, *The First Epistle General of Peter*, 5:41.

37. J. Howard B. Masterman, *The First Epistle of S. Peter (Greek Text)*, p. 64.

5

2. The Thanksgiving for Our Salvation
(1:3-12)

(3) Blessed *be* the God and Father of our Lord Jesus Christ, who according to his great mercy begat us again unto a living hope by the resurrection of Jesus Christ from the dead, (4) unto an inheritance incorruptible, and undefiled, and that fadeth not away, reserved in heaven for you, (5) who by the power of God are guarded through faith unto a salvation ready to be revealed in the last time. (6) Wherein ye greatly rejoice, though now for a little while, if need be, ye have been put to grief in manifold trials, (7) that the proof of your faith, *being* more precious than gold that perisheth though it is proved by fire, may be found unto praise and glory and honor at the revelation of Jesus Christ: (8) whom not having seen ye love; on whom, though now ye see him not, yet believing, ye rejoice greatly with joy unspeakable and full of glory: (9) receiving the end of your faith, *even* the salvation of *your* souls. (10) Concerning which salvation the prophets sought and searched diligently, who prophesied of the grace that *should come* unto you: (11) searching what *time* or what manner of time the Spirit of Christ which was in them did point unto, when it testified beforehand the sufferings of Christ, and the glories that should follow them. (12) To whom it was revealed, that not unto themselves, but unto you did they minister these things, which now have been announced unto you through them that preached the gospel unto you by the Holy Spirit sent forth from heaven; which things angels desire to look into.

That beautiful passage is the outpouring of an adoring heart. Only one who has devoutly contemplated the greatness of our salvation could utter such a magnificent paeon of praise, one that prepares and encourages the suffering soul to steadfastly continue the spiritual battle. It transmutes present suffer-

43

ings and turns them into abiding heavenly treasures; it evokes a song of praise
to God amid present tests and afflictions.

Blessed (*eulogētos*) is a compound verbal adjective that means a person or
thing "well spoken of" and thus praised. In the Septuagint it was used of both
men and God, but in each of its eight occurrences in the New Testament,[1] it
refers to God. When God blesses men, He confers blessings on them, making
them blessed. Whenever men "bless" God, they declare that He, in His infinite
excellence, is infinitely praiseworthy and express their celebration of what He
is and does (cf. our English words, *to eulogize, eulogy*). The devout heart
readily eulogizes God.

There is no verb with the adjective in the Greek construction, as is evident
from the italicized *be* in the ASV quoted above. It was also omitted by Paul in
the identical expression in 2 Corinthians 1:3 and Ephesians 1:3. Omissions of
such finite verbs are common to all parts of the New Testament. Grammarians
have discussed what mode of the verb *to be* is implied in 1 Peter 1:3. The
formula may be taken as a simple declarative as in the *Twentieth Century*'s,
"Blessed is the God and Father of our Lord Jesus Christ."[2] The indicative *is*
(*estin*) appears in Romans 1:25 and 1 Peter 4:11, but in both of those instances
the doxology is introduced by a relative pronoun. In 1:3 the doxology is an
independent construction. Most modern commentators and versions understand the words to be a prayer-wish, giving expression to the writer's actual
adoration of God and his conscious desire that God may be praised. That is
more probable. Lenski, however, suggested that no verb should be supplied.
He gave Peter's words the force of an exultant exclamation—"Blessed the God
and Father of our Lord Jesus Christ!"[3] That reflects the triumphant tone of the
passage.

Jewish piety prescribed that the benediction "Blessed be He" should be
pronounced whenever the name of God was uttered. But it is improbable that
a pious Jewish practice prompted Peter's doxology. His eloquent utterance
is no mere adoration of the divine name; it is a heartfelt outpouring of praise
for the marvelous salvation God has wrought in Christ Jesus. Peter's
utterance is grounded in the fuller New Testament revelation and is a
vital confession of Christian faith; it celebrates God's soteriological acts and
blessings.

Verses 3-12 form one grand sentence. In it are set forth "what God had
already done for the sojourners, and the transcendent greatness and glory of
the salvation, within whose securities they had already entered, as the
foundation on which must rest all ethical instruction in the school of Christ."[4]
Though the whole is constructed as a grammatical unit, its contents readily fall
into three divisions. Viewed from a chronological perspective, Farrar remarks
that the passage contains a "comprehensive glance at the future (3-5), the

1. Mark 14:61; Luke 1:68; Rom. 1:25; 9:5; 2 Cor. 1:3; 11:31; Eph. 1:3; 1 Pet. 1:3.
2. 20th Cent.
3. R. C. H. Lenski, *The Interpretation of the Epistles of St. Peter, St. John and St. Jude*, pp.
29-30.
4. John Lillie, *Lectures on the First and Second Epistles of Peter*, p. 24.

present (6-9), and the past (10-12)."[5] Using a trinitarian perspective, Hart notes that "vv. 3-5 have as their central figure the Father, vv. 6-9 the Son, and vv. 10-12 the Spirit who is at last given, who inspired the prophets of old and now inspires the Christian missionaries."[6] Looked at from the standpoint of the great salvation that Peter celebrated, he gave a description of that salvation (vv. 3-5), reminded his readers of their paradoxical experiences in connection with it (vv. 6-9), and pointed to three realities that magnify it (vv. 10-12).

A. THE DESCRIPTION OF SALVATION (VV.3-5)

Peter described our glorious salvation with a double designation of its author (v. 3a-b), reminded his readers of its two aspects (vv. 3c-4a), and assured them by calling their attention to its two-sided certainty (vv. 4b-5).

1) THE AUTHOR OF SALVATION (v. 3a)

Peter's adoration was not merely religious; it was distinctly Christian. His worship ascended to "the God and Father of our Lord Jesus Christ, who according to his great mercy begat us again." The One whom he worshiped is identified in relationship to the Savior as well as the saved.

a. *His relation to the Savior* (v. 3a). "The God and Father of our Lord Jesus Christ" is a concentrated Christian confession. It is the distinctive title of God in His saving activity toward mankind through the incarnate Son. Only Christians can thus characterize the God whom they worship and serve.

The one article with the two nouns, *the God and Father* (*ho theos kai patēr*), denotes a two-sided relation of the Father to the incarnate Christ. Peter's words could be taken to mean, "God, even (the) Father of our Lord Jesus Christ."[7] But that is not the natural force of the words. That translation cannot eliminate the fact that in Ephesians 1:17 we have the unambiguous phrase, "The God of our Lord Jesus Christ" (cf. Matt. 27:46; Mark 15:34). And on the morning of the resurrection, in His conversation with Mary Magdalene, the risen Lord explicitly expressed His two-sided relation to the Father when He said, "My Father and your Father, and My God and your God" (John 20:17). The double title is Peter's witness to the abiding reality of the incarnation. "For Jesus according to his human nature God is his God, and for Jesus in his deity God is his Father; his God since the Incarnation, his Father from all Eternity."[8]

The double title also witnesses to the subordination of the Son in His redemptive mission (John 14:28; 1 Cor. 15:24-28). It was through the incarnate

---

5. F. W. Farrar, *The Early Days of Christianity*, p. 86.
6. J. H. A. Hart, *The First Epistle General of Peter*, p. 41.
7. The KJV so translates the identical expression in 2 Cor. 1:3 and Rom. 15:6, but not in 2 Cor. 11:31 and Eph. 1:3.
8. Lenski, p. 31.

Son that the Father revealed Himself to mankind (Heb. 1:1-4). And it was the God thus revealed that the early church proclaimed as the true God. "Only as thus revealed in and through the Word made flesh, does the Supreme Being draw to Himself the confidence and confessions of man's guilty heart, and the praises of the redeemed."[9]

"Our Lord Jesus Christ" is the exultant cry of the redeemed. They gladly acknowledge the incarnate Christ, through whom they have been brought into living fellowship with the Father who sent Him, as their Lord. *Lord* (*kurios*) acknowledges Him as their Master and the One to whom they gladly give their obedience.[10] *Our* is confessional; it united Peter with his readers in a common bond in Christ.

The formula, "Blessed be the God and Father of our Lord Jesus Christ," also occurs in 2 Corinthians 1:3 and Ephesians 1:3 (cf. Rom. 15:6). Some writers, like Beare, argue that those words "are borrowed outright from St. Paul."[11] Cook even suggested that Peter "adopted the words expressly to indicate the perfect harmony of feeling, as well as of doctrine between himself and the apostle to the Gentiles."[12] But others insist there is no need to suspect literary dependence on Paul.[13] The phrase was a time-honored Jewish formula that the early church naturally took over with suitable adaptations. As such, it readily "passed into the liturgical and epistolary usage of the church, and so was adopted by our author."[14] But even if the phrase was drawn from the Pauline epistles, the similarity does not establish that Peter could not have written 1 Peter.

b. His act of mercy to the saved (v. 3*b*). The God who revealed Himself in Jesus Christ also acted in our salvation, as the phrase "who according to his great mercy begat us again" indicates. Our English versions prefer to continue with a relative clause, but the original uses an articular participle (*ho anagennēsas*), standing in apposition with *the God and Father of our Lord Jesus Christ*. The God whom Peter adored is further identified by His action toward the saved. He is the One who begat us again. *Us* unites the writer with his readers in the experience of salvation.

The aorist participle translated *begat* is a compound form that means "to beget again, to cause to be born again" and points to a past decisive experience of regeneration into which those addressed had already entered. The active voice presents the experience as God's work in them; it is not procured through human effort but is possible only through the operation of God's mercy and

---

9. Lillie, p. 25.
10. For a fuller discussion and bibliography see "Lord," *NIDNTT*, 2:513-20.
11. Francis Wright Beare, *The First Epistle of Peter*, p. 81.
12. F. C. Cook, *The First Epistle General of Peter*, p. 175.
13. J. N. D. Kelly, *A Commentary on the Epistles of Peter and of Jude*, p. 47; Ernest Best, *I Peter*, pp. 74-75.
14. Best, p. 74.

power. The verb pictures the beginning of the Christian life as a "new birth," the commencement of a drastic new order (2 Cor. 5:17). The verb *anagennaō*, "to cause to be born again," does not occur in classical Greek or the Septuagint. Elsewhere in the New Testament, it occurs only in 1 Peter 1:23. But portraying the inception of the Christian life as a new birth is fully consistent with other New Testament passages. The picture of the "new birth" is developed in Christ's conversation with Nicodemus (John 3:1-8). John 1:13; James 1:18, and 1 John 5:1-4 use "born of God" to refer to the inception of salvation. Titus 3:5 speaks of the beginning of the Christian life as a "regeneration," and Ephesians 2:10 says that Christians have been "created in Christ Jesus." The Christian is "a new creature," "a new creation" (2 Cor. 5:17; Gal. 6:15). The basis of the Christian life is an "actual participation in new God-given life."[15] The beginning of that life implies subsequent growth. "But if, from the time when it is supposed to take place, there is no growth, nothing can be admitted as evidence that it occurred at all."[16]

Beginning in the second century, the verb *anagennaō*, "to be born again," was commonly used in relation to baptism.[17] Accordingly, some interpreters believe that 1:3 refers to baptism,[18] but others, like Selwyn,[19] question that. Plumptre observed that Peter did not mention baptism but referred "further back to the Resurrection of Christ as that without which baptism and faith would have been alike ineffectual."[20] In the early church, conversion was always followed by baptism as a sign of and witness to the inner reality of the new birth.

"According to his great mercy" indicates that God's act in causing us to be born anew was in harmony with His compassionate character. He acted "according to" (*kata* with the accusative), that is "down along the line of" His mercy, the norm for His action. God's act was consistent with His character.[21] *Mercy* (*eleos*) is the feeling of pity and compassion toward the miserable. "It assumes need on the part of him who receives it, and resources adequate to meet the need on the part of him who shows it."[22] We did nothing to merit salvation. God displayed the fullness of His mercy by saving us when we were hopeless and miserable (Eph. 2:4). *Great* (*polu*), "much, great in magnitude or quantity," emphasizes the richness of His love and mercy (Eph. 2:4).

---

15. Alan M. Stibbs, *The First Epistle General of Peter*, p. 74.

16. Nathaniel Marshman Williams, *Commentary on the Epistles of Peter*, p. 12.

17. Charles Bigg, *A Critical and Exegetical Commentary on the Epistles of St. Peter and St. Jude*, pp. 99-100.

18. "The reference being clearly to baptism." Kelly, p. 48.

19. Edward Gordon Selwyn, *The First Epistle of St. Peter*, p. 123.

20. E. H. Plumptre, *The General Epistles of St Peter & St Jude*, p. 94.

21. In the Greek the prepositional phrase stands between the article and the participle; it thus has the force of an attributive adjective, ascribing a quality to the subject (H. E. Dana and Julius R. Mantey, *A Manual Grammar of the Greek New Testament*, p. 118).

22. C. F. Hogg and W. E. Vine, *The Epistle of Paul the Apostle to the Galatians with Notes Exegetical and Expository*, p. 341.

2.) THE NATURE OF SALVATION (vv. 3c-4a)

The salvation that we have received has a present as well as a future aspect. Our new life gives us a present hope grounded in Christ's resurrection (v. 3c) and also makes us heirs of a glorious inheritance yet to be revealed (v. 4a).

a. *The living hope grounded in Christ's resurrection* (v.3c). "Unto a living hope" sets forth the present character of the new pilgrim life. *Unto* (*eis*) indicates the result of our new birth; it has given us a living hope as the energizing principle of the new life. As used here, *hope* is not an objective prospect that the gospel sets before the believer but the subjective attitude of expectancy that grips the newborn soul. Vincent notes that in classical Greek hope (*elpis*) "has the general signification of expectancy, relating to evil as well as to good," but that "in the New Testament the word always relates to a future good."[23] In the present turbulent world, Christians are truly justified in viewing the future with optimism. Our new God-given life has delivered us from hopelessness (Eph. 2:12) and given us a joyous expectancy of what God still has in store for His people.

Peter characterized Christian hope as "living" (*zōsan*), having in itself the very life of the "living God" (1 Thess. 1:9). That hope stands in contrast to the empty, frustrating, deceptive, false hopes of the world.[24] Tribulation cannot destroy the Christian's hope since the living God inspires it and guarantees its fruition.

That personal hope is grounded in the objective reality of Jesus Christ's resurrection from the dead. Some, like Huther, directly connect the phrase "by the resurrection of Jesus Christ" with the verb *begat* and understand that phrase to specify the means by which God has begotten us again.[25] But it is more natural to connect the phrase with the entire preceding statement "the One who begat us again unto a living hope by the resurrection of Jesus Christ from the dead."[26] The resurrection of Christ is the crowning point of His redemptive work and the valid foundation for all of God's saving work, both present and future.

Peter's expression seems to recall "the sudden revulsion of feeling, a veritable birth into a new life, that came to the disciples through the Resurrection of Jesus Christ"[27] (cf. the experience of the Emmaus disciples, Luke 24:13-35). Without His resurrection, there can be no true hope (1 Cor.

---

23. Marvin R. Vincent, *Word Studies in the New Testament*, 1:630.

24. "Living hope as a fundamental religious attitude was unknown in Gr. culture," E. Hoffmann, "Hope, Expectation," *NIDNTT*, 2:239. For examples see Rudolf Bultmann, "The Greek Concept of Hope," *TDNT*, 2:517-21.

25. Joh. Ed. Huther, *Critical and Exegetical Handbook to the General Epistles of Peter and Jude*, p. 56.

26. Lenski, p. 33.

27. J. Howard B. Masterman, *The First Epistle of S. Peter (Greek Text)*, pp. 65-66.

15:12-20). "Without the Resurrection," Hunter remarked, "there would have been no Christian Church. Christianity is an Easter religion. Its theism is resurrection theism."[28]

"From the dead" rounds out the picture of the foundation of our hope. Christ's atoning death on the cross ushered Him into the realm of the dead, the disembodied state between death and the resurrection. But His bodily resurrection from the dead (ek nekrōn), "out from among such as are dead people," was the demonstration "that he is indeed the Son of God and the Savior of the world, and that his dying sacrifice is sufficient to cancel the sins of the world and to satisfy the righteousness of God."[29] His resurrection is the hope and guarantee of the resurrection of His people (1 Cor. 15:12-28). "As surely as He has conquered death and entered upon a heavenly life of joy, so surely will those who are members of the Body, whereof He is Head, follow Him."[30]

b. The glorious inheritance awaiting believers (v.4a). "Unto an inheritance" . . . is parallel to the preceding "unto a living hope" . . . and indicates the second aspect of our great salvation. Those words relate to the objective reality, the paternal estate that awaits believers as members of the family of God. The word inheritance (klēronomian) originally denoted "the portion which one received by lot," hence the portion that one received as his inheritance or possession. It may refer to a present possession (Gal. 3:18; Heb. 11:7), but in 1:4 it clearly refers to an expected possession (Col. 3:24; Heb. 9:15). It is the heavenly kingdom that will be fully manifested at the return of Christ (Phil. 3:20-21). As members of God's family, we are already heirs, yet our full possession of the inheritance awaits the future (Rom. 8:15-17; Eph. 1:13-14). The adjectives that follow were probably intended to establish a contrast between the heavenly inheritance and the earthly inheritance of the Israelites in the land of Canaan.

"Incorruptible" (aphtharton) is a negative adjective denoting something that is not subject to decay and dissolution. Unlike all earthly things, our inheritance does not contain in itself the seeds of decay and death and so is absolutely imperishable. It belongs to the heavenly realm where "neither moth nor rust doth consume" (Matt. 6:20) and shares the nature of the incorruptible God Himself (Rom. 1:23; 1 Tim. 1:17). The root verb of that adjective, meaning "to corrupt, to destroy," was sometimes used of the ravaging of a country by hostile armies. Therefore, some have suggested that Peter meant that our inheritance will never be subjected to outside forces of violence and wasting.[31] But it seems better to understand the word as a reference to the intrinsic nature of the inheritance as totally free from the forces of decay.

28. Archibald M. Hunter and Elmer G. Homrighausen, The First Epistle of Peter, p. 93.
29. Lenski, p. 33.
30. G. F. C. Fronmüller, The Epistles General of Peter, p. 15.
31. F. J. A. Hort, The First Epistle of Peter, p. 36; Masterman, p. 67.

"And undefiled" (*kai amianton*) specifies a second characteristic of our heavenly inheritance. The root verb means "to colour something by painting or staining it."[32] The adjective carried the picture of that which is morally and spiritually free from stain and "unsusceptible of any stain."[33] Uncontaminated by sin, our inheritance has the very character of Christ, our great High Priest (Heb. 7:26). The term suggests that the inheritance is free from defilement since the threat from external evil has been resisted. Wesley suggested that it was incapable "of being enjoyed by any polluted soul."[34]

"And that fadeth not away" (*kai amaranton*) adds the further fact of the permanent beauty of that inheritance. The adjective, occurring only here in the New Testament, projects the picture of a lovely flower that never fades (cf. the kindred adjective [*amarantinon*] in 5:4). The term denies the mutability and perishableness of that inheritance. The attractiveness of the inheritance will never diminish nor will it lose its charm for Christians. "The fountain of immortal youth is there, and in all the universe of God to be found there, and there alone."[35]

The force of those three negative adjectives is not readily reproduced in corresponding English negative adjectives. Rotherham literally translates, "an inheritance incorruptible and undefiled and unfading,"[36] and the NIV reads "an inheritance that can never perish, spoil or fade."[37] MacDonald remarks that those three negative terms picture the inheritance as "death-proof," "sin-proof," and "time-proof."[38] In its internal nature it is free from the germs of destruction; in its outward appearance it is untouched by the stain of sin; in its abiding character it is without diminution of its beauty.

The three negative terms indicate that in seeking to describe the heavenly inheritance, Peter could only tell us what it is not like in terms of our present life. Trench remarked,

It is a remarkable testimony to the reign of sin, and therefore of imperfection, of decay, of death, throughout this whole fallen world, that as often as we desire to set forth the glory, purity, and perfection of that other higher world toward which we strive, we are almost inevitably compelled to do this by the aid of negatives, by the denying to that higher order of things the leading features and characteristics of this.[39]

32. J. I. Packer, "Defile," *NIDNTT*, 1:447.

33. Robert Jamieson, A. R. Fausset, and David Brown, *A Commentary, Critical and Explanatory, on the Old and New Testaments*, 2:499.

34. John Wesley, Adam Clarke, Matthew Henry, and Others, *One Volume New Testament Commentary*, *loc. cit.* (pages unnumbered).

35. N. T. Caton, *A Commentary and an Exposition on the Epistles of James, Peter, John and Jude*, p. 68.

36. Joseph Bryant Rotherham, *The Emphasized New Testament*.

37. NIV.

38. William MacDonald, *I Peter: Faith Tested, Future Triumphant*, p. 16.

39. Richard Chenevix Trench, *Synonyms of the New Testament*, p. 253.

3.) THE CERTAINTY OF SALVATION (vv. 4b-5)

Peter added two passive participles to indicate the certainty of salvation. It is certain from the side of the inheritance itself (v. 4b), as well as from that of the heirs (v. 5).

a. *The safekeeping of the inheritance* (v. 4b). "Reserved in heaven for you" personally assured the readers of the certainty of their glorious inheritance. *Reserved* translates a perfect passive participle (*tetērēmenēn*). The perfect tense denotes that the inheritance was placed under safekeeping and that the preservation is still in force, and the passive implies that God is the One who preserves. The verb means "to watch over, to take care of, to guard against" loss or injury, by keeping an eye on that which is being guarded. The inheritance is certain because of God's watchful care. It is immune from the disasters that often befall an inheritance on earth. Its preservation in heaven (*en ouranois*)[40] adds to the assurance of safety. It is safely beyond the reach of all destructive forces. Its preservation in heaven indicates that the inheritance is not merely the believer's arrival in heaven.

"For you" (*eis humas*)[41] applies the assurance directly to the readers. The trials and sufferings they were experiencing on behalf of their faith would not undermine the certainty of their coming inheritance; they would possess it in due time.

b. *The preservation of the heirs* (v. 5). The articular participial construction, standing in apposition with you, sets before the readers the complementary truth that the heirs themselves were being divinely protected. That is made clear by the statement "who by the power of God are guarded through faith unto a salvation ready to be revealed." Peter emphasized that complementary truth to provide special encouragement to his afflicted readers.

"Guarded" (*phrouroumenous*), "to guard, to protect, to keep," is a military term (2 Cor. 11:32; Phil. 4:7), indicating that the heirs need protection from enemies. The present tense indicates that such protecting activity is continually exercised, and the passive voice indicates the external power that assures their safety. That power is identified by the phrase "by the power of God." The preposition translated "by" (*en*) may bear its regular locative force, "in." If so, it pictures the sphere in which God's keeping power is experienced. God's power is the garrison in which we find our security. His power "is all around them; it is the sphere in which they live and move; no harm can reach them in that all-embracing shelter."[42] But it is more likely that the preposition has an

---

40. The plural denotes the heavenly realm in contrast to the earthly sphere.

41. The Greek Text of Stephanus 1550 reads *hēmas*, "us," but that reading has the support of only a few late cursives. The Textus Receptus as well as all recent editors agree in reading *humas*, "you."

42. B. C. Caffin, *The First Epistle General of Peter*, p. 5.

instrumental force, and should be translated "by," as is generally done in our English versions. If so, the guarding force is itself God's power (*dunamei*), the power inherent in Him as God. And no power is greater (Rom. 8:31-39). Its operation is compatible with suffering for the faith.

The prepositional phrase, *those by God's power being guarded*, which stands between the article and the participle in the original, has the force of an attributive adjective. The operation of that power is an inherent aspect of the Christian's experience of being preserved from the assailing forces of evil.

Peter balanced that objective picture of God's preserving power with a reference to its subjective condition—"by faith." From the human side, faith is the means that activates God's preserving power in the life of the Christian. God deals with Christians as free moral agents and asks that we voluntarily commit ourselves to Him for our preservation. Our response of faith "gives Him His due place, and keeps us in our place of confidence in Him according to His word."[43] The proper human response is to recognize our own inadequacy and in every circumstance, by faith, ask Him to shield us by providing a way of escape (1 Cor. 10:13). Like Peter on the night before the crucifixion, we too will fall whenever we self-confidently presume that we can keep ourselves.

The present operation of God's preserving power in our lives anticipates the goal specified in the phrase "unto a salvation ready to be revealed in the last time." *Salvation* is synonymous with the inheritance already described in v. 4 and is eschatological in scope. The word *salvation*, which occurs three times in this section (1:5, 9-10), is a comprehensive biblical term. It is part of the Christian's past, present, and future experience. In the past, we were saved from the guilt of sin when we trusted the Savior (Eph. 2:8); in the present, we are being saved from the power of sin as we allow the Savior to work in us (Rom. 5:10; 1 Cor. 1:18; Phil. 2:12-13); in the future, we shall be saved from the very presence of sin when the Savior comes again (Rom. 13:11; Heb. 9:28). The future aspect of salvation, which is in view here, is its most glorious aspect and includes the glorification of our bodies (Phil. 3:20-21). Our salvation has both a negative and a positive aspect. Negatively, salvation involves deliverance from present sin and future destruction; positively, it includes entry into the fullness of the blessings that God has bestowed upon believers through the redemption in Christ.

Peter portrayed our future salvation as something "ready to be revealed in the last time." *Ready* indicates that all that was needed for the realization of salvation has been accomplished. It is now ready and waiting to be revealed at the proper moment. The aorist passive infinitive *to be revealed* (*apoka-luphthēnai*) signifies a specific act of uncovering or unveiling and implies the previous existence of that which is unveiled. The term looks forward to the

43. William Kelly, *The Epistles of Peter*, pp. 23-24.

coming day when God will draw back the veil that now hides our glorious salvation from mortal eyes. The unveiling is not deferred because the salvation is not ready, but because the appropriate time in the eternal counsel of God has not yet come.

The unveiling will occur in the last time (*en kairō eschatō*). The word for time (*kairos*), one of two Greek words regularly so translated, embodies the thought of "the right, proper, favorable time."[44] Peter designated that time as "last." It is a reference to the crucial situation that will mark the consummation of the present age and culminate in the visible return of Christ. Peter did not specify when that would be, but his words were intended to engender a sense of expectancy in the hearts of his readers.

Peter did not refer to the time of the believer's death, when the soul departs to be with Christ but the body remains in the grip of death (2 Cor. 5:8; Phil. 1:23). The full realization of our salvation awaits the time when Christ will return in glory and believers will "with him be manifested in glory" (Col. 3:4).

B. THE EXPERIENCES RELATING TO SALVATION (vv. 6-9)

Peter employed a relative clause to introduce the next section of his thanksgiving for our salvation, rather than beginning a new sentence, as we would do in English. Having described salvation in vv. 3-5, Peter focused his readers' attention on their experience of salvation. The construction indicates the close connection between Christian truth and Christian experience.

Peter explained the paradoxical nature of the Christian experience of salvation (vv. 6-7) and reminded his readers of the spiritual realities that sustained them when they were tested for their faith (vv. 8-9).

1) THE PARADOXICAL NATURE OF THE EXPERIENCES (vv. 6-7)

The emotional paradox that salvation evokes is boldly expressed in the phrase "Wherein ye greatly rejoice, though now . . . ye have been put to grief in manifold trials" (v. 6). It is the paradox of "a present rejoicing set in the midst of an environing grief."[45] Sadness and gladness exist side by side.

a. The experience of exultation (v. 6a). The intended antecedent of Peter's relative pronoun *wherein* (*en hō*), "in which" or "in whom," is uncertain. The relative *hō* is either masculine or neuter; therefore, the antecedent cannot be the salvation of v. 5 because it is a feminine noun. If the relative is masculine, it may relate to *the God and Father* at the beginning of the thanksgiving (v. 3). There is abundant biblical precedent for the thought of rejoicing in God, but

---

44. William F. Arndt and F. Wilbur Gingrich, *A Greek-English Lexicon of the New Testament and Other Early Christian Literature*, p. 395.

45. J. H. Jowett, *The Epistles of St. Peter*, p. 11.

the wealth of material between the pronoun and the antecedent makes that connection very improbable. Others, like Bigg,[46] believe that *en hō* has a temporal force, and so connect the relative with *the last time*, which stands immediately before it. Bigg understood Peter to mean that the readers "exult because their sufferings are so nearly at an end, and deliverance and glory are so near."[47] But that raises the problem of a mistaken anticipation. Lenski, who also accepted that connection, argued that *the last time* means "the present period of time in which we now live" and that they exult because "at any moment in this period the revelation may occur."[48] Lenski's interpretation is quite probable. But Selwyn argued that "the words 'the last time' are scarcely a large enough element in the previous sentence to carry the weight of this rich and significant relative clause."[49] According to Bennett, that "would give a sense very difficult to combine with the context."[50] Kelly states that "the fatal flaw" in that understanding "is that the last time, though imminent, is still to come," and would require that the verb *rejoice* be future.[51] It seems best to regard the relative as neuter and to understand the expression *en hō*, "in this," as a summary of the picture drawn in vv. 3-5. The expression looks back to the readers' "gracious privilege, security, and expectation, which had previously been described."[52] That widely accepted view is consistent with the relative clause construction that closely connects those two sections.

In view of the realities described in vv. 3-5, Peter said, "ye greatly rejoice" (*agalliasthe*). The verb, which occurs three times in 1 Peter (1:6, 8; 4:13), denotes an intense joy, "to exult, to be overjoyed," and implies an outward expression of that joy, "a jubilant and thankful exultation."[53] It is a distinctly religious joy (the term was not used in secular Greek). The verb was used "to express both corporate and individual attitudes of thankful joy before God."[54] Peter's use of the verb (it does not occur in the Pauline epistles) seems to be a clear echo of the Lord's use of it in Matthew 5:12, "Rejoice, and be exceeding glad." The present tense indicates that was the characteristic feeling of Peter's readers. It did not vanish at the approach of trouble since their rejoicing "turns to the God who now in Jesus Christ has already inaugurated the eschatological age of salvation and will gloriously complete it on Christ's return."[55]

46. Bigg, pp. 102-3.
47. Ibid., p. 103.
48. Lenski, p. 38.
49. Selwyn, p. 126.
50. W. H. Bennett, *The General Epistles, James, Peter, John, and Jude*, p. 190.
51. J. N. D. Kelly, p. 53.
52. Lillie, p. 38.
53. Rudolf Bultmann, "*agalliaomai, agalliasis*," *TDNT*, 1:20.
54. E. Beyreuther, "Joy, Rejoice," *NIDNTT*, 2:353.
55. Ibid.

The verb is either an indicative or an imperative. Some commentators,[56] as far back as Augustine, take the verb as a command. Thus B. C. Williams translated, "In such a hope keep on rejoicing."[57] That makes Peter's expression parallel to the imperative in Matthew 5:12 and James 1:2. But the context in 1 Peter is not parallel to either of those imperatives. To interpret that verb as an imperative is to make "an abrupt and premature transition to the hortative style, and has nothing of its own to recommend it."[58] As part of Peter's great opening thanksgiving, the context is clearly declarative. The hortatory section of the epistle begins with v. 13.

Others suggest that the indicative has a future meaning. Huther, who joined the verb closely with *the last time*, asserted that "the present tense strongly emphasizes the certainty of the future joy."[59] Here (and in v. 8), John Brown understood the rejoicing to have an eschatological setting. He insisted that the rejoicing is "too strong to describe the Christian's habitual feelings in the present state."[60] But to understand Peter's reference to rejoicing as exclusively future overlooks the paradoxical nature of the Christian experience of salvation. Paul, too, described our experience of salvation paradoxically in 2 Corinthians 6:10. Peter's picture of joy amid persecution is one of the unique features of the Christian life (cf. Acts 16:23-24; 1 Thess. 1:6).

b. The experience of distress (vv. 6b-7). Peter dwelt on the paradoxical nature of Christian experience. He carefully explained it (v. 6b) and indicated the divine purpose behind it (v. 7).

(1) *The nature of the distress* (v. 6b). Peter wrote, "Though now for a little while, if need be, ye have been put to grief in manifold trials." The aorist passive participle *lupēthentes*, "having been put to grief," is grammatically related to the plural subject of the verb *greatly rejoice*; it denotes the definite infliction of grief or pain upon those who habitually exult. Alford believed that the relation of the aorist participle to the verb in the present tense meant that at the time of the rejoicing "the grief is regarded as past away and gone."[61] But Greek could also use an aorist participle to denote action simultaneous with the action of a verb in the present tense.[62] That is clearly indicated in the KJV's "Ye greatly rejoice, though now . . . ye are in heaviness." The use of the aorist indicates that the grief was transito-

56. James Macknight, *A New Literal Translation from the Original Greek of All the Apostolical Epistles*, 5:437; Edgar J. Goodspeed, *Problems of New Testament Translation*, p. 192.

57. Williams.

58. Lillie, p. 35.

59. Huther, p. 61.

60. John Brown, *Expository Discourses on the First Epistle of the Apostle Peter*, 1:62.

61. Henry Alford, *The Greek New Testament*, vol. 4 (part 1), p. 335.

62. James Hope Moulton, *A Grammar of New Testament Greek*, 1:130-32; A. T. Robertson, *A Grammar of the Greek New Testament in the Light of Historical Research*, pp. 1112-14.

ry. But it need not follow that from the standpoint of the rejoicing it had already ceased. The verb *lupeō* does not denote the infliction of pain but the inward feeling of distress or grief caused by outward circumstances.

Peter mitigated his reference to grief with "though now for a little while, if need be." He consoled his readers by assuring them that though their experience of distress was "now for a little while" (*oligon arti*) it would be short-lived. He placed their affliction in a Christian perspective.

"For a little while" (*oligon*) indicates the limited duration of the grief. The comparison may be between the brevity of human life and eternity. But Lillie suggested that the reference is to "the shortness of the interval, which should precede the consummation at the coming of the Lord."[63] Less probable is the suggestion that the term is intended to express degree of grief, "in a small degree."[64] If true, it would serve to minimize the contrast between the two experiences. The translation "for a little while" is better.

"If need be" (*ei deon*) suggests that the readers' distress had a divine purpose. Peter tempered the thought by using a conditional form; but the condition used[65] assumes the reality of the condition, "if necessary, [as it is]." It is consoling to know that God's people are never needlessly afflicted. Peter firmly believed in the reality of God's sovereign presence in the lives of His people. His tender words assure us that "God not only holds out a future release but sympathizes with our present struggle."[66]

"In manifold trials" indicates the circumstances that caused their distress. *Trials* (*peirasmois*) characterizes the readers' environment as one of testing. The term denotes a process of testing for the purpose of displaying the nature or quality of the thing or person tested. Such testing may be good or bad, depending upon the purpose of the one who tests. It is good when the test is applied to demonstrate the strength or noble character of the person tested; it is evil when the aim is to cause the object under testing to fail. As a solicitation to evil, it became a "temptation" (KJV). In 1:6 "trials" has the first meaning, yet because of the weakness of human nature the second is not thereby excluded. The trying experiences of life "either put to the test what is good in a man, or tend to provoke his evil tendencies."[67] Though Peter made a veiled allusion to those testings in the words "are guarded" in v. 5, 1 Peter 1:6 is the first explicit reference to the readers' sufferings, a prominent subject in the epistle.

The trials that were encountered were manifold (*poikilois*). That adjective

---

63. Lillie, p. 42.
64. Bennett, p. 190; Hort, p. 41.
65. First class condition, assuming the reality of the condition (cf. Robertson, pp. 1007-12). The addition of *esti*, "is," in many manuscripts strengthens that reality.
66. A. F. Mitchell, *Hebrews and the General Epistles*, p. 236.
67. Lillie, p. 42.

means "of various kinds, diversified, variegated." Literally, it means "many-colored" and was used to describe "the skin of a leopard, the different-colored veinings of marble, or an embroidered robe."[68] It denotes the many aspects and appearances of the trials that afflicted the believers, not their number. In 4:10 Peter used the term of the "manifold grace of God." Barclay remarks, "There is no colour in the human situation which the grace of God cannot match."[69]

(2) *The purpose behind the trials* (v. 7). In v. 7 Peter developed the idea that there was a divine purpose behind the trials his readers suffered. *That* (*hina* with the subjunctive) introduces the statement of purpose. He pictured the testing of their faith (v. 7a) and described its eschatological outcome (v. 7b).

(a) *The testing of faith* (v. 7a). Peter introduced his thought with the words "The proof of your faith, being more precious than gold that perisheth though it is proved by fire." The phrase *the proof* (*to dokimion*) is problematic. In classical Greek *to dokimion* meant "the means or instrument of testing," and the adjective *dokimon* meant what was "examined, tested, or approved." But Peter was not referring to the means of testing. Papyrological usage has established that in koine Greek *dokimion* was used as an adjective equivalent in meaning to *dokimon*,[70] "approved, genuine." Moulton and Milligan cite the expression *chrusion dokimion*, "standard gold," gold that under testing has proved to be genuine.[71] Peter used the articular adjective *to dokimion* as an abstract substantive to denote "that which is approved, genuine," and so "the genuineness." The expression anticipates the result produced by testing.

"Your faith," understood as genuine faith, is the center of Peter's concern in the passage. The reference is not to the genuineness of the doctrinal content of the readers' faith (true versus false teaching) but to the genuineness of their personal response to the message of God. Thus Williams and others translate the phrase as "the genuineness of your faith."[72]

Peter assured his readers that such genuine faith "is more precious than gold that perisheth though it is proved by fire." That phrase continues his spirit of exultation. Because Christians suffer in terms of God's purposes, exultation overcomes grief and trials.

The comparative "more precious" (*polutimoteron*), "more valuable," under-

---

68. Vincent, p. 632.

69. William Barclay, *The Letters of James and Peter*, p. 209.

70. The variant form used in Papyrus 72, 74 and cursives 23, 56, 69, 206, and 429.

71. James Hope Moulton and George Milligan, *The Vocabulary of the Greek Testament Illustrated from the Papyri and Other Non-Literary Sources*, pp. 167-68.

72. So, Williams, 20th Cent., RSV; similarly, TEV, "that your faith is genuine"; NIV, "may be proved genuine."

scores the high value of tested gold. Gold is one of the most precious and durable metals. But faith is more valuable than gold that perishes (*tou apollumenou*). "Perishing" refers to the temporal realm. Genuine faith, by contrast, belongs to the things that are imperishable (1 Cor. 13:13).

The precise point of Peter's comparison is between genuine faith and purified gold. Though perishable, gold is subjected to the purifying process of fire. Peter's language stresses the testing agent, fire, "even though by means of fire it is proved" (Rotherham).[73] As gold is subjected to fire in order to refine and purify it (Isa. 1:25), so faith is refined and purified by fiery trials. The faith that does not endure under persecution cannot be acclaimed as genuine. The faithful are purged in order to be "pure gold." Best remarks, "This is one, but not the only, answer to the question of suffering in the Christian life."[74]

> (b) *The outcome of the testing* (v. 7b). The ultimate aim of testing is that genuine faith "may be found unto praise and glory and honor at the revelation of Jesus Christ." *May be found* indicates that the ultimate disclosure of the result awaits the coming day of judicial investigation. The result, says Fronmüller, is revealed "already now, since often the enemies of truth are constrained to acknowledge such fidelity of faith, innocence and patience, but more in the last days and in the great day of Christ."[75] Only in that day will there be a full disclosure of what God has achieved in the lives of His suffering saints.

"Unto praise and glory and honor" specifies the result of that coming disclosure. *Unto* (*eis*) introduces the goal God has in store for genuine faith. *Praise* denotes the "recognition or approval" that Christians will receive from the Judge. It is the reward of public commendation, "Well done, good and faithful servant" (Matt. 25:21; 1 Cor. 4:5). *Glory and honor* are essentially attributes of God (1 Tim. 1:17), but He is eager to bestow them upon those who have demonstrated the genuineness of their faith (Rom. 2:7, 10; Heb. 2:7, 9). As bestowed upon believers, *glory* indicates their participation in the radiance and glory of the future life (Luke 24:26; Rom. 8:18) because they have been changed into the likeness of the glorified Christ (Rom. 8:21; Phil. 3:21; 1 Pet. 5:1). *Honor* anticipates the positions of distinction to which God will promote His saints (John 12:26) and the blessings they will enjoy. Mason distinguished the three as follows: "'Praise' is the *language* that will be used about these men's faith; 'honour,' the *rank* in which they will be placed; 'glory,' the fervent *admiration* accorded to them; the three words correspond to the regions of word, act, and feeling."[76] But such distinctions should not be pressed too far.

Faith will be rewarded at the revelation of Jesus Christ, the time when the veil will be withdrawn and the Lord will return in visible glory (cf. v. 5). The

73. Rotherham.
74. Best, p. 78.
75. Fronmüller, p. 17.
76. A. J. Mason, *The First Epistle General of Peter*, p. 390.

faith of Peter's readers was being rewarded with scoffing, rejection, and persecution; but when the Lord Jesus returns, the scene will be reversed (cf. 2 Thess. 1:6-10). Such was the assurance Peter wished to keep before his afflicted brethren. "It is necessary," Calvin commented, "that He should turn our eyes to Christ if we wish to see glory and praise in our afflictions."[77]

2) THE SUSTAINING RELATIONS OF BELIEVERS (vv. 8-9)

Christian exultation amid distress can only be explained by the relations that sustain us. According to Peter, they are our relation to Jesus Christ (v. 8) on the one hand and to salvation (v. 9) on the other.

a. Their dual relation to Jesus Christ (v. 8). At verse 8 Peter turned from the prospect of Christ's return to his readers' relations with Him. Two relations are depicted, and both are stated negatively and positively: "whom not having seen ye love; on whom, though now ye see him not, yet believing, ye rejoice greatly."

Their love for the Christ they had never seen sustained them. "Whom not having seen" (*hon ouk idontes*) indicates the readers had never seen the incarnate Christ. The negative *ouk* with the aorist[78] participle summarily depicts the situation. Though a few Jewish Christians among the addressees may have seen Him when visiting Jerusalem, the vast majority of the readers had no personal contact with Jesus. It is generally thought that Peter's words imply a contrast between himself and his readers. Those who reject Petrine authorship minimize or dismiss that implication;[79] but others, like Cook,[80] see the expression as a mark of authenticity. Lack of personal contact with the Jesus of history did not place the readers at a spiritual disadvantage. By accepting the testimony of those who had seen Him, they entered into a personal relationship with Christ. They knew the blessedness of the Lord's beatitude, "Blessed *are* they that have not seen, and *yet* have believed" (John 20:29). "Whom ye love" indicates the readers' genuine relationship with Christ, the One they had never seen. Their love for Christ had been poured out in their hearts by the Holy Spirit, the One who makes Christ real to believers (Rom. 5:5). Love for the Lord Jesus is the sure mark of a true Christian (John 8:42; 14:21; 1 Cor. 16:22; Eph. 6:24; 2 Tim. 4:8).

Their faith in the Christ they had never seen also sustained them, as is indicated by the phrase "on whom, though now ye see him not, yet believing."

---

77. John Calvin, *The Epistle of Paul the Apostle to the Hebrews and the First and Second Epistles of St Peter*, pp. 235-36.

78. The Textus Receptus reads *eidotes*, "knowing," but the reading *idontes*, "having seen," is better supported and makes better sense. Modern editors agree in reading the aorist, *idontes*. For the evidence see the United Bible Societies text; also Bruce M. Metzger, *A Textual Commentary on the Greek New Testament*, p. 687. But James Moffatt, *The General Epistles, James, Peter, and Judas*, pp. 97-98, accepted *eidotes* as original.

79. Beare, p. 88; Best, p. 79.

80. Cook, p. 178.

The two present participles *see him not* (*mē horōntes*) and *yet believing* (*pisteuontes de*) emphasize the negative and positive aspects of the relationship. *Not seeing* (*mē*[81] *horōntes*) draws attention to the fact that their relationship is not nurtured by any gazing upon His visible presence. Unlike Thomas (John 20:24), they did not demand to see before they would believe. Yet Peter's "now" implied that one day they would see Him (Rev. 22:3-4). *On whom* (*eis hon*) is related to *believing* and denotes that their faith brought them into personal union with the One they had not seen. *Though ye see him not* is concessive; their faith is not sustained by sight.

"Ye rejoice greatly" indicates that the readers' relationship with Christ was marked by continuing love and faith (cf. v. 6). He who was the object of their faith and love also inspired their exultation. The indicative depicts the fact of their rejoicing. The present tense is not to be given a future force; it portrayed their actual experience.

That joy was no ordinary, earth-born joy. Peter said, "ye rejoice greatly with joy unspeakable and full of glory." Two adjectives draw attention to its uniqueness. *Unspeakable* (*aneklalētō*), which occurs only here in the New Testament, may denote what cannot adequately be expressed by human words, what is unutterable, or what human words cannot exhaust. The first possibility seems the most likely. Such joy contradicts the experience of the natural man.

That joy is also said to be *full of glory* (*dedoxasmenē*). The perfect passive participle pictures Christian joy as suffused with glory. It is a joy inspired by, and in a remarkable measure already radiant with, the glory that is yet to come (v. 7). As such, it can only be described in the language of the perfect life to come. That explains why the joy is unspeakable. But it is a joy that is experienced only along the pathway of steadfast suffering for the Lord.

b. Their experiential relation to their salvation (v.9). Peter introduced the topic of the experience of salvation with the words "Receiving the end of your faith, even the salvation of your souls." The participle *receiving* (*komizomenoi*) relates grammatically to the subject of the verb *rejoice greatly*, specifying the ground on which exultation rests. The action of the present participle is simultaneous with the rejoicing. Peter's language involves the tension between the present and the future in Christian experience. The ultimate realization of salvation is still future, awaiting the return of the Lord, yet there is a present appropriation by faith of that future consummation. The participle, as an active verb, means "to bring," as a jar of ointment in Luke 7:37; but in the middle voice, as here, it means "to carry off, get (for oneself), or receive" as wages or a prize.[82] To the simple thought of obtaining or receiving, it "adds the

---

81. The change of the negative from *ouk* to *mē* is not meaningless. Robertson, p. 1138, explains, "Here *ou* harmonizes with the tense of *idontes* as an actual experience, while *mē* with *horōntes* is in accord with the concessive idea in contrast with *pisteuontes*."

82. Arndt and Gingrich, p. 443.

thought of personal appropriation and enjoyment, of taking as one's own for use: Matt. xxv. 27."[83]

That which Christians receive by faith is "the end of your faith, *even* the salvation of *your* souls." What Christians are said to receive can be understood in two ways. The ASV, just quoted, takes *the end of your faith* as the direct object of the participle and *the salvation of your souls* as an explanatory apposition. That appositional force is marked by the addition of *even*. It is equally possible to take *the salvation of your souls* as the direct object of the participle and to understand *the end of your faith* as a predicate accusative. The NASB adopts that view and translates, "obtaining as the outcome of your faith the salvation of your souls." The NASB translation restricts *salvation* to the present experience of the salvation of the soul.[84] Either view is possible, but the former seems simpler and more probable. If that is correct, then the ultimate goal toward which faith is ever moving is already being appropriated in joyous experience.

The end of your faith denotes the end (*telos*), the goal, or final termination toward which Christian faith presses—salvation in its ultimate fullness. That goal is appositionally identified as *the salvation of your souls*, salvation in its full eschatological sense. Peter apparently used the word *soul* (*psuchē*) in a Semitic sense to denote the self or man as a living being (Ex. 1:5; Deut. 10:11). In 3:20 the term certainly denotes the whole human being. *The salvation of your souls* refers to the entire saving activity of God.[85] Therefore, the meaning of the expression need not be limited to the present saving of the soul as distinguished from the body.

The pronoun *your* is problematic. Though a few important manuscripts omit it,[86] the word has good manuscript support. Modern editors disagree concerning its authenticity. The texts of Westcott and Hort[87] and Nestle and Aland[88] omit the pronoun; the text of the United Bible Societies (third edition) places it in brackets (but the first edition included it without brackets)[89]; the text edited by Tasker[90] joins the Textus Receptus[91] and includes it without question. Beare argues that in view of "the all but unanimous testimony of the manuscripts and

---

83. Brooke Foss Westcott, *The Epistle to the Hebrews*, p. 336.

84. "In the 9th verse, salvation is the salvation of our souls, which we have now," W. T. P. Wolston, *Simon Peter: His Life and Letters*, p. 263.

85. See the discussion on "Soul" by G. Harder, *NIDNTT*, 3:676-86.

86. Notably, Codex *B*.

87. Brooke Foss Westcott and Fenton John Anthony Hort, *The New Testament in the Original Greek*.

88. Erwin Nestle and Kurt Aland, *Novum Testamentum Graece* (24th ed., n.d.).

89. Kurt Aland, Matthew Black, Carlo M. Martini, Bruce M. Metzger, and Wikgren, *The Greek New Testament*.

90. R. V. G. Tasker, *The Greek New Testament, Being the Text Translated in The New English Bible*.

91. F. H. Scrivener, *Hē Kainē Diathēkē. Novum Testamentum. Textus Stephanici A. D. 1550*.

versions" it is to be accepted as authentic.[92] Its inclusion makes the thought very personal for the readers.

C. THE MAGNIFICATION OF SALVATION (VV. 10-12)

The final section of Peter's doxology begins with another relative clause, as in v. 6. He incorporated the antecedent in the relative clause (*concerning which salvation*) and enlarged upon the greatness and glory of the salvation that he had just spoken of in v. 9. As Bigg observed, "St. Peter lingers upon the word *sōtēria* [salvation], at each repetition finding something new to say about it."[93] Peter did not seek to prove the truth of his teaching about salvation by showing its agreements with the prophets; rather, he sought to encourage his afflicted readers by demonstrating the importance and comprehensive grandeur of the salvation for which they were being afflicted. He did so by noting "the agents engaged in the ministry of redemption: prophets from the beginning, evangelists in the fullness of time, angels throughout watching and inquiring, all alike overshadowed and energized by the ever-present Spirit of Christ."[94]

1) THE MAGNIFICATION THROUGH PROPHETIC SEARCH (vv. 10-12a)

Peter encouraged his readers by reminding them that the prophets of old eagerly anticipated the great salvation that they were experiencing. Peter developed the relation of the prophets to that salvation at considerable length. Indeed, the salvation that evoked Peter's doxology was a matter of profound interest for those prophets. He depicted their intensive search (v. 10a), their prophetic function (v. 10b), their messianic perplexity (v. 11), and their restricted ministry in relation to that salvation (v. 12a).

a. Their intensive search (v. 10a). According to Peter's words, "Concerning which salvation the prophets sought and searched diligently," the OT prophets intensely investigated the salvation about which Peter wrote. *Salvation*, the subject of their search, has the same meaning here as in v. 9. The original word order, as given in Robert Young's literal translation, "concerning which salvation seek out and search out did the prophets,"[95] reveals that the emphasis is on the nature of their search, not the identity of the prophets. The use of two compound verbs strengthens that emphasis—"sought and searched diligently" (*exezētēsan kai exēreunēsan*). The preposition *ek*, "out," prefixed to both verbs, indicates the thoroughness of the action. The aorist tenses simply state

---

92. Beare, p. 89.
93. Bigg, p. 107.
94. Cook, p. 180.
95. Robert Young, *The Holy Bible Consisting of the Old and New Covenants Translated According to the Letter and Idioms of the Original Languages.*

their activity without marking its duration. The terms are synonymous and some, like Beare, insist that "we need not look for shades of difference in meaning between the two verbs."[96] The two terms obviously are used to intensify the picture of the prophetic search. However, the terms may differ slightly. Lenski said that "the former is more general, the latter more specific."[97] *Sought* (*exezētēsan*) indicates an intensive search or investigation, one that considers the matter from every point of view; *searched diligently* (*exēreunēsan*) indicates a search for something hidden, like "miners engaged in digging for precious metals in the bowels of the earth."[98] The first term may picture an attitude of zealous consideration and reflection and the second a careful investigation of the sources that might provide an answer.

Only here in the New Testament do the two verbs occur together. Kelly suggests that the usage is "perhaps a reminiscence of 1 Macc. ix. 26,"[99] where they are used together to picture an intensive search for certain individuals. Peter's use of those two verbs indicates that the prophets were not merely passive instruments through whom the Spirit delivered His message; they were individuals deeply interested in and moved by the messages they received. "If these words mean anything at all," Ross asserted, "they mean that the intellectual side of a prophet's life was full of an active spirit of enquiry."[100]

The prophets (*prophētai*) is used without the article, making the reference generic. The absence of the article "tends to divert the hearer's attention from the special consideration of individuals to the class itself."[101] The word *prophet* is "made up of the stem -*phē*, to say, proclaim, which always has a religious connotation, and the prefix *pro-*, which as a temporal adv. has the meaning of before, in advance."[102] That etymology suggests the meaning, "one who predicts the future," but common usage indicates that the term has a broader meaning. The prophets functioned as proclaimers of divine revelation, revealing God's will for the present and announcing judgment, as well as predicting the future. Demarest suggested that the preposition *pro-*, "before," should be understood as "referring to place—one who stands before another, declaring the will of his master."[103] Peter stressed the predictive function of the prophets; he viewed them as men whose gaze was fixed on the future.

Peter is commonly understood to have referred to Old Testament prophets. According to Selwyn, however, the reference is to Christian prophets of the

96. Beare, p. 90.
97. Lenski, p. 45.
98. Fronmüller, p. 17.
99. J. N. D. Kelly, p. 59.
100. J. M. E. Ross, *The First Epistle of Peter*, p. 49.
101. John Albert Bengel, *New Testament Word Studies*, 2:730.
102. C. H. Peisker, "Prophet," *NIDNTT*, 3:74. For an elaborate discussion on "Prophet" and massive bibliography see *TDNT*, 6:781-861; *NIDNTT*, 3:74-92.
103. John T. Demarest, *A Translation and Exposition of the First Epistle of the Apostle Peter*, p. 72.

New Testament era.[104] But his arguments have not carried the day; his understanding of the phrase does not fit the context. The passage suggests that a considerable amount of time intervened between the readers and the prophets (cf. v. 12). Selwyn's claim that the terms "sought and searched diligently" do not fit the Old Testament prophets (who authoritatively proclaimed their message as God's word) does not do full justice to Peter's picture. Peter did not suggest that the prophets questioned the truth of what they announced but that they sought to understand the full import of what they declared. There is evidence in the Old Testament that the prophets did seek enlightenment concerning the time and meaning of what they saw (cf. Isa. 6:11; Dan. 7:15-16; 9:1-3; 12:8-9). Peter's picture of those searching prophets seems to be grounded in the words of Jesus in Matthew 13:17 and Luke 10:23-24. Calvin correctly observed that Peter's words do "not refer to their writings or doctrine, but to the private desire with which each one was filled."[105]

b. Their prophetic function (v. 10*b*). The phrase "who prophesied of the grace that should come *unto you*" identifies the prophets in relation to the readers. *Who* is not a relative pronoun in the original but translates an articular participle (*hoi . . . prophēteusantes*) that stands in apposition with the word *prophets*. Their predictive activity united them as a group. But Peter's word order stresses their identity in relation to their message—"who concerning the grace toward you did prophecy" (R. Young). They spoke "of" (*peri*), "concerning," their message centered around "the grace that *should come* unto you" (*tēs eis humas charitos*) "the unto you grace." *Unto you* relates the prophetic message directly to the readers and may either mean the grace that was destined for them or that has now come to them. The latter view would connect the grace with the readers' own experience, and the former views the grace from the standpoint of the prophets. The context favors the former meaning.

The grace indicates the specific, personal grace God had in store for the readers. Grace has the same meaning here as in v. 2. Huther remarked that the grace is larger than the salvation just mentioned: *Grace* comprehends both the present and the future; the *salvation* of v. 9 relates to the future.[106] *Unto you* does not necessarily indicate a contrast between the readers as Gentile believers and *us* as Jewish Christians. Without referring to their background, Peter viewed the readers as recipients of the grace foretold by the prophets.

Foretelling the future was, of course, not the only function of the prophets. They were deeply concerned with the application of God's truth and will to the affairs of their own day. "Inevitably, however, with their eschatological approach to history, their attention was directed to the Day of the Lord, when

---

104. Selwyn, pp. 134; 259-68. See also E. H. Plumptre, *The General Epistles of St Peter & St Jude*, pp. 97-99. For a summary of Selwyn's arguments and answers to them see Best, pp. 83-84; J. N. D. Kelly, pp. 59-62.

105. Calvin, p. 238.

106. Huther, p. 70.

the condemnation of the wicked and the salvation of God's chosen would be fully accomplished, and they scanned the horizon for signs of its advent."[107] The future aspect of the prophets' ministry was of crucial importance for the Christian church since it provided a solid foundation for and authentication of the Christian message.

c. *Their personal perplexity* (v. 11). Their messianic predictions created a problem for the prophets, as Peter's phrase "searching what *time* or what manner of time the Spirit of Christ which was in them did point unto, when it testified beforehand the sufferings of Christ, and the glories that should follow them" indicates. That phrase is closely related grammatically with the preceding words. The nominative plural participle *searching* is related to the plural subject of "sought and searched" in v. 10 and even repeats the second verb.[108] The use of the present participle (*ereunōntes*) pictures the prophets as returning repeatedly to the problem that their predictions created for them. They were concerned to understand the time and circumstances in which their prophecies would be fulfilled (v. 11a), as well as the meaning of a suffering and then glorified messiah (v. 11b).

(1) *The time and circumstances* (v. 11a). The phrase *what* time *or what manner of time* (*eis tina ē poion kairon*) indicates the prophets' basic problem. Peter's words may be interpreted in two different ways. The grammatical problem is whether both interrogative pronouns, *tina* and *poion*, modify *kairon*, or whether *tina* is to be disassociated from *kairon* and understood as personal ("who"). If the first view is correct, the prophets' question relates to the time and attendant circumstances of Messiah's appearing; *or* is conjunctive and indicates an alternative form of the same basic question. That view is represented in the translation of the ASV given above.[109] It is equally possible to understand *tina* as standing alone and meaning "who." If that is correct, then *or* is disjunctive and so indicates a two dimensional search that was concerned with the personal identity and the time and setting of Messiah's coming. The NASB's translation "seeking to know what person or time"[110] is representative of that position.

The latter view allows the assumption that the prophets did not know whether the one they foresaw was the Messiah. But as Kaiser remarks, if that assumption is correct, "Surely Christ should also give the prophets the same

107. J. N. D. Kelly, p. 59.

108. As usual in such repetitions, the preposition *ek* is dropped (A. T. Robertson, *A Grammar of the Greek New Testament in the Light of Historical Research*, p. 563).

109. Similarly, NIV, "the time and circumstances"; Rotherham, "what particular or what manner of season."

110. Similarly, RSV, "what person or time was indicated"; Berkeley, "to find out to whom or to what time."

scathing rebuke that He gave to the men on the road to Emmaus for being ignorant of his person and work from the O.T., if this text of I Peter so classifies them (Luke 24:25-27)."[111] But Peter's words need not be understood to mean that the prophets did not know that they were speaking about the coming Messiah. As Mason said, "They were aware that they were speaking of a *Messiah*; but who the man should be who would hold that office, or at what period of their history he would arise, this was what they longed to know. They foresaw a Christ, but they could not foresee Jesus; they could give to their Christ no definite position in future history."[112] The One whose coming they foresaw did not fit any familiar pattern. "It is very certain," remarks Caton, "that the king the Jews expected bore no resemblance to the Jesus who did come."[113]

But the view that only a single question is implied in Peter's expression, i.e., the time or season of Messiah's coming, seems somewhat more probable. It is the one problem stressed in the context. It is the commonly accepted view. Generally speaking, it has the support of the Greek grammarians. Blass and Debrunner state that the combination of the two interrogatives is a probable example of "tautology for emphasis."[114] Robertson cites some New Testament examples of that tautological usage of those interrogatives and adds that it "may be true of I Pet. 1:11, but not certainly so."[115] That view is accepted by the majority of the commentators and appears in most of our English versions. In support Kaiser notes, "Daniel 12:4, 9, and 13 make it plain that the 'when' of the fulfillment is what is unknown to the prophet. The appointing of certain visions and prophecies 'for many days to come' (Ezekiel 12:27) or for 'that time' (Zephaniah 3:20) only led all the more to the question 'what time? and when shall these things be?.' "[116] If that is correct, then the interrogative *tina* raises the question of the precise date of Messiah's coming and *poion* queries the characteristic features of the time (*kairon*), the favorable season, of His appearing. That understanding of the prophets' inquiry corresponds to the double question that Jesus' disciples asked Him in response to His prophecy about the end of the age (cf. Mark 13:4).

We accept the translation "what or what manner of time" as more probable. But Best minimizes the distinction between the two interpretations. He says, "There is no essential difference in meaning in so far as it is the 'time' of the 'person' which is at issue."[117]

---

111. Walter C. Kaiser, Jr., "The Eschatological Hermeneutics of 'Evangelicalism': Promise Theology," p. 95.

112. A. J. Mason, *The First Epistle General of Peter*, p. 392.

113. N. T. Caton, *A Commentary and an Exposition of the Epistles of James, Peter, John and Jude*, p. 70.

114. F. Blass and A. Debrunner, *A Greek Grammar of the New Testament and Other Early Christian Literature*, p. 155.

115. Robertson, pp. 735-36.

116. Kaiser, p. 95.

117. Best, p. 81.

The phrase "which the Spirit of Christ which was in them did point unto" indicates the source of those prophecies. They were not the product of the prophets' own imaginations or pious musings; they were communicated by "the Spirit of Christ which was in them." According to Peter, the Spirit is no mere impersonal influence but a personal Being whose work within the personality of the prophets enabled them to give utterance to messages that came not from themselves but from God (2 Pet. 1:19-21). The original, *to en autois pneuma*, "the in them Spirit", portrays the Spirit as operating within the personalities of the prophets.

The Spirit is identified as "the Spirit of Christ." Bengel understood the genitive *of Christ* (*Christou*) as objective, the Spirit "testifying of Christ."[118] More probably the genitive is subjective, the Spirit that He possessed and bestowed. Some, like Fronmüller, understand the designation to denote "the spirit belonging to the preexisting Messiah from eternity, and which He was consequently able to impart to the prophets."[119] If that is correct, then the reference is to the preexistent Christ who was with Israel (1 Cor. 10:4; 2 Cor. 3:17). That view, which gives strong testimony to the preexistence of Jesus Christ, was held by many in the early church. *The sufferings of Christ* refers to the historical Messiah; the two instances of Christ in the verse have the same meaning. As applied to the Old Testament prophets, "the Spirit of Christ" might, as Selwyn suggests, be translated "the Messiah-Spirit."[120] For Peter and his readers "the Spirit of Christ" was a natural Christian identification of the Holy Spirit whom they had experienced as followers of the Messiah. He was the Spirit of Jehovah who inspired the prophets.

The imperfect tense "did point unto" (*edēlou*) emphasizes the successive disclosures that the Spirit revealed through the prophets. The root meaning of the verb is to make clear by giving information on a matter (cf. 2 Pet. 1:14). The Spirit continued to set before the prophets specific disclosures concerning the coming Messiah.

> (2) *The sufferings and the glories* (v. 11*b*). The Spirit's disclosures related to two specific matters: "when it testified beforehand the sufferings of Christ, and the glories that should follow them." *When it*[121] *testified beforehand* translates a compound participle (*promarturomenon*) that occurs only here in the New Testament. The compound does not occur in classical Greek or in the Septuagint. Moffatt suggested that the term was coined by Peter.[122] In classical usage the simple verb in the active meant "to witness," and in the middle voice, as here, "to call

118. Bengel, 2:730.

119. Fronmüller, pp. 17-18.

120. Selwyn, p. 136.

121. Modifying the neuter Greek noun *pneuma*, "Spirit," the participle is neuter; it has no bearing on the doctrine of the Person of the Spirit; cf. John 16:13-15 (Gr.).

122. James Moffatt, *The General Epistles, James, Peter, and Judas*, p. 100.

another to witness." The prefixed *pro*, "before," adds the thought of "beforehand" or "publicly." In keeping with classical usage, Masterman suggested that the Spirit was calling upon God to bear witness to the truth of the revelation being made, and he detected in the form a reminder "of the oft-repeated prophetic affirmation, 'Thus saith the Lord.'"[123] But that seems forced and unnatural. Papyrological usage shows that in koine Greek the middle was used with the meaning "to bear witness." The translation of the compound "to testify beforehand" seems amply justified.[124]

The Holy Spirit testified repeatedly in advance concerning "the sufferings of Christ, and the glories that should follow them." Both aspects of that prediction relate to the Messiah in His human nature.

The sufferings "of Christ" (*eis Christon*), "unto Christ," denote the sufferings directed toward or appointed for the Messiah. The thought of divine foreordination is involved. The plural *sufferings* comprehends all the painful experiences that befell Him during His earthly messianic ministry. Jesus accepted those predictions as an intrinsic part of the messianic picture and repeatedly sought to impress that fact upon His disciples. The doctrine of a suffering Messiah was neglected by the Jews of the first century, and its preaching by the church proved a definite stumbling block to them (1 Cor. 1:23; 1 Pet. 2:7-8).

Some interpreters believe that Peter intended his expression *the sufferings unto Christ* (Gr.) to include the sufferings of the church as His mystical body.[125] But the context does not suggest such an extension of the picture.

The second part of the prophetic picture related to "the glories that should follow them" (*tas meta tauta doxas*), literally, "the after these glories." The order indicates that by their very nature those glories follow the sufferings as results (Phil. 2:6-11). The risen Christ Himself emphasized that order in His exposition to the Emmaus disciples (Luke 24:25-6), and that order also holds for the followers of the Messiah (1 Pet. 1:6-7; 4:13; 5:6-10).

The plural *glories*, occurring only here in the New Testament,[126] "corresponds to the plural 'sufferings,'—the one as multiform as the other."[127] The plural apparently suggests the various steps in Messiah's glorification: His resurrection, His ascension, His resumption of glory on the Father's throne (John 17:5; Heb. 1:3; Rev. 3:21), His return and reign in glory (Col. 3:4; 2 Tim. 2:12), and His majestic glory as the Judge of all (Rev. 20:11-15).

Those two phases of Messiah's experiences forseen by the prophets form the

---

123. Masterman, p. 75; Hort, pp. 53-54.

124. H. Strathmann, *"marturomai, diamarturomai, promarturomai," TDNT*, 4:510-12; Beare, p. 92.

125. Calvin, pp. 240-41; Huther, pp. 72-73; Plumptre, p.99; John Brown, *Expository Discourses on the First Epistle of the Apostle Peter*, 1:85-86.

126. The plurals in 2 Pet. 2:10 and Jude 8 are personal, "dignities."

127. Mason, pp. 392-93.

whole story of the gospel. The problem for the prophets was to relate those two aspects to one Person. It was also a problem for the personal followers of the Messiah (cf. Matt. 16:21-28; Mark 9:31-38), until the dilemma was resolved for them by the events of history. The solution lay not in a correction of the revelations but in the apprehension of their proper correlation.

d. *Their restricted ministry* (v. 12a). The words "to whom it was revealed, that not unto themselves, but unto you, did they minister these things" indicate that the prophets received a partial answer to their question. The aorist passive, *it was revealed*, shows that the realization came to them not simply as a conclusion drawn from their investigation, but as an answer given by the Spirit. Whether the answer came to them as part of the Spirit's messianic predictions (cf. Dan. 10:14) or came later in reply to their personal search concerning what had already been revealed is not certain. The latter view is simpler and more natural.

The prophets were told that Messiah's coming and its attendant blessings would not have historical fulfillment in their own day. The explicit date and the circumstances connected with His coming were not disclosed to them; they continued to live under the consciousness of a great "Not Yet." Their eager anticipation of the future was shared by many righteous men (Matt. 13:17; Luke 10:23-24).

The blessings foreseen by the prophets had reached "unto you" (*humin*), to the readers personally. That phrase emphasized the salvation they had experienced. The reading in the KJV, "unto us" (*hēmin*), follows the Textus Receptus.[128] That reading has the support of Codex *K*, minuscule 33, and some versions, but the mass of the manuscript evidence is in support of *you*. The scribal change of the pronoun reflects the natural consciousness of believers that such blessings are a present privilege of each of us. As Cranfield remarks, "The forward-pointing of the Old Testament is an essential part of the foundation of our faith. There is a real distinction between the Old Testament and the New, but also a no less real unity, and that unity—the fact that the forward-pointing fingers and the backward-pointing fingers are all alike focused on one figure, Jesus Christ."[129] The early Christian church refused to impoverish itself by rejecting the efforts of Marcion and the Gnostics to sever its faith from the Old Testament.

As God's agents who made known the coming of the Messiah, the prophets "ministered" to others; they served the interest of others who at some unknown future time would benefit from their work. They were faithful stewards of God's grace in the service of mankind when they foretold "these things" (*auta*), i.e., the sufferings and glories of the Messiah.

Peter's negative statement, "not unto themselves," does not mean that the work of the prophets had no application to or value for their own day. Much of their work was explicitly related to their own time and circumstances. The

128. Scrivener.
129. C. E. B. Cranfield, *I & II Peter and Jude*, pp. 44-45.

negative, absolute in form, is comparative in meaning. The spiritual benefits that they derived from their prophetic announcements were "a partial and so to speak reflected light caught from the far-off dawn of the rising of the Sun of righteousness."[130] *Ministered* (cf. Acts 6:1-6) likens their work to "a spreading of the table, so that others might afterward feed on the food laid on it."[131]

2) THE MAGNIFICATION THROUGH CHRISTIAN PROCLAMATION (12b)

The greatness of Christian salvation was further held before the readers with the reminder of "these things, which now have been announced unto you through them that preached the gospel unto you." Peter's relative construction, *these things, which* (*auta ha*), draws attention to the continuity between the prophetic revelations and the Christian message. But *now* denotes a strong contrast between the time of the prophets and that of the readers. The prophets looked forward to a distant, unidentified future; the readers were reminded of the historical events that had already been rehearsed for them. Peter's words indicate a long interval of time. The readers were the personal recipients of the prophetic fulfillment. "While our modern critical scholars customarily look for that which is new and unique in the Christian message —and indeed the Christian gospel is ever fresh and new to an aged and dying world—it is significant that the earliest Christians authenticated their message by declaring Jesus to be the fulfillment of that which was old."[132]

The readers heard the message "through them that preached the gospel unto you" (*dia tōn euanggelisamenōn humas*), "them that evangelized you," those who brought them the good news. Peter did not identify the agents through whom they first heard the gospel. The expression is general; it is not limited to the preaching of the apostles. It does not compel us to exclude Peter as one of those evangelists, yet it does so by implication. Had Peter meant to include himself among their number, his statement would have been more specific.

The evangelists announced the good news "by the Holy Spirit sent forth from heaven." Their preaching was "by" or "in" a power beyond themselves.[133] The Holy Spirit used them as His agents and empowered their preaching. The Spirit who used the Old Testament prophets to predict Messiah's coming also used the New Testament preachers to proclaim the fact of His coming. The same Spirit prompted and authenticated the message of both.

Peter described the Spirit, the dynamic of gospel preaching, as "sent forth from heaven." That indicates "not only their inspiration, but the Divine attestation to the truth, the importance, and excellency of the salvation made

---

130. Cook, p. 180.

131. Calvin, p. 241.

132. Robert Paul Roth, *I Peter*, p. 419.

133. There is some textual uncertainty concerning the authenticity of "in" (*en*), but it is probably authentic, in keeping with prevailing usage in 1 Peter. See Bruce M. Metzger, *A Textual Commentary on the Greek New Testament*, p. 687. Under either reading the Holy Spirit is the direct agent behind the gospel preaching.

known by them."[134] The aorist tense, *sent forth* (*apostalenti*), denotes the historical event of the Spirit's coming on the Day of Pentecost (Acts 2:1-4), and the passive voice indicates His coming in fulfillment of a divine commission (cf. Gal. 4:4-6). He was sent as God's precious gift to the church.

3) THE MAGNIFICATION THROUGH ANGELIC INQUIRY (v. 12c)

The phrase "which things angels desire to look into" effectively lays the capstone of Peter's magnification of our salvation. Once more a relative, *which things* (*eis ha*), "into which things," relates backward to and summarizes what has gone before. Those great and glorious realities concerning the Messiah that fascinated the prophets and engaged the energies of the messengers of the gospel also are the objects of intense angelic interest. *Angels*, used without the definite article, is qualitative, indicating that no lesser beings than angels are in view. Peter's concluding comment focuses the mind on the heavenly realm.

"Desire" (*epithumousin*) denotes a strong interest or craving. The present tense portrays a present, continued, inner yearning to comprehend. The term does not imply that the desire cannot or should not be fulfilled, but it does mark an enduring angelic effort to comprehend more of the mystery of human salvation.

"To look into" (*parakupsai*) portrays the manifest interest of those angelic beings. The verb literally means to bend over or forward to examine more closely. In Luke 24:12 and John 20:5 and 11 it is used of the bodily posture of individuals at the open tomb of Jesus. In James 1:25 it is used metaphorically of a man stooping over to look intently into the law of liberty. The angels in 1 Peter are pictured as watching the unfolding of the drama of human redemption to understand it more fully. Peter seems to imply that angels stand outside the redemptive realm and cannot understand it in terms of their own experience (cf. Heb. 2:16). First Corinthians 4:9; Ephesians 3:10; and 1 Timothy 3:16 likewise picture the supernatural world eagerly observing God's program of human redemption. The concept seems grounded in Jesus' words in Luke 15:7, 10 where angels are said to rejoice over one repentant sinner.

Looking back over Peter's heartfelt thanksgiving for our great salvation, one is awed by its depth and richness. The paragraph provides an amazingly comprehensive presentation of Christian salvation. The New Testament pictures Peter as a man of aggressive action. First Peter 1:3-12 establishes that he was also a clear thinker, that he had a firm grasp of the great spiritual realities of the Christian gospel. He displayed an impressive ability to present his message in a balanced, cohesive, and comprehensive manner.

Peter's majestic doxology laid a solid doctrinal foundation for the faith of his afflicted readers. Upon that foundation he constructed three cycles of practical exhortations for Christian living.

---

134. Demarest, pp. 76-77.

Part 2
Practical Exhortation
(1:13—5:11)

The opening "Wherefore" of 1:13 marks the turning point in the tone of 1 Peter. It has appropriately been called "the hinge upon which the Epistle turns."[1] It signals Peter's transition from the didactic to the hortatory, from the doctrinal to the practical. His consistent use of the indicative in presenting the glories of Christian salvation (1:3-12) changes to the repeated use of the imperative in setting forth the duties of the Christian life.[2] A hortatory tone characterizes the remainder of the epistle. Though Peter continued to present doctrine with his imperatives, his main emphasis was upon the realities of Christian duty.

---

1. J. Gresham Machen, *The New Testament. An Introduction to Its Literature and History*, p. 252.
2. Our interpretation of Peter's language in 1:13—5:11 finds thirty-five imperatives, though the count in our English versions is usually higher due to the translation of the participles. For example, there is only one imperative form in 1:13, but our English versions generally use two or three imperatives.

First Cycle:

The body of 1 Peter (1:13—5:11) consists of three cycles of exhortations, each logically flowing from what has gone before. The comprehensive picture of salvation in 1:3-12 functions as a foundation for Peter's exhortations to live out that salvation in the Christian life. His threefold portrayal of how the saved should live (1:13—2:3) is undergirded by a rich section that sets forth the reasons for such a life (2:4-10). Those reasons, which draw a contrast between believers and unbelievers, provide a basis for the second cycle of exhortations. That cycle deals with Christian duties in view of our position in the world (2:11—3:12). The third and longest cycle of exhortations focuses on Christian suffering (3:13—5:11). It explains the nature of the true Christian life, as that life is lived in the midst of a world that rejects Christ. The treatment of the experience of Christian suffering from a hostile world formed Peter's basic message for his afflicted readers and proclaimed the reality of Christian triumph amid affliction.

6

The Christian Life in Relation to God
(1:13-21)

Peter's first cycle of practical exhortations (1:13—2:10) is based on his previous description of salvation. In the first cycle he stressed the kind of life that should result from salvation. Christian faith is to manifest its genuineness in Christian conduct. The section naturally divides into two parts. First, Peter depicted the Christian life in terms of three different relationships (1:13—2:3). Then he gave two reasons to motivate believers to live such lives (2:4-10).

A. THE LIFE ARISING FROM SALVATION (1:13—2:3)

Peter gave a comprehensive presentation of the life that should flow from our great salvation. Such a life involves precise duties to God (1:13-21), man (1:22-25), and self (2:1-3).

1) THE CHRISTIAN LIFE IN RELATION TO GOD (1:13-21)

(13) Wherefore girding up the loins of your mind, be sober and set your hope perfectly on the grace that is to be brought unto you at the revelation of Jesus Christ; (14) as children of obedience, not fashioning yourselves according to your former lusts in *the time of* your ignorance: (15) but like as he who called you is holy, be ye yourselves also holy in all manner of living; (16) because it is written, Ye shall be holy for I am holy. (17) And if ye call on him as Father, who without respect of persons judgeth according to each man's work, pass the time of your sojourning in fear: (18) knowing that ye were redeemed, not with corruptible things, with silver or gold, from your vain manner of life handed down from your fathers; (19) but with precious blood, as of a lamb without blemish and without spot, *even the blood* of Christ: (20) who was foreknown indeed before the foundation of the world, but was manifested at the end of the times for your sake, (21) who through him are

77

believers in God, that raised him from the dead, and gave him glory; so that your
faith and hope might be in God.

"Wherefore" (*dio*, "because of this thing, for this reason") is best understood
to summarize all that has been said in vv. 3-12. As Cranfield put it, "Because
God has begotten you again to a living hope by the resurrection of Christ from
the dead, because you have an incorruptible inheritance, a salvation ready to
be revealed in the last time, *therefore* . . ."[1] In typical New Testament fashion,
Peter constructed his ethical superstructure on the doctrinal foundation he had
laid. The transforming experience of salvation and its hope of future glory
should be the driving force in daily duty. But grace must first be experienced
before the obligations of grace become operative.

Peter focused on three aspects of the believer's life in relation to God. It is a
life of steadfast hope (v. 13), personal holiness (vv. 14-16), and rightful
reverence (vv. 17-21).

a. A life of steadfast hope (v. 13). The imperative in Peter's statement,
"Girding up the loins of your mind, be sober and set your hope perfectly on
the grace that is to be brought unto you at the revelation of Jesus Christ,"
portrays the Christian life as an urgent duty. The original makes *hope* the
central and leading thought of the verse. Two participles precede the control-
ling imperative and designate the activities that support hope. Those
participles are grammatically related to the subject of the imperative and
thereby receive an imperatival coloring. But to translate them as imperatives obscures the way they function to support Peter's remarks about
hope.

(1) The supports of hope (v. 13a). Two activities support the life of hope,
the first a decisive action, the other a continuing attitude.

"Girding up the loins of your mind" embodies a figure familiar from daily
oriental experience. The long flowing garments were habitually drawn up and
tucked under the belt in preparation for vigorous activity; they were let down
for repose. Shortening a garment helped to avoid impeding action and also
gave support to the loins. Girding the loins, as a metaphor of preparation for
aggressive activity, is common to both the Old and the New Testament (cf. Ex.
12:11; 1 Kings 18:46; 2 Kings 9:1; Jer. 1:17; Luke 12:35; Eph. 6:14; etc.). It is a
fitting figure for those who as temporary residents and pilgrims (1:1; 2:11) are
to be aggressive and ready to move on. Christians are to banish all slackness
and indolent heedlessness.

"Girding up" (*anazōsamenoi*) is a compound form that is rare in classical
Greek and occurs only here in the New Testament.[2] The preposition *ana*

---

1. C. E. B. Cranfield, *I & II Peter and Jude*, p. 46.
2. The common form *perizōnnumi*, "to gird around," occurs six times in the NT.

("up"), rather than the more familiar *peri* ("around"), stresses the lifting of the robe to avoid entanglement. The middle voice marks it as an action performed for one's own advantage. The use of the aorist tense conveys the sense of a completed action in preparation for a course of activity, a strenuous life of obedience.

Calvin remarked that "Peter doubles the metaphor by ascribing loins to the mind."[3] The attribution of loins, the seat of the strength of the body, to the mind establishes that the picture relates not to physical but to strong mental activity.[4] "Mind," rather than "soul" or "heart," indicates that Peter was concerned with the practical intelligence of his readers. The word *mind* (*dianoia*) properly means what goes through the mind, one's thought processes; but more generally it denotes the mind, including the intellectual and moral faculties (cf. Matt. 22:37; Eph. 2:3; 2 Pet. 3:1). It is a call to bring all of one's rational and reflective powers under control by "cutting off vague loosely flowing thoughts and speculations that lead nowhither, and only hamper obedience."[5] It is an essential preparatory action if Peter's addressees were successfully to resist the dangers that confronted them. "Loose thinking is creative of loose living; mental slovenliness issues in moral disorder."[6] A disciplined mind has a vital place in spiritual living.

"Be sober" (*nēphontes*), literally, "being sober," designates the second activity that supports a life of hope. The present tense calls for a continuing state or habitual temper of sobriety. In the New Testament the verb is not used to mean "not drunk, unintoxicated." The figurative usage assumes the condition of sobriety.[7] It denotes a condition free from every form of mental and spiritual loss of self-control; it is an attitude of self-discipline that avoids the extremes of the "reckless irresponsibility of self-indulgence on the one hand, and of religious ecstasy on the other."[8] It inculcates a calm, steady state of mind that evaluates things correctly, so that it is not thrown off balance by new and fascinating ideas. Such "levelheadedness" is a constant Christian need.

---

3. John Calvin, *The Epistle of Paul the Apostle to the Hebrews and the First and Second Epistles of St Peter*, p. 243.

4. "The loins" is dropped in the NASB and RSV. Other versions replace "girding" with a more contemporary verb such as "prepare" (NIV, Weymouth, Goodspeed), "brace up" (Moffatt, Montgomery, Berkeley). The NEB's "be mentally stripped for action," changes the figure to that of an athlete. Cranfield (p. 47) says, "We should get the same quaint incongruity that the writer intended if we were to render the Greek—'Rolling up the shirtsleeves of your mind' or even 'taking off the coat of your mind.'"

5. Charles Bigg, *A Critical and Exegetical Commentary on the Epistles of St. Peter and St. Jude*, p. 112.

6. J. H. Jowett, *The Epistles of St. Peter*, p. 36.

7. E. M. Blaiklock, *First Peter*, p. 34, notes that it also does not mean "'glum and straight-faced,' the vice alleged against the Puritan."

8. Alan M. Stibbs, *The First Epistle General of Peter*, p. 85.

(2) The call to hope (v. 13b). "Set your hope perfectly on the grace that is to be brought unto you at the revelation of Jesus Christ," Peter said. The hope called for is a personal attitude of expectant reliance on what God has promised He will yet do. The imperative, directed to the will, indicates that the realization of that hope is "not a matter of emotions, but of the will. It calls for obedience."[9] And the use of the aorist tense underlines the urgent need for such hope.

The decisive action called for may be viewed in two different ways. The aorist may be understood as ingressive, "start to hope." Beare supports that view with the remark that "it implies the purposeful adoption of a new attitude of mind and heart."[10] That view assumes that something was deficient in the attitude of the readers and so involves a note of rebuke. More probably, the action is to be viewed as culminative, marking the completion of the action called for, i.e., "effectively set your hope on." That import of the aorist is clear if the adverb perfectly (teleiōs) is related to the imperative.

The position of the adverb perfectly leaves it open to two constructions. Some commentators[11] and versions[12] relate it to the preceding participle, "being perfectly sober." Alford thought that understanding "better satisfies the rhythm of the sentence" but was "persuaded the majority of commentators are right in making it an emphatic adjunct to the great word of exhortation."[13] Selwyn supports relating perfectly to the following imperative. He argues that "it is unusual for an adverb to follow the verb which it qualifies."[14] We agree with Selwyn.

The adverb teleiōs, occurring only here in the New Testament, means "fully, perfectly, completely."[15] It demands that Christian hope not be halfhearted and dispirited. Such hope should be characterized by a finality that leaves no room for doubt and uncertainty.

They were to fix their hope "on the grace that is to be brought unto you at the revelation of Jesus Christ." On the grace (epi and the accusative case) denotes either the ground or the object of hope. As in the parallel construction in 1 Timothy 5:5, it is better to understand Peter's words to denote the object toward which hope is directed. The validity of our hope is determined by its object, here identified as "the grace that is to be brought unto you," the same grace already mentioned in v. 10. It is inseparably associated with the Person of our Lord Jesus Christ. The passive voice draws the readers' attention to the divine agent who bestows grace. "Unto you" personalizes the gift for them.

9. W. H. Griffith Thomas, The Apostle Peter, p. 160.

10. Francis Wright Beare, The First Epistle of Peter, p. 96.

11. F. J. A. Hort, The First Epistle of Peter, pp. 65-66; Bigg, p. 112; Beare, p. 96.

12. NEB, 20th Cent., Goodspeed, Williams.

13. Henry Alford, The Greek New Testament, vol. 4 (part 1), p. 339.

14. Edward Gordon Selwyn, The First Epistle of St. Peter, p. 140.

15. The KJV translation "to the end" does not adequately give the meaning.

That is to be brought (*pheromenēn*) translates a present passive participle, literally, "that is being brought." Because of the present participle, two distinct interpretations have been advocated for the added words, "at the revelation of Jesus Christ."

Some believe the revelation relates to the past, either to the incarnation of Christ, or to the revelation of grace that took place in the gospel. If that is correct, then the past tense "was brought" would have been more appropriate. The expression "the revelation of Jesus Christ" (*apokalupsei Iēsou Christou*) controls the meaning of the verse. Therefore, it is unwarranted to assume that its meaning is different than in v. 7. The fact that it is used without the article and without further specification makes such a change in meaning highly improbable. Moffatt asserted, "*Revelation* is always eschatological in this letter (i. 5, v. 1)."[16] And Fronmüller found that the expression "is never used of His first advent in the flesh, cf. ch. i. 7, iv. 13; v. 1; 2 Thess. i. 7; Rom. viii. 18, 19; 1 Cor. i. 7."[17] If the present participle had not occurred in the construction, relating the revelation to the past would probably not have been suggested.

If Peter referred to Christ's second advent, we must explain why he used a present rather than a future tense. Selwyn explains: "(1) the future, *oisthē-somenēn*, is so cumbrous that a periphrasis would have been almost necessary, (2) the present is in keeping with the thought of our author who regards the object of hope as already virtually possessed; cf. 1. 3, 4; iv. 7."[18] Thus Alford suggested the translation, "which is even now bearing down on you."[19] Possibly, Peter used the present tense to convey the doctrinal certainty of Christ's return. According to Bennett, "The 'revelation' casts its shadow before it; confident expectation of such blessings is rewarded by an earnest of the grace which will spring from full realization."[20]

We believe that Peter's call for hope relates to the future. As Demarest observed, "The possession of present good is enjoyment, the anticipation of future good, hope."[21] Our hope is centered on "the blessed hope" of Christ's return (Titus 2:13). The real hope of the believer is not death but the second advent and includes the redemption of our bodies (Phil. 3:20-21; Rom. 8:23).

b. A life of personal holiness (vv. 14-16). Those who cultivate Christian hope must also cultivate personal holiness. Hope in a coming Savior demands conformity to His nature. The nature of the Christian life carries the obligation

---

16. James Moffatt, *The General Epistles, James, Peter, and Judas*, p. 104.

17. G. F. C. Fronmüller, *The Epistles General of Peter*, p. 21.

18. Selwyn, p. 140.

19. Alford, p. 339.

20. W. H. Bennett, *The General Epistles, James, Peter, John, and Jude*, p. 196.

21. John T. Demarest, *A Translation and Exposition of the First Epistle of the Apostle Peter*, p. 82.

to personal holiness. Peter grounded that obligation in the filial nature of his
readers (v. 14*a*), expounded the demand for holiness (vv. 14*b*-15), and found
the reason for holiness in the nature of God Himself (v. 16).

(1) *The foundation for personal holiness* (v. 14*a*). "As children of obedience" is more than a complimentary recognition of the readers'
conduct. It indicates the foundation for the call to holiness. *As* (*hōs*)
indicates the filial nature of those to whom he wrote. It has the force
of "inasmuch as ye are." The designation is grounded in the fact
of the new birth mentioned in v. 3. The addressees' new births
gave them the ability and the impulse to obey the demands of holiness.

Children of obedience (*tekna hupakoēs*) contains a familiar Hebraism
common in both the Old and New Testaments (cf. Judg. 19:22, KJV; 1 Sam.
2:12, KJV; 10:27, KJV; 1 Kings 21:10, KJV; Luke 16:8; John 12:36; Eph. 2:2-3;
Col. 3:6; 1 Thess. 5:5; etc.). The genitive *of* denotes the characteristic and
ruling nature of the individual; a child is of the same nature as its parents. The
genitive *of obedience* denotes that "the constitution and character of these
children, which is impressed upon them from their very birth, belongs to their
very nature."[22] *Obedience* indicates their character as true believers; it is the
motivating principle imparted in regeneration. Their nature as " children of
obedience" distinguishes them from the unsaved who are "sons of disobedience" (Eph. 2:2; 5:6). Obedience is therefore an important concept for Peter
(1:2, 14, 22; 3:6).

The KJV and numerous modern versions[23] eliminate the Hebraism and
translate "as obedient children." That smooths out the thought for English
reader, but it changes the picture and minimizes Peter's concept. *Obedient
children* refers to Christian conduct, and *children of obedience* designates
their character. We cannot justify converting the designation into an imperative, "Be obedient children," as Moffatt and a few other versions do.[24] Peter's
designation of the Christian is the foundation for the call to holiness, not a part
of the call itself.

(2) *The call to personal holiness* (vv. 14*b*-15). The call to holiness
is formulated as a negative (v. 14*b*) and a positive obligation (v. 15).
The negative duty is expressed by a participial construction that
makes it subsidiary and preparatory to the leading demand in v.
15.

(a) *The negative demand of holiness* (v. 14*b*). "Not fashioning yourselves according to your former lusts in *the time of* your igno-

22. R. C. H. Lenski, *The Interpretation of the Epistles of St. Peter, St. John and St. Jude*, p. 55.
23. "As [or 'like'] obedient children" (RSV, NASB, NEB, NIV, Berkeley, R. Young, Weymouth,
    Montgomery, Goodspeed, Williams, Kleist and Lilly); "As obedient persons" (Rotherham).
24. Moffatt, 20th Cent, TEV, JB.

rance" indicates the former practice that must be terminated. The negative participle is best understood as grammatically dependent on the imperative in v. 15; it carries a hortatory connotation but is best translated as a participle to mark the preparatory aspect of the action.[25]

The negative with the present participle, "not fashioning yourselves" (*mē suschēmatizomenoi*), prohibits a continuation of former practices. Because of their new nature, there must be "an absolute and perpetual divorce from what they most loved and practiced of old."[26] The compound participle, occurring elsewhere in the New Testament only in Rom. 12:2, denotes the practice of adopting for oneself a pattern or mold (*schēma*, our English word "scheme") of life that is changeable and unstable rather than enduring. The preposition *sun*, "with," in the compound denotes a personal assimilation to or conformity with the pattern indicated. Such a pattern or mold for conduct is natural, but it should not be that of the Christian's own sinful past. In Romans 12:2 the pattern to be rejected is that of "this world," the present age in its estrangement from God.

Peter characterized the old pattern of life as being "according to your former lusts in *the time of* your ignorance." As children of obedience, Christians are not to practice their former lusts. The word translated *lusts* (*epithumiais*) is neutral in meaning; it denotes the presence of good or bad strong desires or cravings. In the New Testament it is occasionally used with a good meaning (Luke 22:15; Phil. 1:23; 1 Thess. 2:17), but predominantly the term (as noun or verb) carries an evil connotation. In 1 Peter 1:14 it denotes the sinful cravings and practices that characterized the addressees' lives before they were saved (v. 3) and is properly translated "lusts." That degeneration in the meaning of the term is a revealing commentary on human nature. Left to himself, instead of gaining mastery over his base desires and steadfastly adhering to the good, the individual is characteristically overcome by his evil cravings, so that they become the dominating force of his life. *Former* defines those lusts as part of the old life, not the new.

Those lusts are more precisely characterized as being "in *the time of* your ignorance" (*en tē agnoia*), "in the ignorance," the spiritual ignorance that characterized the lives of the readers before salvation. The phrase, standing between the article and its noun "lusts," attributes those lusts to spiritual ignorance. The picture looks back to the time before the readers came to know God through the gospel. That ignorance evoked and stimulated their depraved desires. Similarly, in Romans 1:18-32, Paul showed how obscuring the knowledge of God is the source of moral corruption.

Peter's words seem to describe Gentile converts. Likewise Paul, in speaking to the Athenians about their idolatry, described it as "the times of ignorance" that God overlooked (Acts 17:30; cf. Eph. 4:17-20 where Paul further

25. The use of the negative *me* with the participle is in keeping with the hortatory context.
26. John Lillie, *Lectures on the First and Second Epistles of Peter*, pp. 66-67.

associated the life of the Gentiles with ignorance and evil conduct). Peter's reference to the past ignorance of his readers was not intended to minimize their dark past but to remind them how much they owed to the gospel. Remembering their past was to serve as a stimulus to help them completely break with such practices.

> (b) *The positive call to holiness* (v. 15). The strong adversative *but* (*alla*) introduces the positive call for personal holiness. Refraining from undesirable conduct is only its prelude.

First, Peter pointed to the pattern for personal holiness— "like as he who called you is holy." *Like as* does not introduce a comparison of equals; it indicates the divine standard for holiness. "God is the Model of all holiness."[27] Close association with Him who is holy can only awaken in us a sense of our need for holiness (cf. Peter's own experience in Luke 5:8).

Peter's designation of God, "he who called you is holy" (*ton kalesanta humas hagion*), is open to two different interpretations. The ASV (quoted above) takes *hagion*, "holy," as a predicate adjective that asserts God's holiness. The NASB's "the Holy One who called you" understands *hagion* with the article as substantival and the participle as an adjective of nearer description. According to the first understanding, "the Caller" is said to be holy; according to the second, "the Holy One" is identified as having called them. The versions[28] and the commentators[29] differ in their preferences. We prefer the latter construction; it seems more in keeping with Peter's practice of placing the modifier between the article and the noun. *The Holy One* is a well-known biblical designation for God (Hosea 11:9; Hab. 1:12; Mark 1:24; 1 John 2:20); Isaiah's favorite designation was "the Holy One of Israel." His use of the title was apparently rooted in his own experience (cf. Isa. 6:1-8).

The characterization of God as holy or the Holy One embodies a basic biblical teaching concern the nature of God. As holy, He is separated from all that is morally impure and evil (1 John 1:5). As the Holy One, He is immutably holy from all eternity; He has revealed Himself as holy and righteous. As holy, He "loves all that is pure and good and hates, abominates, and punishes all that is sinful."[30] As Himself infinitely holy, God's redemptive purpose is to deliver fallen humanity from sin and all unholiness, so that, conformed to the image of His Son, they may be fitted for abiding fellowship with Himself (Rom. 8:29).

"Called you" reminded them that their experience of salvation began with the divine initiative. God's call became effective in their lives at the time of

---

27. Roy S. Nickolson, *The First Epistle of Peter*, p. 270.

28. The reading "is holy" occurs in RSV, NEB, NIV, TEV, Berkeley, Rotherham, R. Young, Darby, Moffatt, and Montgomery. "The Holy One" appears in the NASB, 20th Cent., Weymouth, Goodspeed, Williams, JB, Kleist and Lilly.

29. Alford, Vincent, Bigg, Johnstone, Williams, Lenski, Beare, and Reicke among the commentators prefer "the Holy One."

30. Lenski, p. 57.

their conversion, when they were brought into conscious fellowship with the Holy One. The reality of the divine call was a precious truth to Peter, and he made repeated reference to it (2:9, 21; 3:9; 5:10; 2 Pet. 1:3, 10). God's call made their election effective (1:1; Rom. 8:29-30). It became operative in their lives when by faith they received the truth set forth in the gospel.

Having been brought into fellowship with the Holy One, their duty was, "be ye yourselves also holy in all manner of living." *Ye yourselves also (kai autoi)* sharpened God's demand for their individual response. "God calls; it is man's duty to respond."[31] The aorist imperative *be (genēthēte)*, stands emphatically at the end of the sentence to underline the urgency of the demand.

The imperative *be ye*, from the verb *ginomai*, "to become," has been interpreted in three different ways. Some, like Rotherham, retain the basic meaning of the verb and translate, "become holy."[32] Wuest accepts the verb as an "ingressive aorist here, signifying entrance into a new state."[33] The reference is not to the inner status of the believer who, joined to Christ by faith, is made holy in Him (1 Cor. 1:30). It is a call, a definite yielding to the indwelling Holy Spirit, to enter upon a course of holy conduct.[34] Others prefer to translate "show yourselves to be holy."[35] Hart supported that translation with the observation that it "suits *anastrophē* [manner of living] which is distinctly outward behaviour."[36] Conduct should demonstrate the believer's inner state of holiness. A third commonly held view regards the verb as a substitute for the familiar verb "to be" (*eimi*) that does not occur in the aorist tense.[37] Thus Lenski asserted, "The meaning is not 'become!' but 'be!' i.e. be decisive, settle it once for all that you be holy."[38] Under any view, the context makes it clear that Peter made a demand that Christian conduct should be consistent with Christian character. "Everything we are exhorted to do rests upon what God has done in Christ, both in Calvary's redemption of the past and in the coming grace of the last day."[39]

"In all manner of living" (*en pasē anastrophē*) denotes the scope of Peter's demand for ethical conduct. *All*, used without the article, points to the multiple occasions for the manifestation of holiness in conduct. All the different areas and concerns of daily life are included. "There should be no part of our life which is not to savor of this good odour of holiness."[40] The compound noun

31. Nickolson, p. 270.
32. So also R. Young, Montgomery, Kleist and Lilly.
33. Kenneth S. Wuest, *First Peter in the Greek New Testament for the English Reader*, p. 37.
34. Cf. Paul S. Rees, "Holiness, Holy," p. 270.
35. 20th Cent. Cf. Beare, p. 99; Hort, p.71.
36. J. H. A. Hart, *The First Epistle General of Peter*, p. 49.
37. William F. Arndt and F. Wilbur Gingrich, *A Greek-English Lexicon of the New Testament and Other Early Christian Literature*, p. 159.
38. Lenski, p. 57.
39. Robert Paul Roth, *I Peter*, p. 420.
40. Calvin, p. 246.

anastrophē, conduct, behaviour, denotes a life of movement and action, turning here and there in meeting the varied demands of daily life.[41] It is a favorite word with Peter (1:15, 18; 2:12; 3:1-2, 16; 2 Pet. 2:7; 3:11).[42] Hort remarked, "Different kinds of *anastrophē* are to be spoken of further on in the Epistle: here at the outset St. Peter lays down what is true for them all."[43]

> *(3) The justification of the call to holiness* (v. 16). "Because it is written" introduces the first quotation from the Old Testament in the epistle. It is the formula regularly employed when citing from the Old Testament and implies its acceptance as sacred and authoritative. The perfect tense (*gegraptai*), "it stands written," declares the permanence of the record. Peter's call to holiness is nothing new; it is a clear part of God's recorded will for His people. It is God's command and cannot be trifled with or evaded.

The words "Ye shall be holy" (*hagioi esesthe*)[44] convey an explicit command. The Greek future indicative can be used for the imperative and conveys an authoritative expression of God's will[45] (cf. the Septuagint use of the future indicative in the Ten Commandments, Ex. 20:1-17). It is an expression of God's will directed to the will of His people, God's appeal to those who are "children of obedience" (v. 14).

The reason for God's demand for holiness in His people is "because I am holy." *I* (*egō*) is emphatic; it stresses the nature of God's own character. The quotation thus embodies a call for holiness and insists on the believer's conformity to the character of God. Because the Christian belongs to and lives in fellowship with God, he should be like Him. For such moral conformity there is no substitute.

The words quoted occur three times in Leviticus. In 11:24 they occur in connection with dietary regulations under the Mosaic law. In 19:2 they appear in connection with social and religious duties. And in 20:26 they are used in specifying cultic and demonic dangers. The quotation has abiding significance; conformity to the character of God was insisted on in all areas of the lives of the Old Testament saints.

c. *A life of motivated reverence* (vv. 17-21). *And* relates back to the preceding exhortation to holiness. There is a close connection between a life of

---

41. The translation "conversation" was accurate when the KJV was published in 1611, since the word then referred to the manner in which one conducted oneself in society. It is now misleading since the term has come to mean "to talk" (cf. *The Oxford English Dictionary*, 2:546).

42. It occurs only three times in all of Paul's letters—Gal. 1:13; Eph. 4:22; 1 Tim. 4:12.

43. Hort, p. 72.

44. The use of the aorist imperative, *genesthe*, in the Textus Receptus repeats the verb used in v. 15. It has inferior manuscript support.

45. H. E. Dana and Julius R. Mantey, *A Manual Grammar of the Greek New Testament*, p. 192.

holiness and reverence toward God that is prompted by the precious redemption He has bestowed (2 Cor. 7:1). Though some, like Huther,[46] understand the verses as a continuation of the preceding exhortation, it is more natural to interpret vv. 17-21 (which form one sentence) in the light of the governing imperative in v. 17.

Peter delineated the basis of Christian reverence (v. 17a), issued his call to live such a life (v. 17b), and explained the redemption that should motivate that kind of life (vv. 18-21).

(1) *The basis for reverent living* (v. 17a). "If ye call on him as Father, who without respect of persons judgeth according to each man's work" lays a firm foundation for the duty to live reverently before God. *If*[47] does not imply doubt but assumes the reality of the condition. It has the force of "if, as you do." The use of the conditional construction indicates that the conclusion must logically follow from the fulfilled condition. It could be translated, "Since ye call," as several modern versions do.[48] But the conditional construction is more forceful; it implicitly appeals to the readers to make a confirmatory evaluation of their own practice.

In view of New Testament[49] and papyrological usage,[50] the verb *ye call on* (*epikaleisthe*) may be interpreted two ways. In the active and passive it can mean "to give a name to, to surname," as in Acts 10:18, "Simon, who was surnamed Peter." Then, "If ye *surname* God Father" means that Peter's readers, who had become God's children by their new birth (1:3), were to give public acknowledgement that God was their Father. Thus the Geneva version reads, "And if ye call him Father, which. . . ."[51] In support, Williams cites Matthew 10:25, "If they have called the master of the house Beelzebub, how much more. . . ."[52] That view points to the public testimony of Peter's readers. But it seems better to understand the verb as middle, "to call on, to invoke," i.e., to point to the addressees' filial relation as expressed in prayer. As a present middle indicative, the verb acknowledged their personal practice of calling upon God in prayer. God called them to be His children (v. 15), and they responded by calling on Him, addressing Him as Father. Cook comments, "You

46. Joh. Ed. Huther, *Critical and Exegetical Handbook to the General Epistles of Peter and Jude*, p. 86.
47. "The First Class: Determined as Fulfilled," A. T. Robertson and W. Hersey Davis, *A New Short Grammar of the Greek Testament*, pp. 349-51.
48. So NIV, 20th Cent., and Montgomery. Moffatt, "And as you call upon a Father."
49. Arndt and Gingrich, pp. 293-94.
50. James Hope Moulton and George Milligan, *The Vocabulary of the Greek New Testament*, p. 239.
51. Luther A. Weigle, ed., *The New Testament Octapla*.
52. Nathaniel Marshman Williams, *Commentary on the Epistles of Peter*, p. 20.

cannot be Christians if you do not pray."[53] To commune with the Father is the natural response of those who are "children of obedience" (v. 14).

The noun *Father* stands emphatically forward—"And if as Father ye are invoking him who . . ." (Rotherham). As the predicate accusative, it gives a more precise definition of the One on whom the addressees were to call; it stresses the intimate relationship into which Christians have been brought through Christ. The Jews had long addressed God as the Father of the Jewish people (Isa. 64:8, 16; Jer. 3:19; Mal. 1:6), but Jesus taught His followers to employ the designation in a new and intimate way. "Its use was characteristic of primitive Christianity and in Gentile Christianity it was even preserved in its Aramaic form, Abba (Rom. 8:15; Gal. 4:6)."[54] Peter's expression may be a veiled allusion to the use of the Lord's Prayer (Matt. 6:9-13), but that is not certain.

But the Father is also an impartial judge—"who without respect of persons judgeth according to each man's work." In Him the two relations are inseparably united. One is never lost sight of in the other. The present articular participle *ton . . . krinonta*, "the one judging," may stress the present continuing judgment that God exercises, or the articular participle may specify "the attribute or office: 'Him, who is the judge.'"[55] The latter interpretation portrays God as the moral governor of the world, the former draws attention to His present judicial dealings with His children. Both truths are latent in the expression, but the context emphasizes His judicial dealings. The verb *judge* (*krinō*) basically means to separate or distinguish and then to evaluate and make a decision. It does not indicate an antagonistic attitude but an action designed to discover the true nature of the person or thing judged. God's judgment of His children may result in condemnation or approval.

Peter stressed God's impartial judgment by writing— "who without respect of persons judgeth" (*ton aprosōpolēmptōs*), "the One impartially judging." The adverb, occurring only here in the New Testament, literally means acting "without receiving of face" and indicates that God's judgment is not determined by outward appearance or outward pretensions. The face or mask that people put on is uniformly transparent to Him. The position of the adverb between the article and the noun indicates that God's impartiality is an inherent aspect of Peter's concept of His character. Peter gave expression to that concept in Acts 10:34, when he declared to the Gentile audience in the house of Cornelius, "Of a truth I perceive that God is no respecter of persons." Selwyn observes, "The idea of God's impartiality was Hebraic (cf. Deut. x. 17), but St. Peter was the first to apply it to the equality of Jew and Gentile in relation to the Gospel."[56] God's impartiality is also affirmed by Paul in Romans 2:11; Ephesians 6:9; and Colossians 3:25. God's total impartiality is the striking difference between Him and the ordinary human judge. God had to remind

53. F. C. Cook, *The First Epistle General of Peter*, p. 182.
54. Ernest Best, *I Peter*, p. 87.
55. Alford, p. 340.
56. Selwyn, p. 143.

Samuel, "Man looketh on the outward appearance [face], but Jehovah looketh on the heart " (1 Sam. 16:7).[57]

"According to each man's work" reminded the readers that they would not be exempt from God's impartial scrutiny. *Each* individualizes that solemn reality. The Christian's filial relation will not preclude their heavenly Father from discerning in their lives that which is inconsistent with His yearning for their holiness. God evaluates each life "according to" (*kata*), in strict harmony with "each man's work." The singular *work* (*ergon*) summarizes, whereas the more usual plural would have individualized the deeds (cf. 2:12; 2 Pet. 2:8). God is concerned with individual deeds and their motivation. The singular embraces the inner character as well as the moral activities of believers as members of God's family.

Peter's primary reference is to God's present dealings with His saints in the development of holiness in their lives. But God's judgment of the believer will find final application at the judgment seat of Christ (1 Cor. 3:11-15; 2 Cor. 5:10). That judgment will not be to determine their salvation but their future reward. "The faithful or unfaithful work of saints will make a difference both here and hereafter."[58]

(2) *The call for reverent living* (v. 17b). Peter concluded his conditional sentence with a ringing imperative, "pass the time of your sojourning in fear." In the original the imperative stands emphatically at the end of the sentence.[59] *Pass* (*anastraphēte*) is the verbal form of the noun translated "manner of life" in v. 15. English versions find it difficult to show that connection.[60] Moffatt, who used "conduct" in v. 15, translated, "be reverent in your conduct." The aorist imperative comprehends the remainder of the Christian life under that command.

That duty holds for "the time of your sojourning" (*ton tēs paroikias humōn chronon*, the accusative of extension), however long that may be. The genitive, *of your sojourning*, in an attributive position to mark the inherent nature of the time in view, characterizes Christians as aliens residing in a strange land. The compound noun (*paroikias*) basically means "alongside the house," having the position of an outsider and not a member of the household. It is used in Acts 13:17 of the sojourn of the Israelites in Egypt. The present earthly life of the believer has that character because Christ's call has taken him "out of this world" (John 15:19). The term takes up the thought already expressed in 1:1 (where a different word is used) and prepares for the renewed exhortation in

---

57. See Joseph B. Mayor, *The Epistle of St. James*, pp. 74-75, for an elaborate listing of biblical and ecclesiastical references to partiality in judgment.

58. John Miller, *Notes on James, I and II Peter, I, II, and III John, Jude, and Revelation*, p. 27.

59. The original order, preserved by R. Young, "in fear the time of your sojourn pass ye," makes awkward English.

60. Modern English versions use various verbs, "live," "behave," "conduct yourselves," "spend," "sojourn," or resort to paraphrasing.

2:11. When we have safely reached our heavenly homeland, the exhortation to live "in fear" will no longer be needed.

The words *in fear* stand emphatically at the beginning—"in fear pass the time of your sojourning." The attitude advocated is not the craven, cringing dread of a slave before an offended master, but the reverential awe of a son toward a beloved and esteemed father, the awe that shrinks from whatever would displease and grieve him. It is the mark of a tender conscience and is the safeguard against carelessness toward danger. Its growth is stimulated in part by the consciousness that our Father is an impartial judge from whom no favoritism can be expected. Even more, it is a reverence formed by our experiences of our Father's merciful dealings with us as His failing children. It is "the safeguard of holiness, and it prompts obedience in things which we do not as yet understand."[61] Cranfield notes, "'Fear' is another key-word in I Peter (cf. 2. 17, 18; 3. 2, 15, of, the fear of God; in 3. 6, 14 the fear referred to is a false fear)."[62]

Bennett suggested that "Peter evidently believed that his readers were divided in their minds, conscious of some unfaithful inclination or desire," and felt that "the better side of their nature needed to be reinforced by a wholesome awe of the Father's displeasure."[63] But it seems more charitable to understand the exhortation to have been given as a needed safeguard amid trying circumstances, not in a spirit of condemnation.

(3) *The knowledge that motivates reverence* (vv. 18-21). "Knowing that" (*eidotes hoti*) is a familiar formula used to introduce a familiar fact. The participle, which grammatically relates to the subject of the imperative in v. 17, specifies a reason for the reverence called for. The practical call is grounded in the highest and most sacred doctrinal truths. It is a knowledge that should continually influence daily life.[64] That knowledge is available to the believer, not on the basis of mental acumen or rigorous scholastic effort, but through the quickening of the Holy Spirit.

The redemption that should motivate Christian reverence is portrayed with remarkable fullness. It may well be called "one of the greatest redemption passages of the New Testament."[65] Yet its very fullness has raised questions concerning its origin. J. N. D. Kelly feels that "much of the detail is extraneous to the argument" and concludes that the elaboration "has been filled out with catechetical, credal or liturgical material" drawn from "standardized teaching."[66] We may concede that a simple reference to the redemptive sufferings of

61. Bigg, p. 117.
62. Cranfield, p. 53.
63. Bennett, p. 199.
64. The old second perfect *oida* is used as a present.
65. Charles S. Ball, *First and Second Peter*, p. 255.
66. J. N. D. Kelly, *A Commentary on the Epistles of Peter and of Jude*, p. 72.

Christ would have sufficed to establish Peter's argument; and we need not object to the view that the elaboration is in accord with "standardized Christian teaching." But the New Testament makes it clear that Peter himself would have been one of the main sources for such "standardized teaching." Peter's teaching indicates how precious those truths were to him and that he was anxious to impress them on the hearts of his readers to assure the full impact of their motivating power. A vague perception of Christian truth does not guarantee dynamic daily motivation.

Peter portrayed the priceless means of our redemption (vv. 18-19), the supernatural nature of the Redeemer (v. 20), and the resultant characteristics of the redeemed (v. 21).

> (a) *The means of our redemption* (vv. 18-19). The original word order stresses the precious means of our redemption as a motivating force; "not with corruptible things—silver or gold—were ye redeemed . . . but with precious blood, as of a lamb unblemished and unspotted—Christ's" (R. Young). Peter desired that his readers "not only hold it as an intellectual acquisition, but permit it to become the moulding principle of their entire life."[67]

"Ye were redeemed" (*eluthrōthēte*) states the central message of Christianity as an historical fact. The aorist portrays the fact as already accomplished without stressing the train of events involved. The passive is a reminder that it was the work of another for us, not our own effort or merit (Ps. 49:7; 1 Cor. 9:19b-20).

The verb *redeem*, also used in Luke 24:21 and Titus 2:14, basically denotes the act of deliverance by the payment of a ransom. The same metaphor also appears in related terms used in the New Testament.[68] "In extra biblical Greek," as Cranfield notes, "both noun and verb have to do with the ransoming of prisoners of war, the manumission of slaves, and the redemption of pledges, the noun signifying in each case the price paid."[69] The term was also used of the redemption of the firstborn (Ex. 30:12 LXX). It came to be used metaphorically of deliverance from dangers or distress. God's deliverance of the Israelites from Egyptian bondage is spoken of as a redemption (Ex. 6:6; 15:13) and God as their Redeemer (Ps. 78:35). No thought of a literal ransom payment was involved. "The emphasis here," Harrison suggests, "may well be upon the great output of strength needed to accomplish this objective—strength which itself serves as a kind of ransom price."[70]

Peter's picture of Christ's redemption rules out any attempt to eliminate the concept of a ransom from the atonement. It is present in Christ's reference to

---

67. F. B. Meyer, *"Tried by Fire": Expositions of the First Epistle of Peter*, p. 59.
68. *Antilutron*, "ransom" in 1 Tim. 2:6; *lutrōsis*, "ransoming, redemption," in Heb. 9:12; *apolutrōsis*, "release, redemption," in Rom. 3:24; 1 Cor. 1:30; Eph. 1:7; Col. 1:14; Heb. 9:15.
69. Cranfield, p. 54.
70. Everett F. Harrison, "Redeemer, Redemption," p. 438.

His atoning work in Mark 10:54 and Matthew 20:28. But the concept should not be extended to support the speculation that the ransom was paid to the devil; there is no scriptural basis for that medieval notion. The Bible does not directly say to whom the ransom was paid, but the redemption of the firstborn in the Old Testament implies that the correct answer is, to God. The ransom involved in Christ's sacrificial suffering and death relates to God's holiness and righteous government; His substitutionary death on the sinner's behalf enables God to "be just, and the justifier of him that hath faith in Jesus" (Rom. 3:26.).

"Not with corruptible things, with silver or gold" emphatically portrays the kind of things that did not procure redemption. Excluded are all corruptible things (*phthartois*), those by their nature perishable, subject to decay or destruction. The negative *ou* categorically excludes them. *With silver or gold* names two of the best and most highly treasured means that belong to the category. *Or* is disjunctive; neither silver, nor yet gold, which is more valuable, will suffice. The two nouns are diminutive in form, suggesting the picture of the small silver and gold coins used to procure a slave's freedom from bondage. Such material means count "for nothing in the weighing-chamber of eternity."[71]

The concept of "corruptible—incorruptible" seems to have gripped the mind of Peter in connection with the spiritual life (cf. 1:4, 18, 23; 3:4). Apparently, he was deeply impressed with the teaching of Jesus in Matthew 6:19-21, where the perishable things of this world are set in sharp contrast to the imperishable nature of spiritual goods. That attitude is reflected in Peter's sharp rebuke to Simon Magus in Acts 8:20, "Thy silver perish with thee, because thou hast thought to obtain the gift of God with money" (cf. Acts 3:6: "Silver and gold have I none"). But Farrar goes too far when he asks the readers of the epistle to "notice the Petrine contempt for dross."[72]

Christ's redemption effectively delivered the readers "from your vain manner of life." *From* (*ek*), "out of," indicates their removal from the realm in which they formerly lived. As Israel's redemption was a liberation from their life of bondage, so believers in Christ are freed from their old manner of life (cf. v. 15). The call in v. 15 to be holy was justified because of the nature of their old life. It was vain (*mataias*), futile, unprofitable, void of positive results. The term may have reference to the idolatrous past of the readers. In the Septuagint the adjective is scornfully applied to pagan gods in contrast to the one living and true God (Lev. 17:7; 2 Chron. 11:15; Jer. 8:19; 10:15). In Acts 14:15 the term is used as a specific designation of idols (cf. Rom. 1:21 and Eph. 4:17). Probably, Peter's reference is more general, denoting the futile and ineffectual life of those who live without a knowledge of the true God. As such, the term is an appropriate description of the lives of former Gentiles. Kelly

71. Meyer, p. 60.
72. F. W. Farrar, *The Early Days of Christianity*, p. 87, n. 12.

remarks, "An early Christian would never have described the ancestral upbringing of converts from Judaism in such terms."[73]

The old life of Peter's readers is further described as "handed down from your fathers" (*patroparadotou*). That compound adjective, which occurs only here in the New Testament, characterizes such life as inherited. Their former beliefs and practices had rested on the sanctions of ancestral precedent; "the way had been beaten broad and smooth by the feet of many generations."[74] The power of tradition was strongly developed among the Jews (cf. Gal. 1:14), but the traditional religious beliefs and practices of the Gentile world exercised an equal, if not greater, dominance. Rooted in their own corrupt tendencies, and sanctioned by deep emotional ties of respect and honor for their forefathers, their traditional behavior patterns often proved a tremendous restraining force on prospective converts to Christianity. They were often very reluctant to break with those traditions since that would have implied condemnation of their respected parents, teachers, and statesmen. There is, of course, nothing wrong in maintaining the traditions of our forefathers, if they are compatible with Christian truth. But antiquity is no guarantee of the correctness of an opinion or practice. Peter's readers had come to see the inconsistency between continued adherence to their inherited religious practices and the salvation they had received.

But (*alla*), a strong adversative particle, points to the true means of redemption—"with precious blood, as of a lamb without blemish and without spot, *even the blood* of Christ" (v. 19). The entire statement portrays the true antithesis to the corruptible means just repudiated. The blood of sacrificial animals would not constitute a true contrast to corruptible means since it was quite perishable. Only Christ's blood, the One whose name stands emphatically at the end, offers the true antithesis. *Blood* is used figuratively to denote His "bloody death" for us. It is precious blood because of the true nature of the One who shed His blood as a ransom for fallen humanity. *Precious* (*timios*) has a twofold meaning: precious in the sense of its high value, and "highly esteemed, held in honor." The former meaning predominates. "The cost of Calvary is beyond all human computation; the value of the shed blood of Jesus is beyond all our comprehension."[75] He was indeed "the Lamb of God" (John 1:29), God's sacrificial provision, "a lamb without blemish and without spot." *As* (*hōs*) does not draw a comparison but emphasizes that Christ had the character of an acceptable sacrificial offering, one "without blemish and without spot." Being "without blemish," He had no character defect in Himself; being "without spot," He remained unstained by the evil around Him. The physical perfection of all the animals whose blood was shed to cover the sins of men typified the morally and spiritually perfect Lamb of God. Whether Peter had in mind the Pascal lamb or the prophetic lamb of Isaiah 53 is not certain—perhaps the

73. Kelly, p. 74.
74. Lillie, p. 76.
75. John Phillips, *Exploring Romans*, p. 71.

latter. Acts 8 shows that Christians applied Isaiah's picture to Christ at an early date.

> (b) *The nature of the Redeemer* (v. 20). Two participles, standing in apposition with *Christ*, the last word in v. 19, make unmistakably clear the dual nature of the Redeemer "who was foreknown indeed before the foundation of the world, but was manifested at the end of the times." Two particles, "indeed . . . but" (*men . . . de*, "on the one hand . . . on the other"), balance those two aspects of God's unique Lamb. The first looks back to His transcendent origin; the second focuses on His redemptive appearance in history.

In his opening salutation Peter assured his readers that they were included in the redemptive foreknowledge of God (1:1-2). Now their Redeemer is presented as central in that divine foreknowledge. *Was foreknown* (*proegnōsmenou*) translates a perfect passive participle and designates the central place that Christ had and continues to hold in God's redemptive plan. He foreknew the whole program, and His foreknowledge rested with affectionate favor upon the Christ who had already been chosen as man's redeemer before the foundation of the world. *Before* (*pro*) "carries the thought back to a stage anterior to the Creation, i.e. to the transcendent sphere, cf. Jn. xvii. 24, Eph. i. 4."[76] Before the establishment of the material universe, before there were human sinners to be redeemed, Christ, in the eternal counsel of God (cf. Acts 2:23), had already been chosen as man's redeemer. Christ's work as redeemer was no remedial afterthought. Planned before creation, God's prophets were inspired to foretell the Redeemer's coming, His life, death, and glorious resurrection (cf. 1:11). The foreknowledge of believers in 1:2 does not imply their preexistence, but, as Moffatt conceded, "here the conception of a personal pre-existence is extended to the personality of Christ."[77]

"But was manifested at the end of the times" counterbalances the preceding picture; the preexistent Christ visibly appeared in human history as the Redeemer. *Was manifested* (*phanerōthentos*), an aorist passive participle meaning "to be revealed, to become visible," indicates the point in history when Christ, previously hidden from view in heaven, appeared on earth as a man among men (John 1:14; Heb. 9:26; 1 John 1:2).[78] The aorist summarizes the entire first advent, reaching from Christ's birth to the enthronement in glory. John the Baptist had the unique privilege of declaring the identity of the earthly Jesus as the "Lamb of God" (John 1:29, 31). The knowledge of that manifestation became known to the readers through the preaching of the gospel.

---

76. Selwyn, p. 146.

77. Moffatt, p. 107.

78. In Col. 3:4; 1 Pet. 5:4; and 1 John 3:2, the verb is used of Christ's visible return at the second advent.

That manifestation, Peter noted, occurred "at the end of the times"[79] (*ep' eschatou tōn chronōn*), "upon [the] last of the times." *End*, more literally "last," is used as a substantive and denotes the time of Christ's advent as the termination of all the preceding, anticipatory periods of time (cf. Gal. 4:4 and Heb. 1:1-2).[80] The phrase stands in antithesis to "before the foundation of the world." In the Person of the Redeemer, God embodied the beginning and end of His redemptive program.

"For your sake" makes another direct application of the teaching to the readers. According to Fronmüller, "Believers are the end and aim in the manifestation of the Redeemer: you may therefore view it, as if Christ had come for you only."[81] To become operative in our own lives, that redemption must be personalized (cf. Gal. 2:20, "who loved *me*, and gave himself up for *me*"). That precious realization intensifies the personal obligation to live reverently. Peter's phrase skillfully turns the focus from the Redeemer to the redeemed.

    (c) The characteristics of the redeemed (v. 21). "Who through him are believers in God" (*tous di' autou pistous eis theon*), an articular clause that stands in apposition with the pronoun *your* (*humas*, "you") in the preceding phrase, further characterizes the recipients of Christ's redemptive manifestation. But *through him* emphasizes that Christians are what they are only because of their personal experience of Christ. True knowledge of God is mediated to us only through Christ, the Mediator (John 14:6; 1 John 2:22-23). His redemptive work has once for all opened up man's approach to God (3:18; Rom. 5:1).

The word *believers* (*pistous*) is difficult; a textual problem is involved. The great majority of Greek manuscripts have a participle, *pistountas* ("believing"), rather than the verbal adjective used as a noun.[82] The Textus Receptus[83] has the participle, but modern critical editions of the epistle agree in reading the verbal adjective[84] on the principle that the more difficult reading is more likely to be original. Modern textual critics agree that the participle is an early scribal assimilation to a much more commonplace way of expressing the idea.[85] The reading commonly agreed upon raises the question of its intended force; is

79. The reading of the KJV, "in these last times," is based on a slightly different Greek text that has less manuscript support.

80. The view that the reference is to the present church age as the last period of history is less probable.

81. Fronmüller, p. 24.

82. The verbal is supported by *A*, *B*, 398, and the Latin Vulgate.

83. F. H. Scrivener, *Hē Kainē Diathēkē. Novum Testamentum, Textus Stephanici A. D. 1550.*

84. So the texts of Souter, Westcott and Hort, Nestle and Aland, United Bible Societies, and Tasker.

85. Cf. Bruce M. Metzger, *A Textual Commentary on the Greek New Testament*, p. 688.

the verbal adjective active or passive? If it is active it means "trusting, believing," but if it is passive it means "trustworthy, faithful, loyal." In the New Testament it is usually passive. The passive meaning, "who, through him, are faithful to God" (20th Cent.),[86] has received the support of few commentators.[87] Most, however, agree that the verbal adjective is active. With considerable hesitation, we accept *pistous*, understood as an active verbal adjective, as the more probable reading. The substance remains the same, but the verbal adjective points to what the readers are, "believers," rather than to the act of their believing. The possible intimation of their loyalty need not be rigidly excluded from Peter's designation.

The One in whom his addressees believed is explicitly identified as the God "that raised him from the dead, and gave him glory." He is specifically the God of the Christian gospel, not merely the Creator, or the God of the Jews. Two participles governed by one article identify God in His relationship to the Redeemer. He is the God who acted in Christ Jesus.

"That raised him from the dead" indicates the fundamental feature of saving faith (Rom. 10:9-10). The aorist active participle denotes the historic fact that God acted to raise our Redeemer from the dead (*ek nekrōn*), out from among other individuals who had died. He entered the realm of the dead when He gave His life as a ransom. Without His resurrection, we would have no assurance that His ransom had been accepted. His resurrection eloquently proved that the God of the Christian gospel is truly the Living God. The resurrection held a prominent place in the preaching of Peter as recorded in Acts (Acts 2:32-36; 3:15; 4:10, 33; 10:40).

"And gave him glory" (*kai doxan autō donta*), "and glory to him gave" (Rotherham), closely relates the bestowal of glory with the resurrection. That glory was in part bestowed at the resurrection, but the fuller reference is to Christ's ascension and exaltation at the right hand of the throne in heaven.

His resurrection and glorification illuminate the true work of the Redeemer. "They throw back a halo of Divine glory upon the awful cross; they bring out the beauty and the dignity of the atoning sacrifice; they show that it is accepted, that the work of our redemption is complete."[88]

"So that your faith and hope might be in God" may indicate either the object or the result of God's dealings with our blessed Redeemer. The ASV, quoted above, adopts the former view; the NASB's "so that your faith and hope are in God," represents the latter. Choosing one or the other is difficult since there is a close connection between purpose and result in such a context. We agree that was God's purpose in His mighty display of grace in Christ Jesus; the entire epistle makes it equally clear that His purpose had actually been achieved in the lives of the Christian readers.

Their experience of God's great salvation brought faith and hope into their

86. Rotherham and Weymouth also translate "faithful."
87. So Caffin, *The First Epistle General of Peter*, p. 11; A. J. Mason, *The First Epistle General of Peter*, p. 397.
88. Caffin, p. 11.

lives; both are directed Godward. The faith that they had in Jesus Christ (v. 8) was equally faith in God (*eis theon*). It brought them into living union with the true God. But that salvation also involved hope in Him. Both are features of the new life that the gospel brought to Peter's readers. Bengel noted that "these two are most closely joined, and yet they differ with respect to the present and the future."[89] Here is Peter's third reference to hope in the epistle (1:3, 13). The readers' hope for the future also rested in God. The words *in God* bring Peter's picture of the life of the saved in relation to God to a fitting conclusion.[90]

89. John Albert Bengel, *New Testament Word Studies*, 2:732.
90. The translation of Moffatt, "and thus your faith means hope in God," represents an improbable understanding of the Greek text. In reply to that construction see Bigg, p. 122; Lenski, p. 133; J.N.D. Kelly, p. 78.

7

The Christian Life in Relation to the Brethren
(1:22-25)

In the concluding four verses of chapter 1 (vv. 22-25), Peter continued his description of the life that should result from salvation. The absence of any connecting particle indicates the introduction of a new thought. The discussion has turned from the vertical to the horizontal dimension of the Christian life, emphasizing that Christians are to love their brethren. First Peter 1:22-25 echoes much of what has already been said.

2) THE CHRISTIAN LIFE IN RELATION TO THE BRETHREN (1:22-25)

(22) Seeing ye have purified your souls in your obedience to the truth unto unfeigned love of the brethren, love one another from the heart fervently: (23) having been begotten again, not of corruptible seed, but of incorruptible, through the word of God, which liveth and abideth. (24) For,
　　　　All flesh is as grass,
　　And all the glory thereof as the flower of grass.
　　The grass withereth, and the flower falleth:
(25) But the word of the Lord abideth for ever. And this is the word of good tidings which was preached unto you.

Verses 22-23 form one sentence, and the imperative, "love one another," is its heart. The new life should be lived out in a community setting; it requires relationships of mutual affection among the brethren as the members of God's family. Peter reminded his readers of their experience of inner purification (v.

99

22*a*), emphasized the urgent duty of mutual love (v. 22*b*), and explained that regeneration is the basis that enables the Christian to love (vv. 23-25). Verses 24-25 are an illustrative expansion of the teaching of verse 23.

A. THE EXPERIENCE OF INNER PURIFICATION (v. 22*a*)

This experience is vividly portrayed in the phrase "Seeing ye have purified your souls in your obedience to the truth unto unfeigned love of the brethren." The purification in view is distinctly moral rather than ritual. The order of the original, "your souls having purified" (R. Young), emphasizes that the experience related not to bodily cleansing but to the souls of the readers (*tas psuchas*), the inner life as the seat and center of self-conscious life. The consciousness of sin's defilement of the Christian's inner being has been removed. Though impurities that relate to the use of the body are naturally included (cf. 1:9), the expression clearly shows that the purification is moral, not merely external.

In the Septuagint the concept of purification is usually ceremonial. It also has that ceremonial sense in John 11:55; Acts 21:24, 26; and 24:18. But here, as in James 4:8 and 1 John 3:3, the verb denotes moral purification. It looks back to the thought of verses 2 and 15. The term expresses the moral purity demanded in the life and character of those who have been brought into a personal relationship with the holy God (1:16; 1 John 3:3). Ross points out that various pagan practices bear witness to the innate consciousness of the human heart for the need of such purification.[1]

The perfect active participle, *hēgnikotes*, "having purified," looks back to a specific past experience that has a present result. The cleansing took place at the time of the readers' regeneration, and so they were in a state of being clean (cf. John 13:10; 15:3; 17:19). The impact of that cleansing "extends beyond mere external separation from heathen worship and habits to the abandonment of false principles and beliefs, and evil desires and passions."[2] That purification is a necessary antecedent to life in the Christian community.

The use of the active voice marks the experience of cleansing as a matter that involved the will of the readers. They acted to receive the cleansing by placing themselves under obedience to the word of God. In Acts 15:9 Peter spoke of God cleansing the heart by faith; here the reference is to the human involvement in cleansing. In both instances the reference is to the purification that initiates the Christian life.

Scholars who interpret 1 Peter as a baptismal homily naturally understand the mention of purification as "an archaic description of baptism."[3] That association seems natural to them since they believe that the new birth takes

1. J. M. E. Ross, *The First Epistle of Peter*, p. 78.
2. W. H. Bennett, *The General Epistles, James, Peter, John, and Jude*, p. 202.
3. J. N. D. Kelly, *A Commentary on the Epistles of Peter and of Jude*, p. 78, quoting C. Spicq. Cf. Francis Wright Beare, *The First Epistle of Peter*, p. 109; A. R. C. Leaney, *The Letters of Peter and Jude*, p. 28; Bo Reicke, *The Epistles of James, Peter, and Jude*, p. 86.

place by means of or in conjunction with the ceremony of water baptism. But both Peter and James (1:18) connect the begetting with the word of the gospel, not the waters of baptism. Regeneration is explicitly related to the personal reception of Christ as Savior rather than to an outward ritual. In New Testament times, however, there was no long interval between personal acceptance of the Savior and an open confession of Him in Christian baptism.

"In your obedience to the truth" indicates the sphere in which that purification becomes operative. The trait of obedience has already been mentioned in verses 2 and 14. It is an important element in the Christian life. Our obedience is not the instrument or means that procures purification; it designates the human attitude that enables the Spirit to purify. *Your obedience* (*tē hupakoē*, "the obedience") looks back to the obedience expected from readers when the gospel message came to them. The compound noun conveys the thought of attentively listening to an authoritative pronouncement and then submitting to it in obedience. The words are "but another and fuller way of expressing their faith."[4] It is an obedience that springs from hearing in faith. Such an obedience to the gospel "brings us, not into a state of bondage, but into one of glorious liberty in which the heart is free and the conscience is pure."[5]

But it should be obedience to "the truth" that is "neither abstract or intellectual truth, nor the true philosophical system which explains the universe, but the divine revelation of the gospel (cf. 2 Th. 2:10, 12, 13; Jn 14:6; Eph. 1:13; Col. 1:5; Gal. 5:7)."[6] The genitive "of the truth" (*tēs alētheias*) may be interpreted as subjective, the obedience that truth demands and works in the believer;[7] but more probably the genitive is objective, obedience to the truth as revealed in the gospel. Oberst well observes, "Souls are not purified when one submits to false teaching or deceitful doctrines."[8]

The words "through the Spirit" in the KJV represent the Textus Receptus.[9] Though the words appear in some later uncials and in most minuscules, their absence in important early Greek manuscripts has led modern editors of the Greek text to omit them, but with acknowledged uncertainty.[10] The words are apparently a "theological expansion introduced by a copyist,"[11] but they clarify the truth that the purification in view is the work of the Holy Spirit in the obedient soul.

"Unto unfeigned love of the brethren" specifies the natural tendency

4. William Kelly, *The Epistles of Peter*, p. 102.

5. John Miller, *Notes on James, I and II Peter, I, II and III John, Jude, Revelation*, p. 29.

6. Ernest Best, *I Peter*, p. 93.

7. F. J. A. Hort, *The First Epistle of Peter*, pp. 88-89; J. Howard B. Masterman, *The First Epistle of S. Peter*, p. 89.

8. Bruce Oberst, *Letters from Peter*, p. 42.

9. F. H. Scrivener, ed., *Hē Kainē Diathēkē. Novum Testamentum. Textus Stephanici A.D. 1550*.

10. See the evidence in the United Bible Societies text, *The Greek New Testament*, p. 792.

11. Bruce M. Metzger, *A Textual Commentary on the Greek New Testament*, p. 688.

produced in the heart by the experience of purification. "Before we have purified our souls, there is every thing not only to hinder such affection but to render it impossible."[12] "Unto (*eis*), with a view to," indicates the natural goal that the purification has in view. The result is not merely individual but social.

The noun rendered "love of the brethren" (*philadelphia*) was used in secular Greek of the mutual love of natural brothers and sisters, but in the New Testament it is always used of affection for those who are spiritual brothers in the faith. According to Masterman the term does not mean "brotherly love, but brother-love. Not 'love men *as though* they were your brothers,' but 'love men *because* they are your brothers.'"[13] That affectionate relation to fellow believers, the "noblest jewel in the diadem of early Christianity,"[14] is the sure mark of the new birth (1 John 3:14). Peter insisted that such brother-love should be "unfeigned" (*anhupokriton*), "unhypocritical," without a show of affection that lacks reality. Underlying the adjective is the practice of ancient actors who wore a mask to represent some fictitious character, thus playing a pretended part. Peter well knew that in circles where warm Christian affection was common and expected among its members, there was ever a danger of pretending to have a love that was not truly felt. "Pretense to a good that is not genuinely felt is hateful to God, and unworthy of His child."[15] Peter's demand need not be viewed as a censure of the readers but as a needed warning against the ever-present danger of allowing our affections to become insincere in our dealings with fellow believers.

B. THE DUTY OF MUTUAL LOVE (v. 22*b*)

To those with purified hearts Peter directed an urgent command, "love one another from the heart fervently." The command is an appeal to the will; Peter believed that Christian love can be commanded. The believer should deliberately act to assure its operation. Peter was anxious for his readers to unlock the floodgates, so that the full stream of love might gush forth. The aorist imperative need not be understood as ingressive, "begin to love," as though addressed to baptismal candidates just entering the Christian life. It carries a sense of urgency and demands that Christians should act to let their love operate to its fullest.

The verb (*agapēsate*) is a different term from that just rendered "love of the brethren" (*philadelphia*). Though the two terms have much in common, in New Testament usage there is a discernable difference between them.[16] *Agapēsate* does not make prominent the emotional aspect of *philadelphia*; it is

---

12. William Kelly, p. 102.
13. Masterman, p. 89.
14. Quoted from Gunkel by Archibald M. Hunter, *The First Epistle of Peter*, p. 104.
15. William Kelly, p. 103.
16. See William Barclay, *New Testament Words*, pp. 17-30; "Love," *NIDNTT*, 2:538-51; Ethelbert Stauffer, *agapaō*, *TDNT*, 1:35-55.

rather "the love of full intelligence and understanding coupled with corresponding purpose."[17] It is a love of rational goodwill that desires the highest good for the one loved, even at the expense of self.

Such love should be mutual—"love one another" (*allēlous agapēsate*), "one another love ye." The forward position of the reciprocal pronoun stresses the mutual character of that love. Christian love is not a one-way street; the expression of love should flow in both directions.

Two modifiers, both emphatic by their position, further describe love —"from the heart one another be loving fervently" (Gr.). The former stresses its source, the latter its intensity.

"From the heart" (*ek kardias*) demands that love should flow from within as an expression of the Christian's true inner being. *Heart* as a metaphorical designation denotes the "center and source of the whole inner life, with its thinking, feeling, and volition."[18] As the seat of the inner life, heart stands in contrast with "outer things like lips or the mouth (cf. Matt. 12:34; 15:8)."[19] The Textus Receptus reads "out of a pure heart." *Pure* (*katharas*) has some good early manuscript support and may well be authentic.[20] But most modern critical editors omit it,[21] regarding it as an early interpretive gloss. The adjective brings out the required meaning, but in the context it seems redundant.

The second modifier, *fervently* (*ektenōs*), is a compound adverb, composed of the preposition *ek*, "out," and a verbal root meaning "to stretch." It thus embodies the picture of something stretched out and extended to the limit. The term suggests increased tension or highly energetic activity. Jowett suggests the picture of a stringed instrument, "as when the string of a violin has been stretched to a tighter pitch that it might yield a little higher note."[22] Cranfield suggests the figure of "the taut muscle of strenuous and sustained effort, as of an athlete."[23] Understood either way, the term does not refer to the emotional warmth but to the intensity of Christian love. It is a call for love at full capacity as a deliberate principle of life.

C. THE FOUNDATION IN PERSONAL REGENERATION (vv. 23-25)

Peter well knew that such a life of mutual love should be rooted in a new nature. The new birth makes possible and demands such a life. The crucial importance of regeneration is underscored by the expanded treatment Peter

17. R. C. H. Lenski, *The Interpretation of the Epistles of St. Peter, St. John and St. Jude*, p. 74.
18. William F. Arndt and F. Wilbur Gingrich, *A Greek-English Lexicon of the New Testament and Other Early Christian Literature*, p. 404.
19. Jay E. Adams, *Trust And Obey. A Practical Commentary on First Peter*, p. 50, n. 21.
20. In *The Greek New Testament*, published by the United Bible Societies, it was omitted in the first edition (1966), but in the third edition (1975) the editors place it in the text in brackets and mark the reading as carrying a considerable degree of doubt.
21. It is omitted in the texts of Westcott and Hort, Nestle and Aland (24th ed.), and Tasker, as well as Souter.
22. J. H. Jowett, *The Epistles of St. Peter*, p. 63.
23. C. E. B. Cranfield, *I & II Peter and Jude*, p. 57.

gives it. He notes the fact of the readers' regeneration (v. 23a), the means of that regeneration (vv. 23b-25a), and the evangelization that led to their regeneration (v. 25b).

(1) The fact of their regeneration (v. 23a). "Having been begotten again" emphasizes the abiding reality of regeneration. The phrase is a return to the basic fact with which Peter began his description of salvation (v. 3). In verse 3 the reference was to the initial experience of regeneration; here the thought turns to its abiding result. There the aorist active participle depicted the new birth as the work of God; here the perfect passive participle looks to the essential character of those who have been born again.

The perfect passive participle, "having been begotten again" (*anagennēmenoi*), is grammatically parallel to the perfect active participle, "having purified your souls" (v. 22a). Both participles describe the subject "ye" of the imperative "love ye one another" (v. 22b); they complement each other. In regeneration God works to implant a new nature, and that new nature motivates the development of moral purity of life. "Peter again recalls the roots as he appeals for the fruits of Christian living."[24] Peter's expression indicates the certainty of regeneration.

(2) The nature of their regeneration (vv. 23b-25a). Peter next describes the source and means of the new birth. The source of the new life is described both negatively and positively, "not of corruptible seed, but of incorruptible." *Of* (*ek*), "out of," indicates its source and should be distinguished from the following *through* (*dia*), which denotes its means.

The word "seed" (*sporas*), which appears only here in the New Testament, primarily denotes the activity of sowing and was used figuratively of the act of procreation. It also denoted that which was sown, the seed. Peter may have used *seed* in the sense of "plant seed." Bigg advanced that view and appealed to the parable of the sower for support.[25] But in the context, the picture of the new birth more naturally implies the father's seed out of which the new life springs (cf. John 1:13; James 1:18; 1 John 3:9).

The seed out of which natural life springs is "corruptible" (*phthartēs*), perishable, subject to decay and destruction, and can only give rise to a life that is subject to decay and death. But the new life of the believer is not derived from such a transient source; it springs from that which is "incorruptible" (*aphthariou*), not subject to corruption and death. It has the same nature as the inheritance that awaits the redeemed (v. 4). Thus Peter made a sharp distinction between human and divine generation. The supernatural source of the believer's new life may be viewed as "God's creative grace"[26] that

24. James Moffatt, *The General Epistles, James, Peter, and Judas*, p. 111.
25. Charles Bigg, *A Critical and Exegetical Commentary on the Epistles of St. Peter and St. Jude*, p. 123.
26. Edward Gordon Selwyn, *The First Epistle of St. Peter*, p. 151.

redeemed us "according to his great mercy" (v. 3). Caffin suggests that "the Holy Spirit of God is, in the deepest sense, the Seed of the new birth."[27] Only a supernatural source can account for the new life of the believer.

The parallel phrase, "through the word of God" (*dia logou . . . theou*), specifies the means or instrument used in regeneration. Neither noun has the definite article; that emphasizes the essential quality of the regenerating agent, "God's word" (cf. James 1:18).

Two epithets, both present active participles, "living" and "abiding," describe the means used in regeneration. According to Peter, the regenerating word has a dual character; it is "living," actively possessing life, and "abiding," permanent and unchanging. Living is the primary quality.

It is grammatically possible to connect those two epithets with *God* and render "through means of the word of a Living and Abiding God" (Rotherham).[28] That is done in the Vulgate and by a number of scholars.[29] In support scholars argue that Peter's expression apparently was influenced by the Septuagint rendering of Daniel 6:26, where both terms are applied to God. So understood, Peter's words would mean that the new kinship introduced by the new birth abides because of the living and abiding nature of God Himself. But that understanding of Peter's words is questionable. It is better to relate *living* and *abiding* to *word* (*logou*) and to understand those participles to specify the nature of the means (*word*) used in regeneration. Emphasis on the lasting quality of the regenerating Word is appropriate to the argument. It compliments the following quotation in the text, which places the emphasis upon the abiding nature, not of God, but of the Word of God. That understanding of Peter's phrase is supported by the original word order that places *living* before *God* (*theou*) and *abiding* after it. If *living* was intended to be connected with God, because of the subsequent *and abiding* it, too, should stand after *theou*. The original order closely connects *living* with *word* and then adds that the Word is God's and has the further characteristic of being abiding—literally, "through a word living, God's, and abiding." In what follows Peter identifies that Word with "the word of glad tidings" (v. 25), the gospel message that was preached to the readers. Peter did not refer to Christ directly as "the Logos" (John 1:1).

So two participles portray the continuously living and enduring nature of the gospel message. It has the very character of the God whose message it is (Phil. 2:16; Heb. 4:12). It is also "abiding," never obsolete or irrelevant. It is "intended for all periods of time, never to be superseded by human philosophy."[30] The second epithet follows from the first and introduces the subsequent quotation (vv. 24-25a).

27. B. C. Caffin, *The First Epistle General of Peter*, p. 12.

28. Rotherham. Similarly, 20th Cent., Goodspeed, Williams, JB.

29. John Calvin, *The Epistle of Paul the Apostle to the Hebrews and the First and Second Epistles of St. Peter*, p. 252; Albert Barnes, *Notes on the New Testament, Explanatory and Practical, James, Peter, John, and Jude*, p. 131; Hort, p. 92; Beare, p. 112.

30. Nathaniel Marshman Williams, *Commentary on the Epistles of Peter*, p. 22.

The words "for ever" (KJV) represent the reading of the Textus Receptus. But as Metzger notes, those words (*eis ton aiōna*) are "absent from a wide variety of representative types of text."[31] Scholars generally believe that they are an addition from verse 25. The thought they convey is already communicated by *abiding* and *living*.

"For" (*hoti*), also used in verse 16, introduces a quotation from Isaiah 40:6 and 8 to illustrate and confirm what Peter had just asserted about the nature of the Word of God. The quotation, which links the New to the Old Testament, follows the Septuagint (with some minor variations). It is possible that the text Peter used contained those variations, but it is more probable that Peter introduced them. Mason believed that the quotation "varies between the Hebrew and the LXX in the kind of way which shows that the writer was familiar with both."[32] The New Testament writers were not obligated to quote from the Old Testament with verbal exactness. Their quotations might be drawn directly from the Hebrew; or, as they often did, they might quote from the Septuagint, the Greek Old Testament in common use among Greek-speaking Jews and Christians. And at times they apparently quoted from memory, content to give the essence of the passage they referred to.

"All flesh is as grass" (Isa. 40:6*b*) depicts the transitory nature of human existence. "The life of flesh of man," Miller observes, "is longer than that of grass, but the end is the same."[33] But *flesh* is not to be restricted to the physical flesh; it denotes all of mankind. *As* (*hōs*) underlines the comparison between the grass and human existence; both are frail and temporal. It does not occur in the Hebrew or Septuagint versions but was added by Peter to emphasize the transitory nature of human existence. *Grass* (*chortos*) in the New Testament generally denotes green grass standing in a field or meadow, but the Greek term also includes flowering plants or herbs, which were used as feed for cattle. The parallelism makes it clear that flowering plants are in view.

"And all the glory thereof as the flower of grass" strengthens the poetic picture. *All the glory thereof* centers attention on man's vaunted achievements, "all that man prides himself on—his wealth, rank, talents, beauty, learning, splendour of equipage or apparel."[34] All are short-lived like "the flower of grass"—"the most short-lived part of it."[35] Instead of *thereof* (*autēs*), which refers back to "grass," the Textus Receptus reads "of man" (*anthrōpou*), the reading of the Septuagint. The manuscript support for that reading is poor, and the critical editors agree that it is a scribal correction— it is more probable that a scribe would change the unusual *autēs* to the familiar *anthrōpou* than the other way around.

"The grass withereth, and the flower falleth" announces the inevitable end.

---

31. Metzger, p. 689.
32. A. J. Mason, *The First Epistle General of Peter*, p. 398.
33. Miller, p. 29.
34. Barnes, p. 132.
35. John Wesley, Adam Clarke, Matthew Henry, and others, *One Volume New Testament Commentary*, *in loc.*

Withered pictures the dried up and shriveled state of the once beautiful flower, and *falleth (exepesen)*, "to fall out, fall away," denotes the disintegration of the flower as the leaves fall away from the calyx. Our English versions generally use the present tense to denote an act that is repeated. But the Greek gnomic aorists, though relating a recurring act, portray the action as a quick and startling event. Lenski seeks to represent that dramatic picture by translating, "Withered the grass, fallen the bloom!"[36] In the original the first verb stands before the subject and the second verb stands at the end— "wither did the grass, and the flower of it fell away" (R. Young). The chiasm makes the picture all the more dramatic. To Peter, who like James (1:11) was familiar with the drastic impact of the dry season on the Palestinian flora, the inevitable end of plant life was a standing lesson on the transitoriness of human existence.

"But" *(de)* adds the contrasting fact of the abiding nature of God's word, "But the word of the Lord abideth for ever" (v. 25a). The term rendered "the word" *(to rhēma)* is not the same term rendered "the word" *(logou)* in verse 23. *To rhēma* is the term used in the Septuagint. The same transition occurs in Peter's sermon in Acts 10:36-37. *To rhēma* is more concrete and denotes that which is spoken, the utterance itself. *Logos* is more comprehensive and includes the thought as well as its expression. The term *rhēma*, "utterance" or "message," pointedly designates the message spoken by the mouth of God; it is the divine revelation made known in the Christian gospel (cf. Heb. 1:1-2). The repetition of that term in the next phrase identifies that divine utterance with the gospel proclaimed to the readers. It is indeed "the word of the Lord." But the reading *of the Lord (kuriou)* is a clear departure from the Septuagint reading *of our God (tou theou hēmōn)*, which reproduces the Hebrew. *Kurios* is the Septuagint translation of the self-disclosed name of the covenant-God of Israel, Yahweh, "Jehovah" (ASV: Ex. 6:2-4; 19:3; 20:1-2; Jer. 31:31-34). In the New Testament it is a standard designation for Jesus Christ, whether with the definite article, "the Lord," or without an article, as here.[37] Vincent remarks, "The substitution indicates that Peter identifies Jesus with God."[38] Peter's change to *the Lord* gives the quotation a Christian slant and leads to his identification of the divine utterance with the gospel in the following phrase.

(3) The evangelization leading to their regeneration (v. 25b). "And this is the word of good tidings which was preached unto you." *And (de)* is transitional and does not imply a contrast. It marks the transition from the Old Testament picture of God's abiding Word to the thought of its operation in the lives of the readers. *This (touto)* looks back to the last line of the quotation and connects God's abiding "utterance" with the gospel message that came to them as "good tidings." Peter's words are an echo of the statement in 1:12b. We may more literally translate, "the message that was *evangelized* [proclaimed as good

36. Lenski, p. 75.
37. Bigg, p. 124; Hans Bietenhard, "kurios," *NIDNTT*, 2:510-20; Werner Foerster, "*kurios* in the New Testament," *TDNT*, 3:1086-95.
38. Marvin R. Vincent, *Word Studies in the New Testament*, 1:641.

tidings] unto you." Peter thus authenticated the message that was brought to the readers. The message "that was evangelized" (to euanggelisthen) to them was indeed the good news of salvation. The reference is to the evangelization that resulted in the establishment of the churches that were addressed.[39] Their acceptance of that message resulted in their regeneration. Unto you (eis humas) applied the teaching to the experience of the readers; it implies that the message had entered into their lives as a living force.

---

39. The reading of the KJV, "is preached unto you," generalizes the statement but misses the time indication of the original.

8

The Christian Life in Relation
to Personal Growth
(2:1-3)

Peter's "therefore" closely relates chapter two with chapter one. The inferential particle (*oun*) indicates that the call to spiritual growth in 2:1-3 is a logical and natural consequence of Peter's previous remarks on the new birth in 1:12-25; the Godward and the manward aspects of the Christian life make their inescapable demands on the believer.

3) THE CHRISTIAN LIFE IN RELATION TO PERSONAL GROWTH (2:1-3)

(1) Putting away therefore all wickedness, and all guile, and hypocrisies, and envies, and all evil speakings, (2) as newborn babes, long for the spiritual milk which is without guile, that ye may grow thereby unto salvation; (3) if ye have tasted that the Lord is gracious.

Those three verses constitute one sentence that centers on the imperative "long for." That craving is essential to the healthy growth of the new life. The obligation to grow involves the negative duty to remove all hindrances to growth (v. 1), and the positive duty to actively appropriate nourishment that furthers growth (v. 2). Verse 3 cites past experience as an incentive to growth.

A. THE REMOVAL OF HINDERING VICES (v. 1)

A sweeping removal of all hindrances to growth is needed—"Putting away all wickedness, and all guile, and hypocrisies, and envies, and all evil speakings." The plural participle "putting off" (*apothemenoi*) is grammatically dependent on the plural subject of the imperative "long [ye] for" in verse 2. That connection gives the participle an imperatival force. Some modern English versions, like the NIV, translate it as an imperative, "rid yourselves of all malice."[1] But it is better to retain the participial form to indicate the fact that it is an action subsidiary to the imperative that expresses the main duty. Since both the participle and the verb are in the aorist tense, the action of the participle is best understood as antecedent to that of the verb.[2] Before their yearning for milk can be realized, there must be a definite break with all the evils that hinder spiritual growth.

The image involved in *putting away* has been understood in two ways. In view of Peter's use of the noun in 3:21, some interpreters understand the verb to mean the washing off of defilement.[3] But the verb was commonly used of the putting off of clothes. In Acts 7:58 it is used in the literal sense, but generally the sense refers metaphorically to the removal of evil (cf. Zech. 3:3-4).[4] Peter's words picture someone flinging off a badly stained or infected garment. Either understanding, because of the aorist tense of the participle, demands a definite break with sin; the Christian should remove it entirely. The term repudiates every effort "to cover these unsightly deformities of the old man with the veil of an assumed courteousness and politeness, or sanctimony."[5]

The repeated *all* leaves no room for exceptions in the demand for holiness. Its threefold repetition groups moral evils into three categories. All such evil behavior is a holdover from the old, unregenerate nature. None of it relates directly to God. Peter lists vices that destroy the fellowship of believers. But it is unwarranted to infer that Peter's list describes his recipients. More likely, he was well aware that they were open to scandalous experiences if such evils were not decisively dealt with.

The exact meaning of the first-named vice, "wickedness" (*kakia*), is debated. Barclay calls it "the most general word for evil and wickedness."[6] It denotes the quality of badness or faultiness and is the opposite of that which is good in character and beneficial. Except in Matthew 6:34, where it means "trouble, evil circumstances," in the New Testament it carries an ethical import—that which is morally evil. The translation "all wickedness," wickedness of every kind, understands it to denote moral evil in all its forms. Accepting that general connotation, Lenski notes that the term "covers all the sins against the second

1. So also Weymouth and TEV. Others variously translate "get rid of"—Williams; "put away" —RSV, Montgomery, Kleist and Lilly; "lay aside"—Berkeley; "off with"—Moffatt; "away with"—NEB; "free yourselves from"—Goodspeed.
2. H. E. Dana and Julius R. Mantey, *A Manual Grammar of the Greek New Testament*, p. 230.
3. Charles Bigg, *A Critical and Exegetical Commentary on the Epistles of St. Peter and St. Jude*, p. 125; J. H. A. Hart, *The First Epistle General of Peter*, 5:54; J. W. C. Wand, *The General Epistles of St. Peter and St. Jude*, p. 63.
4. Rom. 13:12; Eph. 4:22-24; Col. 3:8; Heb. 12:1; James 1:21.
5. John Brown, *Expository Discourses on the First Epistle of the Apostle Peter*, 1:203.
6. William Barclay, *The Letters of James and Peter*, p. 224.

table of the law.'"[7] But often in the New Testament it apparently is used more specifically, in lists with other vices, to denote ill will, malice, or malignity. If that is the case here, then Peter referred to the moral baseness that is eager to injure one's neighbor. Wand notes that in that sense the term comes "close to that 'hatred of the human race,' which Tacitus tells us was a regular charge against the Christians at the time of the Neronian persecution" (Annals, xv. 44).[8] Scholars differ on whether Peter's use of the term is to be understood comprehensively—all kinds of moral evil—or more specifically as ill will or malice. If he used it comprehensively, then the thought is that everything that is morally inferior and base must be removed as inconsistent with the nature of the new life in Christ. But in the context the term seems to have a more specific meaning; it refers to the basic attitude of ill will toward others. Kelly notes that that term and the following, both singular, "stand for general attitudes disruptive of community life, while the remaining three words are plurals denoting the practical expressions of hypocrisy, envy and slanderous backbiting."[9] The majority of our modern English versions translate it as "malice."[10]

"And all guile, and hypocrisies, and envies" seem clearly united as a second class of vices by the repeated all. They all flow from the preceding vice, malice.

"Guile" (dolon) means deceit, cunning, or craftiness; it is the attitude that desires to get the better of another by cunning and deception. The term originally meant "a bait for fish," and thus came to denote any cunning contrivance for deceiving and catching. It is the selfish, "two-faced" attitude that deceives and hurts others for personal gain.

The plural "hypocrisies" (hupokriseis) indicates the various forms of pretense that guile resorts to in its endeavor to throw the intended victim off guard. The term basically denotes an actor playing a role, a part that hides his true identity. The term readily developed an evil connotation to denote the hypocrite, "a man who all the time is concealing his real motives, a man who meets you with a face which is very different from his heart, and with words which are very different from his real feelings."[11] Such religious impersonation is seen in the case of Ananias and Sapphira (Acts 5:1-10) who cloaked evil desires behind pious appearances. The unfeigned love called for in 1:22 must be without that terrible quality.

"And envies" (phthonous), a plural noun, denotes the various occasions when envious feelings may arise within the group. "Envy is the feeling of displeasure produced by witnessing or hearing of the advantage or prosperity of others."[12] Envy is the running-mate of hypocrisy. "As hypocrisy has its

---

7. R. C. H. Lenski, The Interpretation of the Epistles of St. Peter, St. John and St. Jude, p. 78.

8. Wand, p. 64.

9. J. N. D. Kelly, A Commentary on the Epistles of Peter and of Jude, p. 83.

10. So NASB, NIV, RSV, NEB, 20th Cent., Darby, Moffatt, Goodspeed, Montgomery, Berkeley, Williams, Kleist and Lilly. Weymouth has "ill will," and the JB has "never spiteful."

11. Barclay, p. 225.

12. W. E. Vine, An Expository Dictionary of New Testament Words, 2:37.

spring in claiming to have the good we lack, envy seeks to deny and defame the real good of others."[13] It is a moral cancer (Prov. 14:30) that plagues "all voluntary organizations, not least religious organizations."[14] It reared its ugly head even among the twelve, while Jesus was yet with them (Mark 10:41). It is "almost the only vice which is practicable at all times and in every place" (Johnson).[15]

"And all evil speakings" adds a third category of vices that must be eliminated. The noun "evil speakings" (*katalalias*), which occurs in the New Testament only here and in 2 Corinthians 12:20,[16] denotes speech that "runs down" or disparages another. It is a vice that deliberately assaults the character of another and usually takes place behind the victim's back. The plural points to the varied forms of such injurious and slanderous speech. It operates "either by denying or darkening a neighbour's virtues, and either by attributing to him evil or imputing to him evil designs in doing good."[17] MacDonald notes that it can even act under the guise of a pious prayer request, "'I mention this only for your prayer fellowship, but did you know that he . . .' and then the character is assassinated."[18] It is usually the fruit of envy. *All* insists that every manifestation of that evil must be eliminated. Let it be replaced by calling attention to the commendable traits of others.

Lenski notes that Peter's list "stops with the misuse of the tongue and does not add base deeds," and then well observes, "defamations are the first outward evidence, and where this is absent, base deeds will not follow."[19]

B. THE CALL TO SPIRITUAL GROWTH (vv. 2-3)

Removing hindering vices must be followed by active efforts to promote Christian growth. The duty to provide needed nourishment is emphasized by the sole imperative of the sentence, "long for." Peter points to the duty of promoting spiritual growth (v. 2a), the aim of such growth (v. 2b), and the spiritual incentive to growth (v. 3).

(1) The duty to promote growth (v. 2a). "As newborn babes, long for the spiritual milk which is without guile." That duty is demanded from those characterized as "newborn babes" (*artigennēta brephē*), a designation occurring only here in the New Testament. As (*hōs*), an adverb of manner, indicates that the designation is figurative. It characterizes Christians as newborn

13. William Kelly, *The Epistles of Peter*, p. 117.
14. Edward Gordon Selwyn, *The First Epistle of St. Peter*, p. 153.
15. Quoted in James Moffatt, "The General Epistles, James, Peter, and Judas," p. 112.
16. The adjective *katalalos* appears in Rom. 1:30; the verb *katalaleō* is used three times in James 4:11 and twice in 1 Pet. 2:12 and 3:16.
17. G. F. C. Fronmüller, *The Epistles General of Peter*, p. 31.
18. William MacDonald, *I Peter: Faith Tested, Faith Triumphant*, p. 34.
19. Lenski, p. 79.

infants with an inborn longing for their mother's milk. The term is not derogative but rather "sets forth the tenderness of their relation to God, and implies the idea of guilelessness."[20]

In classical Greek the term babe (*brephos*) was used of the embryo, the unborn child, but in later writers it was extended to include the suckling child and even small children generally. Those who view 1 Peter as originally a baptismal homily[21] naturally appeal to that designation as confirmation of their view. Thus Beare asserts that the designation "could not be used with any appropriateness of the general body of Christians in the provinces mentioned in the salutation" and insists that "the words are wholly appropriate to the condition of converts who have just been received into the Church by baptism."[22] Admittedly, Peter's designation can be understood to support that view. Kelly remarks, "The adjective need mean no more than that the Asian communities included a substantial proportion of fairly recent converts."[23] It should be observed, however, that Peter's term is clearly figurative and in itself does not establish the claim that those addressed were new converts. Rather, as Selwyn maintains, "The purpose of the adjective is to make the imagery of the passage more vivid. . . . What the author wants to express is the ardour of the suckled child."[24] Such an ardor for spiritual food is essential for spiritual growth. Believers should at all times be *like* infants in their craving for the nourishment that the Lord has provided for their spiritual growth. The imagery is both expressive and challenging!

Peter's picture is apparently based on the teaching of Christ that the kingdom of God must be received as a little child (Matt. 18:3; Mark 10:15). Peter made no mention of a process of growth from infancy to adulthood, where the longing for milk is replaced by the ability to eat solid food. His picture of the readers as babes, unlike that of Paul and the author of Hebrews (1 Cor. 3:1-4; Heb. 5:12-14), is not derogatory. He was eager for them, as those who have been born again (1:23), to maintain the distinctive characteristic of baby-like eagerness for spiritual nourishment. His figure was clearly influenced by the imagery that follows.

Consistent with that designation, Peter challenged his readers to "long for the spiritual milk which is without guile." The original places the object before the verb, thus giving emphasis to both—"for the spiritual milk which is without guile long ye" (Gr.).

The imperative, a compound form (*epipothēsate*), is a strong verb. Some, like Alford, maintain that the preposition *epi*, prefixed to the verb, is directive and means "long after."[25] But it is generally accepted as more in keeping with the

20. Fronmüller, p. 31.
21. See the Introduction.
22. Francis Wright Beare, *The First Epistle of Peter*, p. 114.
23. J. N. D. Kelly, p. 84.
24. Selwyn, p. 154.
25. Henry Alford, *The Greek New Testament*, vol. 4 (part 1), p. 344.

context to regard it as intensive, "to long for greatly, crave."[26] Selwyn remarks that the aorist tense calls for "vigorous action, such as is seen in a child being suckled."[27] Such vigorous craving is the sign of a healthy condition. Beare, advocating a baptismal setting for the term, views the aorist as ingressive, "they must begin to cultivate the taste for spiritual things."[28] But like the imperatives in chapter 1—all in the aorist (1:13, 15, 17, 23), the aorist tense can equally be understood to express urgency. As an appeal to the will of his readers, Peter was anxious that they allow that attitude to be truly characteristic of them.

As newborn babies, the nourishment Christians should crave is "the spiritual milk which is without guile" (to logikon adolon gala). The definite article, "the milk," makes the reference specific, "the divinely-given nourishment supplied by the Gospel."[29] In 1 Corinthians 3:2 and Hebrews 5:12-13, the term is used of the nourishment suitable for babes but not for those who are mature. But Peter did not make that distinction. The nourishment in view is suitable for all who have been born again.

That milk is described by two attributive adjectives. The first, logikon, translated "spiritual" in the ASV, occurs elsewhere in the New Testament only in Romans 12:1. It does not occur in the Septuagint. Its exact force in 1 Peter is much debated. It is composed of the noun logos, "word," and an adjectival suffix (-ikos) that denotes the characteristic nature of that which is described.[30] The form thus points to a kind of milk that is characterized by its connection with "word." It is not literal milk; it is not nourishment for the physical body. Thus Weymouth translates "milk for the soul," and Rotherham renders, "the milk that is for the mind." Those translations suggest that it is milk for the rational nature of man. The term has often been translated "reasonable" or "logical," and that meaning is suitable in Romans 12:1. It may mean "rational" or "intellectual milk" suited to man's rational nature. More probable is the translation "spiritual," indicating that it ministers to the spiritual needs of man. Thus a number of our modern English versions use the term "spiritual." That is perhaps the best available term, yet it is somewhat vague and leaves the milk unidentified. But in view of 1:23, the readers would readily identify it with the Word of God. The suggestion that the intended reference is to Christ as the "Word" (logos) is questionable.

The milk is further described as being "without guile" (adolon), the very opposite of the vice to be removed (cf. v. 1). There is nothing crafty or deceitful in its nature. It is perfectly suited to nurture the guileless life. In the Greek papyri the adjective was regularly used in the sense of "pure" or "unadulterat-

26. Our English versions variously reflect the intensive force in their translations: "desire earnestly"—Darby; "crave"—NEB, NIV, 20th Cent., Rotherham, Goodspeed; "thirst for" —Moffatt, Weymouth, Williams; similarly, Berkeley and TEV.

27. Selwyn, pp. 155-56.

28. Beare, p. 114.

29. Selwyn, p. 154.

30. Bruce M. Metzger, Lexical Aids for Students of New Testament Greek, p. 56.

ed" as applied to foodstuffs.[31] The milk upon which Christians are to feed should be "unmixed or pure; not adulterated, or drugged with vain and deceitful philosophy, or any thrust-in human deceits."[32]

(2) The goal of spiritual growth (v. 2b). Feeding upon the Word has a specific aim, "that ye may grow thereby unto salvation." Active appropriation of the milk is not the final goal; it is rather the means whereby spiritual growth is realized. The new life cannot grow without the nourishing milk of the Word. "Thereby" (*en autō*), "in connection with it," stands before the verb and emphasizes that the needed growth is produced by the imbibed milk, "in order that in it ye may grow." *Grow* (*auxēthēte*) is aorist passive in form and may be translated "be made to grow." It is an activity that is wrought within us by the nourishment supplied. The aorist tense simply pictures that growth as the essential feature of the Christian life. Spiritual growth is not a direct act of human volition. The Christian's responsibility is to diligently appropriate the Word that produces the growth. The verb continues the picture of the readers as "newborn babes." Best remarks, "while the Christian is newborn he is also always in process of growth; it is not his status which requires emphasis but his progress."[33]

"Unto salvation" (*eis sōtērian*) indicates the goal of that growth. Those words are absent from the Textus Receptus, which follows the reading of Codex *L* (which dates from the eighth century) and many late minuscule copies. The omission, as Metzger suggests, was due to either "an oversight in copying or because the idea of 'growing into salvation' was theologically unacceptable."[34] On the basis of the strong manuscript evidence, the words are to be accepted as a true part of the original text. They do not imply that growth produces or merits salvation; rather, they indicate that present spiritual growth moves toward and will consummate in future salvation in all its fullness (cf. 1:5, 7). Then the process of growth as newborn babes will attain its full maturity.

(3) The incentive to spiritual growth (v. 3). "If ye have tasted that the Lord is gracious" is related grammatically with the command, "long for." That yearning for the milk of the word has its stimulus in past experience. *If (ei)*[35] does not imply doubt; it assumes the reality of the past experience. But the conditional construction is an implied invitation to the readers to self-examination on the matter. The verb *tasted* (*egeusasthe*) continues the imagery

31. James Hope Moulton and George Milligan, *The Vocabulary of the Greek Testament Illustrated from the Papyri and Other Non-Literary Sources*, p. 10.
32. John T. Demarest, *A Translation and Exposition of the First Epistle of the Apostle Peter*, p. 98.
33. Ernest Best, *I Peter*, p. 98.
34. Bruce M. Metzger, *A Textual Commentary on the Greek New Testament*, p. 689.
35. The Textus Receptus reads *eiper*, a strengthened form, "if indeed, since." It is probably a stylistic improvement of the simple form *ei*.

of the milk. The verb does not imply a cautious sip on the part of the readers but denotes actual appropriation and enjoyment on their part. The aorist tense looks back to the past experience begun at conversion. "A taste excites the appetite."[36] Peter assumes that the enjoyableness of the past experience will incite them to further appropriation.

Their experience has assured them "that the Lord is gracious." The words are an adaptation of Psalm 34:8, "Oh taste and see that Jehovah is good" (ASV). Peter used the Septuagint translation, omitting the words "and see" as unsuited to his purpose. In the Septuagint *the Lord* (*ho kurios*) translates the ancient Hebrew name of God, commonly referred to as "Jehovah" or "Yahweh." But as the following verse establishes, Peter used it to denote Jesus Christ. The position of the articular designation "the Lord" at the end of the sentence points to the personal identity of Him whom by experience Christians have found to be gracious. It is another evidence of Peter's high Christology.

The context indicates food that is tasted, but our English word gracious does not describe a quality peculiar to food. Though that term (*chrēstos*) is commonly used of persons both in the New Testament and the Septuagint, it was also used to describe pleasant food. In Jeremiah 24:2-5 it is used of delicious figs, and in Luke 5:39 Jesus used it of the mellowness of old wine.[37] The quotation from the psalm is thus consistent with the context. But the food imagery should not be taken to mean that Peter was simply thinking of the blessings of the Lord that we find to be "gracious" or "good." The experience is of the Lord Himself. Christians have found Him to be "gracious" Himself, "kind, loving, and benevolent."[38] Their eager appropriation of the milk of the Word has brought them into direct contact with the Lord who gave the Word. "He and His Word form a unity."[39] The true aim of Bible study is never a mere mastery of its contents but a transforming experience with the Lord who reveals Himself in His Word.

---

36. John Albert Bengel, *New Testament Word Studies*, 2:734.
37. Jesus also used it of the yoke He offers the believer, "my yoke is *chrēstos*" (Matt. 11:30).
38. William F. Arndt and F. Wilbur Gingrich, *A Greek-English Lexicon of the New Testament and Other Early Christian Literature*, p. 894.
39. George Williams, *The Student's Commentary on the Holy Scriptures*, p. 999.

9

The Reasons for Such
a Life of the Saved
(2:4-10)

Grammatically, the weighty and vivid portion in 2:4-10 is closely connected with what precedes. Peter continued his argument with a relative construction (see 1:6, 8, 10). Some interpreters, therefore, view what follows in verse 4 as a direct continuation of the exhortation in 2:1-3. But because of Peter's sudden change of metaphors, centering on a vivid description of our gracious Lord and what is corporately true of those in union with Him, it is preferable to regard the verses as a new paragraph.

If we accept those verses as a distinct unit, their modal coloring is not immediately obvious. The verb in verse 5, "built up" (*oikodomeisthe*), may be understood either as an imperative or an indicative. If understood as an imperative, what follows may logically be interpreted as the concluding exhortation in Peter's first cycle of exhortations (1:13—2:10). But only verses 4 and 5 can naturally be regarded as hortatory; the remainder of the section is clearly descriptive. It seems best, therefore, to accept the familiar view that the verb is indicative (see under v. 5). If that is the case, then verse 4 introduces a new line of thought that provides solid doctrinal justification for the threefold exhortation to holiness in 1:13—2:3. The close grammatical connection indicates that the precious spiritual realities described in verses 4 and 5 are inseparably related to the Lord and the way God expects His redeemed to live. The present doctrinal passage serves as a solid foundation for the preceding exhortations, but its clear distinction between the nature and destiny of the saved and the unsaved also provides a suitable bridge to the second cycle of exhortations in 2:11—3:12.

117

B. THE LIFE OF THE SAVED AS A CORPORATE UNITY (2:4-10)

(4) Unto whom coming, a living stone, rejected indeed of men, but with God elect, precious, (5) ye also, as living stones, are built up a spiritual house, to be a holy priesthood, to offer up spiritual sacrifices, acceptable to God through Jesus Christ. (6) Because it is contained in scripture,

Behold, I lay in Zion a chief corner stone, elect, precious:
And he that believeth on him shall not be put to shame.

(7) For you therefore that believe is the preciousness: but for such as disbelieve,

The stone which the builders rejected,
The same was made the head of the corner;

(8) and,

A stone of stumbling, and a rock of offence;

for they stumble at the word, being disobedient: whereunto also they were appointed. (9) But ye are an elect race, a royal priesthood, a holy nation, a people for *God's* own possession, that ye may show forth the excellencies of him who called you out of darkness into his marvellous light: (10) who in time past were no people, but now are the people of God: who had not obtained mercy, but now have obtained mercy.

The Christian life is lived in Christian community and finds its vitalization in union with Jesus Christ as its corporate head. Peter described what God does for those related to Jesus Christ, the touchstone of human life and destiny (vv. 4-8) and concluded with a vivid portrayal of their corporate nature and function (vv. 9-10).

1) THE DIVINE WORK THROUGH CHRIST WITH BELIEVERS (vv. 4-8)

Peter noted the continued approach of believers to Christ, the Living Stone (v. 4), depicted the corporate character and function of Christians as living stones (v. 5), and enlarged on the human responses to Christ, the touchstone of human destiny (vv. 6-8).

a. The living relation of believers to Christ (v. 4). The relative "whom" in Peter's phrase "unto whom coming" (*pros hon proserchomenoi*) relates to *the Lord* in verse 3. What follows in the paragraph shows "how naturally the N.T. writers interpret O.T. passages that speak about Jehovah (the covenant or salvation title for God) to Jesus Christ."[1] The nominative plural participle "coming" is grammatically dependent on the emphatic subject "ye also" in verse 5—the readers of the epistle. The present participle does not refer to

1. Jay E. Adams, *Trust and Obey*, p. 61.

an individual's initial commitment to Christ for salvation[2] but to the voluntary, repeated, or habitual coming of believers to Christ for sustenance and fellowship. As Mason notes, "From this point the regeneration-idea, which coloured the whole of the preceding portion of the Epistle, suddenly disappears."[3] As believers, the readers' initial taste of the goodness of Christ (v. 3) removed all natural dread of coming into the presence of God; repeatedly, they freely drew near to their Lord. The double use of the preposition *pros*, which has the root meaning of "near" or "facing," underscores the intimacy of that unique relationship. As Harrison notes, "No other faith can claim a living founder who has passed through death and has risen to a triumphant station at God's right hand there to be continually available to the immediate fellowship of each one who trusts Him."[4]

Many modern English versions, interpreting the verb in verse 5 as an imperative, transform the participle in verse 4 into an imperative and translate "Come to Him."[5] Though participles that are grammatically related to imperatives often acquire an imperatival force, that is not likely in this case since, as Best points out, the participle "does not lay down a rule of behaviour."[6] The participle does not command the readers to approach Christ; it describes what they were doing.

The One to whom believers draw near is appositionally identified as "a living stone" (*lithon zōnta*). That paradoxical designation, occurring only here (2:4-5), has no obvious Old Testament parallel. We naturally refer to something as being "stone dead," but for Peter the stone, as a person, is pulsating with life, strength, and coherence.[7] The spiritual reality transcends the natural figure. The absence of the definite article focuses attention on the innate quality of the stone, not its identity. The added modifiers make the reference entirely definite. Peter had already spoken of a living hope (1:3) and the living Word (1:23), both in relation to the living Christ. His fondness for the word "living" is reminiscent of his confession, "Thou art the Christ, the Son of the living God" (Matt. 16:16). As the risen Lord, the stone possesses and imparts life to those united to Him by faith (John 6:51; Rev. 2:8-10). That concept is central to the life-giving gospel.

2. If the reference was to their initial coming in salvation, the aorist tense would have been more natural. Charles Bigg, *A Critical and Exegetical Commentary on the Epistles of St. Peter and St. Jude*, says, "The present participle is used because stones keep coming one after another," p. 128. But that view would distribute the action over the duration of the church age; the present tense of the verb in verse 5 certainly relates to the continuing experience of each individual believer.

3. A. J. Mason, *The First Epistle General of Peter*, p. 400.

4. Everett Falconer Harrison, "Exegetical Studies in I Peter," p. 313.

5. So RSV, NEB, Weymouth, 20th Cent., Montgomery, Moffatt, Goodspeed, Berkeley; "Keep on coming to Him"—Williams; "Come to the Lord"—TEV; "Draw near to Him"—Kleist and Lilly.

6. Ernest Best, *I Peter*, p. 100.

7. The picture of "living stones" is latent in Christ's remark in Luke 19:20 that "the stones will cry out."

The sudden introduction of the stone figure was not inspired by Peter's meditation on the meaning of his own new name; a different word is used. The designation was clearly derived from the prophetic passages about the messianic stone that filled his mind and that are soon quoted. Peter's picture of Christ prepares the readers for his subsequent development of the image of Christians as a corporate structure.

The term translated "stone" (*lithos*) is the usual word used in connection with the construction of a building; Palestinian structures were commonly made of stone. It refers to a prepared stone, one that has been shaped for its place in the building. As such, it is "to be distinguished from *petros*, a loose stone lying on field or roadside, and from *petra*, a rock, or simply rock in contrast with e.g., sand or metal."[8] The term appropriately refers to Christ as One prepared and qualified to carry out the prophetic functions of a messianic stone. Christ used that figure of Himself when he warned the scribes and Pharisees of the fate they were incurring by rejecting Him (Matt. 21:42-44; Mark 11:10-11; Luke 20:17-18). Peter himself applied the figure to the hostile Sanhedrin members (Acts 4:11).

The added description of the stone, "rejected indeed of men, but with God elect, precious," indicates two significantly different viewpoints. Two diametrically opposite evaluations are indicated by the particles: *men*, "on the one hand," and *de*, "on the other." One class refers to human beings (*anthrōpoi*), the other to God. *Men* and *God* are placed before their corresponding verbs to stress their contrasting identity. "The human and the divine viewpoints are often at variance (1 Sam. 16:7; Isa. 55:8; Lk. 16:15), but never more acutely than in the appraisal of the Lord Jesus Christ."[9]

"Rejected of men" is adapted from Psalm 118:22, "The stone which the builders rejected." But instead of *the builders* Peter uses *men* without the article, mankind as such, to mark a perfect antithesis with *God*. As he wrote Peter was aware that Christian belief was a minority viewpoint. *Rejected* (*apodedokimasmenon*), a perfect passive participle, indicates that men applied their tests to the stone but, because it failed to measure up to their expectations and demands, they cast it aside as useless. The perfect tense denotes that they now obstinately continue to adhere to their adverse evaluation. That rejection took place "first of all by the Jews when they crucified Christ, and now by all who hear the Gospel and reject it."[10] It was a painful reality to the persecuted readers. But in the light of God's evaluation, Christians are encouraged to adhere to their experiential evaluation of that stone.

"But" (*de*), in spite of the hostility of the masses of mankind, God's evaluation still stands. *With God* (*para theō*), "alongside of God," in His presence, God standing by as the judge in the matter, the stone is "elect,

8. Edward Gordon Selwyn, *The First Epistle of St. Peter*, p. 158.
9. Harrison, p. 313.
10. Best, p. 100.

precious." The decisive evaluation rests with Him. Christ was indeed God's "chosen" One, selected by Him to be mankind's redeemer. As the one selected for God's building purposes, that stone was "choice" or "excellent" in His sight.[11] Because of Christ's proven character and work, the Father also esteems Him as "precious" (*entimon*), honored and prized, highly valued. The stress is upon the Father's evaluation of Christ, not His own instrinsic value. As Beare remarks, "The rejection of men cannot altar the fixed purpose of God, who has irrevocably chosen Christ for honour."[12]

b. *The corporate character and function of believers* (v. 5). "Ye also, as living stones, are built up a spiritual house" renews the focus on the readers and extends the stunning paradox of *living stones* to them also. The insertion of *as* (*hōs*) implies that Christ in His own right is the living stone of prophecy; but the readers, as believers in Him, have become living stones. Habitually drawing near to Him who is a living stone, "ye also" (*kai autoi*), "also yourselves," now have His unique nature. Through the new birth (1:23), He has imparted His own life to Christians. "Because I live, ye shall live also" (John 14:19c). Christians possess a life that will triumph over persecution and death itself.

The plural "ye" recognizes their existence as individuals, but Peter did not think of them as isolated stones scattered over a field. He pictured them collectively as forming a great spiritual house. They have been brought into a close and permanent union with one another, as fellow members of the house of God. "The Scriptures know nothing of an individual piety that is out of touch with the living body of God's people."[13] Furthermore, a house is not a jumbled pile of stones. The image implies the orderly and purposeful arrangement of the individual stones, each shaped and placed to fulfill its assigned task (cf. Paul's image of the members of the body in 1 Cor. 12:12-31).

The verb translated "are built up" (*oikodomeisthe*) may be interpreted as an indicative or an imperative; scholars are sharply divided. The evidence cited by Goodspeed shows that the English versions through the centuries have differed on the matter.[14] Modern English versions and interpreters likewise disagree. If the verb is an imperative, it may be either in the middle or passive voice. If middle, it may be translated "build yourselves up" (Goodspeed); if passive, "be built up" (Weymouth).[15] Of the two, the passive seems more consistent with the imagery; a house constructed of stones naturally implies

11. William F. Arndt and F. Wilbur Gingrich, *A Greek-English Lexicon of the New Testament and Other Early Christian Literature*, p. 242.

12. Francis Wright Beare, *The First Epistle of Peter*, p. 122.

13. C. E. B. Cranfield, *I & II Peter and Jude*, p. 63.

14. Edgar J. Goodspeed, *Problems of New Testament Translation*, pp. 194-95.

15. Other translations of the imperative middle are, "form yourselves into"—20th Cent.; "keep on building yourselves up"—Williams; "set yourselves close to him"—JB. The passive imperative is used in RSV, TEV, Moffatt, Montgomery, and Berkeley.

the thought of a builder. The NEB translates "Let yourselves be built, as living stones, into a spiritual temple." But as Kelly remarks, that rendering "is not easy to extract from the Greek."[16]

Goodspeed argues for the imperative "in view of the prevalent tone of the letter, which is steadily imperative."[17] Bigg supports that with the assertion that the verb is "the last link of the chain of imperatives extending from i. 13 onwards."[18] But Lenski well replies, "To point to the previous imperatives as proof for the use of another imperative overlooks the fact that the four preceding imperatives [1:13, 17, 22; 2:2] are aorists, which this fifth would not be. This cannot be accounted for by saying that now durative action is in place, whereas such action is not in place in the other imperatives. Quite the contrary."[19] We agree that the imperatives in 1:13—2:3 do not establish that the form here must also be imperative. The mode of the verb is best determined from the context in which it appears. The section in 1:13—2:3 was strongly hortatory, setting forth moral duties. But as Best observes, "The theme of 2:4-10 is not moral instruction but a description of the church."[20] The passage moves in the realm of historical facts. Selwyn notes that "in verse 4 we pass from exhortation to doctrine,"[21] and Elliott insists, "In contrast to 2:1f. the mood is indicative throughout. Analogous to 1:18-21, 1:23-25, 2:21-25, and 3:18-22, this section explicates and substantiates foregoing exhortation."[22] We accept the verb as indicative passive, and translate, "ye are being built up." The verb denotes a present continuing reality. The implied builder is, of course, God.

The edifice being reared is "a spiritual house" (*oikos pneumatikos*).[23] Collectively, Christians constitute the house. The word *house* (*oikos*) may denote either a building or a household; the context requires the former meaning. *Spiritual* indicates its immaterial character. That house is the church (4:17; 1 Tim. 3:15; Heb. 3:5-6; 10:21). But in the context of priesthood and sacrifices, the house obviously "is not domestic but religious and sacerdotal,"[24] a place devoted to the worship of God. Peter's designation serves to contrast that structure with Israel's "material temple, a type and a symbol of the spiritual house that Israel itself was to be, but failed to be."[25] The picture of the

---

16. J. N. D. Kelly, *A Commentary on the Epistles of Peter and of Jude*, p. 89.

17. Goodspeed, p. 194.

18. Bigg, p. 128.

19. R. C. H. Lenski, *The Interpretation of the Epistles of St. Peter, St. John and St. Jude*, pp. 84-85.

20. Best, p. 101.

21. Selwyn, p. 159.

22. John Hall Elliott, *The Elect and the Holy*, p. 16.

23. The nominative case indicates that *oikos* is not the direct object of the verb. It is apparently a "predicative amplification" of the subject *autoi*, "yourselves are being built up, a spiritual house" (A. T. Robertson, *A Grammar of the Greek New Testament in the Light of Historical Research*, p. 401).

24. Selwyn, p. 160.

25. Lenski, p. 90.

church as a spiritual house, capable of indefinite growth, is the nearest that 1 Peter comes to the Pauline image of the Body of Christ (Rom. 12:5; 1 Cor. 10:17; 12:12-27; Eph. 1:23; 2:16; etc.). The adjective "spiritual" (*pneumatikos*) —not the term so translated in 2:2—indicates that the stones of the building are characterized as belonging to the Spirit. They have been regenerated by the Spirit; they form a house where the Holy Spirit dwells (cf. 1 Cor. 3:16; Eph. 2:22). Mason concludes that the designation describes the edifice "not in its capacity of a place for *worship* so much as a place for Divine *inhabitation*."[26]

The addition, "to be a holy priesthood, to offer up spiritual sacrifices," develops and modifies the imagery. The habitation of God actively serves as a temple. *To be* (*eis*),[27] "unto, so as to be," indicates God's purpose with His people. The preceding picture of a spiritual house portrays the nature of the church; the phrase under discussion denotes its function. The translation "for a holy priesthood" (NASB)[28] is possible but should not be understood to mean that the house is built to be indwelt by the priests as separate and distinct from the house.[29] The Old Testament priests did not live in the temple, nor were they usually all there at one time. In Peter's picture those who constitute the house also function as priests; the house and the priesthood are not two separate and distinct entities. The spiritual reality strains the resources of language.

The noun *priesthood* (*hierateuma*) occurs in the New Testament only here and in verse 9 and only twice in the Septuagint (Ex. 19:6; 23:22),[30] Peter's source of the term. It occurs elsewhere only in writings dependent on those biblical occurrences. It may be understood either as an abstract noun, the office of the priesthood, or as a collective singular noun that denotes the body of persons who function as priests. The latter is the meaning in verse 9. That is also probably its meaning here, since it stands alongside the collective term "house."[31] The verses are basic to the precious doctrine of the priesthood of all believers. In the book of Revelation believers individually are called priests (1:6; 5:10; 20:6). Masterman remarks, "We become priests by joining the *hierateuma* [priesthood] of the Church."[32] Since all believers constitute a

26. Mason, p. 400. Italics in the original.
27. The preposition *eis* is omitted in the Textus Receptus but it has strong MSS support. For the evidence see Bruce M. Metzger, *A Textual Commentary on the Greek New Testament*, pp. 689-90.
28. So also Goodspeed, Rotherham, and Williams.
29. That is the implication inaccurately represented in the TEV's "let yourselves be used in building the spiritual temple where you will serve as holy priests."
30. The text of Deuteronomy 23:22 in the Seputagint is an expansion of the received Hebrew text; it reads "If ye will indeed hear my voice, and if thou wilt do all the things I shall charge thee with, and keep my covenant, ye shall be to me a peculiar people above all nations, for the whole earth is mine; and ye shall be to me a royal priesthood, and a holy nation: these words shall ye speak to the children of Israel, If ye shall indeed hear my voice, and do all the things I shall tell thee, I will be an enemy to thine enemies, and an adversary to thine adversaries."
31. Elliott, pp. 66-70; Ernest Best, "I Peter II 4-10—A Reconsideration," pp. 282-88; Gottlob Schrenk, *hierateuma*, *TDNT*, 3:249-51.
32. J. Howard B. Masterman, *The First Epistle of St. Peter*, p. 97.

124   First Peter

priesthood, there is no longer any place for a special office of priests to mediate
between individual believers and God; each believer has direct access to God
Himself.

Such a priesthood should be holy (*hagion*), consecrated, and set apart as
belonging and ministering to God. The term includes all that is meant by
Peter's demand for holiness in 1:14-17. Such holiness was not a permanent
attribute of all forms of priesthood or priestly service. Selwyn thinks that the
term was intended to mark a "contrast with the heathen priesthoods of Asia
Minor, which were at best idolatrous and therefore false, and at worst
immoral."[33]

Such a consecrated priesthood is qualified actively "to offer up spiritual
sacrifices, acceptable to God through Jesus Christ." *To offer up* (*anenengkai*),
an aorist infinitive, records the nature of the ministry being performed without
any reference to the repetition of the action involved. That compound verb
(*anapherō*), "to bring or carry up," was used in the Septuagint of Levitical
sacrifices (Lev. 17:5; Deut. 12:13-14; 1 Sam. 2:19) etc.); it recalls the priestly
act of carrying up the sacrificial animal and placing it upon the raised altar.
James used the term in describing Abraham's act of placing Isaac on the altar
on mount Moriah (2:21). Peter's verb portrays those offerings as true sacrifices, but his designation of them as "spiritual" (*pneumatikos*) distinguishes
them from the Levitical sacrifices and characterizes them as related to the
Spirit. They are offerings befitting a spiritual priesthood that is prompted by
the Spirit and that reflects His nature and essence. They are not sacrifices
offered to make expiation for sins nor to procure personal merit before God.
Such sacrifices have no place in the Christian church since the perfect sacrifice
of Christ on the cross has fulfilled the shadows and symbols of the Old
Testament sacrifices (Heb. 8:1—10:18). The sacrifices Peter mentions are
expressions of worship by the redeemed, offered in gratitude and self-
surrender. The spiritual sacrifices of the New Testament priest are: (1) the
living sacrifice of his body offered to God for service (Rom. 12:1-2), (2) his
praise (Heb. 13:15), (3) his voluntary acts of self-dedication (Phil. 2:17; Eph.
5:1-2), (4) his good deeds (Heb. 13:16), and (5) his material possessions used for
God's service and transmuted by the Spirit into worthy sacrifices (Phil. 4:18;
Heb. 13:16).

"Acceptable to God" (*euprosdektous*) reveals the true criterion for the
evaluation of any sacrifice. That compound adjective literally means "to receive
to one's self with pleasure." Such is God's assured response to all sacrifices that
are truly spiritual.

"Through Jesus Christ" contains "the keynote of every Christian sacrifice."[34]
Through (*dia* with the genitive) denotes agency; all acceptable sacrifices are
related to Him as mediator. His mediation may be understood in two ways,

33. Selwyn, p. 160.
34. Masterman, p. 98.

depending upon the way the phrase is understood. It may be related to the infinitive "to offer" or to the adjective "acceptable." The translation of Williams represents the former understanding—"to offer up, through Jesus Christ, spiritual sacrifices that will be acceptable to God."[35] That means that we offer our sacrifices through Jesus Christ; it is in keeping with the New Testament teaching that man can only approach God through Christ (John 14:6; Acts 4:12; 1 Pet. 3:18; 1 John 2:23). According to the second interpretation, the sacrifices "are acceptable because offered through Him, deriving all their worth from Him who presents them to God, and with whose one sacrifice they are bound up."[36] Hebrews 13:15, "Through him then let us offer up a sacrifice of praise to God continually," supports the former understanding. But the natural order of the sentence, followed by most of our versions, favors the latter. Both views express biblical truths. We may agree with Caffin, "The Greek words admit of either connection and perhaps are intended to cover both relations."[37]

c. *The human responses to Christ the Cornerstone* (vv. 6-8). The mention of Jesus Christ centers attention on Him as the touchstone of human destiny. As the opening formula indicates, what Peter already said about that stone in verses 4-5 is not something new. The Old Testament passages concerning the wonderful stone have been prominent in Peter's thinking in the preceding passage.

"Because it is contained in scripture" (*hoti periechei in graphē*) is an uncommon construction. *Because* (*dioti*), as in 1:16 and 24, introduces a relevant quotation from the Old Testament.[38] The verb is a compound form (*peri*, "round about," and *echō*, "to hold") that means "to contain or encompass." In Luke 5:9 that verb is personal, "he was amazed," literally, "astonishment encompassed him." But here, as in Acts 23:25, the verb is impersonal, "it is contained." The papyri support that impersonal usage.[39] *Scripture* is without a definite article[40] and might be translated "in a writing," but the context makes it obvious that Peter was thinking of the inspired Old Testament (cf. 2 Tim. 3:16; 2 Pet. 1:20). As a technical term it may be translated "the Scripture," but Peter was content simply to refer to an authoritative written account.

The quotations in verses 6-8 are drawn from Isaiah 28:16; Psalm 118:22; and Isaiah 8:14. They center on the concept of Christ as the Stone. Paul, in Romans 9:33, quoted from the first and last of those and fused them. The fact that both

---

35. Charles B. Williams, *The New Testament: A Private Translation in the Language of the People.*

36. Bigg, p. 129.

37. B. C. Caffin, *The First Epistle General of Peter*, p. 70.

38. The Textus Receptus reads *dio kai*, "wherefore also," but *kai* has little MSS support.

39. James Hope Moulton and George Milligan, *The Vocabulary of the Greek Testament*, p. 505. See also Josephus, *Ant.*, XI.7.

40. The Textus Receptus does have the article, but modern editors agree in the omission.

Peter and Paul drew those Old Testament passages together does not prove
that the author of 1 Peter borrowed from Paul or Paul from Peter. Scholars
agree that both drew from a previously formed tradition. Peter quoted Isaiah
28:16 to establish that God acted directly to place the cornerstone (v. 6a); he
then sketched the diverse human responses to that stone (vv. 6b-8).

> (1) *The divine laying of the stone* (v. 6a). "Behold, I lay in Zion a chief
> cornerstone, elect, precious" refers to the voice of God announcing His
> action. *Behold (idou)* calls attention to the importance of the divine
> announcement through Isaiah, an announcement whose amazement
> Peter shared. The quotation follows the Septuagint with a few minor
> variations.[41] God placed His chosen messianic stone "in Zion," appar-
> ently a synonym for the city of Jerusalem (cf. Isa. 40:9; Mic. 3:12).[42]
> Perhaps Peter retained the reference to remind his readers of the
> place where the messianic kingdom originated. But he omitted all
> reference to the laying of a foundation in the original and retained
> three adjectives that indicate the uniqueness of the stone.

First, the stone is characterized as "elect," a quality previously attributed to
it in verse 4. Peter emphasized the fact that it is no ordinary stone but the
specific object of God's approval and selection.

The second adjective, "a chief corner" stone (*akrogōniaion*), which occurs in
the New Testament only here and in Ephesians 2:20, denotes a stone "lying at
the extreme corner." In verse 4 Peter centered his attention on the fact of
Christ being "a living stone," but now the quotation calls attention to the
position of that stone in the building. It is the "cornerstone" that controls the
lines of the building. It is visible, not a buried foundation stone. Some suggest
the picture is that of a stone, located at the top, that holds two walls together;
some extend that idea to mean that Christ holds the Jewish and Gentile walls of
the church together.[43] Though that thought might fit the picture in Ephesians,
it is not suggested by the present context. Others believe that the stone is the
final or locking stone that completes the arch over the gate.[44] Generally, the
stone has been understood as the large stone placed upon the foundation at one
of the corners.[45] That seems to be the meaning in Isaiah 28:16, the one place in
the Septuagint where the rare word occurs. The term does not emphasize the
elevated position of the stone but the fact that it forms the extreme outer
projection of the wall. That seems to be the most probable view. Each of the
positions portrays the importance of the stone for the building.

41. Peter omits all reference to the foundation, substitutes *tithēmi*, "place, put," for *emballō*,
    "throw in, set," and includes *ep' autō*, "on him," which is found in some manuscripts of the
    Septuagint.
42. J. B. Payne, "Zion," *ZPEB*, 5:1063-66.
43. J. H. A. Hart, *The First Epistle General of Peter*, p. 56.
44. Joachim Jeremias, *akrogōniaios*, *TDNT*, 1:792.
45. R. J. McKelvey, "Christ the Cornerstone," pp. 352-59.

Peter's third adjective *"entimon,"* "precious," "valuable, costly," indicates the intrinsic worth of the stone (cf. v. 4). By its very nature it is of inestimable value; that is God's evaluation. Peter, like Paul, understood the stone in Isaiah 28:16 to be a direct reference to the Messiah. Snodgrass points out that the verse had already received a messianic interpretation in pre-Christian Judaism, and that it was due to that fact "that the verse had such attraction for the Church and could be used so effectively."[46]

    (2) The human reactions to the Stone (vv. 6b-8). Men cannot escape the unique stone and its determining impact. Reactions to the stone divide mankind into two classes, the believing (vv. 6b-7a) and the unbelieving (vv. 7b-8).

      (a) The experience of believers (vv. 6b-7a). In Isaiah 28:16 God Himself assures His people of the beneficial impact the stone will have for them, "And he that believeth on him shall not be put to shame" (v. 6b). The opening "and" indicates a natural sequence between the nature of the stone and its impact on humanity. "He that believeth" (*ho pisteuōn*), "the one believing," indicates that continuing faith is the one basic characteristic of the group. Faith alone makes one a member of the class of believers, but it must be a faith "on him" (*ep' autō*), a faith that confidently rests upon the stone (cf. 1:8). In the words of Calvin, "No one can rightly believe except he who has set Christ before him as the One he ought wholly to trust."[47]

The man of faith has the firm assurance that he "shall not be put to shame" (*ou mē*[48] *kataischunthē*), will never be disappointed because the stone failed him, resulting in personal shame and disgrace. Peter used the Septuagint translation of the Hebrew that reads "shall not be in haste," that is, flee in confusion and terror from the danger hanging over him. The Septuagint translation is a valid interpretation of the Hebrew; the one who rests his faith on the stone shall never hasten away in shame and confusion because his misplaced faith has ended in bitter disappointment. The negative is really an understatement; in the hour of crisis the believer will stand firm and unshaken upon the stone.

"Therefore" (v. 7a) applies the prophetic assurance directly to Peter's readers—"For you therefore that believe is the preciousness." *For you* (*humin*), standing emphatically at the beginning, makes the assurance personal. *That believe* (*tois pisteuousin*), "the ones believing," an appositional designation standing emphatically at the end, provides the basis for the

---

46. K. R. Snodgrass, "I Peter II. 1-10: Its Formation and Literary Affinities," p. 106.

47. John Calvin, *The Epistle of Paul the Apostle to the Hebrews and the First and Second Epistles of St. Peter*, p. 261.

48. The double negative strengthens the negation, "shall in no wise." *"Ou mē* is the most decisive way of negating something in the future" (Arndt and Gingrich, p. 519).

application. The prophetic assurance is for them because they belong to the class that God indicated. Rotherham's translation conveys Peter's emphasis; "Unto you, then, is the honour—[unto you] who believe." Peter developed the idea of the contrasted group in vv. 7b-8.

The noun translated "the preciousness" (hē timē), more literally, "the honor," is difficult to interpret. It may either mean "price, value of," or "honor, reverence, respect." The latter seems to be the meaning here. The translation "he is precious" (KJV) or "is the preciousness" (ASV) suggests the emotional response of believers to the stone. But Bigg insisted that the noun is never used "of that value in affection which we call 'preciousness.'"[49] The reference seems to relate to some objective value or honor. But to whom does the value or honor relate? The NIV translates, "In your sight this stone is precious." That implies that the readers ascribe the honor or preciousness to Christ. But Peter's "therefore" indicates that the value or honor is something that the readers themselves possess. The honor seems to be antithetical to the shame mentioned in verse 6. United with Christ, who is Himself chosen and honored with God, they share the honor of the privileged status already described in verses 4-6.[50] The reference is to their present status, further delineated in verse 9, not to their eschatological future. There may, however, be the further implication that just as Christ triumphed over rejection they, too, will yet triumph over their Christ-rejecting opponents when their salvation is consummated at His return.

> (b) The frustration of unbelievers (vv. 7b-8). "But" (de) marks the transition to another group. "For such as disbelieve" (apistousin), God's wonderful stone produces a very different result. That group is designated by a present active participle without an article; the absence of the article leaves those in view quite indeterminate. The only common quality that characterizes them is absence of faith in the messianic stone. Disbelieve does not suggest ignorance of the gospel message but a refusal to believe that message. The term includes all the varied opponents that the readers confronted.

The Textus Receptus reads "be disobedient" (apeithousi), but it is commonly accepted that disbelieve (apistousin) is the original reading. That reading preserves the contrast with the preceding "you that believe." The term "disobedient" seems to have been imported from verse 8.

As one thoroughly familiar with the Septuagint, Peter continued by weaving his quotation into his own sentence, "but for such as disbelieve, 'The stone which the builders rejected, The same was made the head of the corner;' and, 'A stone of stumbling, and a rock of offence'" (vv. 7b-8a). The first part of the

---

49. Bigg, p. 131.
50. John T. Demarest, A Translation and Exposition of the First Epistle of the Apostle Peter, pp. 105-6.

quotation is from Psalm 118:22 and reproduces the Septuagint; the two phrases in verse 8 are drawn from Isaiah 8:14.

In verse 4 Peter clearly had the quotation from Psalm 118:22 in mind, but in verses 7b-8a he quoted it to bring out the application to unbelievers. Those who deliberately tested and rejected God's wonderful stone were "the builders" (*hoi oikodomountes*), the professional builders who regarded themselves as skillful and qualified workers in erecting what they regarded as God's house. During Passion Week Jesus quoted that verse and directly applied it to the hostile scribes and Pharisees (Matt. 21:42; Mark 12:10; Luke 20:7). Peter quoted it to the persecuting Jewish Sanhedrin (Acts 4:11). John Calvin pointedly applied the picture to his own religious opponents and remarked, "Those in office are not always God's true and faithful ministers."[51]

God nullified the rejection of those unbelieving builders—"The same was made the head of the corner." *The same* (*houtos*), "this one," the very stone that the builders rejected, emphasizes that rejection did not dispose of the stone. God's action reversed their action; it "was made the head of the corner" (*egenēthē eis kephalēn gōnias*), "came into a position as corner-head." The reference is not to the shape but to the position assigned to the stone. As noted earlier, there are different views regarding its placement. Some picture it as placed at the bottom corner of the wall; others think of the stone as placed at the top. The latter view is represented in the NIV, "has become the capstone," and in the margin of the NEB, "the apex of the building." The latter position seems more probable if the verse in Psalm 118 reflects a tradition that was current in connection with the building of the temple. According to tradition, during the erection of the temple an unusually shaped stone was sent up from the quarry and rejected by the builders as useless; only later did they discover that it was the very stone they needed to complete the building.

With a simple "and" (v. 8) Peter continued his picture of the destructive effect of God's stone on unbelievers. It introduces two phrases from Isaiah 8:14, "A stone of stumbling, and a rock of offence." The two phrases continue the stone theme drawn from the Old Testament, but now the term "stone" is elucidated by the use of the term "rock" (*petra*), "a rocky mass or cliff."

To the unbeliever, Christ is "a stone of stumbling" (*lithos proskommatos*), "a stone that causes stumbling." The stone has been prepared for a specific place in the building. But since it is not being utilized, the passerby, unmindful of it, collides with it and injures himself. The second phrase, "a rock of offence" (*petra skandalou*), presents a parallel but somewhat different picture. The term "rock" does not denote a building stone but rather portrays a large embedded bolder, a great rock cliff; it is a large rock that human opposition cannot dispose of. The genitive "of offence" points to the calamitous impact of that rock on unbelievers. In classical Greek the term *skandalon* denoted the trigger stick that released a deadly trap. In New Testament usage the term is figurative and denotes enticement to sin and apostasy; it is used to denote that which causes one's fall morally, involving men in sin and its disastrous

51. Calvin, p. 263.

consequences (our English word *scandal* is derived from that Greek term by way of Latin). Those two designations declare that by rejecting God's stone, men only bring about their own injury and ruin. Men cannot evade Him by their unbelief. He meets them in unexpected and unavoidable ways.

Interpreters have noted that the various references to Christ as "the stone" do not convey a uniform image; a single image cannot convey the full reality of that unique stone. As Beare remarks,

> There is a superficial difficulty in the double thought of the Stone as at one and the same time fixed in place in the building for those that accept it, and yet lying in the path to hamper and foil the efforts of those that reject it; but the double image is necessary and true. Christ is too great to be neglected or avoided. For His followers, he becomes the foundation on which all life rests; where He is rejected, there is and can be only chaos and anarchy.[52]

Peter continued his picture concerning unbelievers with the comment "for they stumble at the word, being disobedient." *For they* (*hoi*) is the Greek relative pronoun "who" that continues the description of "such as disbelieve" in verse 7*b*. The verb "stumble" points out the repeated effect the stone of stumbling has on their lives. The remainder of the statement may be interpreted in two different ways, depending on one's interpretation of "the word" (*tō logō*), the saving message concerning Jesus Christ, the living stone. If *the word* is grammatically related to *stumble* and a comma placed after *the word* (cf. ASV), then the Word is the object against which they stumble. It is the Word through which the living stone is presented to them. That view implies a close connection between Christ and *the word*, which is not identified with His person but "with His doctrine, the truth of which He is the manifestation."[53] The added participle, "being disobedient" reveals their character and elucidates their unbelief. The verb "to disobey (*apeitheō*) is a negative compound that means "not to allow one's self to be persuaded."[54] They stumble over the Word in their refusal to accept its message.

Others prefer to relate *the word* to the following participle, placing a comma after *stumble*, "who stumble, to the word being disobedient" (Gr. word order). Then the phrase means that unbelievers stumble precisely because of their willful disobedience to the Word. Alford pointed to 3:1 and 4:17 in support of that interpretation and held that it gives proper prominence to the Word that is the means of Christian growth but is being willfully rejected by unbelievers.[55] Fronmüller argued that that understanding is preferable since the context already implies that Christ is the object of their stumbling.[56] That interpreta-

---

52. Beare, p. 125.

53. F. C. Cook, *The First Epistle General of Peter*, p. 190.

54. Hermann Cremer, *Biblico-Theological Lexicon of New Testament Greek*, p. 475; Joseph Henry Thayer, *A Greek-English Lexicon of the New Testament*, p. 55.

55. Henry Alford, *The Greek New Testament*, vol. 4 (part 1) p. 348.

56. G. P. C. Fronmüller, *The Epistles General of Peter*, p. 34.

tion is represented in the NASB, "They stumble because they are disobedient to the Word."[57] It is the preferable interpretation.

"Whereunto also they were appointed" is a startling conclusion, yet Peter clearly intended the comment to reassure his persecuted readers that what was happening was not outside of God's purpose. *Also* (*kai*), an intensive particle, indicates that the appointment follows from their unbelief and disobedience. The verb "appointed" (*etethēsan*) literally means "to place, put, set," and commonly meant to appoint or destine someone to or for something. *Whereunto* (*eis ho*), "unto which thing," indicates the purpose of the divine appointment. But interpreters differ regarding what they were appointed to. Some believe the phrase refers to their disobedience or unbelief. Calvin asserted, "They had been appointed to unbelief."[58] Demarest said, "God had determined not to give them faith in the Messiah."[59] But surely Peter "does not mean that those who rejected Christ were *destined* to do so apart from any choice to do otherwise."[60] Such a view seems inconsistent with the purpose of the passage or Peter's explicit statement in 2 Peter 3:9 that God does not desire that any should perish but that all should come to repentance (cf. Ezek. 18:32; 33:11; 1 Tim. 2:4). "There has always been room for human choice and responsibility in the dealings of God with man."[61]

The clause seems to mean that those who willfully reject the message of God concerning Christ are destined to stumble as the just and inevitable consequence of their deliberate rejection. As Bigg pointed out, "the antecedent to *eis ho* ['whereunto'] is the main verb *proskoptousi* ['they stumble']: this follows as a necessary consequence from the subordination of the participle" ['being disobedient'].[62] Huther insisted that that view of the antecedent "alone is in harmony with the connection of thought, for it is simply the 'believing' and 'disobedient,' together with the blessing and curse which they respectively obtain, that are here contrasted, without any reference being made to the precise ground of faith and unbelief."[63] God has established Christ, the Living Stone, as His divinely appointed way for human salvation; He has also ordained that men cannot reject His provision with impunity.

2) THE CORPORATE NATURE AND FUNCTION OF BELIEVERS (vv. 9-10)

"But ye" refocuses attention on believers in contrast to the unbelieving. *Ye* (*humeis*) is emphatic and happily marks the contrast between the readers and

---

57. Similarly in NIV, RSV, NEB, Weymouth, Moffatt, Montgomery. Rotherham translates, "Who stumble because unto the word they did not yield."

58. Calvin, p. 264.

59. Demarest, p. 109.

60. Ray Summers, *I Peter*, 12:156 (italics by Summers).

61. A. F. Mitchell, *Hebrews and the General Epistles*, p. 248.

62. Bigg, p. 133.

63. Joh. Ed. Huther, *Critical and Exegetical Handbook to the General Epistles of Peter and Jude*, p. 117.

the unbelieving world around them. It was a contrast both encouraging and humbling for them. But Peter was not thinking of his readers as individuals, nor yet as a number of isolated local congregations in Asia Minor, but as members of the Body of Christ. Though the word *church* does not appear in Peter's epistles, his description of the church comes to its climax in these two verses. Peter's repetition indicates how he rejoiced in the blessings and privileges he set before his readers. He used a series of designations that depicted their corporate identity (v. 9a), stated their divinely intended function (v. 9b), and concluded with a reminder of their changed position (v. 10). Almost every item is drawn from Old Testament language and thought.

a. *Their corporate identity* (v. 9a). "Ye are an elect race, a royal priesthood, a holy nation, a people for *God's* own possession." Each of those titles is a collective singular, declaring what the church already is. The description is not a portrayal of the eschatological future of the church. All of the designations are without a definite article; attention is focused on character rather than identity.

"An elect race" (*genos eklekton*) is drawn from Isaiah 43:20, where the designation refers to the people of Israel. The word *race* (*genos*) denotes the descendants of a common ancestor and thus designates a people with a common heritage, sharing the unity of a common life. The term pictures Christians as a people united by their common heritage through the new birth (1:23). Because of its spiritual birth, the new race transcends all natural distinctions of ancestry, languages, or cultures. But the word *elect*, the fourth and final occurrence of that adjective in the epistle (1:1; 2:4, 6), reminds us that it is the divine initiative that has made Christians a distinct people who no longer belong to the world. It "removes all boasting and yet establishes a dignity of heredity that enables a chosen one to point to God as the father of his race."[64] The oneness of believers in Christ is a reality to be treasured, especially in times of persecution.

The thought of election is precious to Peter. In 1:1 the term was applied to believers as individuals, in 2:4 and 6 to Christ as the living Stone, and here to the church as a whole. Kelly observes that the use of the term "accentuates the parallelism between Christ and His followers."[65]

"A royal priesthood" (*basileion hierateuma*) is drawn from the Septuagint of Exodus 19:6. The first of those two words can be understood either as a noun or an adjective. Both usages occur in the Septuagint, and either is a possible interpretation of the term here.

Some modern interpreters advocate understanding Peter's use of *basileion* as a noun.[66] If that is correct, then the two words of that designation are in apposition to one another; and there are five, rather than four, titles applied to the church. As a noun, especially in the plural, the term means "royal

64. Adams, p. 70.
65. Kelly, p. 96.
66. Best, pp. 107-8; Elliott, pp. 70-73; Kelly, pp. 96-98.

residence" (Luke 7:25). Thus Kelly translates, "You, however, are a chosen race, a royal house, a priesthood, a holy nation, a people for God's possession."[67] So understood, the designation repeats the thought of *house* in verse 5. Attractive arguments are advanced in favor of that view,[68] but that interpretation is faced with the awkwardness of having two nouns placed side by side without any modifiers; all the other terms are qualified by an adjective or a phrase equivalent to an adjective. Furthermore, the translation "a royal house" does not fit the series since all the other terms denote groups of people. We prefer the usual adjectival translation, "a royal priesthood."

The adjective *royal* has been understood in two different senses. Christians may be called royal in the sense that they are "a body of priests attached to the court of the Divine king."[69] They are priests who conduct the worship offered to God as King. That interpretation does not involve their royal status. Or the designation may indicate that as priests they also have royal prerogatives; they are priests with a royal heritage, like the Maccabees.[70] Under the Mosaic law the offices of king and priest were properly regarded as mutually exclusive. When King Uzziah sought to intrude upon the priestly office, he was severely punished (2 Chron. 26:16-21). The author of Hebrews insisted that under the Mosaic law Jesus, because of His royal descent, could not be a priest at all (Heb. 7:13-16). But the prophet Zechariah portrayed the coming Messiah as "a priest upon his throne" (6:13), and the book of Hebrews declares the fulfillment of that prophecy in the person of Jesus Christ who, in establishing a new order of priesthood "after the order of Melchizedek," gloriously embodies in Himself the two offices (Heb. 7:1-28). In view of the intimate relations between Christ and believers depicted in verses 4-5, it seems probable that by that title Peter intended to portray believers as kings and priests. That would be consistent with the celebration in Revelation 5:10 that believers have been made "*to be* unto our God a kingdom and priests; and they reign upon the earth" (cf. Rev. 1:6). We agree with Stibbs "that Christians are here described as sharing with Christ in kingship or sovereignty as well as in priesthood. They are therefore a true hierarchy, called to reign as well as to serve."[71]

In verse 5 Peter described that priesthood as "holy," and here he declared it is also "royal." The adjectives indicate two complementary aspects of the priesthood. MacDonald comments, "As holy priests, they enter the sanctuary of heaven by faith to worship. As royal priests, they go out into the world to witness."[72] Some understand the royal aspect as presently operative in that "as kings, we are to take God to men, revealing the righteousness of Christ in holy living, which honors the 'King of kings.'"[73] But others, in view of passages like

---

67. Kelly, p. 82.
68. For those arguments see the references in footnote 66.
69. Masterman, p. 101.
70. W. H. Bennett, *The General Epistles, James, Peter, John, and Jude*, p. 213.
71. Alan M. Stibbs, *The First Epistle General of Peter*, p. 104.
72. William MacDonald, *I Peter: Faith Tested, Future Triumphant*, pp. 44-45.
73. J. Allen Blair, *Living Peacefully. A Devotional Study of the First Epistle of Peter*, p. 109.

2 Timothy 2:12 and Revelation 20:6, argue that the royal aspect of the priesthood will have its true fulfillment at the time of the future reign of Christ as king over the earth.[74] Peter did not further develop the idea of the royal aspect of the priesthood of believers.

Peter's third designation, "a holy nation" (*ethnos hagion*), is also drawn directly from Exodus 19:6. *Nation* (*ethnos*) means a community of people held together by the same laws, customs, and mutual interests. The term, as Morgan notes, involves "two ideas, those of *government* and mutual *interrelationship.*"[75] It is a common biblical term, especially in the plural, "for the Gentiles as distinct from the Jews or Christians."[76] The term was also used at times of Israel as the people of God united by their covenantal relation to Him, making them distinctly His nation. It is in that latter sense that Peter applied the term to the church, which forms a unique international nation having a common spiritual life from God and committed to His rule. *Holy* indicates its separation from the nations of the world and consecration to God and His service. Its position of separation demands that the members must not, like Israel of old, stoop to the sinful practices of the world (1:15-17).

The fourth designation, "a people for *God's* own possession," likewise has an Old Testament background (cf. Ex. 19:5; Deut. 7:6; 14:2; 26:18; Isa. 43:21; Mal. 3:17). *People* (*laos*), another collective singular noun, again indicates the unity of believers as God's private possession, belonging exclusively to Him. The translators of the Septuagint seized upon the term as "ideally suited for expressing the special relationship of Israel to Yahweh."[77] They were a distinctive people whom God had formed for Himself (Isa. 43:21). So the church, composed of people who have been bought with a price (1 Cor. 6:20; 7:23), constitutes a "special people, the very meaning of whose existence lies in its being possessed by God."[78] God has acted to make them His "own possession" (*peripoiēsin*), something acquired and treasured as one's own, a private possession. That is the meaning of the KJV translation, "a peculiar people."[79] Today, that translation is open to misinterpretation; because of the changed usage of the word peculiar, that translation might appear to mean "different from the usual, singular, odd."

b. *Their God-centered function* (v. 9b). Peter followed his fourfold picture of the church with a purpose clause—"that ye may show forth the excellencies of him who called you out of darkness into his marvellous light." That clause, which Lenski suggests may be read with "an undertone of admonition,"[80] is to be attached to all four preceding designations. The statement of God's purpose

74. J. Nieboer, *Practical Exposition of I Peter*, pp. 132-33.
75. G. Campbell Morgan, *Peter and the Church*, p. 72. Italics in Morgan.
76. Karl Ludwig Schmidt, "*ethnos* in the NT," *TDNT*, 2:370.
77. H. Bietenhard, "*laos*, people," *NIDNTT* 2:796.
78. C. E. B. Cranfield, *I & II Peter and Jude*, p. 66.
79. *The Oxford English Dictionary*, 12:602-3.
80. Lenski, p. 104.

for the church reflects His stated purpose for Israel in Isaiah 43:21, "the people which I formed for myself, that they might set forth my praise." The lofty titles bestowed upon believers in Christ, Peter at once reminds us, are not merely for their personal gratification, or their corporate glory; the service of God is involved. God's purpose in saving us is to reveal Himself to others through us.

The verb "show forth" (*exanggeilēte*), a compound form that only occurs here in the New Testament, means "to tell out, to make widely known." The compound conveys the picture of a message being proclaimed to those outside concerning what has taken place within. It indicates the evangelistic function of the church. The message will be embodied in the transformed life of the witnesses (cf. 3:1-4), but more than the silent witness of conduct and character is implied by the term. Both word and conduct are involved. *Ye* implies that the witness is to be given by the entire membership of the churches addressed. The aorist tense indicates that as the unifying purpose of God for His church; privilege involves responsibility.

The corporate assignment is to proclaim "the excellencies of him who called you." Their message is not to center on their own experience but on "the excellencies" (*tas eretas*) of the God who has saved them. That Greek term, which occurs only four times in the New Testament,[81] by New Testament times had developed several meanings.[82] It is variously understood here. Its basic meaning is that of "eminence," understood either as the result of inherent nature or personal achievement. Its usual meaning is that of "virtue," and Goodspeed translates, "so that you may declare the virtues of him." As applied to God, the term is not the opposite of "vices" but points to those attributes of His nature that manifest His preeminent qualities, His "excellencies"[83] or "perfections."[84] As applied to the proclamation of those divine virtues among men, the term may mean His "praises," the extolling of His glorious attributes and deeds.[85] Polkinghorne supports that translation with the observation that it represents the Hebrew text of Isaiah 43:21 and "accords best with the governing verb 'declare,' which certainly means a verbal declaration."[86] In contemporary pagan usage the term denoted the manifestations of power of a god through his miracles.[87] That meaning is reflected in the RSV, "the wonderful deeds of him who called you," or "the triumphs of him who has called you" in the NEB. That view has the support of several recent commentators.[88] But since Peter identified God by reference to His action, "who called you,"

---

81. Phil. 4:8; 1 Pet. 2:9; 2 Pet. 1:3, 5.

82. Otto Bauernfeind, *aretē*, *TDNT*, 1:357-61; H. G. Link, A. Ringwald, *"aretē*, virtue," *NIDNTT*, 3:925-28; James Hope Moulton and George Milligan, *The Vocabulary of the Greek Testament Illustrated from the Papyri and Other Non-Literary Sources*, pp. 75-76.

83. NASB, Rotherham, Darby, Robert Young, Kleist and Lilly.

84. So Berkeley, Weymouth, Williams.

85. So KJV, NIV, JB.

86. G. J. Polkinghorne, *The First Letter of Peter*, p. 590.

87. Moulton and Milligan, pp. 75-76.

88. Beare, pp. 118, 132; Best, p. 109; Kelly, pp. 99-100.

that translation involves a measure of tautology and leaves out any specific reference to God's character. We prefer the translation "excellencies," for it involves God's preeminence both in what He is and does. The God whom Christians make known to men is not merely another of the "many gods" (1 Cor. 8:5) who were competing for adherents in the first century world; He is unique in His nature as well as His self-manifesting deeds.

Peter identified God by His saving initiative in the lives of the readers, "him who called you out of darkness into his marvellous light." *Who called* (*tou . . . kalesantos*) looks back to the time of their conversion and designates God's call as effective. It was the act of the Father, "the God of all grace" (5:10), to whom elsewhere in the New Testament that saving call is usually ascribed (1 Cor. 1:9; Gal. 1:15; 2 Thess. 2:14).

God's call wrought a crucial change in the lives of the readers, bringing them "out of darkness into his marvellous light." That metaphorical usage of *darkness* and *light* appears in both the Old and New Testaments and was familiar to the religious language of the pagan world. *Darkness* aptly symbolizes the state of sin and spiritual ignorance and the consequent wretchedness of the unsaved (Matt. 6:23*b*; 22:13; 25:30; John 3:19; 2 Cor. 6:14; 1 John 1:5-6). Williams observes that "nothing in the material universe more expressively symbolizes the state of the unrenewed mind."[89] Such darkness is not merely the environment in which the unbeliever finds himself; due to sin, it is also the inner state of his own soul. *Out of darkness* (*ek skotous*) notes that God's saving act constitutes a removal from that condition of darkness (Col. 1:13). Peter's original word order, "who out of darkness hath called you into his marvellous light" (Rotherham), stresses the readers' original condition.

God's saving act transferred them "into his marvellous light." *Light* is not merely a reference to the blessedness and joy of salvation; as "his" (*autou*) indicates, it is the light in which He dwells, the sphere of purity and holiness. *Into* (*eis*) indicates that Christians have been brought into and made partakers of that light (2 Pet. 1:3-4). It has transformed them into "sons of light" (1 Thess. 5:5). God's "light," expressive of His very nature (1 John 1:5), is "marvellous" (*thaumaston*), creating wonder and amazement because of its transcendent and inconceivable nature. It is marvelous as to its origin, nature, and effect.

c. Their changed condition (v. 10). Having just indicated what *God* has done in the lives of his readers, Peter, with a relative pronoun "who" (*hoi*), which relates back to the "ye" of verse 9, concluded the paragraph with a direct remark to his readers. The change wrought involves their external status as well as their inner personal experience.

Verse 10 is not a direct quotation from the Old Testament. Peter clothed his thoughts in terms drawn from Hosea chapters 1-2. Hosea 2:23 seems to have been specifically in his mind. The prophet's words described God's rejection of apostate Israel and the prophetic assurance of Israel's future restoration to His

89. Nathaniel Marshman Williams, *Commentary on the Epistles of Peter*, p. 29.

favor. Peter's use of that prophetic picture does not establish that his readers were Jewish Christians.[90] In Romans 9:25-26 Paul applied Hosea's picture to Gentile as well as to Jewish believers. Israel's apostasy had made them spiritually equal to Gentiles in God's eyes; their promised restoration through grace establishes the depth of God's forgiveness that is now equally offered to believing Gentiles. That unlimited grace is now operative in Christ Jesus.

"Who in time past were no people, but now are the people of God" stresses the contrast between the readers' past and present status. *In time past (pote)* summarizes their pre-Christian lives (cf. 2:25). At that time they could only be characterized as "no people" *(ou laos)*, having no distinct existence as a community of people who were of any usefulness in God's program. They were a "heterogeneous mass of Gentiles, aliens from God and separated from each other by race, language, customs, and religion."[91] Peter, like Paul (1 Cor. 6:11; Eph. 2:11-12; Col. 3:7), believed that it was good for believers occasionally to remember what they once were; it should deepen their gratitude for what they now are, "the people of God" *(laos theou)*, "God's people." They have been "lifted so high as to have become not merely a people, but the people of God—belonging to Him and acknowledged by Him."[92]

The second contrast, "who had not obtained mercy, but now have obtained mercy," emphasizes inner experience. Formerly the readers "had not obtained mercy" *(ouk eleēmenoi)*. The perfect tense portrays their entire preconversion life as characterized by no conscious experience of God's forgiving compassion. *But now* emphasizes the change that had taken place. The aorist passive "have obtained mercy" *(eleēthentes)*, "have received mercy," does not imply an active search for God's mercy but that at a definite time God acted to bestow His mercy on them, thereby terminating their former state.

In glancing back over the last two verses, one cannot escape the impression that Peter clearly intended to establish a parallel between Israel and the church. That parallel is discernible in each of the three areas just considered. The four designations of the corporate identity of the church (v. 9*a*) were all drawn from designations applied to Israel in the Old Testament. That which Israel effectively failed to realize under the law and through law-keeping has now through grace been realized in the church composed of those who by faith have become united to Israel's promised Messiah, Jesus Christ. The assignment given to the nation of Israel to be God's witness concerning Him to the nations was frustrated by their unfaithfulness and sin. The church, now God's chosen people, has the same assignment to be God's witness to the world (v. 9*b*). In Romans 11 Paul points out that Israel's history of failure is a clear warning to the church (11:17-24). A faithless Christendom will likewise fall under God's judgment. The prophetic message of Hosea, declaring God's forgiving grace to Israel, offers an encouraging parallel to all men today; God

---

90. Mason, p. 404; William Kelly, *The Epistles of Peter*, pp.143-44; Tom Westwood, *The Epistles of Peter*, pp. 61-62.

91. Cook, p. 191.

92. John Lillie, *Lectures on the First and Second Epistles of Peter*, p. 124.

will forgive and regard with His favor all who by faith appropriate His unique
provision of salvation in Jesus Christ (v. 10). It does not naturally follow from
the parallel between Israel and the church that Peter believed that the church
has permanently replaced Israel and that the latter will not again enjoy a
separate existence under the favor of God. Israel's future is inseparably
connected with its acceptance by faith of the returning Messiah (Zech.
12:10—14:11; Acts 3:19-26; Rom. 11:25-27).

Second Cycle:

EXHORTATIONS IN VIEW OF OUR POSITION IN THE WORLD
(2:11—3:12)

Peter's second cycle of practical appeals flows naturally out of the preceding paragraph (2:4-10) that sets forth the sharp contrast between believers and unbelievers. Confronted with the hostility of a godless and unbelieving world, the readers were urged to glorify God through becoming Christian conduct. The underlying theme in this cycle of exhortations is the need for a spirit of submissiveness on the part of believers in daily life. Peter began with a general exhortation to appropriate individual conduct (2:11-12), stressed the duty of submission to the state (2:13-17), elaborated on the duty of submission in household relations (2:18-25), dealt more specifically with Christian duties in marital relations (3:1-7), and concluded with an appeal to becoming corporate conduct (3:8-12).

10

A. The Appeal for Appropriate Personal Conduct
(2:11-12)

(11) Beloved, I beseech you as sojourners and pilgrims, to abstain from fleshly lusts, which war against the soul; (12) having your behavior seemly among the Gentiles; that, wherein they speak against you as evil-doers, they may by your good works, which they behold, glorify God in the day of visitation.

That brief exhortation is "at once resumptive and prefatory,"[1] forming a beautiful transition to the second cycle of practical exhortations. In essence, verse 11 summarizes the first cycle (1:13—2:10) and verse 12 the second. Peter indicated his attitude in making the appeal (v. 11a), stated the appeal's two aspects (vv. 11b-12a), and recorded the reason for the conduct called for (v. 12b).

1) THE TONE OF THE APPEAL (V. 11a)

"Beloved, I beseech you" reflects Peter's personal attitude. Beloved (agapētoi), the first of two occurrences of that form of address in the epistle, expressed the apostle's own warm affection toward his readers, who faced a hostile world. Kelly notes that that form of address "is rarely used in non-Christian Greek to mark an affectionate relationship,"[2] but it is frequent in

---

1. Edward Gordon Selwyn, *The First Epistle of St. Peter*, p. 169.
2. J. N. D. Kelly, *A Commentary on the Epistles of Peter and of Jude*, p. 103.

the New Testament epistles.[3] Peter's heart reflected the love that he had already urged upon the readers in 1:22 as a manifestation of a holy life. His appeal came from a friend who had the true interests of his readers at heart. Thus he drew them "closely to his heart with intelligent, purposeful love, a love that will call forth in them a corresponding love and a readiness to obey."[4] The expression reflects not only the writer's love but also the more important fact that they were the objects of God's love in Christ.

Some modern versions employ the translation "Dear friends."[5] Use of that current English idiom gives a contemporary flavor, but it fails to convey the depth of the original *beloved* and is equally susceptible to becoming an empty formula. Somewhat more acceptable is the translation of the JB, "My dear people."[6]

"I beseech you" for the first time makes Peter's appeal distinctly personal. *Beseech* (*parakalō*) reflects Peter's tender attitude. That verb, which basically means "to call alongside," is capable of a variety of translations, depending on the occasion for calling someone alongside.[7] Perhaps "urge" or "appeal to" may be used to express the import of the term here. Peter did not command his readers; he appealed to their own sense of what is right. True holiness is not procured by the application of a compelling external authority but by awakening and strengthening the personal desire and will of those appealed to. *You* is not expressed in the original, but it is readily supplied to designate the recipients of the appeal. Its absence places the emphasis on the contents of the appeal.

2) THE CONTENT OF THE APPEAL (VV. 11*b*-12*a*)

That which Peter urged upon his readers is introduced by the infinitive "to abstain from" and indicates the inner and private aspect of the appeal. The following participial clause, "having your behavior . . . ," indicates the outward and public duty. The order shows that personal holiness is basic to social righteousness.

A. THE INNER SELF-DISCIPLINE CALLED FOR (v. 11*b*)

"As sojourners and pilgrims, to abstain from fleshly lusts." The insertion of a comma after *pilgrims* in the ASV raises the question of the relation of the

---

3. The adjective *agapētos* occurs nine times in the synoptic gospels, each time of the Father's relation to the Son; once in Acts 15:25; twenty-eight times in the epistles of Paul; once in Hebrews 6:9; and twenty-three times in the general epistles. It occurs twice in 1 Peter (2:11; 4:12) and six times in 2 Peter (1:17; 3:1, 8, 14-15, 17).

4. R. C. H. Lenski, *The Interpretation of the Epistles of St. Peter, St. John and St. Jude*, p. 107.

5. *Dear friends* in the NEB, NIV, 20th Cent., Goodspeed, Berkeley.

6. JB.

7. Our English versions use a variety of terms: "appeal"—Moffatt, TEV; "beg"—NEB, Goodspeed, Williams; "beseech"—KJV, RSV, Montgomery; "call upon"—R. Young; "entreat" —Weymouth; "exhort"—Rotherham, Darby, Kleist and Lilly; "implore"—Berkeley; "urge" —NASB, NIV, 20th Cent., JB.

metaphorical designation "sojourners and pilgrims" to its context. Due to its position, that phrase may be related to the preceding verb "beseech" or to the following infinitive "to abstain from."

The insertion of the comma implies that Peter appealed to his readers "as sojourners and pilgrims." Their status motivated his appeal. Bigg supports that understanding by pointing to the absence of the word "you," the nominative case of the following participle "having," as well as the fact that some important uncial manuscripts read the imperative, "abstain ye" (*apechesthe*), rather than the infinitive, "to abstain" (*apechesthai*). That is the more natural understanding if the verbal form is imperative and, as Bigg believed, the original reading.[8] The imperative, which is the easier reading, probably arose through a confusion of the nearly identical vowel sounds ending the two forms. Modern editors agree with the Textus Receptus in reading the infinitive.[9] If the infinitive is the original reading, then those two nouns may with greater force be joined to it. When that is done, the two terms stand emphatically forward and underscore the reason the readers must abstain from fleshly lusts. The Berkeley version reflects that understanding, "I implore you, dear friends, as aliens and exiles to keep from gratifying the fleshly desires."[10] They must abstain because of what they are. We accept that understanding as the more probable.

The two metaphorical designations have already appeared separately. The first was used as an abstract noun in 1:17 and translated "your sojourning;" the second appeared in 1:1 as "sojourners" (see the discussions in both places). The combination appears in the Septuagint in Genesis 23:4 and Psalm 39:12 (LXX 38:12). Abraham's application of the two terms to himself in Genesis may have inspired Peter's designation.

The two terms are closely related in meaning. "Sojourners" (*paroikous*) denotes people living in a foreign country where they do not have the rights of citizens. In Ephesians 2:19 it is used of those who are without citizenship in God's kingdom. *Pilgrims* (*parepidēmous*) indicates that they are temporary residents in a place that is not their permanent home. Our English word *pilgrim*, which is commonly used to denote a traveler passing through a country on his way to his destination, does not convey the exact force of the original, though the image conveyed is true in itself. Our English versions resort to a variety of terms to give the force of that combination.[11] The

8. Charles Bigg, *A Critical and Exegetical Commentary on the Epistles of St. Peter and St. Jude*, p. 135.

9. For the manuscript evidence for the imperative see Erwin Nestle and Kurt Aland, *Novum Testamentum Graece*. The editors of the United Bible Societies text, *The Greek New Testament*, do not even list the textual evidence for the imperative as a probable variant reading.

10. Berkeley.

11. "Aliens and exiles"—RSV, Berkeley, Goodspeed, Williams; "aliens and strangers"—NASB, NIV; "aliens in a foreign land"—NEB; "pilgrims and exiles"—Montgomery; "pilgrims and strangers"—20th Cent.; "sojourners and exiles"—Moffatt; "sojourners and pilgrims" —Rotherham; "strangers and foreigners"—Weymouth; "strangers and pilgrims"—KJV, Kleist and Lilly; "strangers and refugees"—TEV; "strangers and sojourners"—Darby, R. Young; "visitors and pilgrims"—JB.

doubling of the nouns emphasizes the "foreignness" of believers in this Christ-rejecting world; they are citizens of a heavenly country. That implies that the standards of life in their native land are superior to those of the pagan culture in which they find themselves. Hence they must not adopt its immoral customs (v. 11), but they must conduct themselves honorably and generously toward those amid whom they now reside (v. 12). The concept of the historical environment of the churches being addressed provides an appropriate basis for the ethical injunctions that follow. Like all the New Testament writers, Peter did not use the "otherness" of believers as a motive for escapist withdrawal from the world but rather as a motive for holiness in daily conduct.

In view of what the readers are, their standing duty is "to abstain from fleshly lusts." That is the negative aspect of sanctification. "To abstain" (*apechesthai*), a present middle infinitive, is literally "to be holding yourselves off from," and marks that as a constant need. The decisive "putting away" of the old evils called for in 2:1 must be maintained in daily practice. Such abstinence is essential for victory over "fleshly lusts" (*tōn sarkikōn epithumiōn*), "the fleshly lusts" against which Christians must struggle as citizens of the heavenly kingdom. The article groups together the desires that have that nature. The implication is "that the fallen nature whose power over the believer was broken when he was saved is still there with its sin-ward pull."[12] But victory over the allurements of those lusts is available to the Christian (Gal. 5:16).

The noun translated "lusts" (*epithumiōn*) is a neutral term, denoting strong desires or cravings, whether good or bad.[13] In Luke 22:15; Philippians 1:23, and 1 Thessalonians 2:17 it has a good connotation; but generally in the New Testament, it has an evil meaning. In this verse, the readers' evil nature is highlighted by the genitive "fleshly" (*sarkikōn*), having the nature and characteristics of the flesh. Wand understands the reference to be to "those desires that have their seat in our bodily nature."[14] But Peter's words should not be interpreted to mean that desires related to our physical nature are evil, as though the human body in itself was evil. The thought is not limited to sensual indulgences; Peter's words circumscribe all those cravings associated with the entire nature of man as a fallen being, whether they express themselves through the body or the mind. *Flesh* is used in its ethical sense to denote fallen mankind as characterized by depraved and corrupting desires.[15]

Peter further characterized them as desires "which war against the soul."

---

12. Kenneth S. Wuest, *First Peter in the Greek New Testament for the English Reader*, pp. 58-59.
13. William F. Arndt and F. Wilbur Gingrich, *A Greek-English Lexicon of the New Testament and Other Early Christian Literature*, p. 293; H. Schonweiss, "Desire, Lust" in *NIDNTT*, 1:456-58.
14. J. W. C. Wand, *The General Epistles of St. Peter and St. Jude*, p. 74.
15. Arndt and Gingrich, pp. 750-52; A. C. Thiselton, "Flesh" in *NIDNTT*, 1:671-82.

Which (*haitines*), "which are such as," as a qualitative relative pronoun places all those cravings in one category as being contrary to the readers' spiritual welfare, for they "war against the soul." The verb "war" (*strateuontai*) indicates an attitude of enmity and active hostility. The figure is not that of hand to hand fighting but of a planned military expedition against a military objective. Those lusts constitute an army of soldiers engaged in constant warfare against the soul, aimed at capturing the believer and making him useless to God. Ross remarks, "The pilgrim of God, as we see him, carries about a battlefield inside his own personality."[16]

"Soul" seems to be used to denote man's inner moral nature, the seat and center of self-conscious human life. Human experience reveals that to allow those corrupt cravings of our fallen nature to dominate is destructive of human welfare. They not merely injure the body, they also "pervert desire, enslave the will, and darken the understanding. They deepen the spirit of disobedience against God."[17] But since Peter's appeal is addressed to believers, his expression denotes man's inner being as animated by the new life received from Christ. Best observes, "It is his redeemed soul, not some pre-existing divine spark, which is here set in contrast with his flesh."[18]

B. THE OUTWARD WINSOME CONDUCT NEEDED (v. 12a)

"Having your behaviour seemly among the Gentiles" shifts the focus from the inner spiritual battle to the attractive conduct required of the believer. The conduct called for constitutes the visible fruit of victory in the struggle against the inner cravings of the old nature. Grammatically, the construction is somewhat irregular in that the participle "having" (*exhontes*) is in the nominative case.[19] Alford noted that that disjunction in the construction "serves to give vividness to the description, . . . depicting, as it were, the condition recommended as actually existing."[20] Since the present tense denotes continuing action, the participle might well be translated "holding to" or "persevering in" to suggest the steadfast maintenance of the standard of conduct indicated.

"Your behaviour" (*tēn anastrophēn humōn*), the object of the participle "having," stands emphatically at the beginning of the verse. It denotes the varied activities of daily life (cf. 1:15) lived under the watchful eyes of "the Gentiles," their non-Christian neighbors. Some, like Wand,[21] suggest that the

---

16. J. M. E. Ross, *The First Epistle of Peter*, p. 102.

17. Everett Falconer Harrison, "Exegetical Studies in I Peter," p. 461.

18. Ernest Best, *I Peter*, p. 111.

19. Under the control of the infinitive, it would be in the accusative as the accusative of general reference. See the same disjunction in Ephesians 4:1-2.

20. Henry Alford, *The Greek New Testament*, vol. 4 (part 1), pp. 349-50.

21. Wand, pp. 74-75.

term *Gentiles* implies that the readers were Jewish Christians; but the term is equally appropriate if they had a non-Jewish background since the expression well marks the present contrast between them as Christians and their Christ-rejecting neighbors. The Jews used the term to designate the non-Jewish masses as sinful and idolatrous, as "the heathen" (cf. 1 Cor. 12:2; 1 Thess. 4:5). For Peter the term readily indicated the distinction between believers in Christ and the pagans whose evil practices they once shared (4:4).

The readers' behavior must be "seemly" (*kalēn*), morally noble, and praiseworthy—conduct that commends itself to the moral judgment of those around them. The position of the term at the end of the clause makes the adjective emphatic—"having your behaviour among the nations honourable" (Rotherham).[22] Peter was anxious that their Christian conduct be attractive and winsome. Kelly observes, "This concern for the Church's fair name among non-Christians is frequent in the NT (1 Cor. x. 32; Col. iv. 5; 1 Thess. iv. 12; 1 Tim. iii. 7; v. 14; vi. 1; Tit. ii. 5-10; also ii. 15; iii. 1)."[23]

3) THE AIM OF THE APPEAL (V. 12b)

"That" (*hina*), "in order that," introduces the aim behind the appeal. Peter's concern was not merely the vindication of believers before a hostile world; he was also interested in "the evangelising influences of a chaste and winsome character."[24] Behind the existence of the church is a missionary motive.

The phrase, "wherein they speak against you as evil-doers, they may by your good works, which they behold, glorify God in the day of visitation," indicates a double purpose: to disarm hostility and to lead to conversion. *Wherein* (*en hō*), "in which thing," draws attention to the conduct of believers as the occasion for the slanders that were hurled against them. Though the pronoun may be masculine (as in Mark 2:19), here it is neuter and relates to the circumstance that evoked the hostility, the readers' withdrawal from further participation in the pagan practices of their neighbors. Unable to understand that withdrawal, their pagan neighbors "speak against" (*katalalousin*), revile, and slander them. The compound verb literally means "to speak down on" (cf. the noun "evil speaking" in 2:1) and denotes critical and derogatory speaking with the malicious intention of harming those spoken against by turning others against them. Such speech overlooks the good traits of those criticized, concentrating on their faults as perceived by the speaker.

Peter's readers were charged with being "evil-doers" (*kakopoiōn*), "doers of baseness."[25] The adjective, used as a noun, stamped them as individuals

22. Rotherham.
23. Kelly, p. 105.
24. J. H. Jowett, *The Epistles of St. Peter*, p. 78.
25. Lenski, p. 106.

engaged in the practice of base and evil activities that deserved to be punished. Used in a general sense, it denotes that which is base or morally evil or, specifically, that which is criminal. In John 18:30, its only occurrence outside of 1 Peter, it has the connotation of *criminal*, one engaged in deeds liable to punishment by the magistrates. Its use in conjunction with *speak against* suggests that the more vague meaning is preferable. Being compelled as Christians to withdraw from degrading heathen customs and religious rites, the believers were misunderstood and slandered. Those slanders gave Christians a bad reputation, fulfilling the warning that Jesus had given his followers (Matt. 5:11). The warning had become personally relevant to the churches addressed. In the words of Cook,

> Christians were specially attacked by Gentiles, generally at the instigation of Jews, on political grounds as enemies of the state (cf. Acts xvii. 6, 7); on religious grounds as atheists, *i.e.* rejecting the objects of heathen worship; on ethical grounds as introducing unlawful customs, and, as it was believed, abominable impurity, Acts xvi. 20, 21. These points are commonly alleged by opponents of Christianity, and are specially noticed by apologists in the first two centuries. . . . Hebrew and Gentile Christians were of course alike objects of such calumnies, but the latter were peculiarly hateful to the Gentiles as apostates from their own religion; and considering the character of many converts before they were rescued from the unspeakable pollution of heathenism (cf. 1 Cor. vi. 9, 11), it is not surprising that strong prejudices were entertained, and that calumnies invented by the deadly enemies of the Cross were readily believed by the Gentiles.[26]

It was the general acceptance of those vicious charges against the believers in Rome that enabled Nero to use Christians as the scapegoat by which he divested himself of the charge of ordering the burning of Rome in A.D. 64. Thus Tacitus (c. A.D. 55-117) reported that "Nero fastened the guilt and inflicted the most exquisite tortures on a class hated for their abominations, called Christians by the populace." He added that that "most mischievous superstitition" had been only temporarily checked in Palestine by Pilate, and he classed it as among all the "hideous and shameful" things to be found in Rome.[27] And Suetonius (born. c. A.D. 70), in his life of Nero, with unconcealed approval, recorded that the Emperor inflicted punishment "on the Christians, a class of men given to a new and mischievous superstition."[28] With varying degrees of intensity, the enmity against Christians prevailed in the various parts of the empire.

Peter encouraged his readers to refute those slanders and to change the attitude of their detractors "by your good works, which they behold." *By* (*ek*), "out of," may have a partitive force and indicate that the opponents will only

---

26. F. C. Cook, *The First Epistle General of Peter*, pp. 192-93.

27. P. Cornelius Tacitus, *The Annals and the Histories*, Annals, 15:44.

28. Gaius Suetonius, *The Lives of the Twelve Caesars*, p. 250.

need to observe some of their noble deeds to be convinced.[29] More probably, *ek*
points to the source of influence that will effect the anticipated change, namely,
their "good works" (*kalōn ergōn*), deeds that are seen to be "noble, beautiful, and morally excellent" (it is the same word rendered "seemly" just
above). Such a life of good works is unfolded in the paragraphs that follow
and encompasses the whole range of the outward relations of believers in
society.

"Which they behold" (*epopteuontes*), "beholding, observing," indicates the
essential condition for the expected change in the opponents. The term, which
occurs only here and in 3:2 in the New Testament, pictures the close, personal
scrutiny of an eyewitness. In 2 Peter 1:16 the noun is translated "eyewitness-
es." The present tense of the participle depicts the intense and prolonged
scrutiny to which Christians were to expose themselves. The term denotes
that they would indeed be a spectacle (1 Cor. 4:9) to the world around them.
When Christians are misunderstood and slandered, the proper answer is not
withdrawal from the world nor contemptuous disregard of the opinions of one's
opponents but manifest purity of conduct.

The enemies of Peter's readers had only superficially observed their lives;
a close, careful scrutiny should have convicted them of their error. What
they would discover would lead them to "glorify God in the day of visitation." *Glorify* (*doxasōsin*), to honor, magnify, adore, stands in antithesis to
speak against you and underlines the anticipated change produced by the
inspection. The implication is not that the enemies will praise the noble
deeds of the Christians, though themselves remaining pagans. Rather,
the evangelistic hope is that, like the centurion at the cross (Mark 15:39),
the opponents will themselves be led to glorify God (*ton theon*) and to
worship the true God (1 Tim. 1:17) whom Christians already know and
serve.

"In the day of visitation" (*en hēmera episkopēs*) is literally "in a day of
inspection" (R. Young) and may denote a magisterial investigation associated
with mercy or with judgment. The expression, without the definite article,
depicts a day when God confronts man and brings matters to a crisis,
rewarding or punishing as He finds occasion. Some, like Bennett,[30] William
Kelly,[31] and others, think that the reference is to the day of judgment at the
second coming of Christ.[32] If men are brought before the judgment bar as
pagans, then they must be viewed as the unwilling means of glorifying God in
that day. But such a view seems unsuited to the context. It suggests that after
a thorough investigation they will be led to accept and magnify the God
believers already love. Such, for example, was the experience of Justin Martyr

29. John T. Demarest, *A Translation and Exposition of the First Epistle of the Apostle Peter*, p.
    118.

30. W. H. Bennett, *The General Epistles, James, Peter, John, and Jude*, p. 216.

31. William Kelly, *The Epistles of Peter*, p. 150.

32. The view that the reference is to the judgment upon the Jews in the destruction of the city of
    Jerusalem and the Jewish state is improbable. See Bruce Oberst, *Letters from Peter*, pp. 59-60.

(c. A.D. 100-165), according to his own testimony (*Second Apology*, xii). So understood, the reference is to a visitation when God brings home the truths of the gospel to the individual heart and that person is led to accept His mercy. The persecutors could not be said to glorify God in the day of judgment unless they had previously been converted. In Luke 19:44 Jesus lamented the fact that Israel was blind to its time of visitation, when her Messiah came with His offer of grace and blessing. The parallel of Peter's picture with the words of Jesus in Matthew 5:16, "Even so let your light shine before men; that they may see your good works, and glorify your Father who is in heaven," supports the view that the reference is to a visit in mercy. It also agrees with Peter's evangelistic note in 2:9. We agree with Lillie that most probably the reference is "to a day of gracious visitation—the very day which had then just dawned, and which is still shining, during which, according to James's description of the first calling and conversion of the Gentiles through Peter's ministry, 'God is visiting the Gentiles to take out of them a people for His name,'"[33] cf. Acts 15:14. So understood, the comment of Farrar is apt, "Notice the large-hearted absence of any spirit of revenge. He only desires that the heathen, when they find how base were their calumnies, how cruel their conduct, may be led to glorify God! No anathemas here."[34]

33. John Lillie, *Lectures on the First and Second Epistles of Peter*, pp. 134-35.
34. F. W. Farrar, *The Early Days of Christianity*, p. 89, n. 7.

11

B. The Duty of Submission to the State
(2:13-17)

The life of believers before the world that will silence the slanders against them (2:11-12) is now elaborated in three broad areas: obedience to the state (2:13-17), in household relations (2:18-25), and in marital relations (3:1-7). Peter began with the broadest area, the believer's duty to the state. Similar teaching occurs in Romans 13:1-7 and Titus 3:1-2.

Bigg notes that discussions of social duties were "a missionary's common-place."[1] Such lists of moral duties in various social relations are found elsewhere in the New Testament (Eph. 5:21—6:9; Col. 3:18—4:1; 1 Tim. 2:8-15; 6:1-2; Titus 2:1-10), as well as in other early Christian writings (e.g., *The Didache*, 4.9-11; *Epistle of Barnabas*, 19.5-7; *1 Clement* 1.3; 19.6-9; Polycarp, *To the Philippians*, 4.2—6.2). Similar codes of moral conduct were common in contemporary Jewish and pagan literature.

> (13) Be subject to every ordinance of man for the Lord's sake: whether to the king, as supreme; (14) or unto governors, as sent by him for vengeance on evil-doers and for praise to them that do well. (15) For so is the will of God, that by well-doing ye should put to silence the ignorance of foolish men: (16) as free, and not using your freedom for a cloak of wickedness, but as bondservants of God. (17) Honor all men. Love the brotherhood. Fear God. Honor the King.

Peter commanded the readers to be submissive to the state (v. 13a), described the civil powers to whom obedience is due (vv. 13b-14), elaborated on

---

1. Charles Bigg, *A Critical and Exegetical Commentary on the Epistles of St. Peter and St. Jude*, p. 139.

the believer's submission to the state (vv. 15-16), and concluded the paragraph with a summary of the scope of Christian well-doing (v. 17).

1) THE DUTY OF CHRISTIAN SUBMISSION (V. 13a)

The duty of submission to the state is bluntly introduced with no transitional particle[2] by the bald statement: "Be subject to every ordinance of man for the Lord's sake." The aorist imperative, "Be subject" (*hupotagēte*), conveys a sense of urgency, making a decisive demand. It points "less to the continual course of submission than to the act of decision by which this policy of submission is adopted."[3] The compound verb means "to station or rank under" and thus denotes subordination to a superior authority. The form is passive and is strictly translated "be subjected;" but it is generally accepted that here the verb has a middle force[4] and may be translated "submit yourselves,"[5] or "put yourselves in the attitude of submission to."[6] It is not a derogatory concept, demanding forced submission, but rather a voluntary acceptance of a position of obedience to a superior authority. It is not the cringing obedience of spineless weaklings but the free acceptance of the duty of submission to governmental authority. Of that submission Hort says,

> It consists not in the sacrifice of the individual to the community, the weakness of the ancient social life, but in the recognition that the individual attains his own true growth and freedom only through devotion to the community, and submission to the various forms of authority by which society is constituted.[7]

Jesus explicitly taught the duty of "rendering unto Caesar the things that are Caesar's" (Matt. 22:21), a duty to which many Jews at the time were reluctant to submit. When Peter wrote, the unfounded charges and prevailing suspicions against Christians made it imperative that they should not be remiss in their obedience to government. The duty of submission, which is prominent in the second cycle of exhortations, is an essential aspect of the Christian life.

Believers should submit "to every ordinance of man" (*pasē anthrōpinē ktisei*), a debated expression that literally means "to every human creation" or, possibly, "to every human creature." The noun *ktisis* occurs nineteen times in the New Testament, and only here is it translated "ordinance" or "institution."[8]

---

2. The Textus Receptus does have *oun*, "Therefore," but it is not strongly attested.

3. Edward Gordon Selwyn, *The First Epistle of St. Peter*, p. 172.

4. See the discussion in James Hope Moulton, *A Grammar of New Testament Greek*, 1:162-63.

5. Our versions variously translate: "Be subject"—ASV, RSV, R. Young; "be in subjection" —Darby; "submit yourselves"—KJV, NASB, NIV, NEB, TEV, Rotherham, Montgomery; "submit"—Weymouth, 20th Cent., Moffatt, Goodspeed, Williams; "be submissive"—Berkeley, Kleist and Lilly.

6. Kenneth S. Wuest, *First Peter in the Greek New Testament for the English Reader*, pp. 60-61.

7. F. J. A. Hort, *The First Epistle of St. Peter, I. 1—II. 17*, p. 139.

8. "Ordinance of man"—KJV, ASV; "human institution"—NASB, RSV, NEB, Darby, 20th Cent., Berkeley; "Social institution"—JB; "authority instituted by man"—NIV; "human authority"—Moffatt, Goodspeed, Williams, Montgomery, Kleist and Lilly; "authority set up by men"—Weymouth; "human creation"—Rotherham, R. Young.

In all the other occurrences the reference is to God as Creator of the world or to the new creation in Christ. Due to that prevailing New Testament usage some, like Foerster[9] and Kelly,[10] maintain that we should translate "to every human creature." In support Foerster points to Philippians 2:3 as a parallel and argues that "Peter's admonition to the congregations is that they should be subject to men of every sort."[11] The difficulty with the view that the noun *ktisis* denotes individuals is the addition of the adjective "human" (*anthrōpinē*), belonging to the realm of the human. In the context the reference is not to humans as such but to individuals by virtue of their position of authority. Since it is literally impossible to be subject to every human creature, the term is best understood as impersonal and taken to refer to the various fundamental human orders of authority in society. So understood, Peter's expression should be taken as deliberately comprehensive; it includes all the various fundamental human relationships that are discussed in the following sections. That generalization is reflected in the translation of the JB, "accept the authority of every social institution." But such a generalization is not evident from the immediate sentence since "whether to the king . . . or to governors" limits the reference to civil rulers.

Macknight interpreted Peter's expression to mean "every human creation of magistrates" since "both Greeks and Romans called *the appointment* of magistrates, *a creation* of them."[12] If that is correct, then the reference is to the holder of the office as embodying the authority of the institution. In secular Greek the noun "creation" (*ktisis*) was not only applied to things made, whether by the gods or men, but was used of the founding of cities or colonies with their governmental institutions.[13] The adjective "human" points to an institution founded by men; it is not an institution established at the explicit command of God but one given specific shape and development by men. The expression does not stipulate any specific form of human government, though the form in view is that of the Roman Empire. It is unwarranted to assume that Peter regarded civil government as purely a human development. He would certainly have agreed with Paul's teaching in Romans 13 that all human government has a divine origin. Peter was not dealing with the source of governmental authority but with the existing institutions, whatever their form, that are indeed a human creation. Whatever the precise form of civil government under which believers may live, Peter's words demand obedience to it on their part. Christianity is independent of any form of human government, though through its influence it may be an agent in establishing a better form of government.

9. Werner Foerster, *ktizō, ktisis, ktisma, ktisēs, TDNT,* 3:1034-35.

10. J. N. D. Kelly, *A Commentary on the Epistles of Peter and of Jude,* p. 108.

11. Foerster, p. 1035.

12. James Macknight, *A New Literal Translation from the Original Greek of all the Apostolical Epistles,* 5:459.

13. Henry George Liddell and Robert Scott, *A Greek-English Lexicon,* p. 852.

Peter's condensed instructions did not deal with the problem of the believer's response whenever government demands that which is contrary to the Christian faith. In Acts 4:19 and 5:29 we have the example of Peter himself concerning the Christian's response under such conditions. For the Christian the state is not the highest authority, and whenever a government demands that which is in conflict with the dictates of the conscience enlightened by the Holy Spirit and the Word, then the Christian must obey the Word of God and suffer the results. "The Church soon learned by bitter experience that there are some things which the state has no right to do, and that therefore the counsel of submission has its limitations."[14] But under ordinary circumstances, believers should actively support civil government in its promotion of law and order.

Obedience to the government is to be rendered for the Lord's sake. That is a distinctly Christian motive for obedience. The human motive of obedience to avoid punishment is not precluded (cf. Rom. 13:5), but it is not distinctly Christian. Christian obedience is motivated by loyalty to "the Lord" (*ton kurion*), most naturally understood as a reference to the Lord Jesus Christ. Except in quotations from the Old Testament, that is the meaning of the term in Peter's epistles. In Him believers find freedom to subordinate themselves to others (cf. 2 Cor. 4:5b). *For the Lord's sake* may mean a submission yielded out of regard for His authority, since He explicitly taught submission to government and its demands (Matt. 17:27; 22:21; Mark 12:17). Christian allegiance to Him, far from annulling or impairing that demand, should add to the force and sacredness of the duty. Or the words may be understood to denote concern for His cause—not to bring dishonor on His Name or increase persecution of His church by disobedience and unruly conduct. Both views are valid motives.

2) THE CHARACTERIZATION OF THE CIVIL POWERS (VV. 13b-14)

With "whether . . . or" Peter indicated two classes of civil authorities to whom submission is to be rendered. The picture of the supreme ruler and his subordinate rulers is of course drawn from the governmental structure of the Roman Empire. But the absence of the definite article makes all the nouns qualitative and denotes a graded power structure that is characteristic of human governments generally.

A. THE SUPREME RULER (v. 13b)

"Whether to the king, as supreme" denotes the Roman emperor as the supreme authority. Though the term *rex* ("king") was odious to Roman citizens, the designation was freely applied to the emperor in the Greek-speaking provinces. Though the term is frequently applied to subordinate

14. J. M. E. Ross, *The First Epistle of Peter*, p. 115.

rulers in the New Testament, it is also applied to the emperor (John 19:15; Acts 17:7; 1 Tim. 2:2).

"As supreme" portrays the emperor as one who held power over others as their overlord, as the personal representative of all power inherent in the state. Our acceptance of the authenticity of this epistle involves the conclusion that when Peter wrote, the emperor was Nero (A.D. 54-68), an evil and unworthy man. The personal unworthiness of the office holder does not cancel the duty of obedience to the office.

B. THE SUBORDINATE RULERS (v. 14)

"Or unto governors, as sent by him" marks those rulers as subordinate representatives of the emperor. The noun "governors" (*hēgemosin*) means those who stand in a position of leadership and guidance and so are also over others, themselves supreme in their lesser spheres of authority. The term was used of the governors in the provinces, such as Pilate (Matt. 27:2), Felix (Acts 23:24), and Festus (Acts 26:30), who were commissioned by the emperor himself. Peter did not stop to distinguish between imperial and senatorial governors; he used the term in the wider sense of all administrators of the various Roman provinces. As sent by the Roman government, they represented the central Roman authority. Though the *de facto* rule of those governors had been established by the tyrannical power of the Roman Empire, as the actual rulers of their areas, their authority was to be accepted.

Though Peter is silent concerning the origin of the authority of the king, he clearly indicates the derived power of those governors. "As sent by him" (*di' autou*) is best taken to mean the emperor, not the Lord. If the intended reference was to God as the sender, it would have been more natural to use *hupo* to indicate the ultimate source, rather than *dia* as the agent of sending. That view would involve the incongruity of predicating a divine mission for the subordinate rulers but not of the supreme governmental power. The present participle "sent" (*pempomanois*), "being sent," pictures those governors being commissioned by the emperor one by one, from time to time.

The purpose in sending the governors indicates the double function of government: "for vengeance on evil-doers and for praise to them that do well." They represent the emperor in executing that two-sided function, implying that it is likewise the function of the supreme government. Though not always fully or impartially administered, the Roman government operated through the enforcement of prescribed laws. Peter, like Paul in Romans 13, was speaking of the normal functions of rulers.

"For vengeance on evil-doers" indicates the restraint of evil as a major function of government." *Vengeance* (*ekdikēsin*) is the act of vindicating justice through appropriate punishment of those who commit injustices or evil acts (cf. 2:12). The punishment may be mild, but it should not lose its character as punishment for the evil done. Bigg remarks, "Though the individual Christian is forbidden to take the law into his own hands and avenge his own injuries

(Matt. v. 39), yet it is the duty of the civil power to avenge them for him; and
unless this duty is firmly discharged the State cannot exist."[15] That negative
function of government is a witness to the evil tendencies of human nature.
The welfare of society makes it necessary.

"For praise to them that do well" states a second function of human
government, by its very nature not as prominent as the first. *Praise* stands as
the opposite of *vengeance* and denotes the commendation or laudatory recognition bestowed on those who won the approval of the rulers. That implies that
civil government is responsible not only for the security of its citizens but
should also foster their moral well-being. It does so by giving appropriate
recognition on occasion to those individuals who habitually do that which is
good and beneficial. Bigg points out that under the Roman philosophy of
government the ruler was father as well as magistrate and that "owing to this
paternal jurisdiction 'praise' was much more directly and frequently the
function of the ancient magistrate than of his modern counterpart."[16]

It has been noted that the motives to which the state appeals are basically
selfish, but the alternative is anarchy. Cranfield well observes,

> The motives to which the State appeals are not the highest, for the State (even a
> Christian State) is not the Church, but includes those who deliberately reject the
> gospel. It is a provision of God's mercy for fallen man, for the curbing of the worst
> excesses of man's sinfulness and the maintenance of a degree of order in a world
> disrupted by man's disobedience.[17]

3) THE ELABORATION OF THE BELIEVER'S SUBMISSION (VV. 15-16)

"For" (*hoti*), a causal conjunction, introduces the reason for the command to
the readers to submit themselves to governmental authorities (v. 13). Peter
elaborated on that duty by pointing out the anticipated impact upon opponents
(v. 15) and further reminded them of the demand it placed on them personally
(v. 16).

A. THE INTENDED IMPACT UPON FOOLISH MEN (v. 15)

The Christian motive for submission to government has already been
indicated by "for the Lord's sake" (v. 13*a*). Peter now portrayed the readers'
submission in relation to their opponents: "So is the will of God, that by
well-doing ye should put to silence the ignorance of foolish men."

The adverb "so" (*houtōs*), "thusly, in this manner," may be retrospective,
relating to the injunction to submit themselves (v. 13). If that is correct, then
the meaning is, "God's will is realized by your being dutifully obedient to the
authorities," and the remainder of the verse is a loosely attached afterthought

15. Bigg, p. 140.
16. Ibid, pp. 140-41.
17. C. E. B. Cranfield, *I & II Peter and Jude*, p. 76.

of the effect of such submission.[18] But that adverb may also be viewed as looking forward, "thusly," in the manner described in what follows, meaning that the will of God is that by their well-doing they will silence the ignorance of foolish men. We accept the latter as the more probable connection.

"The will of God" (*to thelēma tou theou*) indicates that which is willed by "*the* God," the true God whom the readers know and represent. His will for Christians is to effectively realize the conduct described by the remainder of the verse. The participle "by well-doing" (*agathopoiountas*) describes God's will as it relates to the believers themselves. Reicke asserts that the term, standing in contrast to *evil-doing*, "does not specifically denote pious deeds, but acting rightly in general with regard to society, proper civil behavior in contradistinction to criminality."[19] But that compound term, which occurs only here in the New Testament, is broad enough to include all aspects of Christian well-doing. The present tense portrays good and beneficial activities as characteristic of believers.

The anticipated result of such lives is expressed by the phrase "ye should put to silence the ignorance of foolish men." *Put to silence* (*phimoun*) means "to tie shut, to muzzle," like a vicious dog. Metaphorically, the verb means to stop the mouth so that the objector is unable to say anything further, like Jesus silencing the Sadducees in Matthew 22:34. The implication is that "the attacks thus far have been by word rather than deed."[20] The enemies have their mouths open rather than their eyes. Such vicious verbal attacks are best answered not by indignant self-defense but by open well-doing. The present tense implies that the silencing of the attackers is to be a recurrent result.

Those attacks were prompted by "the ignorance of foolish men" (*tēn tōn aphronōn anthrōpōn agnōsian*). The definite article with both nouns makes each specific, "the ignorance of the foolish men." *Ignorance* is not the more common term *agnoia*, used in 1:14, but *agnōsia*, also used in 1 Corinthians 15:34, which does not so much denote intellectual inadequacy as a religious failure to perceive the true nature of the Christian faith and life. It implies a stronger sense of blameworthiness. The perspectives of their own pagan religious life and their innate hostility to the life-style manifested by the adherents of the new religion produced an obstinate, culpable ignorance concerning Christianity that readily manifested itself in their vocal opposition to the Christians. Their reaction exposed them as "foolish men." The definite article, "the foolish men," points them out as a specific group, those already mentioned in verse 12. The adjective "foolish" (*aphronōn*) characterized them as acting without reason, as though they lacked mental sanity. *Men* (*anthrōpōn*) is general, human beings, and thus is broader than "the Gentiles" in verse 12. Their ignorance, which gives rise to unfounded charges against Christians, is essentially characteristic of such foolish individuals.

---

18. Kelly, p. 110.
19. Bo Reicke, *The Epistles of James, Peter, and Jude*, p. 137, n. 21.
20. J. W. C. Wand, *The General Epistles of St. Peter and St. Jude*, pp. 77-78.

B. THE TRUE CHARACTER OF THOSE SUBMITTING (v. 16)

The absence of any finite verb indicates that the verse is descriptive. "As free, and not using your freedom for a cloak of wickedness, but as bond-servants of God" describes the character and conduct of believers who will be able to silence the slanders of their opponents. Without any connecting conjunction or term of contrast, the description stands prominently alone.[21]

"As free" is Peter's approving acknowledgment of the spiritual status of his Christian readers. The Christian message of the freedom experienced in Christ was a treasured part of the faith of the early church (John 8:36; Gal. 5:1, 13). They were constantly being reminded that they were citizens of a heavenly kingdom (Phil. 3:20; Col. 1:5; Heb. 10:34-35; 1 Pet. 1:3-4). But that teaching of Christian freedom was capable of being misinterpreted and misused. Their freedom in Christ was "not political but that interior liberty of the Christian which results from breaking the yoke of bondage to sin or the law."[22] As living in this world, it did not relieve them of their duty of submission to the civil powers. Believers should render due submission "for the Lord's sake" (v. 13) without feeling that they are the slaves of government.

"And" (*kai*), not *but* (*de*), introduces a second perversion of Christian freedom that must be avoided: "not using your freedom for a cloak of wickedness." *Your freedom* (*tēn eleutherian*), the liberty that Christians possess and cherish, should not become a pretext for antinomianism. It was a danger against which Paul warned the Galatian churches (Gal. 5:13) and one that on various occasions has plagued the Christian church.[23] Peter warned against using spiritual liberty as a "cloak" (*epikalumma*) or pretext for evil practices. The noun translated "cloak" occurs only here in the New Testament and does not denote a garment put on but a veil or a cover thrown over that which is to be concealed. Christian freedom is not license under the guise of liberty to practice "wickedness" (*tēs kakias*), "the evil" (R. Young) that the readers had already been called upon to put away (2:1). *Wickedness* is used in its general sense to denote all that is morally base and corrupt (cf. 2:1). Prevailing false teaching made the warning appropriate. "Judaizers claimed exemption from human law; Gentile sophists confounded liberty with libertinism, and held that grace implied deliverance from the restraints and penalties of divine law."[24]

21. The intended connection of the verse is differently understood. The nominative plural adjective "as free" may be viewed as a continued description of the subject "ye" of the verb "be subject" in verse 13. If that is correct, then the verse describes those who should submit to rulers. But the large amount of material intervening makes that connection improbable. It seems better to view the verse as an epexegetical elaboration of the duty in verse 15, adding an important complement to the injunction to silence the opponents by well-doing. The view that the verse is to be joined with verse 17 is improbable in the light of the contents of that verse.

22. Wand, p. 78.

23. Hugh J. Blair, "Antinomianism," *The New International Dictionary of the Christian Church* (*NIDCC*), p. 48.

24. F. C. Cook, *The First Epistle General of Peter*, 4:194.

"But as bondservants of God" categorically asserts the true status of those who have found spiritual freedom in Christ. Christian freedom consists not in freedom from a master but in the voluntary submission to God as our rightful master. As (*hōs*) does not compare believers to slaves but marks their actual relationship to God as His "bondservants" (*douloi*), as belonging wholly to Him and bound to be doing His will. The use of such a strong term, "slaves," does not imply involuntary servitude for the believer but stresses the unconditional, absolute obedience due to his Master. The Master's will is that His servants should be dutiful citizens.

4) THE SCOPE OF CHRISTIAN WELL-DOING (V. 17)

Four ringing imperatives without any connective particles summarize the duty of the paragraph: "Honor all men. Love the brotherhood. Fear God. Honor the king." Those rapid-fire commands mark out the scope of the duty of Christian well-doing. As they are kept, the Christian's life will silence the ignorant charges of foolish men.

Based strictly on grammatical considerations, those four commands seem naturally to group into one and three: the first is a decisive aorist; the following three are durative present tenses. Alford and Lenski[25] view the first as setting forth the initial urgent duty, followed by three present imperatives that elaborate it. The contents of those commands led Williams to note: "The apostle ascends from men in general to men of spiritual relationship; from these he ascends to God himself, and ends by dropping to the key-note: 'Honor the king.'"[26] Others, like Kelly, feel that the change in tense, though puzzling, is not to be pressed, and that the contents of the verse are best viewed as grouping the commands "into two pairs, with *all* balanced by *brotherhood* and *God* by *emperor*; and these are also arranged chiastically, the second verb having a richer content than the first and the third than the fourth."[27] That arrangement into two pairs suggests two contrasts, the first between the humanitarian and the Christian relationship, the second between the divine and the human authority believers live under. Such a grouping of those commands is suggestive, but we do not believe that thereby the force of the initial aorist should be ignored. The initial aorist states the specific action, the categorical duty of adopting an attitude of honoring all men, and the translation of that attitude into daily life follows in the durative commands.

"Honor all men" (*pantas timēsate*), by its very order, "to all give ye honour" (R. Young), makes the scope of the duty emphatic. The masculine plural "all" (*pantas*) is not defined by an added noun. Some, like Demarest,[28] would limit

25. Henry Alford, *The Greek New Testament*, vol. 4 (part 1), p. 352; R. C. H. Lenski, *The Interpretation of the Epistles of St. Peter, St. John and St. Jude*, p. 115.

26. Nathaniel Marshman Williams, *Commentary on the Epistles of Peter*, p. 33.

27. Kelly, p. 112 (italics by Kelly).

28. John T. Demarest, *A Translation and Exposition of the First Epistle of the Apostle Peter*, p. 123.

the reference to "all rulers;" but the context does not require such a narrow definition. Others, like Bengel, understand Peter to mean, "all to whom honor is due."[29] But it is generally accepted that it is best to give the undefined term its natural broad scope, "all human beings." So understood, the command "was the utterance of a new spirit, when Christ's Apostles proclaimed to God's redeemed children, the excellent of the earth, the duty of *'honoring all men'*—all sorts and conditions of men."[30] The command is striking in view of the biblical picture of mankind in its unsaved state. Sinners are still the objects of God's love; He seeks to save them at infinite cost to Himself. God urges the saved to have an attitude toward the lost in keeping with His own. They should have respect for all men as His creatures, in whom the image of God at present is not utterly defaced (James 3:9-10)—beings capable of regeneration and reconciliation with Him. Their dignity as human beings should be respected; they must not be regarded and treated as mere things to be exploited. The duty to honor—not the same as love or obey—demands that Christians evaluate and fix a price on human personality and so treat it with respect. It is the opposite of "to treat with scorn and contempt," an attitude that has been distressingly common on the part of the self-assumed elite through the ages. Huther comments, "This exhortation is all the more important for the Christian, that the consciousness of his own dignity can easily betray him into a depreciation of others."[31]

"Love the brotherhood" (*tēn adelphotēta agapate*), literally, "the brotherhood keep on loving," centers the attention on a narrower circle. *The brotherhood*, a term occurring only in 1 Peter (here and 5:9), denotes all believers considered as a collective unity. It is Peter's term for "the church," a term that does not appear in his letters. Christian love should not be restricted to a few individual believers but be directed to the whole body. Christian love must be interested in and desire the welfare of the entire body of God's people. Masterman remarks, "With the loss of this sense of corporate life we have lost the wideness of Christian love, and are too often contented to limit our affection to those who attract, or who prove responsive; and since love is our power for service we correspondingly narrow the scope of our influence."[32]

The third command, "Fear God" (*ton theon phobeisthe*), "God keep on revering," at first may seem somewhat out of place in the series. Peter already called upon the readers to live their lives in reverential awe before God as their Father and impartial Judge (1:17). The call for fear does not imply fright and cringing terror before God but a habitual attitude of awe and reverence. Such a fear of God is the source of true wisdom (Prov. 1:7; 8:13) and enables the believer rightly to carry out his duties toward men. It is the safeguard against the temptation to abuse Christian liberty.

29. John Albert Bengel, *New Testament Word Studies*, 2:738.
30. John Lillie, *Lectures on the First and Second Epistles of Peter*, p. 153.
31. Joh. Ed. Huther, *Critical and Exegetical Handbook to the General Epistles of Peter and Jude*, p. 133.
32. Masterman, p. 110.

"Honor the king" (*ton basilea timate*), "the king be honoring," appropriately concludes the paragraph. He is to be shown all due respect as the supreme representative of civil authority. Such honor is shown by obedience to the laws of the land as well as by prayer for him (1 Tim. 2:1-2).

Peter apparently derived that last pair of commands from Proverbs 24:21, "My son, fear thou Jehovah and the king," but with a significant alteration. Peter accepted that fear or reverential awe is the proper attitude toward God, but the proper attitude toward the king is honor. It was a distinction vital to a church confronted with the demand of emperor worship. But both of those responses were essential for the welfare of the Christian church: "The antinomian had to learn the fear of God, the zealot his duty to the king."[33]

33. Cook, p. 195.

12

C. The Duty of Submission in Household Relations
(2:18-25)

(18) Servants, *be* in subjection to your masters with all fear; not only to the good and gentle, but also to the froward. (19) For this is acceptable, if for conscience toward God a man endureth griefs, suffering wrongfully. (20) For what glory is it, if, when ye sin, and are buffeted *for it*, ye take it patiently? but if, when ye do well, and suffer *for it*, ye shall take it patiently, this is acceptable with God. (21) For hereunto were ye called: because Christ also suffered for you, leaving you an example, that ye should follow his steps: (22) who did no sin, neither was guile found in his mouth: (23) who, when he was reviled, reviled not again: when he suffered, threatened not; but committed *himself* to him that judgeth righteously: (24) who his own self bare our sins in his body upon the tree, that we, having died unto sins, might live unto righteousness; by whose stripes ye were healed. (25) For ye were going astray like sheep; but are now returned unto the Shepherd and Bishop of your souls.

In that paragraph the Christian duty of submission is pressed on a more restricted group, the slaves of the household. Since their status involved the most difficult relations of everyday life, the duty is portrayed with a marked increase of vividness and intensity. Christian slaves constituted a significant element in the early Christian churches (1 Cor. 7:21-23; Eph. 6:5-8; Col. 3:22-25). Lumby argues that "most of those whom" Peter addressed "were slaves."[1] In directing his exhortations to different groups within the churches Peter, unlike Paul, addressed slaves first. Peter did not discuss the existing institution of slavery; he gave instructions to the slaves of his day. His aim was to give comfort and guidance to suffering believers in the existing social situation.

1. J. Rawson Lumby, *The Epistles of St. Peter*, p. 699.

The institution of slavery "was a deeply rooted part of the economy and social structure of the ancient Near East and of the Graeco-Roman world."[2] In Rome and the larger cities of the empire, more than half of the total population in New Testament times were slaves. Conditions and treatment of slaves naturally varied greatly, but their lot in life was a lowly one and often very difficult. However, as Rupprecht warns, "one must be exceedingly careful not to assign the barbaric treatment of slaves by the Romans in the pre-Christian centuries to the early Christian era."[3] He cites evidence that the legal status of the slaves at that time was much improved.[4]

Like the other New Testament writers, Peter did not make a frontal attack on the institution of slavery, but he was keenly aware of the abuses it promoted. His heart went out to the ill-treated slaves and he honored them above other believers by reminding them that in a special way they had the opportunity of following the example of their suffering Savior. Christianity discouraged all violence and rebellion on their part, well aware that "where there is no inner freedom, outward freedom leads only to new slavery."[5] Its primary goal for the believing slave was not release from slavery but a Christ-like life (Rom. 14:7-8; 2 Cor. 5:15). As Kelly observes,

> It was the burning conviction of these early Christians that, through their fellowship with Christ, they had entered into a relationship of brotherhood with one another in which ordinary social distinctions, real enough in the daily round of life in the world, had lost all meaning (Gal. iii. 28; I Cor. xii. 13; Col. iii. 11; Phm. 8-18). . . . They were not so much concerned with natural ethics as with the ethics of the redeemed community.[6]

Peter did not stress the rights of the slave but his Christian responsibility. Slaves should not make their Christian liberty an excuse for evildoing (cf. 2:16). The conduct of the slave should not be governed by the character of his master, whether he be kindly or brutal, but by his own inner consciousness of his personal relationship to God.

In this weighty paragraph Peter stated the slaves' duty of submission to their masters (v. 18), asserted that such submissive suffering has God's approval (vv. 19-20), and motivated such suffering through a display of the sufferings of Christ (vv. 21-25).

1) THE DUTY OF SUBMISSION BY HOUSE-SERVANTS (V. 18)

"Servants" (*hoi oiketai*) indicates the specific group addressed. The articular plural apparently is the vocative of address, "Ye domestics" (Rotherham); but

---

2. A. Rupprecht, "Slave, Slavery," *ZPEB*, 5:453.
3. Ibid., p. 458.
4. Ibid., pp. 459-60.
5. H. L. Ellison, *1 and 2 Peter, 1, 2 and 3 John, Jude, Revelation*, p. 9.
6. J. N. D. Kelly, *A Commentary on the Epistles of Peter and of Jude*, p. 115.

it may be the subject of the verse with no verb expressed (cf. 3:1, 7). The absence of a connecting participle indicates the new subject.

Peter's term is not the usual word translated "servants." It occurs elsewhere in the New Testament only three times (Luke 16:13; Acts 10:7; Rom. 14:4). The term could be used to denote those in one's household, including the women and children, but generally it was used as synonymous with *doulos*, "slave."[7] It certainly has the latter connotation here, as also in its other New Testament occurrences. But the term "does not bring out and emphasize the servile relation so strongly as *doulos* does."[8] It points to slaves working in the household and thus standing in close relation to the family, "a house-servant, a domestic." The meaning of the term could include freedmen who continued to reside with their former masters, but the context as well as the other New Testament occurrences establishes that slaves are in view. Hart surmises that Peter chose the term "as suggesting the parallel between slaves and Christians who are God's household (ii. 5)."[9] As suggesting such a close household relationship, Peter's term is milder than the ordinary word "slave." Macknight asserts, "The slaves who were employed in the house were more exposed to suffering from the vices and bad temper of their masters, than those in the field."[10] But those employed in the fields were equally subject to capricious suffering at the hands of vicious masters.

The over-arching duty of those house-servants was to "*be* in subjection to your masters with all fear." As indicated by the italics, "*be* in subjection" (*hupotassomenoi*) is grammatically not an imperative but a single participle, marking a connection in thought with a preceding imperative. Some, like Fronmüller, believe that the simplest understanding is to connect the participle with the preceding imperatives in verse 17.[11] But the context favors the common view that in thought the participle relates back to the imperative, "be subject," in verse 13. In force, the participle may be viewed as a substitute for the imperative, but the construction used makes clear that the exhortation is dependent on a thought already expressed (see the similar construction in 3:1, 7-8). In the words of Lenski, "This is good Greek, the effect being to make all of these admonitions a continued chain by means of participles."[12]

The present participle indicates that it is the standing duty of slaves to submit themselves to the authority of their masters. "It is a built-in fact of life that in any society or organization, there must be authority on the one hand, and obedience to that authority on the other."[13] *Your masters* (*tois despotais*), the term from which we derive our word *despot*, is used in its usual secular

---

7. Henry George Liddell and Robert Scott, *A Greek-English Lexicon*, p. 1029.

8. Richard Chenevix Trench, *Synonyms of The New Testament*, p. 33.

9. J. H. A. Hart, *The First Epistle General of Peter*, p. 60.

10. James Macknight, *A New Literal Translation from the Original Greek of All the Apostolical Epistles*, 5:462.

11. G. F. C. Fronmüller, *The Epistles General of Peter*, p. 45.

12. R. C. H. Lenski, *The Interpretation of the Epistles of St. Peter, St. John and St. Jude*, p. 116.

13. William MacDonald, *I Peter: Faith Tested, Future Triumphant*, p. 55.

sense[14] to denote the master of the house as one who exercises absolute ownership and unlimited control over the things and persons in his household. Lenski observes, in the light of 2:13, that slavery "is only 'human' and not a divine arrangement. God did not institute slavery, men did that, but Christian slaves bow submissively to this human bondage."[15] But, as Cook points out, such submission "does not include evil compliance, such as was held by Roman legists to be a *duty* on the part of freedmen and of *necessity* on the part of slaves."[16]

Submission to their masters was to be given "with all fear" (*en panti phobō*). *Fear*, as in verse 17, is to be understood as meaning "fear of God" rather than servile fear of one's master, a cringing fear that submits to avoid punishment. As Christians they were to be motivated by fear or reverence for God that is concerned not to displease Him by failing to do their Christian duty toward their masters. *All* intensifies the thought; no half-hearted attitude will do. Such a fear-prompted submission stands in opposition to pretense or forced subjection. Such an attitude is constructive and, in the words of Wand, "gives the key to the right Christian attitude towards that ultimate residuum of physical and mental suffering from which none can hope to be exempt. Rebellion increases the trouble; resignation gives no spring of energy; willing acceptance for and in Christ develops the Christ-like character."[17]

Such an attitude should motivate the submission of slaves in all cases: "not only to the good and gentle, but also to the froward." That twofold classification shows that Peter had primarily heathen masters in view. It was comparatively easy to submit to masters who were good and gentle in character and action. *Good* (*agathois*) characterizes them as benevolent in their inner disposition and their treatment of their slaves; *gentle* (*epieikesin*) indicates their indulgent and sweet-tempered nature in dealing with failures. They were willing to moderate the harsh demands of the law according to circumstances. Peter assumed that there were such kindly masters.

Peter also knew that some masters were "froward" (*tois skoliois*), literally, "the crooked, bent," the opposite of straight. The figure aptly depicts their moral perversity; in their treatment of their slaves they deviated from what was right and just, being cruel and unfair in their reactions. Mason characterized them as "unreasonably exacting, capricious, and cross-grained."[18] Wuest suggests that they were probably irritated by the transformation in the conduct of the Christian slaves; it was a powerful testimony to the gospel.[19]

It is noteworthy that Peter, unlike Paul, had no words of instruction for Christian masters. That need not imply that there were no Christian masters

---

14. Karl Heinrich Rengstorf, *despotēs, TDNT*, 2:48.
15. Lenski, pp. 116-17.
16. F. C. Cook, *The First Epistle General of Peter*, p. 195.
17. J. W. C. Wand, *The General Epistles of St. Peter and St. Jude*, p. 80.
18. A. J. Mason, *The First Epistle General of Peter*, p. 408.
19. Kenneth S. Wuest, *First Peter in the Greek New Testament for the English Reader*, pp. 63-64.

in the assemblies addressed.[20] That there were no Christians in the Roman provinces to which his letter is directed who were wealthy enough to own slaves would be an unwarranted assumption (cf. 1 Tim. 6:17). Perhaps Peter did assume that Christian masters could for that reason be expected not to mistreat their slaves. The obvious explanation is to be found in Peter's purpose: "he is dwelling in this section of his epistle upon the Christian graces of submission and meekness."[21]

2) THE APPROVAL BY GOD OF SUBMISSIVE SUFFERING (VV. 19-20)

"For" introduces justification for the difficult demand for submission to cruel masters. In verse 19 Peter identified the kind of suffering that is assured of God's approval, and in verse 20 he distinguished two kinds of suffering, reminding those house-servants that it is only the latter kind that is assured of divine approval.

A. THE ASSURED ACCEPTABLENESS OF SUCH SUFFERING (v. 19)

"This is acceptable, if for conscience toward God a man endureth griefs, suffering wrongfully." The first class conditional sentence assumes that the indicated condition was being fulfilled. Such suffering was a reality to those house-servants. The two parts of the conditional sentence are reversed, placing the assurance emphatically at the beginning.

"This is acceptable" (*touto charis*) announces the true evaluation of the trying situation in view. The demonstrative neuter pronoun "this" summarizes the conduct described in the remainder of the verse. Such suffering is declared to be "acceptable" (*charis*), the noun commonly translated "grace." Its force is variously understood. In verse 20 Peter repeated the expression and for clearness and impressiveness added "with God" (*para theō*), "alongside God, in His presence." Some scholars believe that it is simpler and more forceful to translate "this is grace" and so understand Peter to mean either "this is a mark of grace," that is, it indeed shows that they were Christians, or "this is a gift of grace," a response so supernatural and God-like that the ability to endure could only have come from God. That view relates grace to the believer. But if it is correct, we would have expected Peter in verse 20 to have added *from God* (*para theou*), rather than "with God," which points to the divine regard for such suffering. The cast of thought in verses 19-20 favors the view that the reference is to another's evaluation of the believer's patient suffering. Peter's expression is probably to be regarded as "an abbreviation of the O.T. idiom *to find favor with God*."[22] The expression is reminiscent of Christ's language in

20. So Edward A. Maycock, *A Letter of Wise Counsel. Studies in the First Epistle of Peter*, p. 61. The churches at Ephesus and Colossae were within the scope of the churches addressed by Peter (cf. 1:1).

21. Charles R. Erdman, *The General Epistles*, p. 68.

22. Hart, p. 61.

Luke 6:32-34, where the same idiom is repeated three times and translated "What thanks have ye?" If we accept that nontechnical meaning for *grace*, Peter's words in verse 19 have the general meaning "This is a matter for thanks," and in verse 20 he added, "This is a matter of thanks before God;" it brings God's favor, or approval. It is obvious from verse 20 that the resultant approval is by God rather than the master.

The entire clause, "if for conscience toward God a man endureth griefs, suffering wrongfully," stands in apposition to *this* (*touto*) and makes explicit the kind of suffering that receives God's approval. *For conscience toward God (dia suneidēsin theou)* points out the motivating power for such conduct; the patient endurance of suffering is in itself not a matter worthy of thanks except as it is motivated by the sufferer's relation to God. Mason declared, "A resignation which comes from stolid want of feeling, or stoical fatalism, or from a sense that it is no good to seek redress—such resignation is sinfully defective."[23] It is the sense of the reality of God in life that gives Christian conduct its true moral value.

The exact force of the phrase "for conscience of God" has been differently understood. The compound term "conscience" (*suneidēsis*) means "with knowledge," and in the reflexive sense means "conscience," "the reflexive action of the mind, the mind's conference, so to speak, with itself."[24] In the New Testament, generally speaking, the term has the force of our word *conscience.*[25] If that is correct, then the added genitive, "of God," should be understood as objective, "conscience toward God"—a conscience that is aware of its accountability toward God. But such a knowledge of duty is not enough to enable anyone to accept undeserved suffering with patient endurance. The expression seems best understood in the sense of "consciousness of God," or "spiritual awareness of God."[26] The Christian servant's knowledge of God, shared with fellow believers, and his inner awareness of God's will and presence stimulates and enables him to endure such suffering. His enlightened conscience prompts him to accept that as his duty, but his personal awareness of God's approval enables him to do so. The indefinite pronoun *tis*, translated "a man," implies that such a response is not limited to the Christian house-slave but is for all believers.

The compound verb "endureth" (*hupopherei*) means "to bear up under" and conveys the picture of something sustaining a weight that is placed on it. The present tense conveys the thought of constancy, of not succumbing under the load. The load imposed is termed "griefs" (*lupas*), the plural pointing to the varied experiences of trouble and vexation that cause an inner feeling of grief.

"Suffering wrongfully" stresses Peter's evaluation of the moral nature of the sufferings in view. Those sufferings were primarily physical, as the next verse

---

23. Mason, p. 408.
24. Robert Johnstone, *The First Epistle of Peter*, p. 172.
25. See H. C. Hahn, "Conscience," *NIDNTT*, 1:348-53.
26. William F. Arndt and F. Wilbur Gingrich, *A Greek-English Lexicon of the New Testament*, p. 794.

indicates, but the moral element is stressed by the adverb "wrongfully" (*adikōs*), placed emphatically at the end of the sentence. The adverb, occurring only here in the New Testament, indicates that those sufferings were unjustly inflicted and morally undeserved. Peter knew that masters can act unjustly toward slaves. Aristotle, in his *Ethics* (v. 10. 8), taught that justice, in the proper sense of the word, did not exist between a man and his chattels: they were his own and he could do with them as he liked. But Peter refused to think of the slave as merely a living tool with no personal rights; he dignified him as a person with moral rights and responsibilities. Plumptre commented:

> Natural impulse, one might almost say natural ethics, sanctions the burning indignation and desire to retaliate which is caused by the sense of wrong. Here, as in the Sermon on the Mount (Matt. v. 39), which this teaching distinctly reproduces, that is made the crucial instance in which the Christian is to shew that the law of Christ is his rule of life.[27]

B. THE TRUE IDENTITY OF ACCEPTABLE SUFFERING (v. 20)

With "For" Peter frankly reminded those slaves that there is another side to the sufferings that they may have to endure. Two different kinds of suffering are described in two conditional sentences. The *if* clauses are arranged chiastically.[28]

There is suffering that is not praiseworthy: "What glory is it, if, when ye sin, and are buffeted *for it*, ye shall take it patiently?" The interrogative pronoun "what" (*poion*), "what kind of," indicates that there are sufferings that have little or no value for the teaching in view. The word "glory" (*kleos*), which does not occur elsewhere in the New Testament, does not denote the divine glory but points to the human reputation or fame acquired by a certain course of action. The reference is to the good opinion of men concerning an individual as the rumor or report about his conduct spreads. His action adds to his credit in the evaluation of others. The pursuit of reputation is not a distinctly Christian virtue and should generally be shunned as a specific aim; but Christians cannot be indifferent to the opinions of non-Christians toward them. Peter had just urged his readers to live in such a manner that false opinions about them would be refuted (2:12, 15). But the conduct depicted is valueless to produce such a result.

Two closely connected participles describe the suffering being reproved: *hamartonontes kai kolaphizomenoi*, "sinning and being buffeted" (R. Young). Both are in the present tense, describing a course of wrong-doing rather than an isolated instance. *Kai* (*and*) relates them as cause and effect. *Sinning* may not carry its full theological implication since in the next clause it is balanced by the term "doing well." It denotes a falling short of what is expected; but for

27. E. H. Plumptre, *The General Epistles of St Peter & St Jude*, p. 117.
28. The rhetorical figure in which the corresponding *if* clauses are placed crosswise to form the figure of an X, the Greek letter Chi.

the Christian, sin is involved since he fails to do what is God's will for him. Personal guilt is involved, too. Disobedience to the master's rightful commands has a logical result, "are buffeted," literally, "struck with the fist, beaten," and so mistreatment in general. Such beatings, expressing the master's ill-will toward the slave, were common occurrences. In Matthew 26:67 and Mark 14:65 the term is used of the abuse heaped on Jesus by the Jews the night before His crucifixion. In 2 Corinthians 12:7 the verb is used figuratively of a painful illness, pictured as a physical beating by a messenger of Satan.

The future verb "ye shall take it patiently" (*huomeneite*) is future in reference to the admonition given. The verb pictures the slave as remaining under the punishment justly inflicted. People do not naturally regard the endurance of deserved punishment as something meritorious. It is not the kind of suffering that receives divine approbation.

"But" (*all'*), a strong adversative, introduces a contrasted kind of suffering: "If, when ye do well, and suffer *for it*, ye take it patiently." Again, the experience is described by two closely related participles, *agathopoiountes kai paschontes* ("doing well and suffering"). The two terms denote characteristic actions and are best viewed as standing in a cause and effect relation. Their beneficent conduct aroused the master's anger. Johnstone pictures it as follows:

> It accords with universal experience that a brutal, low-minded master, irritated by that feeling of moral inferiority which was awakened in him by the sight of the virtuous conduct of his slave, might in many cases subject the slave to cruel treatment, professedly perhaps for some pretended fault, but really, as the slave himself, and everybody around knew, because of the well-doing.[29]

The switch from the impersonal "a man" (*tis*) in verse 19 to the personal "ye" indicates that Peter knew that his readers were undergoing such experiences.

The true evaluation of such suffering is placed emphatically at the end, "this is acceptable with God." *This is acceptable* must have the same meaning as in verse 19. The added words "with God" indicate that God's evaluation is in view. F. B. Meyer commented that whenever there is such suffering "there is a thrill of delight started through the very heart of God, and from the throne God stoops to say, *Thank you*."[30] It is an approbation that the most menial Christian servant can evoke.

3) THE MOTIVATION FROM THE EXAMPLE OF CHRIST (VV. 21-25)

With another confirmatory "for" Peter passed from duty to motivation with a graphic picture of the suffering Christ. In these verses there are numerous allusions to Isaiah 53, the prophetic portrait of the Suffering Servant of the

29. Johnstone, p. 174-75.
30. F. B. Meyer, *"Tried by Fire": Expositions of the First Epistle of Peter*, p. 101.

Lord.[31] Peter confirmed the call to submissive suffering by citing the example of Christ (v. 21), and then painted an elaborate picture of His exemplary and redemptive sufferings (vv. 22-25).

A. THE CALL TO SUFFER CONFIRMED BY CHRIST'S EXAMPLE (v. 21)

"Hereunto were ye called" (*eis touto eklēthēte*), "unto this ye were called," looks back to what has just been said. *Touto* ("this") has the same force as in verse 19, to suffer for and while doing good. "It is to this kind of living that you were called" (Williams). The verb looks back to the time of the reader's conversion and implies that God Himself acted in calling them to such a life. *Ye* is a direct reference to the house-servants being addressed. In calling them, God gave them a new dignity: to suffer as His people, and a new motivation: to follow the example of their Savior and spiritual Master. But since that call "applies to them not as slaves but as believers, it holds true at the same time of all Christians."[32] It is a clear reminder to all believers "that through many tribulations we must enter into the kingdom of God" (Acts 14:22). Jesus Himself repeatedly stressed that being His disciple involved cross-bearing (Matt. 10:38; 16:24; Luke 14:27).

"Because Christ also suffered for you" introduces a compelling motivation to accept suffering willingly while doing good. *Also* emphasizes the similarity between Christ's sufferings and those of Peter's readers. "Nothing seems more unworthy," Calvin observed, "and therefore less tolerable, than undeservedly to suffer, but when we turn our eyes to the Son of God, this bitterness is mitigated, for who would refuse to follow Him as He goes before us?"[33] The fact that Christ had Himself suffered undeservedly was an inherent element in the gospel message that they had received. That, and the fact that a servant is not above his Lord, strongly motivated them to accept similar sufferings. The fact that Christ had suffered "for you" (*huper humōn*)[34] made His example personal and compelling. The preposition *huper*, "over," in the context conveys the picture of Christ bending over the readers to shield them from danger and destruction. He acted for their good, their personal advantage. The preposition was also used to convey the thought of substitution, a truth brought out in the latter part of the picture (vv. 24-25).

"Leaving you an example, that ye should follow his steps" describes the abiding import of Christ's example. *You* (*humin*),[35] "to you," standing emphati-

---

31. For a convenient display of the parallels, see Archibald M. Hunter and Elmer G. Homrig-hausen, *The First Epistle of Peter*, p. 118.

32. Joh. Ed. Huther, *Critical and Exegetical Handbook to the General Epistles of Peter and Jude*, p. 138.

33. John Calvin, *The Epistle of Paul the Apostle to the Hebrews and the First and Second Epistles of St Peter*, p. 275.

34. The Textus Receptus reads *hēmōn*, "us," but modern textual editors hold that manuscript evidence and transcriptional probabilities support the second person, "ye," as original. For the evidence see the United Bible Societies, *The Greek New Testament*.

35. The Textus Receptus again reads the first person. See note 34.

cally forward, emphasizes the significance of His experience for those house-servants. His treatment as a much-abused slave made His example a standing inspiration for those who were mistreated. *Leaving (hupolimpanōn)*, "leaving behind," a verbal form found only here in the Greek Bible (NT and LXX),[36] implies that His exemplary experiences on earth terminated with His ascension, but the present tense indicates their abiding significance for His followers.

Christ left His followers "an example" *(hupogrammon)*, another rare term appearing only here in the Greek Bible, denoting a model to be copied by the novice. The term, literally an "underwriting," could refer to a writing or drawing that was placed under another sheet to be retraced on the upper sheet by the pupil. More probably, the reference is to the "copy-head" that the teacher placed at the top of the page to be reproduced by the student. It is also possible that the reference is to an artist's sketch, the details of which were to be filled in by others. According to each of those views, the example was not left merely to be admired but to be followed line by line, feature by feature.

"That ye should follow his steps" states the purpose of Christ's example. The explanation changes the figure: the example becomes the guide along a difficult way. *His steps*, elaborated in what follows, is the guide to direct the course of the Christian's life. Those footprints beckon him to follow. Those who have accepted Christ as Savior are challenged to follow His example. His footsteps lead into the valley of humiliation, even to its lowest and darkest depths; but they also surely and confidently lead through the valley, ending at the throne in glory.

"Follow" *(epakolouthēsēte)* translates a compound verb meaning "to follow upon, to devote oneself to" that which is followed, and so denotes a close and diligent following. The aorist tense denotes actual following. The preposition *epi*, "upon," does not literally mean *"in* his steps."[37] Nor does its use in Mark 16:20 and 1 Timothy 5:10 require that translation here. The force of the preposition apparently is not intensive, to "follow closely," but indicates the direction: Christians must follow the line Christ's footprints mark out. As failing human beings we cannot always place our feet fully in His footprints; but, though falling short, we can follow where His tracks lead.[38] In his work on *Patience*, Tertullian (c. A.D.160/170—215/220) developed at some length the various aspects of Christ's patient sufferings and concluded, "Patience such as this no mere man had ever practiced!"[39] Sinful men need more than a perfect example; they first of all need a Savior.

---

36. It is a by-form for *hupoleipo*, which occurs in the LXX as well as the N.T.

37. So in NASB, NIV, RSV, TEV, NEB, Rotherham, Darby, 20th Cent., Weymouth, Montgomery, Berkeley, Kleist and Lilly. "Follow his steps"—KJV, R. Young, Moffatt, Goodspeed, Williams. "Follow the way he took"—JB.

38. "Like a little boy following his father through the snow. The father takes far too long steps for the boy to step in them, but he can go the same way his father went," J. Niebor, *Practical Exposition of I Peter*, p. 168.

39. Tertullian, *Patience*, ch. 3, p. 197.

B. THE PORTRAYAL OF CHRIST'S SUFFERINGS (vv. 22-25)

Four successive relative clauses skillfully develop the picture of Christ's sufferings. In verses 22-23 the focus is on His exemplary sufferings, and in verses 24-25 His redemptive sufferings are described.

(1) The Exemplary Sufferings of Christ (vv. 22-23). The portrayal of the model sufferer is both negative and positive. Four features declare what He did not do (vv. 22-23a), and one fundamental feature marks what He did do (v. 23b). He is the perfect example in both areas.

(a) *What He did not do* (vv. 22-23a). The first relative clause portrays the unmerited nature of His suffering. "Who did no sin" asserts His innocence in conduct. The aorist tense (*epoiēsen*) indicates that not in a single instance did He succumb to an act of sin. Peter knew that Christ had been assailed by the Tempter, but never once had He fallen short of the divine standard. That testimony, by one who was closely associated with Jesus during His entire earthly ministry, cannot lightly be set aside. In 1:19 Peter affirmed Christ's unblemished character. Here he drew attention to His unique, sinless conduct. Christ's sinlessness is explicitly declared in 2 Corinthians 5:21; Hebrews 4:15; 7:26; and 1 John 3:5, is asserted by Christ Himself in John 8:46 and 14:30, and is verified by the testimony of history. He demonstrated that sinlessness under the most intense provocation and undeserved suffering.

Neither were His sufferings due to sinful speech; "neither was guile found in his mouth." "Sinlessness as to the *mouth* is a mark of perfection"[40] (cf. James 3:2). The verb "found" (*heurethē*), stronger than "was," indicates that His speech passed the most rigorous scrutiny of His enemies. No evidence of guile (see 2:1), so characteristic of fallen man, could be detected in His words. That confirmed His purity of heart (Matt. 12:34-35). And it was that aspect of Christ's example that was "particularly applicable to slaves in the empire, where glib, deceitful speech was one of their notorious characteristics, adroit evasions and excuses being often their sole means of self-protection."[41] Christian slaves were reminded that in their trials they should look to the Lord Jesus and strive to copy His innocence and truth.

The second relative clause depicts Christ's patient endurance; it describes two negative features of it (v. 23a), in word and in action. Both statements are alike in structure, a present participle that pictures the scene taking place, followed by an imperfect indicative that permits us to contemplate Christ's resolute refusal to engage in the kind of response contemplated. Both are further manifestations of His uniqueness.

---

40. Robert Jamieson, A. R. Fausset, and David Brown, *A Commentary, Critical and Explanatory, on the Old and New Testaments,* 2:506.

41. James Moffatt, *The General Epistles, James, Peter, and Judas,* p. 127.

"Who, when he was reviled, reviled not again" (*hos loidoroumenos ouk anteloidorei*) may more literally be translated, "who being reviled was not reviling again" (Rotherham). Though none of the gospels employs that verb of the experiences of Jesus, they do record various occasions when He was reviled, was abused by having bitter and vicious words hurled against Him. His enemies "said he was possessed with a devil. They called him a Samaritan, a glutton, a wine-bibber, a blasphemer, a demoniac, one in league with Beelzebub, a perverter of the nation, and a deceiver of the people."[42] Though the present participle makes room for all those varied charges, it seems that Peter specifically focused on the scenes during Christ's trials and crucifixion —events during which the normal human urge to "revile again" (*anteloidorei*) would be especially strong. The use of the compound form creates a wordplay not found elsewhere in the Greek Scriptures. When our Lord at times did speak in severe words to His bitter opponents (cf. Matt. 23), He was not simply returning abuse for abuse but was seeking to convict them of their error. What He said was never a mere outburst of personal hatred against His detractors.

"When he suffered, threatened not" (*paschōn ouk ēpeilei*), "suffering, he was not threatening," heightens His negative response in His reactions. Though the linear action of the verbal forms may be understood of His habitual conduct, the Passion scenes seem clearly in view. He was subjected to severe physical sufferings: He was struck in His face, crowned with thorns, beaten with a reed, scourged, forced to bear His own cross, and crucified. Yet through it all He never threatened retaliation on His tormentors, nor even predicted that they would be punished for it. Some of the early Christian martyrs could not resist the natural urge to threaten their executioners with divine punishment. Even the apostle Paul, on one occasion, when abused in court, did not resist the temptation (Acts 23:3). Mistreated slaves at times threatened revenge in some near or distant future.

Peter's picture of what Jesus did not do was molded by his memory of the teaching in Isaiah 53:6-7. Yet he did not quote those verses but gave his own confirmatory witness, thereby underlining the veracity of the prophetic picture.

> (b) *What He did do* (v. 23b). "But" (*de*) does not function to introduce a contrast to preceding material so much as it introduces a new statement of the subject in a positive form. He "committed *himself* to him that judgeth righteously." The phrase gathers up the essence of His positive response to unjust suffering. He did so repeatedly as injustice after injustice was being heaped on Him. "Committed" (*paredidou*), "to hand over," was commonly used of delivering up a criminal to police or court for punishment (Matt. 26: 14-16; Mark 14:41-42; John 19:11, 16). Here it indicates Christ's own action of handing over or committing to, with the dative of the one to whom the commitment is made. The form is active, not reflexive, but no object of

42. Macknight, p. 464.

what is committed is added. Rotherham reflects the lack of a stated object by translating, "was making surrender unto him that judgeth righteously." Different suggestions about the implied object have been made. Various commentators[43] and versions[44] agree that *himself* is the intended object. That is consistent with the nature of Peter's example, the Passion story, the explicit use of the verb in Galatians 2:20 and Ephesians 5:2, 25, and offers a parallel to the case of the suffering slaves being addressed. It is also possible to supply "his cause"[45] in keeping with the following reference to the righteous judge. Kelly, who finds support for that formula in Jeremiah 11:20 and in Josephus (*Antiquities*, 4.33; 7.199) asserts, "The point is, not that the Lord was concerned about His own fate, but that, confident though He was of His righteousness, He preferred to leave its vindication to God rather than take action Himself against His enemies."[46] If that is correct, then the message to the suffering servants was that they should avoid all retaliation because of unjust treatment and leave matters in the hands of a just God. Less likely is the suggestion of Alford that *them*, that is, His enemies, should be supplied. He saw support for that in the prayer of Jesus on the cross, "Father, forgive them" (Luke 23:34).[47]

The active voice of the verb "committed" indicates that that was the deliberate, volitional response of Jesus. And it is precisely here that suffering believers can truly walk *in* His steps. As failing mortals they cannot fully place their feet in His sinless footprints, but by His grace they can resolutely determine to follow His example of unreservedly committing themselves to God in all circumstances.

Christ committed Himself "to him that judgeth righteously" (*tō krinonti dikaiōs*), the One characterized as the righteous Judge.[48] In 1:17 Peter described God as impartial in His judgments, judging "without respect of persons." His judgments are the outcome of His character. He judges righteously in full conformity to the standard of truth and holiness. Christ could therefore, with full assurance, commit His vindication into God's hands. Stibbs suggests another aspect of that commitment: "Because voluntarily, and

43. So Bigg, Lenski, Beare, Stibbs, and others.
44. "Himself"—KJV, NASB, NIV, R. Young, Darby, 20th Cent., Berkeley, Kleist and Lilly.
45. "His cause"—NEB, Weymouth, Montgomery. "His case"—Goodspeed, Williams; "everything"—Moffatt.
46. Kelly, p. 121.
47. Henry Alford, *The Greek New Testament*, vol. 4 (part 1), p. 354.
48. The Vulgate has the singular reading "to him that judged Him unjustly," as though the Greek adverb were negative, *adikos*. The reading has no manuscript evidence to support it and deserves mention only because of its peculiarity. According to that reading the reference is to Pilate.

in fulfillment of God's will, He was taking the sinner's place and bearing sin, He did not protest at what He had to suffer. Rather, He consciously recognized that it was the penalty righteously due to sin."[49]

(2) *The redemptive sufferings of Christ* (vv. 24-25). The third relative clause brings the reader to the topic of Christ's redemptive sufferings. For Peter, a picture of the suffering Christ would be fatally incomplete without that truth. "Christ was not only a Model but a Mediator."[50] At the heart of the gospel is the message that our salvation was accomplished through His atoning work. But Christ's sufferings for sin have practical implications for believers.

Peter declared the nature of Christ's redemptive sufferings (v. 24a), indicated their redemptive purpose (v. 24b), and concluded with the resultant experiences of the redeemed (vv. 24c-25).

(a) *The nature of His redemptive sufferings* (v. 24a). "Who his own self bare our sins in his body upon the tree" declares the essence of those sufferings. Our sins are closely related to His sufferings. *Our sins* stands emphatically forward, and *his own self* stresses His personal identity: *hos tas hamartias hēmōn autos anēnegken*, "who our sins himself bare up." The sins of mankind in all ages made necessary those sufferings. *Sin* is "the most comprehensive term for moral obliquity" in the New Testament.[51] It portrays a falling short of the target, missing the mark, and thus characterizes sin as a falling short of God's standard and purpose for our lives. But in the New Testament the concept is not merely negative; it also involves a positive element of willful disobedience to the known will of God. The plural "sins" (*tas hamartias*) indicates the multitudes of sins committed. *Our* (*hēmōn*) is confessional; Peter united himself with his readers in acknowledging his own share in the mass of sins.

Those sins He, "his own self" (*autos*), bore on the cross. Alone, He suffered to deal with those sins: "there being *none other but Himself* who could have done it."[52] Unlike the imperfects in verse 23, *bare* (*anēnegken*) is an aorist—a definite event, not a repeated practice. The verb means "to carry up," to bring from a lower place to a higher, and is a ritual term. In the Septuagint it is used of bringing a sacrifice and laying it upon the altar (Gen. 8:20; Lev. 14:20; 17:5; 2 Chron. 35:16; etc.). In James 2:21 it is used of Abraham bringing his son Isaac up to the altar. Clearly, Isaiah 53:12 was in Peter's mind, "he bare the sins of many." Peter's thought centered on the final sacrificial act, not the preparatory bringing up. But he did not imply that our sins were the sacrifice that Christ laid upon the altar, an impossible thought, since nothing unholy could be

49. Alan M. Stibbs, *The First Epistle General of Peter*, p. 119.
50. Charles S. Ball, *First and Second Peter*, p. 263.
51. W. E. Vine, *An Expository Dictionary of New Testament Words*, 4:32.
52. Jamieson, Fausset, and Brown, p. 2:506.

offered to God as a sacrifice. Rather, Christ Himself, the sinless One (2:22), was so identified with our sins that as our substitute He bore the consequences of our sins. "He took the blame for them; suffered the 'curse' of them (cf. Deut. xxi. 23, quoted in Gal. iii. 13), which is separation from God; and endured their penal consequences."[53] "Him who knew no sin he made *to be* sin on our behalf" (2 Cor. 5:21*a*). In fulfillment of Isaiah 53, "Jehovah hath laid on him the iniquity of us all" (v. 6), "made his soul an offering for sin" (v. 10) as "he poured out his soul unto death" and "bare the sin of many" (v. 12). His death was not that of a heroic martyr dying for a rejected cause; it was redemptive and substitutionary in nature.

"In his own body" does not mean that His redemptive sufferings were limited to His body in contrast to His soul. His body was the means through which his self-sacrifice was accomplished (Heb. 10:5). The crucifixion scene was naturally described with reference to His body that was suspended on the cross. The One who suffered on that cross was no docetic Christ who only seemed to have a human body. The mention of His body ties those redemptive sufferings to the incarnate Christ of history.

"Upon the tree" is a typical Petrine expression for the cross (cf. Acts 5:30; 10:39). *Tree* (*xulon*), "wood," or "made of wood," can denote a wooden instrument used for punishment, whether stocks for the feet (Acts 16:24) or a wooden beam on which a criminal was suspended, as here. Plumptre suggested that Peter "in writing to slaves, may have chosen it as bringing home to their thoughts the parallelism between Christ's sufferings and their own."[54] But Peter apparently preferred the term because in the light of Deuteronomy 21:22-23 (cf. Gen. 46:19; Josh. 10:26) it implied that the One thus suspended on wood was under a curse (Gal. 3:13). It involved the deep shame of implied criminality. He expiated the curse of sin on the cross in our stead.

> (b) *The purpose of His redemptive sufferings* (v. 24*b*). There was a glorious practical purpose behind those sufferings: "that we, having died unto sins, might live unto righteousness." The negative aspect relates to the believer's sinful past, and the positive depicts God's purpose for his present life. An experiential realization of the former makes possible a vital personal entry upon the latter.

"Having died unto sins" looks back to the time of the readers' conversion. The word translated "having died" (*apogenomeoni*) occurs only here in the New Testament and not at all in the Septuagint. Its root meaning is "to be off from, to have no part in" something; in classical writers it was used to mean "cease to exist" as a euphemism for death. The dative "sins" (*tais hamartiais*) indicates the relationship that has been terminated: "to have ceased in relation to the sins." The plural denotes the various sins in our past, those for which Christ died. In our union with Christ, whose death effected the termination of

---

53. Edward Gordon Selwyn, *The First Epistle of St. Peter*, p. 180.
54. Plumptre, p. 119.

sin's guilt and domination, we have been freed from the demands of sin upon us (Rom. 6:2; Col. 3:3). In Him the power of the tyranny of sin in our lives has been broken, enabling us to conquer sin and by the indwelling Spirit to claim our liberation (Rom. 6:11; 8:12-13).

Redemption from sin is intended to have a practical effect in daily life, "that we . . . might live unto righteousness." Peter's word order, (tō dikaiosunē zēsōmen), "to the righteousness we might live" (R. Young), makes prominent the new relationship in that life. The goal of the new life is "the righteousness," the righteousness that God's righteousness and holiness require in His people and that the indwelling Holy Spirit works in and through them. The singular, "righteousness," in contrast to the plural, "the sins," implies the unitary nature of the new life, marked by daily submissive obedience to God and His will. That (hina), with the aorist subjunctive, "should live," means that the redeemed should actually live righteous lives. Only thus is the full purpose of the cross realized.

> (c) The result of His redemptive sufferings (vv. 24c-25). The fourth relative clause, "by whose stripes ye were healed," states the result of the Redeemer's sufferings in the experience of the redeemed. The words are an allusion to Isaiah 53:5, "with his stripes we are healed," but the change to the second person, "ye," brings the whole picture sharply back to its application to the suffering servants.

The reference to the means of healing, "by whose stripes," touched a tender cord in the hearts of the slaves. Their Lord's experience of such great ignominy poignantly appealed to many of their personal experiences. Stripes (mōlōps) means the bruise or bloody welt that results from a sharp blow to the flesh. The noun, used only here in the New Testament, is singular and is best viewed as collective. The literal reference is to the scourging that Christ endured, but possibly the picture is to be understood to include all the sufferings that terminated in His death. McNab suggests that the singular term "is used figuratively of the stroke of divine judgment administered vicariously to Christ on the cross."[55]

By Christ's stripes the wounds that sin had inflicted on the souls of Peter's readers "were healed" (iathēte), not merely will be healed. The forgiveness of sins in regeneration marked the experience of imparted spiritual wholeness. Such healing must be received from the divine Healer; spiritual self-healing from the wounds of sin is a delusion. Peter's words involve a striking paradox, well summed up by Theodoret (c. A.D.393-458) in his oft-quoted exclamation: "A new and strange method of healing; the doctor suffered the cost, and the sick received the healing!"

The context indicates that the reference is not to the healing of physical sickness or disease. The passage cannot be used to teach that bodily healing is available in the atonement, as salvation from sin is found at the cross.

---

55. Andrew McNab, The General Epistles of Peter, p. 1136.

The conjunction "for" (*gar*, v. 25) is explanatory; it reveals how and from what state the readers came to their experience of spiritual healing. *Ye were going astray like sheep* pictures their former lost condition. The explanation changes the figure; the reference to straying sheep is an allusion to Isaiah 53:6, "All we like sheep have gone astray." But *ye* applied the figure to the slaves, no longer characterized as slaves but as ordinary fallen sinners. Possibly Peter also had in mind the Lord's picture in Matthew 9:36. The comparison of sinners to straying sheep is a common biblical figure. It is not a complimentary comparison since sheep are notoriously dull, prone to stray, and helpless to find their way back. Straying sheep, lost in the wilderness or mountains and exposed to wild beasts and destruction, present a wretched picture of the needy state of the lost. If the figure of straying is pressed to imply the original union of the sheep with its master, the straying portrays mankind's alienation from God through the Fall.

"But" (*alla*), a strong adversative, indicates the decisive change that has taken place. Peter's readers "are now returned unto the Shepherd and Bishop of your souls." *Now* (*nun*) emphasizes the contrast between their past and present states.[56] *Are returned* (*epestraphēte*), "were turned about," records their conversion. They were headed in the wrong direction, away from God, but they were arrested and turned about. *Returned* does "not mean that they were once walking with Him and have now resumed doing so after an interruption. It means that inasmuch as their former wandering was leading them away from Him, they have now turned completely towards Him."[57] Best remarks that the expression implies "that the natural place for the sheep is in the flock with the shepherd and that the readers by their conversion and baptism have found this place."[58]

Their conversion brought them "unto the Shepherd and Bishop of your souls." They had been brought into personal union with "the Shepherd and Bishop" (*ton poimena kai episkopon*), one individual identified under two related aspects. The reference to the readers as sheep naturally calls forth the shepherd image of the One with whom they were happily related. In the Old Testament the figure of "shepherd" was at times used of the leaders of Israel (Jer. 23:1-4; Ezek. 34:1-10; 37:24; Zech. 11:17); at other times it is used of Jehovah (Pss. 23:1; 80:1; Isa. 40:11). In the New Testament it is a familiar figure for Christ (Mark 14:27; John 10:1-18; Heb. 13:20; 1 Pet. 5:4; Rev. 7:17). Though some, like Mitchell, refer the figure to "God the Father,"[59] the natural reference is to Christ who performs the functions of the shepherd in relation to His sheep. In 5:4 Peter called Him "the chief Shepherd."

The term "Bishop" (*episkopon*), used of Christ only here in the New Testament, is closely related to "Shepherd." Derived from the verb *episkopeō*,

---

56. Any suggestion that "now" implies that the reference is to new converts being baptized is not justified by the context.

57. Wand, p. 84.

58. Ernest Best, *I Peter*, p. 123.

59. A. F. Mitchell, *Hebrews and the General Epistles*, p. 257.

which means "to look at, to care for, to oversee," the noun designates one who inspects and keeps watch over, hence an "overseer."[60] In the New Testament the term is used in close association with the shepherd or pastoral function (Acts 20:28; 1 Tim. 3:2; 1 Pet. 5:2-4). The verb and its cognates "stress active and responsible care for that which has been seen."[61] The double designation assured the afflicted readers of Christ's care for His own. He not only leads, feeds, and sustains His own, but also guides, directs, and protects them.

He is the Shepherd and Bishop "of your souls" (*tōn psuchōn humōn*), their true inner selves (cf. 1:9, 22). Their bodies may have been subject to the power and caprice of harsh masters, but their inner life was under the constant watchcare of their Great Shepherd.

The rich development of Peter's message can only leave the reader with a strong assurance of "the overflowing fullness of the Christian message. . . . The Apostle starts his paragraph with a counsel to domestics on their behavior; he ends with these rich splendours of the evangel. . . . It is the glory of Christianity not only that it is divine: it brings the divine to our level. It works in clay, and transfigures it. It touches duty, and transforms it."[62]

---

60. Modern versions avoid the term "Bishop." Some have "Overseer"—NIV, Rotherham, R. Young, Darby, Williams. Others prefer "Guardian"—NASB, RSV, NEB, 20th Cent., Weymouth, Moffatt, Goodspeed, Montgomery, Berkeley, JB, Kleist and Lilly. TEV has "keeper."
61. L. Coenen, "Bishop, Presbyter, Elder," *NIDNTT*, 1:189.
62. J. M. E. Ross, *The First Epistle of Peter*, p. 125.

13

D. The Duty of Submission in Marital Relations
(3:1-7)

(1) In like manner, ye wives, *be* in subjection to your own husbands; that, even if any obey not the word, they may without the word be gained by the behavior of their wives; (2) beholding your chaste behavior *coupled* with fear. (3) Whose *adorning* let it not be the outward adorning of braiding the hair, and of wearing jewels of gold, or of putting on apparel; (4) but *let it be* the hidden man of the heart, in the incorruptible *apparel* of a meek and quiet spirit, which is in the sight of God of great price. (5) For after this manner aforetime the holy women also, who hoped in God, adorned themselves, being in subjection to their own husbands: (6) as Sarah obeyed Abraham, calling him lord: whose children ye now are, if ye do well, and are not put in fear by any terror.

(7) Ye husbands, in like manner, dwell with *your wives* according to knowledge, giving honor unto the woman, as unto the weaker vessel, as being also joint-heirs of the grace of life; to the end that your prayers be not hindered.

The theme of Christian submission is now applied to the marriage relation, the most intimate and restricted human relationship. That relation involves one of the most fundamental aspects of the Christian life. In addressing wives and husbands, Peter did not stress the rights of each partner but the duties that are to be discharged in their relations to each other. This section of 1 Peter has parallels in Ephesians 5:22-33, Colossians 3:18-19, and Titus 2:4-5,[1] though in the last instance there is no mention of the duties of husbands.

---

1. The instructions for Christian men and women in 1 Tim. 2:8-15 appear in a context regulating assembly worship.

More space is devoted to Christian wives because many of them had husbands who were indifferent or opposed to the Christian faith. No specific group of members in the churches was more in need of understanding, warm encouragement, and wise spiritual counsel. The social status of the wife in the Roman provinces addressed often left much to be desired; when the wife accepted a new "religion" apart from her husband, that action generally produced acute problems for her. Peter's primary concern was not to improve the social status of wives; his concern was to offer the Christian wife a strategy that would enable her to avoid violence, disarm the opposition of her unbelieving husband, and lead him to Christ. Counterbalancing his compassionate suggestions to the wives of non-Christian husbands (vv. 1-6), Peter added a concise directive to Christian husbands (v. 7).

1) THE SUBMISSION OF THE WIVES (VV. 1-6)

"In like manner" (*homoiōs*) implies that the paragraph is another in a series devoted to the subject of Christian submission. That adverb does not imply that the submission of wives to their husbands is comparable to the submission of slaves to their masters. But it does indicate that submission of the wife is as much a sacred duty as the submission of the slave. Both are to submit from the same motive: the mastery of their lives by the redemptive love of Christ their Lord.

"Ye wives" indicates the recipients of Peter's instruction. The use of the definite article (*hai gunaikes*)[2] is textually uncertain. Some important manuscripts omit it, making the designation qualitative, "such as are wives, not slaves."[3] Positionally, they form a unique group. Peter indicated their duty to submit to their husbands (v. 1a) and the saving import of such submission for unsaved husbands (v. 1b), advised wives concerning their personal adornment (vv. 3-4) and cited past examples of such (vv. 5-6a), and pointed out the significance of godly submission for those addressed (v. 6b).

A. THE ACCEPTED DUTY OF THE WIFE'S SUBMISSION (v. 1a)

The present participle, continuing the construction of 2:18, indicates that the wife's submission to her husband is her assumed duty. Peter did not question that view, whose roots are in the Garden of Eden (Gen. 2-3). Paul grounded it in the order of creation, as well as the Fall (1 Tim. 2:9-15). It is a matter of administration and in no way implies the inferiority of the wife. The home,

---

2. See the evidence in Nestle-Aland, *Novum Testamentum Graece* (26th. ed.), which has the article in brackets. The article was omitted in the editions of Westcott and Hort, Souter, Nestle and Aland (24th ed.), and Tasker. The editions of the United Bible Societies Greek text have it in brackets. The Textus Receptus reads it without question as carried by the majority of the Greek manuscripts. Editorial omission of the article is based largely on its absence in the uncials *Aleph*, *A*, and *B*.

3. R. C. H. Lenski, *The Interpretation of the Epistles of St. Peter, St. John and St. Jude*, pp. 129-30.

like every human institution, to operate effectively must have a head, someone who is the final authority. God assigned that position to the husband. But Scripture and human history alike confirm that "the moment we divorce the thought of subjection from that of affection, we have lost its God-given significance."[4] The divine pattern and spiritual motivation for the voluntary submission of the Christian wife to the authority of her husband is profoundly explained in Ephesians 5:22-33. Wherever the love of Christ holds sway in the lives of both husband and wife, her submission to her husband will be an occasion of deep joy, not one of grief and groaning.

"To your own husbands" (*tois idiois andrasin*) indicates the close ties between husband and wife. *Own* (*idiois*), "one's own," underlines the private and unique relationship established by the marriage tie. The closeness and exclusiveness of her relation to her husband should motivate the wife's submission. Fronmüller believed the term meant that Peter would remind them "of the duty of chastity, and warn them of all suspicious obedience to strange men."[5] It is unwarranted to eliminate the note of exclusiveness in the term and to make Peter mean "your husbands."[6] Though Peter's expression guards against the suggestion that he called for a general subjection of women to men, his use of *own* underlines the legitimacy (cf. 1 Cor. 7:13) and exclusiveness (1 Cor. 7:2) of the marriage tie.

B. THE SAVING IMPACT OF THE WIFE'S SUBMISSION (v. 1b-2)

Peter taught that it is the duty of the Christian wife to submit to the authority of her husband whether or not he is saved (cf. vv. 5-6). That submission acquires a saving significance if the husband is not a Christian: "that, even if any obey not the word, they may without the word be gained by the behavior of their wives" (v. 1b). The purpose clause, *that* (*hina*), "in order that," indicates that under that undesirable condition her submission assumes an evangelistic function. Though Peter gave no absolute assurance that such a husband would be saved, he extended that hope as a real possibility. *Even if* (*kai ei*) shows that not all Christian wives face that distressing situation, but the conditional construction indicates that many of them do (cf. Acts 16:1-2; 17:4). According to Peter, such a situation was not the result of a Christian woman marrying an unbeliever (cf. 2 Cor. 6:14); it was the result of the wife in a pagan marriage becoming a Christian. Peter did not accept that her conversion dissolved the marriage.

"If any obey not the word" describes those cases where the husbands persistently reject the call of *the word*, a technical designation for the Christian gospel. Either during public evangelistic meetings or visits by the missionary to the home, both husband and wife had been confronted with the call of the gospel of Christ. The wife experienced its saving power by faith,

---

4. Tom Westwood, *The Epistles of Peter*, p. 91.
5. G. F. C. Fronmüller, *The Epistles General of Peter*, p. 52.
6. J. N. D. Kelly, *Commentary on the Epistles of Peter and of Jude*, p. 127.

but the husband continued to reject the message. The negative verb *obey not* (*apeitheousin*), literally, "to be unpersuaded," portrays those who deliberately and persistently set themselves against the claims of the gospel. According to 1 Peter 2:8, to persist in such a refusal is fatal. Because the early Christians believed that the supreme act of disobedience was to refuse to submit to the truth of the gospel, some interpreters propose that the term simply denotes an unbeliever.[7] It is more forceful, however, to accept the verb's full meaning (cf. Acts 14:2; Heb. 3:18; 11:31). Such an antagonistic attitude toward the gospel created great difficulty for Christian wives, but Peter assured them that the situation was not hopeless.

The wife was ordinarily expected to follow the religion of her husband. If she alone accepted the gospel, she thereby placed herself in a very difficult situation. Peter, therefore, proposed a strategy to win those husbands: "that they may without the word be gained by the behavior of their wives; beholding your chaste behavior *coupled* with fear" (vv. 1*b*-2). Peter's word order indicates that the wife's behavior is an effective evangelistic means: "in order that . . . through the wives' behaviour, without a word, they will be gained." *Behavior* (*anastrophē*), translated "manner of living" in 1 Peter 1:15, denotes the deportment of the Christian wives in all the daily affairs of life. As in 1 Peter 2:12, Peter believed in the power of Christian example. The gracious submission and Christlike conduct of the wife, prompted by faith and love, may be able to achieve that which the spoken word of the evangelist is not able to do.

"Without the word" (*aneu logou*) does not mean that the husband's conversion will be affected apart from the Word of the gospel; it alone is God's regenerating agent (1 Pet. 1:22; James 1:18). Used without the definite article, *word* denotes the oral pleas of the wife. If the husband will not yield to the authoritative spoken word of the gospel, he may be reached by the wife's silent demonstrations of its transforming power in her daily conduct. Instead of trying to coax and argue her husband into becoming a Christian, she will be more effective by quietly living out its saving power before him. His conscience will be forced to admit the presence of a divine power in her faith that he has often mocked.

Such a Spirit-powered strategy gives wives the comforting hope that their husbands "may be gained" (*kerdēthēsontai*),[8] "will be gained" in that way. The future tense portrays the result in relation to the time when the wife adopts the recommended strategy. *Gained* denotes much more than the husband's conciliation to her faith; his conversion is not only a gain for her but also for Christ and His church. In 1 Corinthians 9:19-22 Paul repeatedly used that verb in the sense of winning converts to Christ. The expression shows the value of the individual soul saved from eternal death. In that manner the wife would

---

7. William F. Arndt and F. Wilbur Gingrich, *A Greek-English Lexicon of the New Testament and Other Early Christian Literature*, p. 82.

8. In Koine Greek the future indicative may follow *hina* in a final clause (A. T. Robertson, *A Grammar of the Greek New Testament in the Light of Historical Research*, p. 984).

have the joy of being the personal agent of her husband's salvation. The story of Monica (A.D. 331-387), the mother of the noted Augustine, is a perfect illustration of Peter's teaching.[9]

"Beholding your chaste behavior *coupled* with fear" (v. 2) explains how the victory will be achieved. The strategy closely involves the wife in her husband's conversion. *Beholding (epopteusantes)*, as in 1 Peter 2:12, draws attention to the husband's close, eyewitness observation of the daily conduct of his wife. His attention to the gospel would be won through the eye rather than the ear. *Beholding*, an aorist active participle, is grammatically related to the plural subject of the verb, "they may be gained," thus specifying the husband's part in the process. The aorist tense, which summarily records the process of his observation without indicating its duration, denotes action slightly preceding the action in the verb; his observation preceded and led to his conversion. The aorist tense, which may more exactly be translated, "having beheld" (a past fact), "sets us at the moment of the triumph of the wife's conduct."[10] Today, when words seem impotent, the power of the living Word still changes lives.

According to Peter, the husband's attention was captured by "your chaste behavior *coupled* with fear." *Your behavior* indicates that the wives are in view. Their manner of life (cf. 1:15, 18; 2:12) is described by two terms that portray their conduct. *With fear (en phobō)* may refer to the wife's reverential awe toward her husband, to her deep concern to show proper respect and not to be remiss in any duty.[11] But it is more likely that the reference is to her reverence toward God (cf. 1:17; 2:17), an essential ingredient of a holy life, that which offers strength and motivation for daily conduct.

The wife's conduct is also characterized as *chaste (hagnen)*, "pure" or "holy." The concept is not to be limited to sexual chastity; it denotes that purity in character and conduct that should characterize all of the Christian life (Phil. 4:8; 1 Tim. 5:22; Titus 2:5; James 3:17; 1 John 3:3). It is a positive quality, "innocence refined by testing."[12] Such a life will not fail to convince the pagan husband of the reality of the Christian message and will awaken in him a sense of his own need of the gospel.

C. THE TRUE ADORNMENT OF THE SUBMISSIVE WIFE (vv. 3-4)

With a relative clause Peter's thought moved from the general conduct of wives to their personal adornment. He knew that his strategy for winning unsaved husbands raised the issue of the wives' making themselves attractive to their husbands. His use of the relative "whose" (*hōn*), "of whom," gives his teaching on that topic an impersonal tone. The present imperative "let it be" (*estō*) characterizes that teaching as authoritative guidance. As the italics

9. Augustine, *The Confessions of Saint Augustine*, pp. 143-45.
10. A. J. Mason, *The First Epistle of St. Peter*, 6:259.
11. E. M. Zerr, *Bible Commentary*, 6:259.
12. William Evans, *Peter, The Epistles of "The Living Hope,"* p. 30.

indicate, the translation of the ASV, "whose *adorning* let it not be the outward adorning . . . but *let it be* the hidden man of the heart," is not strictly literal, since neither the verb "be" nor "adorning" are repeated. The exhortation is in two antithetical parts, but the precise form is not easily expressed in translation. The negative aspect of the exhortation in verse 3 has "the outward adorning" and its modifiers as the subject, and "the hidden man" is the subject of the positive aspect (v. 4). We may translate very literally, "whose let be, not the outward adorning of braiding of hair and of placing around things of gold nor of putting on of garments, but the hidden man of the heart expressing itself in the incorruptible quality of a meek and quiet spirit." Peter's words imply the use of the right kind of adornment.

(1) Not mere external adornment (v. 3). The negative "not" (*ouk*) is a categorical prohibition. But as in John 6:27, "Work not for the food which perisheth, but for the food which abideth unto eternal life," the force is relative; wives should not depend upon external adornment but upon a beautiful spiritual character.

As Christian women they should not depend on traditional ways to attract men, "the outward adorning of braiding the hair, and of wearing jewels of gold, or of putting on apparel." In the original all the modifiers stand between the definite article and the noun (*ho . . . kosmos*), making all the modifiers attributive.[13] Adorning of that kind is inadequate for the wives' purpose. The adverb "outward" and the three substantial phrases describe the inherent quality of that adorning. The noun "adorning" (*kosmos*), from which we derive "cosmetics," is used in its original sense of an orderly arrangement, hence adornment or decoration (elsewhere in the New Testament the term signifies "the world" as an orderly system). The reference is to that innate desire, especially among wopmen, to resort to orderly external arrangement to make one's appearance beautiful and attractive. Peter sanctioned that desire.

That adorning is first characterized as "outward" (*exōthen*), "from the outside," consisting in what is external to the true inner being. It consists of material things or activities designed to draw attention. Three substantial clauses elaborate that kind of adorning.

"Braiding of hair" does not denote a convenient way of handling the hair but designates a highly cultivated art of feminine adornment. *Braiding (emplokē)*, used only here in the New Testament, denotes action, not the use of braids but the elaborate process of braiding that involves the services of a professional hairdresser. In Peter's day the hairstyles of fashionable Roman ladies consumed much time and attention and were highly artificial and ostentatious. *And (kai)* continues the portrayal, "the wearing of jewels of gold." The towering hairdo was secured with costly combs and with hair nets of gold. But

---

13. "An adjective is in the attributive relation when it *ascribes* a quality to the noun which it modifies. . . . An adjective is in the predicate relation when it *makes an assertion* concerning the noun which it modifies," H. E. Dana and Julius R. Mantey, *A Manual Grammar of the Greek New Testament*, p. 118 (italics in Dana and Mantey).

Peter's term is broader; "wearing" (*peritheseōs*) is literally "putting around." It includes the common practice of placing various golden objects (chains, rings, bracelets, etc.) around the neck, ankles, arms, and fingers, and suspending glittering ornaments from the ears. The reference to the use of such golden objects for adornment implies that there were women of at least moderate wealth in the congregations addressed. The use of *or* (*ē*) before the third item implies an alternative method of extravagant display, "or of putting on apparel." *Putting on* (*endueōs*), a term not used elsewhere in the New Testament, is another noun of action and apparently indicates the practice of appearing in a great variety of dresses, "the frequent changing of frocks."[14] The Greek term refers particularly to the outer garments worn. Though no direct reference is made to the costly nature of those garments (cf. 1 Tim. 2:9), the description indicates their sumptuous nature. They were put on for show, for a display of personal vanity. Such "undue absorption of mind and heart, time and substance, in the business of mere bodily decoration" has been called "the easily besetting sin of female vanity."[15]

It goes without saying that the design of the passage is not to encourage slovenliness or sordid indifference toward female attire. Neither does it constitute an absolute prohibition of braids or the use of any items of jewelry any more than it forbids the actual putting on of clothes. It is a warning against extravagance and self-centered display. It is possible to be guilty of the evil Peter rebuked by wearing too little as well as wearing too much. Appropriate Christian dress should be a reflection of our inner spiritual life. F. B. Meyer commented, "The one law is to dress as becomes the station in which He has placed us, and in such a way as not to attract notice to ourselves."[16] For the Christian wife simply to rely on external, gaudy, immodest adornment like the world uses would give her husband a wrong impression of her and would frustrate her spiritual purpose.

(2) *Inner spiritual character* (v. 4). *But* (*alla*), the strong adversative conjunction, indicates the true adornment that Christian wives should rely on to win their unsaved husbands. Their inner spiritual beauty should moderate and reflect itself in the proper use of external personal adornment. The Christian wife's true beauty is "the hidden man of the heart, in the incorruptible *apparel* of a meek and quiet spirit." It constitutes the lasting adornment that will reach the husband's heart.

"The hidden man of the heart" (*ho kruptos tēs kardias anthrōpos*) marks a contrast to the external, visible, conspicuous ornaments just repudiated. The inner man is the regenerated nature and does not flaunt itself in open display. *Of the heart*, an appositional genitive, further defines that inner being, the renewed personality, as the seat of life. The inner work of grace has implanted a spiritual beauty that is real and abiding, contrary to the external, artificial

14. J. W. C. Wand, *The General Epistles of St. Peter and St. Jude*, p. 90.
15. John Lillie, *Lectures on the First and Second Epistles of Peter*, p. 188.
16. F. B. Meyer, *"Tried by Fire": Expositions of the First Epistle of Peter*, p. 116.

ornaments that can be removed at will. "This beauty cannot be hung around the neck like a flashing pendant. It grows within like a lovely flower."[17]

The inner life should reflect itself "in the incorruptible *apparel* of a meek and quiet spirit." The translation "the incorruptible *apparel*," as the italics indicate, is an articular adjective (*tō aphthartō*) that designates the quality of not being subject to corruption (cf. 1:4). The noun *apparel* was supplied from the context; other versions supply "ornament," "adornment," or "jewel."[18] If those translations are correct, then the meaning is that their true adornment consists not in outward perishable things but in the inner garment of the soul. Others understand the articular neuter adjective to have the force of an abstract noun. Selwyn translates "the incorruptibility."[19] The NIV suggestively translates, "the unfading beauty of a gentle and quiet spirit."[20] Perhaps the best translation is "the imperishable quality of a gentle and quiet Spirit."[21] That imperishable quality of the inner life will reflect itself in the inner spirit manifested by the godly wife in the everyday relations of life.

"Of a meek and quiet spirit" (*tou praeos kai hēsuchiou pneumatos*) defines the manifested nature of the inner life. The definite article with *spirit*, "the spirit," points to that well-known spirit that characterizes the saintly believer's relations to others. Some, like Best, see "a reference to the Spirit of God which endows the Christian with a new being."[22] But, as Kelly observes, "since this gentle spirit is commended as pleasing to God, it can hardly be the divine Spirit."[23] More natural is the view that *spirit* refers to the ethical temper or disposition of the believer. Peter had the whole inner nature of the believer as transformed and illuminated by the indwelling Spirit of God in view.

That Spirit-wrought inner disposition is described as "meek and quiet"; it beautifully manifestes itself in the wife's submission. The former adjective (*praeos*) describes her bearing as gentle, considerate, and unassuming in its relations to others. The second adjective, *quiet* (*hēsuchiou*), is more general in scope; it pictures a quiet disposition as contrasted to a noisy, boisterous attitude. It is "a spirit which calmly bears the disturbances created by others and which itself does not create disturbances."[24]

"Which is in the sight of God of great price" gives comforting assurance to the tested wives. *Which* (*ho*) may relate to *spirit* (*pneuma*) as its antecedent, or more generally to the entire preceding clause. Whatever the world may think of such an unassuming and mild disposition, for the believer the final test is whether it wins God's approval. God notes and evaluates both the quality of

---

17. Paul S. Rees, *Triumphant in Trouble. Studies in I Peter*, p. 72.
18. "Ornament"—KJV, NEB, JB, Rotherham, Darby, Weymouth, Montgomery; "Adornment" —Kleist and Lilly; "Jewel"—RSV.
19. Edward Gordon Selwyn, *The First Epistle of St. Peter*, p. 184.
20. Similarly, 20th Cent., Moffatt.
21. Similarly, Berkeley, Williams.
22. Ernest Best, *I Peter*, p. 126.
23. Kelly, p. 130.
24. M. J. Harris, "Quiet, Rest, Silence, Sound, Voice, Noise," *NIDNTT*, 3:112.

the inner disposition and its manifestation in daily conduct. In His eyes it is a spiritual gem "of great price" (*poluteles*), "very costly," of infinitely more value than perishable outer adornments. It shone brilliantly in the person of God's dear Son (Matt. 11:29; 21:5).

D. THE PAST EXAMPLES OF GODLY SUBMISSION (vv. 5-6a)

The appeal for proper adornment is undergirded by the example of godly women in the past. "For after this manner aforetime the holy women also, who hoped in God, adorned themselves, being in subjection to their own husbands" (v. 5). Four words emphasize the connection: For (*gar*) introduces an explanation: "after this manner" (*houtōs*), "thusly, in the manner described" in verse 4. "Aforetime" (*pote*), "at some time" in the past, is a vague reference to Old Testament history; "also" (*kai*), the fourth word in the verse, reminded the readers that the saintly wives of the Old Testament themselves did what he is asking them to do.

Those exemplary women are identified as "the holy women" (*hai hagiai gunaikes*), a specific, unnamed group, "those women of blessed memory."[25] That they were married women is obvious from the reference to "their own husbands" (cf. v. 1). They were "holy" because they were members of God's chosen people, set apart as belonging to the God of Israel. As enshrined in the Old Testament records, they possessed a personal dignity and spiritual importance for the Christian women whom Peter counseled. Best remarks that "the Christian church was not yet itself long enough in existence to furnish examples."[26]

Peter described those exemplary wives as those "who hoped in God" (*hai elpizousai eis theon*). The articular present active participle describes them as a group with the characteristic activity of hoping "in God" (*eis theon*), having a hope that reached up and was resting in God. They lived their daily lives with the expectancy that God would accomplish what He had promised. According to Peter such a hope should be the true attitude of God's people (1:3. 13, 21; 3:15). Such a living hope would enable wives to be submissive under difficult and trying circumstances and would free them from the snare of being preoccupied with excessive external adornments.

Those saintly Old Testament matrons "adorned themselves" (*ekosmoun heautas*); they made a practice of adorning themselves with that meek and quiet spirit that Peter advocated. "Holiness has its own beauty and charm."[27] *Being in subjection to their own husbands* reminded the readers of the time when those holy women thus adorned themselves. With that reference to submission, Peter returned to the primary theme of the paragraph.

From among those holy women Peter singled out one example: "as Sarah obeyed Abraham, calling him lord" (v. 6a). *As* (*hōs*) indicates that she was a

25. Fronmüller, p. 52.
26. Best, p. 126.
27. Selwyn, p. 185.

submissive wife. Sarah was held up by the rabbis as the model of submissiveness. Peter did not enter into the full story of Sarah; he had Genesis 18:12 in mind, which he regarded as characteristic of her attitude toward Abraham. *Obeyed (hupēkousen)* is in the aorist tense but the action is not to be limited to that occasion; the aorist summarizes her habitual response toward Abraham, viewed as a characteristic whole. *Calling him lord* indicates her submissiveness. *Calling (kalousa)*, a present participle, specifies her customary, respectful response toward Abraham. Genesis 18:12 is the only time where Sarah uses *lord (kurion)* of Abraham, and then no actual act of submission to him is involved. But on that occasion she is represented as "employing the term in speaking to *herself*—a kind of discourse which brings out with special exactness the real habits of thought and feeling."[28] Some, like Best, regard that as "a somewhat arbitrary use of the Old Testament,"[29] but Peter felt that the occasion did in fact reveal Sarah's customary way of addressing Abraham. That Sarah was not faultless in all her dealings as Abraham's wife is obvious from the biblical account.

E. THE PERSONAL SIGNIFICANCE OF GODLY CONDUCT (v. 6b)

The example of Sarah is applied to Peter's readers: "whose children ye now are, if ye do well, and are not put in fear by any terror." *Ye now are (egenēthēte)* is a historical aorist and may more accurately be translated "ye became." It looks back to the time of their conversion. Having by faith been implanted into the family of God, they had a spiritual likeness to Sarah and may be spoken of as her spiritual "children." As Abraham is spoken of as the father of believers (Rom. 4:11-12; Gal. 3:7, 16, 29; Heb. 2:16; etc.), so believing women are characterized as the daughters of Sarah. In Isaiah 51:1-2 Abraham and Sarah appear as the spiritual progenitors of the people of God. "As Abraham is the 'father of the faithful,' so Sarah is the mother of the obedient."[30] The verb "became" most naturally implies that the readers were former Gentiles. Lillie remarks that Peter's phraseology "was doubtless intended to certify his hearty acquiescence, as the Apostle of the circumcision, in the full adoption of the Gentile believers into all the dignities and privileges of the household of faith."[31]

Two present participles, *agathopoiousai* and *phoboumenai*, ("doing good" and "fearing"), conclude verse 6; their intended grammatical connection has been differently understood. As indicated in the margin of the ASV,[32] some

28. Robert Johnstone, *The First Epistle of Peter: Revised Text with Introduction and Commentary*, p. 205.

29. Best, p. 127.

30. J. Howard B. Masterman, *The First Epistle of S. Peter*, p. 121.

31. Lillie, p. 192.

32. ". . . being in subjection to their own husbands (as Sarah obeyed Abraham, calling him lord, whose children ye now are), doing well, and not. . . ." That is based on the margin of the Westcott and Hort Greek text.

propose to take all of verse 6 before those participles as a parenthesis. If that is correct, then these two participles are parallel to the participle "being in subjection" (v. 5); and all three participles relate to the subject of the verb, "adorned themselves." That interpretation further expands on the conduct of the godly women in the last part of verse 6. But such a lengthy parenthesis is doubtful; the context does not suggest it; it leaves the statement "whose children ye have become" bald and isolated. Best argues that the two participles should be "taken as imperatives and the whole clause read as an independent sentence, 'Do right and let nothing terrify you.'"[33] But it is doubtful that they have such an imperatival force. It seems best to connect them with the subject of the nearest verb, "ye became" (*egenēsthēte*), as expansions on the subject "ye." They offer descriptive evidence of the reality of regeneration; they provide proof that they are the daughters of Sarah.

"If ye do well" translates a single participle (*agathopoiousai*), literally, "doing good." The conditional translation is questionable. To accept a conditional force would "imply that the readers were believing women through their good works."[34] Doing good is not the cause of salvation but the evidence of it. The action of the present participle is subsequent to the aorist verb "ye became." The present participle pictures the subsequent course of doing good following conversion. Its force is complimentary, not admonitory.[35] It portrays the moral activities of those Christian wives, here particularly in regard to the marriage relation.

The second participial phrase turns the reader's attention from the wife's conduct to her inner feelings: "and are not put in fear by any terror." The expression is apparently a reminiscence of Proverbs 3:25 (LXX). The negative with the present participle (*mē phoboumenai*)[36] prohibits a continued feeling or attitude of "fear, being afraid, being frightened." The analogous accusative noun "terror" (*ptoēsin*), which is used only here in the New Testament, may mean either an act of terrifying, intimidation, or the subjective feeling of fear that such an act induces. Either meaning is possible, and the total picture seems to involve both aspects. As godly believers, wives should not allow any event designed to terrify them to get a grip upon them. External causes of fear might arise from the attitudes of society in general, the treatment received from hostile neighbors, or the threats and intimidations of an unbelieving husband. *Any* (*mēdemian*), "not one such occurrence," sweeps away every such occasion as a justifiable cause for nervous terror and excitement. "The meek and quiet spirit" of the Christian wife has nothing in it

---

33. Best, p. 127, following the suggestion of W. C. Van Unnik, "The Teaching of Good Works in I Peter," pp. 100-101.

34. Best, p. 127.

35. Lenski, p. 138.

36. The classical distinction between objective *ou* and the subjective *mē* is not rigidly maintained in the New Testament and Koine Greek. There is a tendency to use *mē* regularly with the participle.

of weakness, irresolution, or cowardice. She will not allow the threats of an unbelieving husband to scare her out of her Christian faith.

2) The Obligations of the Husbands (v. 7)

This verse is not to be viewed as an independent paragraph but as a corollary to the preceding verses to prevent a false assumption concerning the husband's relation to his submissive wife. It is a brief but singularly comprehensive statement of the duties of the Christian husband. Unlike Paul in 1 Corinthians 7:12, Peter made no mention of a Christian husband living with a non-Christian wife. But even in such a mixed marriage, the lot of the husband would not be nearly as difficult as that of a believing wife. Generally, the Christian husband could expect his wife to follow him in his acceptance of the gospel.

"In like manner" (*homoiōs*) firmly links the verse with the preceding material. The subject of submission is not mentioned, yet Peter maintained that marriage lays specific obligations on the husband that he should discharge from the same sense of Christ's lordship. "The spirit which made the wife 'meek and quiet' would make the husband kind and attentive."[37]

The participial construction is continued (cf. 2:18; 3:1). Two participles set forth two coordinated duties, "dwelling with" and "assigning honor" (Rotherham). The present tenses portray the continuing duties of the Christian husband. The duties are not new but they are basic to the Christian husband-wife relationship.

"Ye husbands, in like manner dwell with *your wives* according to knowledge." The compound verb "dwell with" (*sunoikeō*) occurs only here in the New Testament, though the two parts of the compound are common. It can have a general or a specific meaning. In the Septuagint it usually means "to live together as husband and wife, to cohabit."[38] In view of its Septuagint usage, a few commentators accept that meaning here.[39] Thus Demarest insists that Peter means, "live chastely with your wives; cohabit with them alone."[40] But others recognize that "the tie is deeper than mere marital intercourse."[41] It is better to understand the term as a global reference to all aspects of a shared home life and not as a mere euphemism for sexual relations. Masterman stated that the expression "is the nearest equivalent in Greek to our English expression 'making a home for.'"[42]

---

37. W. H. Bennett, *The General Epistles, James, Peter, John, and Jude*, p. 226.

38. So in 5 of its 6 occurrences: Gen. 20:3; Deut. 22:13; 24:3; 25:5*b*; Isa. 62.5. Only in Deut. 25:5*a* is the meaning broader.

39. D. D. Whedon, *A Popular Commentary on the New Testament*, 5:207; John T. Demarest, *A Translation and Exposition of the First Epistle of the Apostle Peter*, pp. 152-53; James Hope Moulton and George Milligan, *The Vocabulary of the Greek Testament*, p. 611.

40. Demarest, p. 152.

41. James Moffatt, *The General Epistles, James, Peter, and Judas*, p. 134.

42. Masterman, p. 122.

The husband's relations to his wife should be "according to knowledge" (*kata gnōsin*); they should be in harmony with and governed by "knowledge." Demarest, who restricts the meaning of the participle to sexual relations, understands the expression to mean "with prudence" and takes it as a warning to husbands to "behave, not as brute beasts, but as intelligent beings."[43] True enough, but that view is again too restricted. All husband-wife relations should be governed by "knowledge," a knowledge derived from reason and common sense as well as an understanding of Christian principles directing the marriage relationship. That involves the husband's understanding of the nature of his wife.

The translation of the ASV, "giving honor unto the woman. as unto the weaker vessel," raises the problem of the intended connection of the words "unto the woman, as unto the weaker vessel." Are those words to be joined to the second participle of the verse, or are they to be connected to the first, "dwelling with"? The difference is evident from a comparison of the ASV and the NASB: "Dwell with *your wives* according to knowledge, giving honor unto the woman, as unto the weaker vessel, as being also joint-heirs of the grace of life" (ASV). "Live with your wives in an understanding way, as with a weaker vessel, since she is a woman; and grant her honor as a fellow heir of the grace of life" (NASB). The first combines the two "as" clauses with the second participle and involves an inversion of part of the sentence. If that is correct, then the meaning is that in intelligently living with his wife, the husband should honor her as the weaker vessel and accept her as spiritually a joint-heir with himself. According to the second interpretation, the husband should live with his wife according to an intelligent understanding of her nature as a weaker vessel, and, as a second duty, he should honor her as a spiritual co-heir of eternal life. The second interpretation is more consonant with the original, avoids an inversion or rearrangement of part of the phrase, and gives a better balance to the two parts of the sentence. We believe that the words translated "unto the woman, as unto the weaker vessel" properly belong to the first participle and present an aspect of the knowledge husbands need to live with their wives.

We prefer to follow the literal order of the original and to translate, "dwelling together according to knowledge as with a weaker vessel, the wifely one." The husband's life with his wife should be governed by an intelligent acceptance of her as a weaker vessel. The comparative "weaker" (*asthenesterō*) implies that Peter thought of both husband and wife as frail vessels or instruments used by God for His purposes. The imagery of human beings as vessels for God's service was readily drawn from the creation account in Genesis 2 and appears in both Testaments (cf. Jer. 18:1-6; Acts 9:15; Rom. 9:21-23; 2 Tim. 2:20-21). Both husband and wife are God's handiwork, designed for each other.

Peter specifically identified the weaker of the two vessels with an articular adjective, "the womanly," or "the wifely" (*tō gunaikeiō*). The designation is

43. Demarest, p. 153.

abstract, not "the wife" but "the female element."[44] The recognition of her greater weakness is not derogatory and does not imply inferiority. Generally speaking, the wife is physically weaker than the man; but it is unfair to imply that she is intellectually or morally inferior to him. By and large commentators have understood *weaker vessel* as a reference to physical strength, but Susan Foh suggests an attractive alternative: "The wife may be considered weak because of her role as wife. She, by marrying, has accepted a position where she submits herself to her husband. Such a position is vulnerable, open to exploitation. The husband is commanded not to take advantage of the woman's vows of submission."[45] Her acceptance of a position of weakness in submission to him is a call to her husband for consideration and thoughtful support. "Christian knowledge will accord the wife all the consideration and the thoughtfulness which God intends for her 'as a weaker vessel' in the 'wifely' relation."[46]

The second participle, "giving honor" (*aponemontes*), "continuing to show honor," specifies a further obligation of the husband toward his wife. In effect it is an elaboration of how they are to live together "according to knowledge." That compound participle, which appears only here in the New Testament, has the basic meaning of "to assign, to apportion to" someone. In a papyrus document it is used of an officer who is commended for giving to all their just dues. The husband should give his submissive wife her just due and not take liberties with her rights. Peter demanded that the wife should be accepted as fully worthy of respect and loving esteem. Macknight interprets *honor* to mean "maintenance," a reference to supplying one's wife with the necessities and conveniences of life.[47] Though the noun can mean "honorarium" or "compensation," such a translation is prosaic, especially in view of the "as" clause that immediately follows. Christian husbands should apportion due honor to their wives "as being also joint-heirs of the grace of life."

"As also" (*hōs kai*) reminded the husbands that their Christian wives were likewise heirs of God's grace with them.[48] In the marriage relationship the husband and wife complement each other. In their personal standing before God, there is equality; they are accepted by God on the same basis (Mark 12:25; Gal. 3:28). Wives, like husbands, believe in the same Savior, are redeemed by the same ransom, live by the same grace, and look forward to the same eternal destiny. Recognition of that reality will end domestic tyranny. Mitchel calls that "perhaps the most uplifting ethical thought in the Epistle."[49]

44. Bo Reicke, *The Epistles of James, Peter, and Jude*, pp. 102, 137-38.
45. Susan T. Foh, *Women and the Word of God*, p. 133.
46. Lenski, p. 141.
47. James Macknight, *A New Literal Translation from the Original Greek, of All the Apostolical Epistles*, 5:472-73.
48. The Textus Receptus reads "joint-heirs" (*sungkleronomoi*) as nominative plural, making it refer to the husbands. Modern editors prefer the dative plural as the more difficult reading; then the reference is to the wives as also being heirs with their husbands. The two readings leave unchanged the fact that the wives are heirs of grace along with others.
49. A. F. Mitchell, *Hebrews and the General Epistles*, p. 262.

Together the husband and wife have the dignity of being "joint-heirs" (*sungklēronomois*), co-sharers in the mutual inheritance that is "the grace of life" (*charitos zōēs*). The exact combination, which occurs only here, may mean "the grace that consists in life" (appositional genitive), or "the grace that has the bestowal of life as its object" (objective genitive). The latter seems preferable. Used without an article, both nouns are qualitative. It is a grace characterized as the unmerited favor of God toward sinners that freely bestows life upon its recipients—life in the truest and fullest sense. Christians already possess that life, but its full manifestation awaits the return of Christ.

Such a relationship is assured of a contemplated result: "to the end that your prayers be not hindered." *To the end that* (*eis to* with the infinitive) may denote purpose, but here it more likely indicates a contemplated result. According to the former view, husbands are urged to do their duty toward their wives in order to avoid that tragic result; according to the latter view, Peter was motivating them to continue what they were already doing because of the assured result. Either interpretation indicates that a man's domestic relations have a profound impact on his own spiritual fellowship with God. *Your prayers* apparently has direct reference to the prayer life of the husbands themselves. Prayer is a normal feature of the Christian life and Peter assumed that those Christian men were men of prayer. But *your prayers* may also include family worship, where the wife and children join the husband. "If husband and wife live together without mutual reverence and affection, there can be no sympathy in united prayer."[50] Such a failure in personal relations will "hinder" their prayers. The compound infinitive "be hindered" (*engkoptesthai*) is apparently a military metaphor and means "to cut in on, throw obstacles in the way," or "cut up the road" so that normal movement is made impossible. Unworthy home relations hinder prayers, so that they do not rise to the divine throne. The alternative reading of the Textus Receptus, *ekkoptesthai*, "to be cut off," means that the husband's failure to maintain right relations with his wife will cut off his practice of prayer, so that he will hardly pray at all. A man's fellowship with God is closely related to his relations to his fellow beings (Matt. 5:22-23; 18:19-35; James 4:1-4; 1 John 4:19-21).

---

50. B. C. Caffin, *The First Epistle General of Peter*, p. 130.

14

E. An Appeal for Becoming Corporate Conduct
(3:8-12)

(9) Finally, *be* ye all likeminded, compassionate, loving as brethren, tenderhearted, humbleminded: (9) not rendering evil for evil, or reviling for reviling; but contrariwise blessing; for hereunto were ye called, that ye should inherit a blessing. (10) For,

> He that would love life,
> And see good days,
> Let him refrain his tongue from evil,
> And his lips that they speak no guile:
> (11) And let him turn away from evil,
> And do good;
> Let him seek peace, and pursue it.
> (12) For the eyes of the Lord are upon the righteous,
> And his ears unto their supplication:
> But the face of the Lord is upon them that do
> evil.

The connection of this paragraph with the preceding series of exhortations is shown by the continuation of the participial (and to some extent of the adjectival) construction (cf. 2:18; 3:1, 7). It constitutes an appropriate conclusion to the series of exhortations that specify how to produce a right impression on a hostile world. The detailed duties of the different groups are now bound together in a general statement portraying the essentials of Christian character.

"Finally" (*to de telos*) or "And finally," is adverbial and marks the conclusion of the second cycle of exhortations (2:11—3:12). The literal expression, "now the end," suggests the thought of bringing a discussion to its conclusion or climax. Peter began the series with an appeal for becoming individual conduct fitted to silence a hostile world. His emphatic *all* (*pantes*) turns the attention from the duties of individual groups to the demand that rests on all Christians to silence and disarm the hostility of an unbelieving world.

Peter pictured the corporate conduct that is needed (vv. 8-9) and then confirmed his appeal with a quotation from the Old Testament (vv. 10-12).

1) THE PORTRAYAL OF THE DESIRED CONDUCT (VV. 8-9)

The absence of a finite verb (note *be* in italics) indicates the continuation of the series. Peter used five adjectives, which describe the desired conduct (v. 8), followed by the participial construction in verse 9. The adjectives describe the conduct in relation to fellow believers (v. 8), and the participles in verse 9 in relation to a hostile world.

A. THE CHARACTERISTICS OF BELIEVERS (v. 8)

The five virtues Peter described are social and specify how Christians are to relate to one another. They constitute an ideal portrait of the church.

"Likeminded" (*homophrones*) is more a call for unity of disposition than uniformity of opinion. The adjective does not occur elsewhere in the New Testament, but Paul used an infinitive phrase (*to auto phronein*), "to be minding the same," to express the same thought (Rom. 12:16; 2 Cor. 13:11; Phil. 2:2; cf. 1 Cor. 1:10; Eph. 4:3; Phil. 1:27; 3:15). Barclay suggests that that concern goes back to the prayer of our Lord in John 17:21-23 for the unity of Christians.[1] The oneness called for by that adjective is an inner unity of sentiment and disposition, aim, or purpose, a unity of heart because of a similar inner experience. It is a unity that arises from having the mind of Christ (Phil. 2:5). Williams observes, "Christendom has long needed more oneness of doctrine, but much more has it needed oneness of heart."[2]

"Compassionate" (*sumpatheis*), or "sympathetic," basically means "sharing fellow-feelings," whether those feelings be joyous or sorrowful. It connotes that readiness to enter into and share in the feelings of others that enables one to "rejoice with them that rejoice" as well as "weep with them that weep" (Rom. 12:15). The kindred verb is used in Hebrews 4:15 and 10:34 with the thought of sharing in the sufferings of others. But the use of the adjective, which occurs only here, was not so limited. "Those who are united by a

---

1. William Barclay, *The Letters of James and Peter*, p. 266.
2. Nathaniel Marshman Williams, *Commentary on the Epistles of Peter*, p. 46.

common spiritual mind, should be moved by, or be sensitive to, the same spiritual emotions."[3]

"Loving as brethren" (*philadelphoi*) is another adjective that appears only here; the noun occurs in 1:22. In secular Greek the term was used of the love of physical brothers and sisters, but in Christian literature the usage is always figurative, denoting "the mutual love which is the bond of brotherhood in Christ, not of an all-embracing 'brotherly love.'"[4] That love is the sign that we have passed from death unto life (1 John 3:14; 4:20) and the badge of true Christian discipleship (John 13:35). As Calvin remarked, "Where God is known as a Father, there and only there brotherhood really exists."[5] Mutual love was the hallmark of the early Christian church.

"Tenderhearted" (*eusplangchnoi*), which occurs also in Ephesians 4:32, depicts a warm and tender attitude—an affectionate sensitivity toward the needs of others. The adjective is derived from the noun *splangchna*, the internal organs—the heart, lungs, and liver—which were thought of as the seat of the emotions. It is comparable to our English term "heart." In the Septuagint and the New Testament, it denotes the deepest human emotions, especially love and compassion. In the synoptic gospels the verb is generally used of Jesus Himself in the sense of being deeply touched, "moved with compassionate tenderness." Such tenderhearted, compassionate feelings toward the needy know no frontiers and naturally find expression also toward those outside the church.

"Humbleminded" (*tapeinophrones*) is accepted as the authentic reading. The reading of the KJV, "courteous," follows the Textus Receptus (*philophrones*), "friendly minded, courteous." It makes good sense, but its manuscript support is weak.[6] As Barnes remarks, "Though Christianity requires that we should be courteous and gentlemanly in our treatment of others, *this* text can hardly be relied on as a proof-text of that point."[7] *Humbleminded* is not used elsewhere in the New Testament, but it is appropriate in the concluding exhortation in a series that has called for submission, since it marks the inner attitude of those who are voluntarily submissive to authority over them. It is the opposite of haughty and high-minded, and it does not brag about and push self; it rejoices over the successes of others. Paul made much of it in Philippians 2. It also forms a proper transition to the social relations mentioned in verse 9. In the words of Lillie,

> As nothing more unfits a man for any kindly consideration of others than an overweening estimate of himself, so the lowliness of heart which is produced by

3. Alan M. Stibbs, *The First Epistle General of Peter*, p. 129.
4. Francis Wright Beare, *The First Epistle of Peter*, p. 160.
5. John Calvin, *The Epistle of Paul the Apostle to the Hebrews and the First and Second Epistles of St Peter*, p. 284.
6. For the evidence see Nestle-Aland, *Novum Testamentum Graece*, (26th ed.). Codex *L* of the 8th century and a few later manuscripts exhibit both adjectives.
7. Albert Barnes, *Notes on the New Testament, Explanatory and Practical—James, Peter, John, and Jude*, p. 165.

genuine repentance, and the experience of God's saving mercy in Christ, though it
has never been allowed a place on the scale of natural ethics, is not only itself of
great price in the sight of God, but by far the best soil for the culture of the social
virtues.[8]

B. THE RESPONSE TO HOSTILITY (v. 9)

Peter first portrayed the believer's response to a hostile world and then
indicated the motivation for such a response. The participial construction is
again used to present the picture: "not rendering evil for evil, or reviling for
reviling; but contrariwise blessing."

The negative aspect of the response involves both deed and word. The
negative (*mē*) with the present participle prohibits any continuation of the
practice of returning evil for evil. Such a response is natural to unregenerate
human nature; we do not have to be taught to do so. But we must be taught and
urged not to retaliate (Rom. 12:17; 1 Thess. 5:15). The teaching of the apostolic
church was grounded in the teaching of our Lord Himself (Matt. 5:38-48; Luke
6:27-36) and in His personal conduct (2:23). The participle "rendering"
(*apodidontes*) strictly means "giving off," but in the context it receives the
force of "giving back, rewarding, recompensing," whether in a good or bad
sense—here the latter. By returning "evil for evil"—anything that we regard
as injurious to our own welfare and interests—evil is only increased and not
restrained. And the extent of the evil returned is measured by the size of the
evil received. The natural tendency is to return the evil in full measure or
more. Thus evil is only multiplied. To break the vicious chain someone must
voluntarily endure evil without retaliation.

"Or reviling for reviling" brings the prohibition into the realm of speech. The
duty laid upon the suffering slaves in 2:23 is extended to all believers. For the
unregenerate nature that prohibition is even harder to obey. An individual
may have enough self-restraint not to resort to active violence but may yield to
the less violent urge to use insolent and abusive language against another who
has injured him. But as Trapp remarked, "To render railing for railing, is to
think to wash off dirt with dirt."[9] The believer should refrain from all
vengeance as the prerogative of God (Rom. 12:19).

The duty of the new nature is also positive, "but contrariwise blessing." *But*,
the particle *de*, indicates that something more must be said, for Christian
ethics is not merely negative. The emphatic adverb "contrariwise" (*toun-
antion*) indicates that the very opposite kind of response should follow,
namely, "blessing" (*eulogountes*), which is not a noun but a present active
participle. Instead of reviling, the Christian's response should be the practice
of invoking God's blessings on those who show themselves hostile. Though
verbally the direct opposite of reviling, such blessing is the appropriate
antithesis of both preceding activities. Selwyn comments that "intercession for

---

8. John Lillie, *Lectures on the First and Second Epistles of Peter*, p. 210.
9. John Trapp, *Trapp's Commentary on the New Testament*, p. 711.

enemies, beneficence towards them and speaking well of them, are all comprised in the term."[10]

"For" (*hoti*), or "because," recalls that that obligation accorded with the readers' Christian calling: "for hereunto were ye called, that ye should inherit a blessing."[11] "Ye were called" looks back to the time of the readers' conversion; it is the fourth reminder that God acted to call them unto Himself (1:15; 2:9, 21). That fact was not to be forgotten as they faced a hostile world. But does the phrase "hereunto" (*eis touto*), "unto this," look back to what has just been said or does it look forward to the clause that follows?

Some believe that "unto this" looks backward and is similar to the use of the phrase in 2:21. Christians should bless their persecutors because that is the kind of life to which they were called at conversion, when God freely forgave all their own sins and hostility toward Him. In keeping with their calling, they should manifest such a response toward others "so that you may inherit a blessing" (NIV). We "increasingly enter into the full enjoyment of the blessing of God's forgiveness and goodwill only if we learn ourselves to extend similar forgiveness and goodwill to others (see Mt. vi. 12, 14, 15, xviii. 32-35; Mk. xi. 25, 26)."[12] We do not earn the blessing, which is God's gift, but we ourselves experience it as we obey such teachings (Luke 6:36-38).

Others believe that *hereunto* or *unto this* looks forward to the following clause. That is clearly the view in the NASB, "for you were called for the very purpose that you might inherit a blessing." That connection is favored by the use of the phrase in 4:6 (cf. John 18:37; 1 John 3:8). The Christian's glorious call to inherit a blessing places him under the noble obligation to bless others. He should do unto others as he would be done unto. "Christians bless others, not in order that they should inherit a blessing, but because it is God's will and their duty; and that duty follows from the fact that God has made them inheritors of his blessing."[13] Either view makes good sense, but the latter seems more simple.

2) THE CONFIRMATION FROM OLD TESTAMENT SCRIPTURE (VV. 10-12)

The opening "For" (*gar*) is not part of the following quotation but was introduced by Peter to confirm and elucidate his exhortation. As usual in the epistle, no formula of citation is given. The quotation is from Psalm 34:12-16 (33:12-16 LXX) and follows the Septuagint with some variations. The passage quoted has aptly been called "an ancient recipe for a happy life."[14] It sets forth the dominating desire (v. 10a), the demanding activities (vv. 10b-11), and the divine response (v. 12) to the kind of life Peter had just set before his readers.

10. Edward Gordon Selwyn, *The First Epistle of St. Peter*, p. 190.
11. The reading "*knowing* that ye are" (KJV) has inferior textual support. See the evidence in Nestle-Aland.
12. Stibbs, p. 131.
13. B. C. Caffin, *The First Epistle General of Peter*, pp. 130-31.
14. Edgar Young Mullins, *The Life in Christ*, pp. 58-66.

A. THE DOMINATING DESIRE (v. 10a)

The double statement of the desire that should characterize the life commended reflects the parallelism of the Hebrew poem being quoted: "He that would love life, and see good days." The articular present participle, *ho thelōn*, "the one wishing" or "desiring," pictures an individual dominated by a unifying desire or purpose, namely, "to love life" (*zōēn agapan*), "life to be loving." Not length but quality of life is in view—to live zestfully, to participate in life with full intelligence and purpose. Peter, like David, was thinking of "life" here on earth, but the revelation in Christ has now made it life indeed—begun here but continued in the life beyond. He was convinced that life can be worth living in spite of the hostility encountered. The parallel line expounds the first: "and see good days," to experience days that are really beneficial, not empty and meaningless. They are good because of the moral quality of his life. With God in control even persecution cannot make good days bad (Rom. 8:28; 2 Cor. 6:4-10). Wand remarks, "There are not many writers ancient or modern who would think of having 'good days' (a good time) under threat of persecution."[15]

Peter's quote skillfully rephrased the Septuagint, which fairly represents the Hebrew: "What man is he that desireth life, and loveth many days, that he may see good?" (Ps. 34:12). He made the picture more intense by dropping the rhetorical question and stressing the dominating desire that characterizes the life he commended. That alteration enabled him to change from the second to the third person singular imperative in setting forth the activities that should characterize such a life.

B. THE NECESSARY ACTIVITIES (vv. 10b-11)

Those activities relate to both speech and conduct. The demands upon speech relate to its negative aspect (v. 10b), again in the form of poetic parallelism: "Let him refrain his tongue from evil, and his lips that they speak no guile." *Let him refrain* (*pausatō*) is an aorist imperative and implies energetic restraint of the tongue when tempted to speak a word of evil. It indicates the impetuous nature of the tongue that must be carefully kept under control (James 3:6-8). *Evil* (*kakos*) is a general term and includes all speech that is of a base and degrading nature, "whether in the way of profane, or slanderous, or impure, or merely idle and unprofitable discourse."[16] The parallel line narrows and intensifies that evil: "And his lips that they speak no guile." The aorist infinitive with the negative *mē* depicts single occurrences, or perhaps better, the entire life as characterized by such restraint. *Guile* (cf. 2:1) is the evil of saying one thing and meaning something else to lead another astray. Both the Old and the New Testament frequently and vehemently

15. J. W. C. Wand, *The General Epistles of St. Peter and St. Jude*, pp. 94-95.
16. Lillie, pp. 213-14.

denounce the sins of the tongue. A lying tongue is one of the things especially hateful to God (Prov. 6:16-17).

The further parallelism in verse 11 presents the demands in the realm of deed: "And let him turn away from evil, and do good; let him seek peace, and pursue it." *And* (*de*), though omitted by various manuscripts, implies that something more than matters of speech must be considered. The way of happiness involves both speaking and doing. *Turn away* (*ekklinatō*) means "to incline or bend out" and pictures the individual as leaning over or swerving aside to avoid an encounter with evil, whatever its nature or form. He takes evasive action because of his holy aversion to evil. The void left by the negative should be filled by the positive: "and do good" (*poiēsatō agathon*), "and let him do good," that which is morally good and constructive. "As a general rule engaging in active goodness is a fairly efficient method of avoiding evil."[17]

The second half of the parallelism is more specific: "Let him seek peace, and pursue it." The Christian should not only desire but aggressively search for peace, harmonious relations conducive to life and welfare. When its attainment is elusive and remote, he accepts the need to pursue (*diōxatō*), to chase it, hunt for the peace that in the excitement and turmoil of life is apt to take to flight. He should aggressively be a peacemaker.

C. THE DIVINE RESPONSE (v. 12)

The opening "for" (*hoti*), or "because," was added by Peter to emphasize the motivation for such a life. In the Hebrew and Septuagint there is no formal conjunction. He assured the readers that God watches both the persecuted and the persecutor. The Hebrew parallelism here is doubled, "each of the two main statements having attached to it a sister statement, which elucidates the primary one by setting forth explicitly the nature and issue of the divine 'seeing', in the one gracious and helpful, in the other stern and punitory."[18] The first half is a message of consolation for the persecuted: "The eyes of the Lord are upon the righteous, and his ears unto their supplication." God's all-seeing eye rests upon the righteous (*dikaious*); the absence of the article makes the term qualitative, "such as are righteous," conforming to the standard of right or justice. The consciousness that God unceasingly observes our conduct, purposes, and aspirations, as well as our perils and tears, is indeed comforting assurance. His watchfulness also assures us that His ears are open to our supplication (*deēsin*), our cry of need; He bows down to catch our faintest whisper. That assurance of answered prayer cannot be separated from the righteous life of those praying.

The second half of the parallelism gives solemn assurance concerning the persecutors: "But the face of the Lord is upon them that do evil." *But* (*de*) marks a contrast; God also watches those who do evil (*poiountas kaka*), those

---

17. Gordon H. Clark, *Peter Speaks Today. A Devotional Commentary on First Peter*, p. 115.

18. Robert Johnstone, *The First Epistle of Peter: Revised Text, with Introduction and Commentary*, pp. 222-23.

who are engaged in the performance of evil things. *The face of the Lord* denotes God's personal presence intently watching them. But Peter did not quote the fourth line of the parallelism that sets forth the result of the divine observation: "To cut off the remembrance of them from the earth" (Ps. 34:16*b*). He stopped short of that dreadful result, leaving room for possible repentance. "The day of wrath and revelation of the righteous judgment of God" (Rom. 2:6) is still future. Peter found no delight in picturing the fate of the wicked; he was concerned with aiding and encouraging the suffering saints.

Third Cycle:

EXHORTATIONS IN VIEW OF CHRISTIAN SUFFERING (3:13—5:11)

The third cycle of exhortations, devoted to the problem of Christian suffering, again flows naturally out of what has gone before. The position of God's people amid a hostile world leads to the development of the theme of suffering inflicted by those who reject Christ. The opening "And" (*kai*) indicates a connection with what has preceded but does not define its nature. The truth set forth in 3:12 (God watches over those who do good as well as those who practice evil) forms an easy and natural transition to this final cycle of practical exhortations. Kelly calls it "the main section of the letter"[1] since it deals with the primary reason for its composition.

The thought of suffering for the Christian faith has, thus far, hovered in the background; only occasionally has it been brought into the open (1:6-7; 2:12, 15, 19-21; 3:9). From now on it constitutes the central theme of the epistle. Peter wrote to enlighten and comfort his afflicted readers, to encourage and strengthen them to stand firm in the midst of sufferings, and to fortify them for what loomed ahead.

In developing the theme of suffering for the Christian faith, Peter began with the unnatural experience of suffering for righteousness's sake (3:13-17), elaborated on Christ's experience of suffering for righteousness (3:18-22), discussed the needed equipment for suffering as Christians (4:1-11), stressed the need for steadfastness in Christian suffering (4:12-19), and concluded with appropriate appeals to both leaders and members of the local churches in view of such sufferings (5:1-11).

---

1. J. N. D. Kelly, *A Commentary on the Epistles of Peter and of Jude*, p. 139.

15

A. The Experience of Suffering for Righteousness
(3:13-17)

(13) And who is he that will harm you, if ye be zealous of that which is good? (14) but even if ye should suffer for righteousness' sake, blessed *are ye*: and fear not their fear, neither be troubled; (15) but sanctify in your hearts Christ as Lord; *being* ready always to give answer to every man that asketh you a reason concerning the hope that is in you, yet with meekness and fear: (16) having a good conscience; that, wherein ye are spoken against, they may be put to shame who revile your good manner of life in Christ. (17) For it is better, if the will of God should so will, that ye suffer for well-doing than for evil-doing.

In beginning this new cycle of exhortations, Peter dropped the participial construction and employed a rhetorical question. He recognized the unnaturalness of suffering for righteousness (v. 13), indicated the blessedness of such suffering (v. 14a), delineated in practical directives the qualifications needed to rightly undergo such sufferings (vv. 14b-16), and offered assurance to those who suffer for well-doing (v. 17).

1) THE UNNATURALNESS OF SUFFERING FOR RIGHTEOUSNESS (V. 13)

"And who is he that will harm you, if ye be zealous of that which is good?" The rhetorical form gives intensity to the matter of the unexpectedness of such suffering and identifies the individual who thus reacts to their well-doing as one who acts unnaturally. Based on our experience and sense of justice, the question expects a strong negative answer. The interrogative "who" (*tis*), together with the articular participle (*ho kakōsōn*, "the one who will harm"), seeks the identity of the individual who would thus react to the practice of goodness.

Peter did not promise his readers that they would escape such suffering. The teaching of Jesus, his own experience, as well as his insight into the perversity of human nature, made him fully aware that there were exceptions. His very purpose in writing was to prepare his readers for such experiences.

The verb "harm" (*kakoō*) continues the concept of evil (*kakos*, v. 12) that lies at the root of Christian suffering. The verb denotes mistreatment and implies that real damage is done through such actions. Elsewhere in the New Testament the verb occurs only in Acts, where it is used of the oppression of the Israelites by the Egyptians (7:6, 19) and of antagonism toward the church—expressed either in active persecution (12:1; 18:10) or in vicious attitudes toward believers (14:2). Here the term includes any hostile and injurious attitude or activity that produces essential damage.

"Will harm" is not a future indicative but an articular future participle (*ho kakōsōn*), a rare form in Greek. A future participle may denote purpose, but here the form apparently is a substitute for the future indicative and has a futuristic force.[2] The expression may be understood in two ways. It may mean "who will do so," implying that normally no one would be expected to act in that way. Thus the NEB translates, "Who is going to do you wrong if you are devoted to what is good?" And it is still true that normally a life of active beneficence toward others disarms those who might otherwise be hostile. If that is correct, then the emphasis is that anyone who is actually disposed to injure those who help others is acting in a perverted way. But Peter knew that his readers were being subjected to such unnatural treatment, as the next verse indicates.

Others believe that Peter meant "who is able to harm you?" Because the readers were under God's watchful care (v. 12), no one was able to do them any real and essential harm.[3] If they met the stated condition, the question became a shout of assurance that the persecution encountered could inflict no real damage.

We rejoice in the theological truth contained in the latter interpretation, but in view of the concession in verse 14, we believe that the former is more probably the intended meaning.

"If ye be zealous of that which is good" states the assumed condition for the rhetorical question. *If ye be* (*ean* with the aorist subjunctive), "if ye may have become," leaves open the fulfillment of that condition but implies that its fulfillment is expected. The reader's own life and conduct will determine the outcome. Being zealous of that which is good is the true basis for a reasonable

---

2. F. Blass and A. Debrunner, *A Greek Grammar of the New Testament and Other Christian Literature*, p. 179; A. T. Robertson, *A Grammar of the Greek New Testament in the Light of Historical Research*, p. 878.

3. Ernest Best, *I Peter*, pp. 131-32; Kelly, pp. 139-40; C. E. B. Cranfield, *I & II Peter and Jude*, p. 97-98; Paul S. Rees, *Triumphant in Trouble*, p. 85; J. W. C. Wand, *The General Epistles of St. Peter and St. Jude*, p. 97.

assurance that God will protect Christians from evil. The condition is not an occasional good deed but being zealous (*zēlōtai*), literally, "zealots" of the good. The use of the noun, rather than the adjective, implies not merely the possession of zeal but its active embodiment in the readers' lives. It conveys "the idea of wholeheartedness and singleness of purpose."[4] They had become "enthusiasts" for the doing of good. Moffatt paraphrases, "if you have a passion for goodness." They aggressively seek to perform the good. Ellison shrewdly observes, "We are far more likely to suffer, if we are zealous for other people to do right, than if the zeal is applied to our own lives."[5]

The KJV reading, "followers" (*mimētai*), literally, "imitators," follows the variant reading of the Textus Receptus. That reading is not as well supported.[6]

That which they zealously promoted is indicated by the genitive "of that which is good" (*tou agathou*), an articular adjective used as a noun. It stands emphatically at the head of the conditional clause, "if of the good zealots ye may have become." The emphasis strengthens the contrast between doing harm and good. The neuter singular sums up and presents as a unit "all the various forms of moral excellence which have been spoken of separately in vv. 10, 11."[7] Christian goodness has a unitary character.

Some commentators have taken *tou agathou* as masculine, "the Good One," understood as a reference to Christ. Thus Robert Young translated, "if of Him who is good ye may become imitators." But that view is likely only if the inferior reading "imitators" is adopted, a reading that Alford suggested may have arisen as a reminiscence of 3 John 11 in the mind of some scribe.[8]

2) THE BLESSEDNESS OF SUFFERING FOR RIGHTEOUSNESS (V. 14*a*)

"But" (*alla*) marks a strong antithesis: "But even if ye should suffer for righteousness' sake, blessed *are ye*." Peter knew that aggressive well-doing did not always disarm the persecutor. *Even if ye should suffer* (*ei kai paschoite*)—one of a few instances in the New Testament of the optative mood in conditional sentences—indicates that such suffering, though naturally remote, may come upon believers. But the optative suggests that the readers were not to overrate the danger; it suggests a possibility, not a certainty. The verb *suffer* (*paschō*) is more general in meaning than *harm* (*kakoō*) in verse 13; it occurs no less than twelve times in 1 Peter,[9] more often than in any other

---

4. Andrew McNab, *The General Epistles of Peter*, p. 1138.
5. H. L. Ellison, *1 and 2 Peter, 1, 2 and 3 John, Jude, Revelation*, p. 12.
6. For the evidence see Nestle-Aland, *Novum Testamentum Graece* (26th ed.).
7. Robert Johnstone, *The First Epistle of Peter*, pp. 226-27.
8. Henry Alford, *The Greek New Testament*, vol. 4 (part 1), p. 361.
9. See 2:19-21, 23; 3:14, 17-18; 4:1 (twice), 15, 19; 5:10.

New Testament book. It means to experience something that falls to one's lot, whether good or ill. Only in Galatians 3:4 does it refer to a pleasant experience. In all of its forty-one other occurrences, it denotes an unpleasant or hurtful experience of some kind. Though the suffering of death may be involved, generally lesser forms of suffering are denoted, such as those mentioned by Jesus in Matthew 5:11: "when *men* shall reproach you, and persecute you, and say all manner of evil against you falsely, for my sake." The use of the present tense indicates that such experiences may be the repeated lot of Christians.

"For righteousness' sake" (*dia dikaiosunēn*) specifies the kind of sufferings in view; not all sufferings that come to believers as human beings belong to that category. They are sufferings inflicted because of a Christian's righteousness, not in the usual Pauline sense of justifying righteousness, but the righteous deeds that flow out of the experience of justification. *Righteousness* is synonymous with "that which is good" in verse 13 and reflects the words of Jesus, "for my sake" in Matthew 5:11. The unbeliever "does not hate benevolence in itself, but if it is coupled with the Name of Christ it arouses his murderous anger. He applauds good conduct, but bitterly hates good conduct 'in Christ' (v. 16)."[10] The suffering in view implies that the life of the believer should be characterized by the practice of righteous deeds.

If such sufferings are their lot, "blessed *are ye*" (*makarioi*). The adjective "blessed" is left without a verb, giving it the force of an exclamation. It clearly reflects the words of Jesus in Matthew 5:10. Instead of being an unmitigated evil, such sufferings contribute to the Christian's spiritual well-being and foster a blessedness that reaches into the life beyond. Christians should not be fearful and despairing but reckon themselves highly privileged: "Rejoice, and be exceeding glad: for great is your reward in heaven" (Matt. 5:12). The term "blessed" refers to "the distinctive religious joy which accrues to man from his share in the salvation of the kingdom of God."[11] It is the second of two terms translated "blessed" in 1 Peter. "The first (*eulogētos*), found in 1:3 with a cognate form in 3:9, focuses attention on the divine source of blessing; while the second (*makarios*), used in 3:14 and 4:13 as also in the Sermon on the Mount, concentrates on the happy result."[12]

3) THE DIRECTIVES TO THOSE SUFFERING FOR RIGHTEOUSNESS (VV. 14b-16)

To consider oneself blessed when suffering persecution is not natural, and so Peter offered practical guidance. The Christian response has its demands, both negatively and positively. Negatively, Christians should not yield to the natural reactions of fear and agitation (v. 14b). Positively, they should keep

---

10. George Williams, *The Student's Commentary on the Holy Scriptures, Analytical, Synoptical, and Synthetical*, p. 1001.

11. F. Hauck, *makarios, makarizō, makarismos, TDNT*, 4:367.

12. G. J. Polkinghorne, *The First Letter of Peter*, p. 593.

Christ central in their lives and make appropriate responses to their adversaries (vv. 15-16).

A. THE HUMAN RESPONSE PROHIBITED (v. 14b)

"And" (*de*) indicates that more must be said. The Christian's personal realization of blessedness in suffering for righteousness involves his refusal of an inappropriate response: "fear not their fear, neither be troubled." The words are drawn from Isaiah 8:12 without a formula of citation.

The natural response of fear when suffering is categorically prohibited: "fear not their fear" (*ton phobon autōn mē phobēthēte*), literally, "the fear of them do not fear." The negative command, in the aorist tense, prohibits yielding to any kind of fear, and the articular noun, already involved in the verb, strengthens the concept of the fear being prohibited. Christians should not allow a feeling of fright and terror to grip them.

The force of the genitive *autōn* ("the fear *of them*") can be differently understood. It may be taken in a possessive, subjective sense, "their fear," the fear that your opponents themselves feel. That is the meaning of the Septuagint translation of Isaiah 8:12, the fear that gripped the people. For that reason, Demarest[13] and Mason[14] support that meaning. If that is correct then Peter urged his Christian readers not to fear the things that their non-Christian opponents themselves dreaded. That is the interpretation of the NIV, "Do not fear what they fear." But the context does not call for that meaning. It is more natural to understand the expression to mean the fear that their enemies sought to instill in them. That is the view of the NASB: "And do not fear their intimidation." Or the genitive may be viewed as having an objective relation to *fear*, a fear of the people themselves who opposed them. That is the view of the RSV, "Have no fear of them."[15] If that is correct then the meaning is, do not fear your threatening opponents. That is the view of Best, Kelly, Selwyn,[16] and others. The second and third views are closely related and either is possible. Because of the context, we prefer the meaning, Do not fear their threats.

"Neither be troubled" (*mēde tarachthēte*) carries the prohibition to its climax. The verb means to shake up or agitate, like water in a glass that has been sharply jarred; it conveys the picture of agitation and confusion. In John 5:4 (KJV) the verb is used literally of the troubling of the waters of the pool of Bethesda and in John 12:7 figuratively of Christ's troubled soul. The term pictures the result of yielding to the assault of fear; it describes "the agitation, distractions, surgings to and fro of thought and feeling, which are brought on by strong fear, and which tend to impede all the exercises of spiritual religion,

---

13. John T. Demarest, *A Translation and Exposition of the First Epistle of the Apostle Peter*, p. 163.
14. A. J. Mason, *The First Epistle General of Peter*, p. 418.
15. So also NEB, TEV, Goodspeed.
16. Best, p. 133; Kelly, p. 141-42; Edward Gordon Selwyn, *The First Epistle of St. Peter*, p. 192.

and to overthrow that restfulness of heart in God which should characterize the Christian."[17] The aorist prohibits any entry into such a state.

B. THE CHRISTIAN REACTIONS ENJOINED (vv. 15-16)

The negative directives prepare the way for and make effective the positive. "But" (*de*) marks the contrast between those two aspects. Peter stressed the basic duty of making Christ supreme in the inner life (v. 15a) and then set out supporting personal requirements for an effective testimony to the adversaries (vv. 15b-16).

(1) The personal enthronement of Christ as Lord (v. 15a). "Sanctify in your hearts Christ as Lord" specifies the primary positive demand. Here *sanctify* (*hagiasate*) does not mean "to purify, make holy," but "to treat as holy," to "set apart, enshrine as the object of supreme, absolute reverence, as free from all defilement and possessed of all excellence."[18] He must be set above all other allegiances. The aorist imperative demands that once for all Christ deliberately be given that position.

"In your hearts" specifies the inner sanctuary where Christ is to be enthroned and worshiped as sovereign. His acknowledged supremacy must begin in the readers' innermost beings, so dominating all of life. It creates a personal consciousness of the sanctity of life, setting them apart from the world and its evils.

"Christ as Lord" (*kurion ton Christon*) alone must have that position in their hearts. In the original those words stand emphatically before the verb: "as Lord the Christ sanctify in your hearts." The expression is an allusion to Isaiah 8:13 where the word "lord" (*kurion*) is the usual Septuagint translation of the Hebrew tetragrammaton YHWH, "Jehovah" or "Yahweh."[19] Peter's application of that term to Christ is another indication of his identification of Jesus Christ with the Yahweh of the Old Testament. The Greek expression may be translated in two different ways. It may be translated "the Lord Christ."[20] Lenski, a supporter of that translation, insists that the anarthrous *kurion* ("lord") is a proper name and thus needs no article and that the definite article with *Christon* ("the Christ") indicates that it is a second name standing in apposition to the first, thus making a unitary designation "the Lord Christ."[21] According to that view, Peter's expression is analogous to the common Septuagint expression *kurios ho theos*, "the Lord God" (cf. Gen. 2:4, 15-16; Rev. 19:6; 22:5). But the translation "Christ as Lord" is equally possible. The view that *kurion* is predicate is favored by its emphatic position at the very beginning of the clause as well as the introduction of the *de* ("but") after it,

17. Johnstone, p. 233.
18. Ibid., p. 234.
19. J. C. Connell, "God, Names of," *NBD*, p. 478.
20. So NEB, JB, Rotherham, Darby.
21. R. C. H. Lenski, *The Interpretation of the Epistles of St. Peter, St. John and St. Jude*, p. 151.

which is represented in neither the Hebrew or the Greek of Isaiah 8:13. Thus viewed, Peter's thought seems to linger specifically on Christ as their Lord, whom both he and his readers acknowledged as "the Christ," the incarnate fulfillment of the Old Testament messianic prophecies.[22] That is the view followed by the ASV and other recent English versions.[23] Selwyn supports that view with the assertion that it "surely" gives a better sense, and does more justice to the order of the words.[24] With Him as the Lord of their lives, Christians will have the grace and strength to stand firm in the midst of suffering for His sake.

(2) *The ready witness to all concerning their Christian hope* (vv. 15b-16). Out of our enthronement of Christ as Lord should flow a personal readiness to explain to opponents the nature of the hope that dominates our lives as Christians. It seems obvious that the directives offered were inspired and molded by Peter's own experiences. He insisted on a personal readiness to defend the hope Christians have (v. 15b), pointed out the personal requirements for effectiveness in witnessing (vv. 15c-16a), and indicated the contemplated impact of such a witness on those who slander believers (v. 16b).

(a) *The necessary readiness to defend their Christian hope* (v.15b). The directive to be ready to explain their Christian hope is added without an expressed verb: "*being* ready always to give answer to every man that asketh you a reason concerning the hope that is in you." The adjective "ready" (*hetoimoi*) relates grammatically with the second person plural subject "ye" of the imperative "sanctify," thus transferring to the adjectival addition an imperatival force. The sanctification of Christ as Lord involves the duty to witness concerning Him.

They should be "ready always" (*hetoimoi aei*), "never unprepared, never unwilling, never timid"[25] to respond to those who question them. That implies that Christianity had aroused public attention and created a curious interest in its nature. As committed believers, the readers were to be ready to state and defend their Christian stance. That does not mean that they had to be able to answer all the subtle questions critics might raise or solve all the problems that might be advanced against Christianity, but they were to be willing to defend it against malicious attacks for the sake of the truth as well as the questioner.

22. Instead of *ton Christon* the Textus Receptus, following the later uncials *KLP* and many minuscules, reads *ton theon*, "God." Textual and transcriptional evidence supports the reading *Christon*. See Bruce M. Metzger, *A Textual Commentary on the Greek New Testament*, p. 691.
23. RSV, NASB, NIV, Goodspeed, Moffatt, Montgomery, Berkeley, Weymouth, Williams.
24. Selwyn, p. 192.
25. Nathaniel Marshman Williams, *Commentary on the Epistles of Peter*, p. 49.

They were to be able to give an intelligent account of what they believed and had experienced. "Our faith must be a first-hand discovery, and not a second-hand story."[26]

Whenever confronted, Christians should be prepared "to give an answer" (*pros apologian*), literally, "for an apology," not in the modern sense of apologizing, but in the sense of making a defense. The compound noun denotes "a reasoning off" by way of removing misconceptions and answering objections, thus making a defense of one's position. In the post apostolic age there were certain Christian men called Apologists, like Justin Martyr (c. A.D.100-165), who wrote formal treatises in defense of Christianity. By life and testimony that should be the function of every believer. The term implies lack of sympathy toward or open opposition to believers.

The term "an apology" was used in connection with a formal public self-defense (Acts 22:1; 25:16; 2 Tim. 4:16), but it was also used of more private and informal utterances of that nature (2 Cor. 7:11). It is arbitrary to limit the meaning of the term to judicial examinations before a court of law. It obviously applies to occasions when Christians were called upon to defend themselves before a magistrate, but Peter's directive is not to be limited to such occasions. A broader picture is evident from the fact that the readers were told to reply "to every man" (*panti*), to every individual who makes an inquiry, not just to officials. Selwyn notes that the verb "asketh" (*aiteō*) "is a quite informal term, and indicates conversation rather than police enquiry."[27] The picture is best understood as offering guidance to the members of the church when "put upon their defense, whether by officious neighbours or by a magistrate."[28]

Whenever confronted, Christians should be prepared to give "a reason concerning the hope that is in you." *Reason* (*logon*) denotes a rational account given in response to inquiry (cf. Luke 16:2). *Concerning* (*peri*) pictures the inquiry as clustering around "the hope that is in you" (*tēs en humin elpidos*), literally, "the in you hope." The attributive position of the phrase "in you" indicates that in the mind of the questioner that hope was a characteristic feature of Christians as he had observed them. Some, like Best and Selwyn,[29] suggest that *in you* should be understood collectively as a reference to the Christian community. But it is more natural to accept the meaning as personal, "in your hearts" as a vital personal conviction. It is significant that the inquiry concerning the readers' Christianity is designated as "the hope" rather than "the faith," as we might have expected. An inquirer would naturally be interested in the doctrinal aspects of Christianity, but the term suggests that in an age of widespread frustration and uncertainty, it was the element of hope in the lives of the believers that aroused special interest. Though the questioner doubtless had but a vague understanding of the true nature of that hope and perhaps considered it one of the most absurd features of the new

26. William Barclay, *The Letters of James and Peter*, p. 273.
27. Selwyn, p. 193.
28. Wand, p. 98.
29. Best, p. 134; Selwyn, p. 194.

religion, he recognized its dynamic power in the lives of those believers amid their trials and afflictions. It is the living hope (1:3) to which we have been begotten again by God, a hope centered in the God who has revealed Himself in Christ, imparting present salvation and the hope of future glory (1:20-21). The experience of present salvation brings with it an assured hope concerning the future (Rom. 8:23-24), the blessed return of our Savior and Lord.

(b)*The personal factors for an effective witness* (vv. 15c-16a). The particle translated "yet" (*alla*) suggests contrast.[30] Apparently mindful of the arrogance so characteristic of their interrogators, Peter counseled his readers to reply "with meekness and fear." In facing their opponents they should manifest a different spirit. *Meekness* (*prautētos*) is not to be confused with weakness. It is the manifestation of an inner strength that enables an attitude of "gentleness, humility, courtesy, considerateness"[31] even toward those who do not manifest such a spirit. Though having full confidence in their own faith, Christians should avoid an attitude of arrogant belligerence in their defense of it. They must guard against giving an impression of haughty superiority toward their ignorant opponents. A personal modesty and genuine humility, suffused with a radiant hope, make for a winsome testimony.

Their answer should also be marked by fear (*phobos*). The reference is not to the fear of men that produces timidity. Nor does the view that it means the fear of God seem to fully satisfy the context. Rather, as G. Williams observes, "'Fear' may be understood to mean both reverence and caution—reverence because of the solemnity of the subject, and caution lest in the earnestness of discussion anything might be said which would give an opponent occasion to accuse the Christian to the civil magistrate."[32] There should be a conscious concern lest through their personal infirmity or lack of restraint the truth of God be brought into disrepute. Such a fear was needed whenever "inquirers" poured scorn and ridicule upon Christians and their faith. Luther, based on his own experience at Worms and elsewhere, commented,

> Then must ye not answer with proud words and bring out the matter with a defiance and with violence as if ye would tear up trees, but with such fear and lowliness as if ye stood before God's tribunal . . . so must thou stand in fear, and not rest on thine own strength, but on the word and promise of Christ. Matt. x. 19, 20.[33]

"Having a good conscience" (v. 16a) posits a further requirement for an effective witness. In making their defense Christians should maintain a good

---

30. A few uncials and most cursives have no particle; so the Textus Receptus.
31. William F. Arndt and F. Wilbur Gingrich, *A Greek-English Lexicon of the New Testament and Other Early Christian Literature*, p. 705.
32. G. Williams, p. 1001.
33. Quoted in Alford, part 1, pp. 362-63.

conscience in word, deed, and attitude. The original order, *suneidēsin echontes agathēn*, "a conscience having good," places the emphasis upon the adjective *good*; it stresses the moral quality of the conscience. That ascription of a moral quality to *suneidēsis* indicates that the term is used in the familiar sense of conscience, rather than consciousness (as in 2:19). Conscience is that God-implanted ability to evaluate the moral quality of human actions, our own (Rom. 9:1; 2 Cor. 1:12) or those of others (2 Cor. 5:11). Its operation makes us moral creatures. *Good* implies that the conscience has been cleansed and enlightened by God's grace to know what is right and wrong, and further, that its possessor obeys its dictates. The maintenance of such a conscience enables one to face an opponent without fear and effectively to defend the truth.

(c) *The contemplated impact upon vicious opponents* (v. 16*b*). "That" (*hina*) introduces the expected result of self-defense in the spirit indicated: "that, wherein ye are spoken against, they may be put to shame who revile your good manner of life in Christ." Though the antagonists will not always be silenced, something will be accomplished.

"Wherein ye are spoken against" (*en hō katalaleisthe*)[34] indicates that the opposition manifested itself in misrepresentations and slanderous lies, rather than official government persecution (cf. 2:12). The present tense denotes that repeatedly such charges were hurled against believers. But Peter was confident that the readers' rational defense in expounding their position as Christians would result in the opponents being put to shame (*kataischunthō-sin*)—effectively shamed and humiliated by the demonstration that their charges were false. Bigg noted that in 2:12 Peter "speaks of the righteousness of the Christian as likely to promote the conversion of the heathen, here simply as stopping the mouths of his defamers."[35] But even that would be a desirable result for the church.

"They . . . who revile" (*hoi epēreazontes*) is a strong designation for the opponents. The verb used conveys a more vicious attitude than the synonymous "speak against" (*katalaleō*) just before. It means "to threaten, mistreat, or abuse," and in Luke 6:28 (and in Matt. 5:44 as a variant reading) it is translated "despitefully use you." Johnstone notes that the verb involves "not thoughtless misrepresentation or insult merely, but an element of meanness and malignity."[36] The present participle pictures individuals habitually engaged in the practice of abusing and defaming them.

The enemy attacks were directed against "your good manner of life in

34. The KJV translation, "they speak evil of you, as of evildoers" represents the Textus Receptus. It apparently arose as a scribal conformation to the reading in 2:12. For the evidence see the United Bible Societies text *The Greek New Testament.*

35. Charles Bigg, *A Critical and Exegetical Commentary on the Epistles of St. Peter and St. Jude,* p. 159.

36. Johnstone, p. 241.

Christ," suggesting that the enemy's hatred was primarily generated by the way the Christians lived (cf. 4:4). The readers' manner of life was a vital concern to Peter. That is the sixth and last reference to it in the epistle (cf. 1:15). Two attributive modifiers (*tēn agathēn en Christō anastrophē*) describe the essential nature of that life. The first declares that the readers' conduct "being good in its character or constitution, is beneficial in its effect."[37] It is morally honorable and approved of God (note the repeated mention of *good* in the paragraph). In the closest connection with its moral character is the fact that it is in Christ. The excellence of the Christian life derives from its spiritual union with Christ. That distinctly Pauline phrase occurs only three times in 1 Peter (here; 5:10, 14). Outside of its repeated appearance in the Pauline letters, it does not occur elsewhere in the New Testament, but the thought is common to the apostle John. As applied to the lives of the readers, it pictures Christ as the sphere or atmosphere in which they lived and moved and had their being. As intimately united to Him, an attack upon their lives was an attack on Him. In verse 15 Peter pictured Christ as being in their hearts; here their life is in Christ. It is a union of essential being. In 5:10 Peter notes that that union has eschatological significance.

4. THE ASSURANCE AMID SUFFERING FOR RIGHTEOUSNESS (V. 17)

"For" (*gar*) can be understood to introduce a substantiation of the call for a good conscience (v. 16). But it may indicate a closing comment on the topic of the paragraph. The verse brings us back to the theme begun in verse 14 and offers encouragement to those suffering for righteousness. The encouragement, which was already extended to the household servants (2:20), is applied to the whole Christian community.

"It is better" (*kreitton*) indicates the contrast between the two conditions of suffering mentioned in the verse. Neither kind of suffering is pleasant, but their moral significance differs greatly. Suffering for well-doing is better "for you yourselves, because so you are in fellowship with the suffering Christ, and also because even a sense of injustice brings not so keen a smart as the prick of conscience. It is better also for the gainsayers if it silences them or brings them to a better mind."[38]

The original order, as reproduced by Robert Young, "it is better doing good, if the will of God will it, to suffer, than doing evil," makes prominent the activity of the sufferer who receives the assurance. *For well-doing* (*agathopoiountas*) may also be translated "while doing good." That would indicate the condition under which the suffering takes place. The other translation, indicating the reason for the suffering, seems more in keeping with the context. If that is correct, then it is an instance of the persecutors being incensed by the good behavior of those they attack.

---

37. W. E. Vine, *An Expository Dictionary of New Testament Words with Their Precise Meanings for English Readers*, 2:163.

38. Wand, p. 99.

"If the will of God should so will," an emphatic pleonasm, stresses the improbability of such suffering under ordinary conditions by the use of the optative mood.[39] Though the unlikely was happening, it was not a matter of blind chance. The unusual wording calls strong attention to the operation of the divine will in the matter. *The will of God* (*to thelēma tou theou*) personifies the divine will as involved in the situation, while *so will* (*theloi*) indicates the action itself. The suffering of God's people for well-doing is not God's usual but His unusual will for them. As living under His grace, His will is involved in whatever happens to us. If He permits suffering, it is for our good. As Luther remarked, "Go on in faith and love; if the cross comes, take it; if it comes not, do not seek it."[40]

Suffering for well-doing is vastly better than suffering for evildoing. If a believer, because of his sin or foolishness, endures the latter kind of suffering, there is no merit in it. Then he must hang his head in shame and seek divine forgiveness.

39. A fourth class condition: "Undetermined with Remote Prospect of Determination," A. T. Robertson and W. Hersey David, *A New Short Grammar of the Greek Testament*, p. 354.

40. Quoted in G. F. C. Fronmüller, *The Epistles General of Peter*, p. 60.

16

B. The Experience of Christ Suffering for Righteousness
(3:18-22)

(18) Because Christ also suffered for sins once, the righteous for the unrighteous, that he might bring us to God; being put to death in the flesh, but made alive in the spirit; (19) in which also he went and preached unto the spirits in prison, (20) that aforetime were disobedient, when the longsuffering of God waited in the days of Noah, while the ark was a preparing, wherein few, that is, eight souls, were saved through water: (21) which also after a true likeness doth now save you, *even* baptism, not the putting away of the filth of the flesh, but the interrogation of a good conscience toward God, through the resurrection of Jesus Christ; (22) who is on the right hand of God, having gone into heaven; angels and authorities and powers being made subject unto him.

That paragraph is notoriously obscure and difficult to interpret. A study of that much-debated portion readily brings to mind the Petrine comment concerning the Pauline epistles, "wherein are some things hard to be understood" (2 Pet. 3:16). The difficulty arises in the central part of the paragraph, which presents "one notorious centre of controversy, which involves serious doctrinal implications (the 'preaching to spirits' in verse 19), and a fairly obscure piece of typology (the Flood as a type of Christian baptism, verses 20-21)."[1] But it is a matter of gratitude that the commencement of the passage, which declares the aim of Christ's vicarious suffering (v. 18), and the conclusion, which depicts the culmination of His suffering in triumph (v. 22)—matters that are essential to our faith—are clear and unambiguous.

1. R. T. France, "Exegesis in Practice: Two Samples," p. 264.

The unifying theme of that perplexing section is the undeserved suffering of Christ for righteousness. As the initial "because" (*hoti*, v. 18) indicates, it is intended to encourage the readers to persevere in their own suffering and also to assure them of the coming triumph in Christ as risen and exalted.

Attempts have been made to find in it fragments of a primitive hymn or creed. Selwyn suggested that the passage "rests in all probability on the creedal hymn quoted in I Tim. iii. 16."[2] Efforts have even been made to reconstruct the original hymn being quoted.[3] Others, like Cullmann,[4] are impressed with the creedal character of the passage and suggest that an early Christian creed is being drawn on. That the passage does reflect creedal elements already in use in the Christian church is commonly accepted today. But scholars do not agree about the extent of the hymnal or creedal material being quoted. We concur with Kelly that "the element of sheer guesswork in such reconstructions makes them of doubtful value."[5] Fragments of hymnal or creedal extraction may possibly be found in verses 18 and 22, but verses 19-21, with their involved structure, are not poetic in form and read much more like an independent construction of the writer. Though some of the material was apparently used in the early church in expressions of Christian faith, the paragraph is best viewed as Peter's own formulation.

The treatment of Christian suffering for righteousness in verses 13-17 prompted Peter to refer to Christ's undeserved suffering (v. 18*a*); that elicited an involved treatment of the consequences of His suffering (vv. 18*b*-21), concluding with a declaration of its triumphant culmination (v. 22).

1) THE CHARACTER OF HIS SUFFERING (V. 18*a-b*)

"Because Christ also suffered for sins once, the righteous for the unrighteous, that he might bring us to God" are words that have aptly been characterized as "one of the shortest and simplest, and yet one of the richest, summaries given in the New Testament of the meaning of the Cross of Jesus."[6]

Because (*hoti*) indicates that Peter was offering encouragement to his afflicted readers. Some, like Huther[7] and Bigg,[8] relate what follows to the immediately preceding idea as giving the ground for the *better* in verse 17. But

---

2. Edward Gordon Selwyn, *The First Epistle of St. Peter*, pp. 17-18.

3. See Ernest Best, *I Peter*, pp. 135-37; William Joseph Dalton, *Christ's Proclamation to the Spirits*, pp. 90-102; Jack T. Sanders, *The New Testament Christological Hymns, Their Historical Religious Background*, pp. 95-96.

4. Oscar Cullmann, *The Earliest Christian Confessions*, p. 20.

5. J. N. D. Kelly, *A Commentary on the Epistles of Peter and of Jude*, p. 147.

6. J. M. E. Ross, *The First Epistle of Peter. A Devotional Commentary*, pp. 151-52.

7. Joh Ed. Huther, *Critical and Exegetical Handbook to the General Epistles of Peter and Jude*, p. 174.

8. Charles Bigg, *A Critical and Exegetical Commentary on the Epistles of St. Peter and St. Jude*, p. 159.

others, like Lenski[9] and Dalton,[10] argue that the connection is with the entire preceding paragraph (vv. 13-17), which they believe offers a firm basis for the call to suffer for righteousness. Such suffering brought the readers into close identity with the experience of their Lord and Savior. It is "clear proof," Macknight observes, "that sufferings are no evidence of the wickedness of the sufferer, nor of the badness of the cause for which he suffers."[11]

"Christ also" (*kai Christos*), or perhaps, "Christ himself,"[12] indicates something of a parallel between Christ and His followers. Peter had already touched on that parallel in 2:21, where Christ is held up as our example in suffering. But the statement here makes it clear that Christ's suffering "is not presented as an example, but rather as something quite unique, beyond imitation; it does not present so much a standard of behaviour as the objective ground and cause of salvation."[13] Believers cannot share His redemptive suffering; His suffering assures their own eventual victory amid present suffering.

A. THE PORTRAYAL OF HIS SUFFERING (v. 18a)

"Christ also suffered for sins once, the righteous for the unrighteous" indicates the fact and the redemptive nature of His suffering. Some textual variants call for attention. Most significant is the question whether *suffered* (*epathen*) or *died* (*apethanen*) is the original reading. The manuscript evidence for *died* is stronger, but due to critical considerations textual editors are divided.[14] *Died* is the reading followed in most recent English versions.[15] In favor of *suffered* is the fact that that term occurs eleven times elsewhere in 1 Peter, but *died* does not occur elsewhere in the epistle. *Died* abruptly introduces a new idea; *suffered* better carries on the thought of verse 17. *Died* seems more likely to be a scribal change because of the added words "for sins." The thought is not materially affected by either reading since the reference is clearly to Christ's Passion. Later scribes probably changed *suffered* to *died* to make that clear because they failed to observe that early Christian usage included Christ's death in His suffering. A number of manuscripts also have the words "for us" or "for you,"[16] but they seem to be scribal glosses to make the statement more personal.

9. R. C. H. Lenski, *The Interpretation of the Epistles of St. Peter, St. John and St. Jude*, p. 157.
10. Dalton, pp. 103-12.
11. James Macknight, *A New Literal Translation from the Original Greek of All the Apostolical Epistles, with a Commentary, and Notes*, 5:478.
12. So translated in 20th Cent., TEV, JB, Moffatt, Goodspeed, Williams.
13. Dalton, p. 104.
14. *Epathen* ("suffered")—Scrivner, Souter, Nestle-Aland (26th ed.), United Bible Societies (3d ed.). *Apethanen* ("died")—Westcott and Hort, United Bible Societies (1st ed.), Nestle-Aland (24th ed.), Tasker.
15. So NASB, NIV, RSV, NEB, TEV, Berkeley, JB, Rotherham, 20th Cent., Weymouth, Moffatt, Goodspeed, Williams, Kleist and Lilly.
16. For the diversity of the readings see Bruce M. Metzger, *A Textual Commentary on the Greek New Testament*, pp. 692-93.

Peter's Gentile readers may have understood *Christ* as a proper name, but for Peter the term implied the messianic identity of the sufferer (Matt. 16:16). Peter once strongly objected to the thought of the Messiah suffering (Matt. 16:22), but here he firmly declares that historical fact. The original places the verb prominently at the end of the clause, "Christ also once for sins suffered."

Two terms characterize His suffering. "Once" (*hapax*) or "once for all," together with the aorist tense of the verb, indicates the uniqueness of Christ's work as something that cannot be repeated.[17] The word conveys "a note of triumphant vindication implicit in the 'it is finished' from the Saviour's own lips on the Cross (Jn. 19:30)."[18] The once-for-all offering of Christ stands in contrast to the annual sacrifice of the Jewish high priest on the day of Atonement and portrays the absolute sufficiency of His atoning work (Heb. 9:24-28; 10:12). *For sins* (*peri hamartiōn*) reveals that Christ's suffering was more than just exemplary; His suffering gathered around or centered on the mass of human sins in a way that the sufferings of mortal men could never do. According to Whedon, the preposition *peri* ("for") "represents Christ throwing himself down upon and around sins in such a manner that the falling curse of the broken law would surely strike him."[19] *For sin* (*peri harmartias*) is the regular phrase in the Septuagint for the sin-offering (Lev. 5:7; 6:30; etc.) and conveys the thought of atonement. But the use of the plural may indicate that the sacrificial parallel was not consciously in mind. The plural points to the mass of sins that He bore for mankind in His death.

"The righteous for the unrighteous" (*dikaios huper adikōn*) directs attention to the character of the sufferer as well as those who benefit from His sacrificial death. Used without an article, the two antithetical terms bring into effective contrast the moral character of both parties, "a righteous One in place of unrighteous ones." The designation "the righteous," was apparently a title for Christ in the early church (Acts 3:14; 7:52; 22:14), but Peter stressed His moral character, which fully qualified Him to deal with sin, not His identity. As righteous (*dikios*), "His whole nature and action are in conformity with the norm of the divine will."[20] His sinlessness qualified Him to act for (*huper*), "instead of," "as the substitute for," those who failed to conform to the divine standard of right. The designation indicates the vicarious nature of Christ's death.[21] "The one Man, whose perfect righteousness meant that He never deserved to die, endured the pains of death on behalf of those who deserved to

---

17. "The Roman Catholic mass is a denial of the phrase that Christ died once. . . . The mass is said to be a propitiatory sacrifice, and is rightly offered for sin and satisfaction, or atonement. And the same Christ dies every time the mass is celebrated." Gordon H. Clark, *Peter Speaks Today*, pp. 122-23.

18. G. J. Polkinghorne, *The First Letter of Peter*, p. 593.

19. D. D. Whedon, *A Popular Commentary on the New Testament*, 5:209.

20. Gottlob Schrenk, *dikaios*, *TDNT*, 2:186.

21. For the use of *huper* in the papyri to indicate substitution see A. T. Robertson, *The Minister and His Greek New Testament*, chap. 3; *A Grammar of the Greek New Testament in the Light of Historical Research*, pp. 630-32.

die."[22] The picture is apparently based on Isaiah 53. It was the expressed mission of the Messiah voluntarily "to give his life a ransom for many" (Mark 10:45), a message that lies at the very heart of the Christian gospel of forgiveness and salvation (Rom. 8:3-4; 2 Cor. 5:21; Gal. 3:13-14; 1 John 2:2). Peter had already indicated the vicarious nature of Christ's sufferings in 2:24.

B. THE AIM OF HIS SUFFERING (v. 18b)

"That he might bring us to God" gives a clear, concise statement of the great purpose in the once-for-all death of Christ on behalf of sinners. That was well-doing in the highest sense. The statement implies the effectual realization of the purpose on Christ's side; that sinful men must accept the provision He made is assumed. "And the fact that the Son of God loved men, and gave himself a sacrifice for them, enduring such bitter sorrows, is the most powerful appeal which can be made to mankind to induce them to return to God."[23]

"Might bring us to God" indicates mankind's universal need. We were "at a distance from God; and this implies ignorance of His character and will —enmity and alienation—moral dissimilarity—and the want of any favorable intercourse and fellowship."[24] But through His atoning death sin-estranged human beings may be restored to fellowship with God (tō theō), the true God whom believers know personally. The dative implies a direct personal relationship with God. We are restored to His gracious favor now; hereafter we shall be restored to His blissful presence. The manuscripts differ between the personal pronouns "us" (hēmas) and "you" (humas).[25] The textual editors[26] and the English versions[27] differ on the reading accepted as original. The confusion, present elsewhere, reflects the similarity of pronunciation of the two forms in New Testament times. The first person seems more natural as denoting all believers, but it may be argued that copyists would be more likely to change the second person, which applies the teaching to the readers, to the first person. The meaning is clear with either reading.

The compound verb "may bring" (prosagagē), in the aorist tense, implies actual entry into an intimate personal relationship. The verb is used with varied associations, and different suggestions have been offered for the intended metaphor that underlies Peter's expression. Suggested figures are (1) the presentation of a sacrifice for reconciliation with God, (2) the entry of the high priest into the Holy of Holies on the Day of Atonement, (3) the

---

22. David H. Wheaton, *I Peter*, p. 1244.

23. Albert Barnes, *Notes on the New Testament, Explanatory and Practical—James, Peter, John, and Jude*, p. 175.

24. John Lillie, *Lectures on the First and Second Epistles of Peter*, p. 233.

25. See the evidence in the United Bible Societies text, *The Greek New Testament* (3d ed.).

26. "Us" (hēmas)—Textual Receptus, Souter, Tasker. "You" (humas)—Westcott and Hort, Nestle-Aland, United Bible Societies.

27. "Us"—NASB, RSV, NEB, JB, Berkeley, KJV, Rotherham, R. Young, Darby, Weymouth, Montgomery, Moffatt, Williams, Kliest and Lilly. "You"—NIV, TEV, 20th Cent., Goodspeed.

presentation before the judge in a court of law, (4) the bringing in of an individual for an audience with the king and, (5) even the bringing in of the initiate before the savior-god in the mystery cults. A mystery religion background is totally unwarranted, for such was completely outside of Peter's experience and viewpoint. Neither need an Old Testament sacrificial scene be read into the picture since there is no clear indication of any sacrificial terminology in the expression. It seems best to understand the statement in a nontechnical manner as a statement of the aim of the work of Christ to bring about man's reconciliation with God. The most natural figure would be that of the forgiven sinner being brought into the presence of the king by Christ, our Redeemer (cf. Rom. 5:2, where the noun form is used).

2) THE CONSEQUENCES OF HIS SUFFERING (VV. 18c-21)

That terse statement characterizing Christ's suffering is followed by an involved and difficult elaboration of its consequences. Peter believed that Christ's sufferings should be viewed in the light of their glorious consequences. He mentioned the violent death and quickening of the sufferer (v. 18c), depicted His preaching to the spirits in prison (vv. 19-20b), and commented on the typological significance of those saved through the Flood (vv. 20c-21).

A. THE DEATH AND RESURRECTION OF THE SUFFERER (v. 18c)

The portrayal of the suffering Savior is presented in two balanced phrases: "being put to death in the flesh, but made alive in the spirit." The use of *men . . . de*, "on the one hand . . . on the other hand," marks the antithesis; the construction is identical, indicating intended balance and correspondence between its members. There is evident contrast between the verbs as well as the nouns.

"Put to death in the flesh" (*thanatōtheis men sarki*) indicates the violent death of Jesus that terminated "the days of his flesh" (Heb. 5:7), His life as a man here on earth. *Put to death*, an aorist passive participle, recalls the violent action of men against Him in crucifying Him. Humanly speaking, it was a miscarriage of justice, yet the sovereign God overruled it to fulfill His redemptive purposes (Acts 2:22-24). *In the flesh* (*sarki*) points to the reality of His death as a real human being. He was no docetic phantom who only appeared to have a human body. *Flesh* refers to the humanity that Christ assumed at the incarnation (John 1:14; 1 Tim. 3:16). Used without an article, *flesh* is qualitative and characterizes Him as a human being, a man among men here on earth.

"But made alive in the spirit" (*zōotoiētheis de pneumati*) offers a glorious antithesis to the preceding declaration of His death. The passive indicates the operation of an outside power; God acted to make Him alive again (cf. Acts 2:36; 4:10; Rom. 8:11; 1 Pet. 1:21). In view of *in the spirit* (*pneumati*) some interpreters believe that the reference is not to Christ's bodily resurrection but to the quickening of His spirit, which, set free from the limitations of His body, entered into a new life in the spiritual realm and engaged in spiritual activities in the spiritual world.[28] According to that view, what follows in verse 19 naturally relates to a time between Christ's death and resurrection. But the antithetical structure of those two clauses more naturally suggests His resurrection, not His death. The verb, which occurs in ten other places, refers to the resurrection of the dead (John 5:21 twice ; Rom. 5:17; 8:11; 1 Cor. 15:22, 36, 45) or denotes the giving of spiritual life (John 6:63; 2 Cor. 3:6; Gal. 3:21). It means to give life where before it had ceased to be or where it had never been. In Romans 8:11 it is used synonymously with *raised up* (*egeirō*) as an affirmation of the resurrection. That supports the reference to Christ's resurrection here.[29] The redemptive victory of Christ was not complete until His resurrection. It does not refer to a quickening of His disembodied spirit that did not die.

The balanced grammatical structure also implies an antithesis between *flesh* (*sarki*) and *spirit* (*pneumati*), suggesting that the two nouns should be understood to be in the same case.[30] The latter term may readily be regarded as instrumental, "by the spirit" (KJV), to denote that Jesus was raised by the Holy Spirit; but the former term cannot be given a parallel meaning, for Jesus was not put to death by the flesh."[31] The two terms are best taken as datives of reference, "as regards flesh . . . as regards spirit." But how are *flesh* and *spirit* to be understood?

Some have understood the two terms to denote the material and the nonmaterial sides of the man Jesus. Such a view faces the problem of how His nonmaterial soul or spirit can be said to have been raised to life. Either the verb must be given the meaning "to preserve alive" or we must accept that His nonmaterial being actually died and was brought back to life. Neither alternative is acceptable. Such a dichotomous understanding of the nature of man is influenced by Greek philosophical views. A contrast between *flesh* and *spirit* as denoting corporeality and incorporeality is foreign to the Old Testament, which nurtured Peter's views; nor can it be readily established in the New Testament.[32]

Others believe that the contrast is between the human and divine natures of our incarnate Lord. Thus Whedon, who adopts that view, explains the situation as follows:

28. John Albert Bengel, *New Testament Word Studies*, 2:746; B. C. Caffin, *The First Epistle General of Peter*, p. 133; A. J. Mason, *The First Epistle General of Peter*, p. 420; J. W. C. Wand, *The General Epistles of St. Peter and St. Jude*, p. 100.

29. Ernest Best, *I Peter*, p. 139; Rudolf Bultmann, *zōopoieō*, *TDNT*, 2:874-75; Dalton, pp. 126-27; Kelly, p. 150; Selwyn, p. 197.

30. Whedon rejects the view that the two nouns must be in the same case and asserts that the case is fixed by the meaning of the two participles (p. 211).

31. John Calvin, *The Epistle of Paul the Apostle to the Hebrews and the First and Second Epistles of St Peter*, explains that death as due to "the weakness of the flesh" (p. 292).

32. Dalton, pp. 124-32; J. A. T. Robinson, *The Body, A Study in Pauline Theology*, pp. 26-33.

As God-man he was *dead*; and, though his human soul still lived in union with his divine nature, while held in the bonds of death he was powerless to apply the benefits of his dying. By his resurrection he became "Lord both of the dead and living," (Rom. xiv. 9,) and won that power.[33]

Thus understood, that view is plausible. But Dalton indicates that such a reference to the divinity of Christ is not in keeping with the flesh-spirit distinction found in the New Testament.[34]

We accept as most probable the view of those scholars who see a reference to the whole Christ in both terms.[35] Both *flesh* and *spirit*, used without an article, emphasize quality and denote two contrasted modes of our Lord's existence, before and after the resurrection. As the incarnate Christ, both involve His body. In the words of Kelly:

> By *flesh* is meant Christ in His human sphere of existence, considered as a man among men. By *spirit* is meant Christ in His heavenly, spiritual sphere of existence, considered as divine spirit; and this does not exclude His bodily nature, since as risen from the dead it is glorified.[36]

The contrast is between Christ's death as a real man here on earth and His risen life as the glorified Lord. *Flesh* and *spirit* thus denote two successive spheres of existence of the incarnate Christ. *Made alive in the spirit* does not refer to Christ *disembodied*, the period between His death and resurrection.

B. THE PREACHING TO "THE SPIRITS IN PRISON" (vv. 19-20b)

The difficulties of this paragraph cluster around the words of verse 19, taken in connection with the last phrase of verse 18: "in which also he went and preached unto the spirits in prison" (*en hō kai tois en phulakē pneumasin poreutheis ekēruxen*). Each of the nine words in the original has been differently understood; they have promoted much speculation and served as a basis for unscriptural teaching. The literature on the problem is voluminous.

The passage poses a series of intriguing and baffling questions: Who are "the spirits in prison"? Where is the prison? When did Christ preach to them? What was His message? Those and other questions have received various answers. As France remarks, "There is probably no more agreement about its exegesis now than there ever has been."[37] We propose to take the words in the order of the text and let them pose the various problems.

The manuscripts present no textual problem for verse 19, yet at various times some scholars have suggested a textual emendation for the opening

---

33. Whedon, p. 211.
34. Dalton, pp. 132-34.
35. Best, p. 139; Dalton, pp. 124-34; Kelly, pp. 150-51.
36. Kelly, p. 151.
37. France, p. 264.

words "in which also."[38] It has been suggested that due to similarity of sound, those first three Greek words (*ENOKAI*) should read "in which also Enoch" (*ENOKAIENOX*). That suggestion was popularized by J. Rendall Harris and was adopted in the translations of Moffatt and of Goodspeed. The conjecture has received little support from modern scholars. Kelly dismisses it as "a brilliant but untenable guess."[39] It does not add to the intelligibility of an already obscure passage; it only adds a new note to a difficult passage dealing with the work of Christ. The conjecture is without a shred of manuscript evidence to support it.

Peter mentioned Christ's preaching to the imprisoned spirits (v. 19) and added a further characterization of them (v. 20a-b).

(1) The activity in relation to "the spirits" (v. 19). It seems obvious that Peter expected to be understood when he wrote, "in which he also went and preached unto the spirits in prison." His purpose seems to have been to encourage his afflicted readers with evidence of the victory of the suffering Christ. But subsequent ages have been perplexed about his exact meaning.

"In which" (*en hō*) raises the question of the antecedent on which the pronoun depends. Most interpreters agree that the neuter pronoun relates back directly to the immediately preceding *spirit* (*pneumati*). If that is correct then the reference is to an activity of Christ in His resurrected state. But others regard the whole preceding phrase as the antecedent and would translate "in which process"[40] or "on which occasion."[41] If that is correct then the activity relates to the disembodied Christ and took place between His death and resurrection. The use of the relative in 1:6; 2:12; 3:16; and 4:4 seems to support that broad view of the antecedent. But in none of those instances is there a masculine or neuter noun in the preceding clause that could naturally be taken as the antecedent. Here such an antecedent for the relative is immediately available in the noun *spirit*. We believe that *in which* refers directly to Christ in His resurrection life, rather than to a time between His death and resurrection.

"Also" (*kai*), to be taken with the following words, indicates that a further activity of Christ is presented. Peter had already mentioned the redemptive activity of Christ suffering to bring us to God (v. 18). His achievement of bringing sinful man back into fellowship with God was grounded in His atoning suffering. But its effectual operation in human experience required His resurrection. It is as the risen Lord that He brings us to God (cf. Rom. 4:23—5:2). That truth was precious to the hearts of Peter's readers. But as a further encouragement, a second activity of the risen Christ, which took place in the sphere of the spirit world, is mentioned. Christ was victor also in the world of evil spirits.

38. Edgar J. Goodspeed, *Problems of New Testament Translation*, pp. 195-98.
39. Kelly, p. 152.
40. Selwyn, p. 197.
41. So Reicke, *The Disobedient Spirits and Christian Baptism*, p. 113.

The original word order draws attention to the recipients of that ministry: "in which also to the in prison spirits having gone he proclaimed" (Gr.). They are emphatically identified as "the spirits in prison" (*tois en phulakē pneumasin*). The attributive position of the prepositional phrase "in prison" (*en phulakē*) most naturally implies that it was as imprisoned spirits that Christ preached to them.[42]

There is no agreement regarding the identity of those spirits, but there are three main views. The latest view of their identity understands them as men alive after Pentecost to whom the gospel was preached by Christ through the apostles—men in a natural prison-house of bondage to sin and Satan.[43] The men of Noah's day are seen as a notable example of the sinful race. Ephesians 2:17 and Acts 26:23 are appealed to in support of that interpretation of Christ's preaching. But the view is beset with difficulty. Such a highly figurative meaning for *prison* seems unlikely and is contrary to the prevailing meaning of the term in Scripture as a place of confinement for criminals, real or supposed. Nor does the aorist participle, "having gone," fit such an extended ministry; it empties the term of real significance. As Johnstone points out, "The fatal objection to the exegesis lies in its making the principal clause and the subordinate apply to different sets of persons."[44]

Another view (which goes back at least as far as Augustine)[45] understands the spirits who are now in prison as the disembodied souls of the people who perished in the Flood and argues that the preincarnate Christ preached to them through Noah, warning them of the coming Flood and urging them to repent. That view found wide acceptance in the Medieval western church and was adopted by many leaders after the Reformation. The view is attractive and has strong advocates today.[46] It agrees with Peter's reference to Noah as "a preacher of righteousness" in 2 Peter 2:5. The idea of Christ preaching through Noah can be understood on the principle of Ephesians 2:17. It eliminates any reference to the difficult doctrine of Christ's descent into hell (Hades). But there are difficulties for that interpretation. That Christ's preaching should suddenly be equated with the preaching of Noah is not obvious. The word "preached" in the aorist tense naturally implies a specific event rather than a series of admonitions extending over long years. It empties

---

42. Matthew Poole, *A Commentary on the Holy Bible*, circumvents the natural force of the attributive position as follows: "The Greek participle of the present tense is here to be supplied, and the word thus read, preached to the spirits which are in prison, viz, now at this time; and so the time of their being in prison is opposed to the time of their being disobedient" (3:911). So the NASB, "made proclamation to the spirits *now* in prison."

43. John Brown, *Expository Discourses on First Epistle of the Apostle Peter*, 2:463-75; W. H. Griffith Thomas, *The Apostle Peter*, pp. 214, 216-17.

44. Robert Johnstone, *The First Epistle of Peter*, p. 261.

45. In the letter of Augustine (A.D. 354-430) to Euodius. For the history of the view, see Reicke, pp. 37-47.

46. So Arno C. Gaebelein, *The Annotated Bible*, 9:78-80; C. E. B. Cranfield, *I & II Peter and Jude*, p. 102; William MacDonald, *I Peter: Faith Tested, Future Triumphant*, pp. 80-81; Ray Summers, *1 Peter*, p. 164. The monograph *The Preaching to Spirits in Prison, 1 Peter III. 18-20*, by William Kelly, defends that view but devotes itself to a refutation of divergent views.

the participle translated "he went" (*poreutheis*) of its personal significance and reduces it to an empty pleonasm. It evades the natural implication of Peter's word order that the preaching was to imprisoned spirits. Also the description of them as "aforetime disobedient" implies a period antecedent to the time of the preaching.

Apparently, the oldest identification of those imprisoned spirits understood them as the fallen angels of Genesis 6. That view was widely known and generally taken for granted in the apostolic era. It is strongly presented in the Book of Enoch, a composite, pre-Christian, Jewish apocryphal writing widely known in the early Christian church; the Book of Enoch fell into disfavor with the fourth-century church.[47] The angelic transgression was always understood as having taken place just prior to the Flood. Proponents of that view point to 2 Peter 2:4-5 and Jude 6 as evidence that it was known and accepted in the early Christian church. In 2 Peter 2 the reference to the imprisonment of sinning angels is immediately followed by a reference to the Flood. Proponents note that Peter's terminology is in harmony with that identification. They point out that in the New Testament *spirits* is regularly used to denote supernatural beings; *unclean spirits* occurs frequently in the gospels of supernatural beings (Mark 1:23, 26, 27; 3:11; 5:2, 8; etc.). The only clear instance in the New Testament where *spirits* is used of the surviving part of man after death is in Hebrews 12:23, but that is immediately indicated by the addition: "of just men made perfect."[48] References to spirits as supernatural beings, either good or bad, occur in the intertestamental literature (Tobit 6:6; 2 Macc. 3:24; Jubilees 15:31; Testament of Dan 1:7; 5:5) and in the writings from Qumran (1 QS 3:17ff; 1 QM 12:8f; 13:10). France argues that Peter's terminology "would unquestionably be understood in this sense by a contemporary reader, especially one at all familiar with Jewish apocalyptic and other inter-testamental literature."[49] Though we do not believe that Peter drew from such a source, it is clear that his words reflect acquaintance with such teaching. We believe the identification with fallen angels is the most probable in view of the parallel teaching in 2 Peter 2:4 and Jude 6.[50]

The words "went and preached" (*poreutheis ekēruxen*) have likewise received voluminous discussion. The participle "went," used with the verb, "marks the act of having gone as subsidiary to that of speaking as a herald."[51] The participle naturally denotes a specific change of location on the part of the herald. Those who see a reference to the preincarnate Christ preaching through Noah feel that no personal movement need be implied and that the participle is pleonastic. But if the reference is to Christ Himself, there seems to be no more justification for eliminating personal movement here than in

47. H. G. Andersen, "Enoch, Books of," *ZPEB*, 2:310-11.

48. In Luke 24:37, 39 the word "spirit" means a ghost or man's angelic counterpart. In Luke 23:46 and Acts 7:59 "my spirit" is probably a substitute for the personal pronoun.

49. France, p. 269.

50. For a full presentation of that identification see Dalton, chaps. 5-8.

51. Lenski, p. 165.

verse 22, where movement is obvious. But in what direction did He go? Dalton insists that since the participle in verse 22 definitely refers to the ascension, it must also do so here.[52] The term is neutral in itself and does not determine the direction of the movement. In verse 22 the upward movement is indicated by the words "into heaven." If those spirits in prison are to be equated with the angels that sinned in 2 Peter 2:4, the movement was clearly downward, to Tartarus (Gr.), which in Greek thought and in Jewish apocalyptic literature was understood as a place of punishment lower than Hades. The time of that descent, not mentioned elsewhere in Scripture, is not certain.

"Preached" (*ekēruxen*), here used absolutely, is another crucial term for the interpretation. The verb occurs only here in the Petrine epistles but appears sixty-one times in the New Testament. It means "to announce, to proclaim aloud," as a herald, to make a public proclamation. The content of the proclamation must be indicated by the context. Though the New Testament uses the verb in a neutral sense (Luke 12:3; Rev. 5:2), in the vast majority of its occurrences, it refers to the preaching of the gospel. Because of that prevailing usage, many interpreters agree with Best: "There is no reason to reject the normal NT meaning of 'preach,' i.e., that it relates to salvation. What is not clear is the result."[53] Thus interpreted, that verse has been appealed to in support of the so-called larger hope, or, more correctly, a second chance. But there are difficulties with such an interpretation. The original meaning of the term is consistent with the fact that in the Septuagint, with which Peter certainly was familiar, the verb is used of bringing bad news as well as good (cf. Jonah 1:2; 3:2, 4 [LXX]). France observes that "the statement in verse 22 that all spiritual powers are subject to Christ would cohere better with a proclamation of his victory than with an offer of salvation." He further remarks, "The purpose of the letter, to boost the morale of persecuted Christians, would be better served by a mention of Christ's triumphing over evil powers than of an offer of salvation to them."[54] The apocryphal story of Enoch's mission to the fallen angels, which was familiar to the apostle Peter, involves a proclamation of judgment, not of mercy (1 Enoch 14:4-5). We do not believe that Peter said that Christ preached the gospel to those imprisoned spirits; he taught that Christ announced His triumph over evil, which was bad news for them. For Peter's readers, however, it meant comfort and encouragement.

(2) The characterization of the "spirits" (v. 20a-b). "That aforetime were disobedient" (*apeithēsasin pote*), "unyielding at one time" (Rotherham), summarily characterizes those spirits by their former conduct. The verb conveys more than an attitude of unbelief; it involves deliberate disobedience, conscious resistance to authority. Here, as in Peter's three previous uses of it (2:7-8; 3:1), the opposition is Godward. *Aforetime* (*pote*), "formerly, at some time in the

52. Dalton, pp. 159-61.
53. Best, p. 144.
54. France, p. 271.

past," indicates that their disobedience took place prior to their imprisonment and Christ's announcement to them. If our identification of those spirits is correct, the reference is to the angelic transgression of God's command (Gen. 6; Jude 6-7). The aorist participle, without an article, describes them by their governing characteristic: they belong to that class. If applied to Noah's contemporaries, the term describes them as notorious examples of those who reject God's word and warning.

The time and circumstances of that disobedience are more specifically indicated in the following clauses: "when the longsuffering of God waited in the days of Noah, while the ark was a preparing." That time reference agrees with the tradition concerning those fallen angels, which always links them with the events before the Flood. The double compound verb "waited" (*apexedecheto*),[55] standing emphatically before the subject, indicates continued eager waiting for something to happen, an attitude of waiting it out. In all of its other New Testament occurrences, that verb is used of the Christian expectation of the Parousia. Only here is it used without an expressed object. If any expressed object of God's waiting is to be understood, it must be the voluntary termination of the evil being carried on. The term does not suggest optimism; it emphasizes God's patient forbearance of evil before judgment falls. Peter's expression, "the longsuffering of God," personifies God's patience with evil—a veritable manifestation of the divine.

The disobedience in view occurred "in the days of Noah," during his lifetime. The reference does not settle the question of the identity of the spirits in prison since it can apply either to the people of Noah's day or to the fallen angels whose activity is uniformly related to the era before the Flood. The added designation, "while the ark was a preparing" (*kataskeuazomenēs kibōtou*)—a genitive absolute—further defines and limits the time of waiting. Noah constructed the ark at God's command (Gen. 6:13-14)—a huge construction project. The present participle "preparing" indicates the prolonged activity. Its construction and outfitting, extending over an unknown number of years, was itself a message of coming judgment. God's patience with obstinate evil is marvelous, but it does have its limits.

C. THE SALVATION THROUGH WATER TYPIFYING BAPTISM (vv. 20c-21)

The mention of the ark enabled Peter to shift his thought from those upon whom judgment fell to those who were saved. He mentioned the few who were saved (v. 20c) and elaborated on the typological significance of that event (v. 21).

(1) The statement of the event (v. 20c). "Wherein few, that is, eight souls, were saved through water" tersely records the outcome of the flood that terminated the period of waiting. *Wherein* (*eis hēn*), literally "into which," conveys the double thought of entry into the ark and being saved in it through

---

55. The Textus Receptus does not have the double compound, reading *exedecheto*.

the floodwaters. *Few* pointedly reminds us of the contrast between the small number saved and the masses, corrupted by evil, who perished. It was an encouraging reminder to the readers who "must have been painfully conscious of their small numbers and relative feebleness compared to the pagan majority among whom they lived. But Noah and his crew were an even smaller minority."[56] The contrast is made more explicit by giving the exact number, "that is, eight souls." Kelly surmises that *eight* was mentioned to remind the readers of the day of Christ's resurrection, "the eighth day *par excellence*."[57] *Souls* denotes the living persons who were saved. Beare suggests that by the use of that term Peter conveyed "an underlying implication that the physical salvation from the Flood was at the same time a moral and spiritual salvation, a salvation from 'the Wrath of God' (cf. Rom. 5:9 1 Thess. 1:10), resting upon faith in Him."[58]

"Were saved through water" (*diesōthēsan di' hudatos*) records the transition from the old to the new world. *Were saved* is a compound verb, the preposition *dia* giving the force of a complete deliverance—"were brought safely through." The passive voice indicates that the ark was the actual agent of their salvation. *Water* is a collective singular, the overwhelming waters of the flood through which they were saved. *Through* (*dia*) may have an instrumental force, "by means of water," but it is difficult to see how the floodwaters can be viewed as the means of their salvation, when in reality the ark saved them. A local meaning of the preposition is more probable: saved in passing through the floodwaters. Yet the picture contains the paradoxical truth that the floodwaters that brought death to the wicked were the very means of their deliverance; the waters buoyed up the ark and brought Noah and his family safely through to the new world.

(2) The typology in the event (v. 21). Peter understood the salvation of Noah and his family as a prefiguration of Christian baptism: "which also after a true likeness doth now save you, *even* baptism." The typological relation, expressed in seven words in the original (*ho kai humas antitupon nun sōzei baptisma*), involves some complexities of grammar as well as perplexities for the interpreter. It is the only direct mention of baptism in the epistle.

"Which" (*ho*), a nominative neuter relative pronoun, is strongly attested as the original reading,[59] but it is difficult to construe. That difficulty is attested by the variations in the manuscripts.[60] Erasmus adopted the dative on the basis of some cursive manuscripts, thus forming the basis for the reading in the Textus Receptus. On the basis of textual evidence, Westcott and Hort retained

56. France, p. 272.
57. J. N. D. Kelly, p. 159.
58. Francis Wright Beare, *The First Epistle of Peter*, p. 173.
59. See the evidence in the United Bible Societies Greek text.
60. Some witnesses omit the word; others read *hō* or *hōs*.

the nominative, though Hort regarded it as "a primitive error."[61] A few modern scholars favor the dative,[62] but the neuter nominative is commonly accepted as original. The antecedent to that relative cannot be the *ark* since it is a feminine noun. The antecedent is either *water* or, more simply, the intended antecedent may be the entire preceding picture of Noah and his family in the ark being saved through water. We prefer the latter interpretation because it is more precise.

"Also you" (*kai humas*), the object of the verb, stands emphatically forward. Peter assured his afflicted readers that they likewise were recipients of that grace that saved Noah and his family. The Textus Receptus reads *us* (*hēmas*), and that reading has fair textual support; but the support for *you* is stronger.[63] It is another instance of the confusion common for those two forms in the Greek manuscripts. *You* agrees better with the personal thrust of the text. Grammatically, it is also uncertain whether the following adjective *antitupon*, familiar under the English concept of antitype, refers to *you* or to *baptism*. According to the former view, the correspondence lies directly between Noah and his family in the ark and the Christian readers. According to the latter view, the similarity is God's saving act at the time of the Flood and the salvation portrayed in Christian baptism. It is more probable that the reference is to saving acts of God than to groups of people.

The adjective *antitupon*, translated "after a true likeness," describes something as corresponding to what has gone before. Though Peter may be understood to mean that baptism is the fulfillment of an Old Testament type, it is more probable that *similarity* or *correspondence* is all that is meant. The parallel lies in the saving experience of Noah and his family in the ark passing through the floodwaters to a new world and Christian baptism as that which denotes the believer's passage from the old life to the new life. The only other New Testament occurrence of the word *antitupos* is in Hebrews 9:24, where it refers to the Mosaic sanctuary as a "copy" of the true heavenly sanctuary. References to Old Testament people or events as types or prefigurations of Christian realities occur elsewhere in the New Testament (Luke 11:29-32; Rom. 5:14; 1 Cor. 10:1-10; Melchizedek in Hebrews). The principle underlying such typology is that "God works according to a regular pattern, so that what he has done in the past, as recorded in the Old Testament, can be expected to find it counterpart in his work in the decisive period of the New Testament."[64]

That which was thus prefigured, Peter explicitly identified as "baptism" (*baptisma*). Though some, like Unger,[65] maintain that the reference is to spirit baptism (1 Cor. 12:13), most interpreters agree with Wuest that "water

61. Brooke Foss Westcott and Fenton John Anthony Hort, Introduction and Appendix to *The New Testament in the Original Greek*, vol. 2, "Notes on Selected Readings," p. 102.
62. Selwyn, p. 203; Beare, p. 174.
63. See the Nestle-Aland Greek text (26th ed.).
64. France, pp. 273-74.
65. Merrill F. Unger, *The Baptism and Gifts of the Holy Spirit*, pp. 129-31.

baptism is clearly in the apostle's mind."[66] The specific term used does not occur in pagan or Jewish literature before the time of the New Testament. It always occurs in the singular and is the distinctive New Testament designation for John's baptism (Matt. 3:7; Mark 11:30; Luke 7:29; Acts 1:22; etc.) and for Christian baptism (Eph. 4:5; Col. 2:12). It does not denote the act of baptizing but the rite of Christian baptism in its true significance. Beasley-Murray suggests that the New Testament writers apparently adopted the term "to express their consciousness that Christian baptism was a new thing in the world, differing from all Jewish and pagan purificatory rites."[67]

Peter made the arresting assertion that baptism "now saves" (*nun sōzei*). The *now* has been appealed to as support for the view that 1 Peter is really a baptismal homily and that the reference is to the act of baptism that has just been administered.[68] But it is more natural to understand it as a word that "simply denotes the time of the New Dispensation."[69] The use of *now* is a marked feature of the epistle (1:6, 12; 2:10, 25; here). It indicates the experience of salvation that characterizes the new era in which God is forming a new people from among Jews and Gentiles (Eph. 2:13-18). By their acceptance of Christian baptism, the readers had announced to their former companions in sin that they now belonged to the people of God. In saying "doth now save you," Peter's use of the present tense (*sōzei*) indicates that the salvation imparted at their new birth (1:3, 23) was not yet complete, had not yet been brought to its final consummation. Their union with Christ in His death and resurrection, proclaimed in their baptism (Rom. 6:3-8), should result in a present spiritual transformation to be consummated at the return of Jesus Christ.

Peter's categorical assertion that baptism "saves you" has been misinterpreted, but the statement is not unparalleled in the New Testament (cf. Rom. 6:3-5; Gal. 3:27; Col. 2:12). The material waters of Christian baptism are not the outward instrument that produces an inner spiritual regeneration; baptism is an act of obedience that bears witness to the inner union by faith with Christ, the Savior. Peter, like Paul, assumed that in true Christian baptism the outward sign and the inner reality are kept together; the rite without the inner reality is useless, just as the dollar sign on a check is valueless apart from the monetary reality in the bank. To avoid any misunderstanding of his assertion, Peter added two appositional clauses that define the nature of baptism. It is only the baptism thus described that saves.

Negatively, Christian baptism is "not the putting away of the filth of the flesh" (*ou sarkos apothesis rhupou*). It is not the aim or function of baptism to remove physical filth. Beare remarks that the need to combat such an erroneous view implies "that the baptism was done by immersion; such a phrase would be meaningless in relation to a baptism by sprinkling (cf. Heb.

---

66. Kenneth S. Wuest, *"First Peter"* in *The Greek New Testament for the English Reader*, p. 108.
67. G. R. Beasley-Murray, "Baptism, Wash," *NIDNTT*, 1:150.
68. See the Introduction.
69. Cranfield, p. 106.

10:22)."[70] Though the term "filth" (*rhupos*), which means "dirt," could be used metaphorically of inner sordidness or meanness, *of the flesh* (*sarkos*) limits the meaning to literal, physical uncleanness. Baptism is not a Jewish rite of purification; such lustrations were well-known in both Jewish and pagan religious practices and apparently form the background for Peter's expression. But the designation "the putting off" (*apothesis*) is unusual for the removal of dirt with water. Both the noun and the cognate verb generally suggest a physical putting away of something, like the removal of a coat, or metaphorically, the putting off of the body as in 2 Peter 1:14 (the only other New Testament occurrence of the noun). Dalton argues that the term indicates that Peter was referring to circumcision.[71] Though such a reference would be intelligible to Jewish readers, it is unlikely that Peter's predominantly Gentile recipients[72] would perceive the implication. The picture of circumcision does not naturally fit the occasion. Peter may have used the term in view of the fact that for his readers their public baptism was an open repudiation of their former lives of sin.

"But" (*alla*) indicates a strong contrast with the preceding negative; baptism is "the interrogation of a good conscience toward God" (*suneidēseōs agathēs eperōtēma eis theon*). Structurally, that positive statement exactly parallels the preceding negative. The genitive *of a good conscience*, like the preceding *of the flesh*, stands before the central noun, and *toward God*, like *filth* in the preceding, stands after the noun. The key word in both expressions is the noun in the center.

The noun "the interrogation"' (*eperōtēma*) occurs only here in the New Testament. Its basic meaning is "a question, an inquiry," hence the translation of the ASV. The cognate verb (*eperōtaō*) is commonly translated "to ask, to question, to inquire." But it is difficult to extract a plausible meaning from such a translation because we would expect there to be some indication of the nature of the question asked. In Matthew 16:1 the verb is used with the meaning "to request" (so also in Ps. 137:3 [136:3 LXX]). On that basis some suggest translating "a request for (or, proceeding from) a good conscience." But it is not clear that the noun was used with that meaning. Since the verb can mean "to request," Greeven suggests the translation "but prayer to God for a good conscience."[73] Such a translation does not readily fit the context and lacks linguistic support.

The papyri show that the noun *eperōtēma* was at times used in a technical sense to denote the question-and-answer process in establishing a formal agreement.[74] Though etymologically the term might be expected to denote only the asking of a question, usage included the response as well. That

---

70. Beare, p. 175.
71. Dalton, pp. 215-24.
72. See the Introduction.
73. Heinrich Greeven, *eperōtēma*, *TDNT*, 2:688.
74. James Hope Moulton and George Milligan, *The Vocabulary of the Greek Testament*, pp. 231-32; Reicke, pp. 184-85.

expanded usage—to include the whole procedure— made the term suitable to juristic language, where it was used to denote a legal contract.[75] That usage was also suitable to the solemnities related to Christian baptism, involving the questions asked of the baptismal candidate and his personal response concerning his faith and commitment. The New Testament gives hints of such a procedure in connection with Christian baptism (Acts 8:37[76]; Rom. 10:12). Modern interpreters generally view Peter's expression in the light of that usage. It may be translated "a pledge to God out of a good conscience" (if *conscience* is a subjective genitive), or "a pledge to maintain a good conscience" (if *conscience* is an objective genitive). Several other terms appear in our modern English versions.[77]

In view of that question-and-answer usage of the noun, the translation in the KJV, "the answer of a good conscience toward God," is quite acceptable. That translation makes it clear that the believer's acceptance of baptism is his answer to the Spirit's questions that stir his conscience and result in his conversion. His answer is given out of a good conscience, a conscience purified by the blood of Christ and assured of personal acceptance with God. His baptism is his answer to the work of God in his heart, bearing witness before the world to what God has done for him. That forms a good contrast to the preceding negative.

It is not certain whether the phrase "through the resurrection of Jesus Christ" is a direct continuation of the preceding words or is to be related to the word "saves." The former understanding mars the balance between the two preceding clauses, but the latter makes clear the true source of salvation. Without Christ's resurrection, which presupposes His death, baptism would be an empty form. His resurrection is the ground of righteousness and guarantee of victory.

With that reference to Christ's resurrection, the thought returns to the triumph of the suffering Christ in verses 18-19. It forms a natural transition to the picture of the culmination of His suffering.

3) THE CULMINATION OF HIS SUFFERING (V. 22)

"Who is on the right hand of God, having gone into heaven." The picture is crystal-clear, and in the center stands the Savior's throne. *Who is on the right hand of God* affirms His present triumphant position. Peter did not pause to mention that Christ is seated at God's right hand, as other New Testament references do (Luke 22:69; Eph. 1:20; Col. 3:1; Heb. 1:3; 10:12; 12:2), indicating the fulfillment of Psalm 110:1. *On the right hand of God (en dexia theou)*

---

75. Hermann Cremer, *Biblico-Theological Lexicon of New Testament Greek*, p. 717.

76. Textual critics hold that Acts 8:37 is not a part of the original text, but it clearly represents an early church practice.

77. "Appeal"—NASB, RSV, NEB; "search"—20th Cent.; "craving"— Weymouth, Goodspeed, Williams; "earnest seeking"—Berkeley; "prayer"—Montgomery, Moffatt; "promise"—TEV; "pledge"—NIV, JB.

denotes the position of honor and authority next to God. He is there in glory, associated with the Almighty in the government of the universe. He is present there as our incarnate Lord, exalted and ever able to aid His suffering saints. Beare notes that the New Testament presents Christ's heavenly ministry in various ways:

> The Session is sometimes related particularly to the gift of the Holy Spirit, and the spiritual gifts communicated to the Church (Acts 2:33-35; Eph. 4:7-8); elsewhere to His office as Intercessor for us (Rom. 8:34; Heb. 9:24), or more generally, to His office as High Priest (Heb. 8:1ff); but more frequently, the emphasis is upon His power, His dignity, and His victory over the powers of evil (Matt. 26:64 and parallels; Acts 7:55; Phil. 2:9-11; Eph. 1:20-24; Heb. 12:2).[78]

Immediately after the words "on the right hand of God," the Vulgate has a remarkable gloss: "swallowing down death, that we might be made heirs of life everlasting."[79] The clause was in the pre-Vulgate text of Augustine, apparently the translation of a Greek gloss. Though not authentic, it is instructive since it reveals how in the mind of the student who wrote it the thought of the quickened Christ as the Life-giver ran through the paragraph concerning His suffering.

Peter added two participial clauses that refer to events prior to Christ's heavenly enthronement. "Having gone into heaven" (*poreutheis eis ouranon*) indicates an event that culminated in the heavenly enthronement of the risen Christ. There are very few passages in the New Testament that depict that historical event (Mark 16:19; Luke 24:51; Acts 1:6-11), and the first two are beset with textual difficulties. The only detailed account is that given in Acts 1. Peter's words constitute the passing reminiscence of an eyewitness to that unforgettable event. The New Testament writers generally thought of Christ's resurrection as leading to His present exaltation, thus assuming the reality of the ascension.

The second participial clause, "angels and authorities and powers being made subject unto him," portrays the universality of Christ's dominion. The aorist passive participle, "having been made subject" (*hupotagentōn*), stands emphatically forward and stresses the actual subjection to Christ's authority. The passive voice indicates that they now stand in subjection to Him; the term itself does not settle the question whether the subjection was voluntary or compelled on the part of the angels. As a genitive absolute, the clause portrays the fact of the subjection as the background for Christ's present sovereignty. In Matthew 28:18 the risen Christ declared to His followers, "All authority hath been given unto me in heaven and on earth." In Ephesians 1:20-22, Philippians 2:9-11, and Colossians 2:15 Christ's dominion over all things is portrayed as a present reality, and in 1 Corinthians 15:24-28 the ultimate realization of that dominion is related to the final eschatological victory of

78. Beare, p. 176.
79. *The Holy Bible, Douay Version.*

Christ. Colossians 2:14-15 declares that the cross is the basis for that domination. Masterman observes, "The thought of subjection, that has been in the mind of the Apostle throughout these chapters, reaches its climax here."[80]

"Angels and authorities and powers" apparently indicates different groups or ranks of angelic beings. The expression may imply three different ranks of spiritual beings—coordinated by *and* (*kai*)—or only two groups may be indicated, angels of authority and of power. According to the latter understanding, the reference may be to their different spheres or realms of operation. Later Jewish speculations ran riot concerning angelic grades and orders. More important is the question of whether Peter referred only to good angels or also included evil angels. Some, like Lenski,[81] maintain that the reference is to good angels. That would be obvious if the expression is to be closely linked with *heaven* just before it. But the genitive absolute construction relates the picture to Christ's all-inclusive domination. If the designation is read in the light of Colossians 2:14-15, the inclusion of evil angels seems clear. Christ's sovereignty over all spiritual forces is a precious assurance to afflicted believers. Surely Peter's readers, who were facing a very real onslaught from evil powers through their enemies, would find real encouragement in that remark.

80. J. Howard B. Masterman, *The First Epistle of S. Peter (Greek Text)*, pp. 136-37.
81. Lenski, p. 177.

17

C. The Equipment for Suffering for Righteousness
(4:1-11)

(1) Forasmuch then as Christ suffered in the flesh, arm ye yourselves also with the same mind; for he that hath suffered in the flesh hath ceased from sin; (2) that ye no longer should live the rest of your time in the flesh to the lusts of men, but to the will of God. (3) For the time past may suffice to have wrought the desire of the Gentiles, and to have walked in lasciviousness, lusts, winebibbings, revellings, carousings, and abominable idolatries: (4) wherein they think it strange that ye run not with *them* into the same excess of riot, speaking evil of *you*: (5) who shall give account to him that is ready to judge the living and the dead. (6) For unto this end was the gospel preached even to the dead, that they might be judged indeed according to men in the flesh, but live according to God in the spirit.

(7) But the end of all things is at hand: be ye therefore of sound mind, and be sober unto prayer: (8) above all things be fervent in your love among yourselves; for love covereth a multitude of sins: (9) using hospitality one to another without murmuring: (10) according as each hath received a gift ministering it among yourselves, as good stewards of the manifold grace of God; (11) if any man speaketh, *speaking* as it were oracles of God; if any man ministereth, *ministering* as of the strength which God supplieth: that in all things God may be glorified through Jesus Christ, whose is the glory and the dominion for ever and ever. Amen.

That hortatory section flows logically out of the didactiac passage in 3:18-22. The opening *oun*, here translated "then,"[1] shows that a practical application is

---

1. Our English versions generally use "then" or "therefore" (RSV, NASB, NIV, Goodspeed). The NEB omits the particle but translates, "Remembering that Christ endured bodily suffering."

being made from Christ's own experience of suffering for righteousness. Peter linked his appeal to the readers directly to the person of the victorious Christ since they too were being subjected to suffering for righteousness. The Christian life is a happy life, but it is extremely costly. For victory in suffering, Peter set forth the need to be equipped with a proper attitude toward it (vv. 1-6), as well as to live fruitful Christian lives inspired by the hope of the future (vv. 7-11).

1) THE NEEDED EQUIPMENT IN VIEW OF PRESENT SUFFERING (VV. 1-6)

Peter issued an urgent call for the readers to properly equip themselves to suffer for righteousness (vv. 1-2) and gave three reasons to motivate them to appropriate the needed equipment (vv. 3-6).

A. THE CALL TO BE ARMED WITH THE PROPER ATTITUDE (vv. 1-2)

Peter's appeal summarily recalled the suffering of Christ (v. 1a), urged the readers to arm themselves with "the same mind" (v. 1b), characterized the one who is victorious in suffering (v. 1c), and held before them the goal they should strive for in so equipping themselves (v. 2).

(1) The example of Christ's suffering (v. 1a). "Forasmuch then as Christ suffered in the flesh" (*Christou oun pathontos sarki*) is a summary reference to the teaching in 3:18 and the fourth direct reference to Christ's suffering in the epistle (1:11; 2:21; 3:18). The expression is a genitive absolute and depicts the background against which the following imperative is issued; it was to have a causal impact on the conduct of the readers. *Suffered in flesh* records Christ's experience as a real man on earth. The tense of the verb (aorist) refers to the past fact; the term may include the total experience of the incarnate Christ, but the primary reference is to His crucifixion. There is considerable manuscript support for the addition "for us" (*huper hēmōn*) or "for you" (*huper humōn*), but the shorter reading has strong early support[2] and best explains the other readings as probable scribal additions that express the teaching in 2:21 and 3:18. The addition, though true, does not bear on Peter's purpose, which was to emphasize Christ's relation to His people as their great example. The inclusion of the phrase in either form would call for gratitude to the great atoner; left out, there is an easier transition to the challenge from the example of Christ as the great sufferer.

(2) The call to be armed with the same mind (v. 1b). The challenge from the Master's example is clear: "arm ye yourselves also with the same mind" (*kai humeis tēn autēn ennoian hoplisasthe*), "ye also with the same mind arm

2. See the United Bible Societies text, *The Greek New Testament*; Bruce M. Metzger, *A Textual Commentary on the Greek New Testament*, p. 694.

yourselves." *Ye also*, standing emphatically forward, makes the challenge personal. In sharing the Master's experience of suffering for righteousness, the readers should also have the same mind He had. The word *mind (ennoia)*, also used in Hebrews 4:12, means "what is in the mind." Originally denoting the act of thought, it came also to denote "the result: thought, realization, insight, disposition."[3] The word thus indicates an idea or viewpoint that expresses itself in determined action. *The same mind* called for an acceptance of Christ's attitude on the part of the readers; they too were to be willing to suffer for righteousness in doing God's will. His insight into the true nature of sin and its consequences led Him deliberately to set His face toward the cross (Luke 9:51). His followers should have the same abhorrence of sin that would prompt them to willingly suffer for righteousness.

"Arm yourselves" (*hoplisasthe*), an aorist imperative, requested the readers to adopt that attitude. The verb, used only here in the New Testament, means "to equip" or "to arm" with the appropriate tool or weapon. The expression need not involve a military metaphor, but since the Christian life is a truceless war with sin, the military connotation is very probable. It was a favorite with the apostle Paul (Rom. 13:12; 2 Cor. 6:7; 10:4; Eph. 6:11-17). The aorist tense called for an act that demanded resolution and determination, and the middle voice reminded the recipients of their personal responsibility and interest in it. Only as girded with that mind could they be victorious in the conflict facing them. Peter was concerned to equip them for the more serious troubles ahead.

(3) The character of the victorious sufferer (v. 1c). "For he that hath suffered in the flesh hath ceased from sin" (*hoti ho pathōn sarki pepautai hamartias*). The conjunction *hoti*, which initiates the enigmatical statement, can mean either "that" or "because." If the first meaning was intended, then the words present the content of the mind the readers were to have. That is the view of Moffatt who translates, "let this very conviction that he who has suffered in the flesh gets quit of sin, nerve you." That makes good sense. But if it is correct then the phrase "the same mind" implies that Christ also has ceased from sin. But Christ never sinned and never ceased from sin. It is better, therefore, to adopt the common view that *hoti* is causal; it specifies the reason for the readers arming themselves. The stated reason may be in the form of a proverbial expression. Beare categorically asserts that the statement is "certainly a proverbial expression, found in a different wording in Romans 6:7—'for he that has died is freed from the claims of sin.'"[4]

The expression has been differently understood. Some, like Fronmüller, argue that the expression is "best applied to Christ Himself" as a definition of the preceding call.[5] But that involves the problem of Christ having ceased from sin. Though Christ belongs to the category of the victorious sufferers, He is

3. G. Harder, "Reason, Mind, Understanding," *NIDNTT*, 3:123.

4. Francis Wright Beare, *The First Epistle of Peter*, p. 179.

5. G. F. C. Fronmüller, *The Epistles General of Peter*, p. 73.

only indirectly in view in His relation to the Christian sufferer. Accepting that the statement specifies a reason, some understand it as a strand of Jewish thought that portrays physical suffering, if rightly borne, as that which can purify the sufferer from sin (which has its seat in the flesh). Others think the meaning is that physical suffering disciplines the flesh so that it is unable to exert its desires. Still others understand the statement as a reference to Christian martyrdom that places the believer beyond the realm of further sin. A different interpretation sees the suffering as a figurative denotation of the believer's union with Christ in death and resurrection as symbolized in Christian baptism.

The articular aorist participle, "he that hath suffered" (*ho pathōn*), indicates one who has victoriously endured such an experience. The expression is generic; it denotes one who is representative of the class. In the first part of verse 1, the term recorded the suffering and death of Christ, and some, like Lenski, believe that the aorist also indicates that "the sufferer has reached death."[6] But the term in itself does not demand that death has taken place; it may simply mean that he has effectively passed through the experience of suffering, now viewed as terminated. The view that the suffering is figurative, denoting the believer's mystical union with Christ in His death and resurrection as declared in his baptism, is improbable; *in the flesh* (*sarki*) denotes that the reference is to actual physical suffering. But the context makes it clear that not just any physical suffering is in view; it is suffering that has been endured for the cause of righteousness as a believer.

"Hath ceased from sin" (*pepautai hamartias*) depicts the spiritual state of the victorious sufferer. It carries a note of triumph; he has effectively broken with a life dominated by sin. It need not mean that he no longer commits any act of sin, but that his old life, dominated by the power of sin, has been terminated. The verb, which does not occur elsewhere in the New Testament in the perfect tense, may be viewed as either middle or passive: if middle, it asserts the fact, "has ceased from sin, has done with sin;" if passive, there is an implied reference to the divine agent who brought the victory, "has been caused to cease from sin."[7] According to either view, the perfect tense records a definite break with sin (*hamartias*); the singular means that his old life, dominated by the power of sin, has ended. Some manuscripts read the dative plural, "to sins" (*hamartiais*).[8] That would mean that he has ceased to engage in the practice of sin. The singular is generally accepted as the correct reading.[9] He who in loyalty to Christ and in His power has steadfastly endured persecution rather than join in the wicked practices of the pagan world has demonstrated that the pursuit of sin in his life has ended.

---

6. R. C. H. Lenski, *The Interpretation of the Epistles of St. Peter, St. John and St. Jude*, p. 182.

7. Though the simple verb *pauomai* in the perfect does not occur elsewhere, the compound *anapauomai* does occur in the perfect in 2 Cor. 7:13 and Philem. 7, in both instances with the passive meaning.

8. It was adopted by Westcott and Hort in their Greek text.

9. See the United Bible Societies text for the manuscript evidence.

(4) The goal in appropriating the equipment (v. 2). "That ye no longer should live the rest of your time in the flesh to the lusts of men, but to the will of God" delineates the outcome that is assured to those who live by means of the equipment being called for. The words are to be joined with the preceding imperative, "arm ye yourselves," and not with the phrase immediately before, "hath ceased from sin." *That ye* (*eis to* with the infinitive) points to the blessed result that will ensue. The Greek construction does not express any pronoun, "ye," "we," or "he." Our versions are divided on their choice.[10] The use of "he" continues the singular of the preceding phrase, but the plural "ye," expressed in the imperative, marks the connection more clearly.

"No longer should live the rest of your time" involves a measure of tautology that is very natural in such an intense appeal. *No longer* (*mēketi*) looks back and indicates that the time they had lived in evil practices as pagans was more than enough. The memory of their sinful past was to serve as a sharp goad against any tendency to relapse into that kind of living. *The rest of your time in the flesh* looks to the future and reminded them of the brevity of the remainder of their earthly lives. That perspective was to inspire them in their efforts to redeem the time. Moffatt well notes that the expression suggests "that capital punishment was not expected as the normal outcome of faithfulness."[11] The verb "should live" (*biōsai*), used only here in the New Testament, "denotes life in its concrete outward manifestations."[12]

Because of their conversion, the readers were conscious of two different types of life. As Christians they were no longer to live "to the lusts of men, but to the will of God." The two dative designations indicate contrasted rules or standards of living. To live "to the lusts of men" (*anthrōpōn epithumiais*) refers to a life ruled or controlled by the varied cravings or sinful desires that characterize fallen human beings (cf. 1:14). *Of men*, standing emphatically forward, carries something of a depreciatory tone—ordinary sinful human beings rather than the redeemed members of the family of God.

"But" (*alla*) marks the sharp contrast between a life lived "to the lusts of men" and a life lived "to the will of God." There is no middle course between them. God's will (*thelēmati*) denotes that which He wills for His people. When living such a life, "His will is our law, His word our rule, His Son's life our example, His Spirit rather than our own soul the guide of our actions."[13] His will should ever be the pole-star for the believer. The plural "lusts" indicates the many and variable cravings of fallen human nature, and the singular, *will*, indicates the unitary, harmonious, and abiding will of God for His people. His nature assures that His will for Christians is righteous and beneficent.

10. "He"—KJV, NIV, NEB, Goodspeed, Williams, Berkeley, JB, Kleist and Lilly. "His" —Darby, 20th Cent. "Ye"—Rotherham, ASV. "You"—Weymouth, Montgomery, Moffatt, TEV. No expressed pronoun—NASB, RSV, Young.

11. James Moffatt, *The General Epistles—James, Peter, and Judas*, p. 146.

12. H.-G. Link, "Life, *bios*," *NIDNTT*, 2:475.

13. Lancelot Andrewes, quoted in Edward Gordon Selwyn, *The First Epistle of St. Peter*, p. 210.

B. THE MOTIVATION TO EFFECTIVELY ENDURE SUFFERING (vv. 3-6)

Willingness to suffer for righteousness is not natural; to endure such suffering victoriously requires strong motivation. With *for* (*gar*) Peter introduced such motivation, drawn from the past (v. 3), the present (v. 4), and the future (vv. 5-6).

(1) The motivation from a sinful past (v. 3). "The time past may suffice to have wrought the desire of the Gentiles." The memory of the ignominy of their own past conduct was to undergird the readers' present suffering for righteousness. *The time past may suffice* (*arketos ho pareléluthōs chronos*), "sufficient is the bygone time" (Rotherham), stresses that their past sinful conduct could not be condoned, and (as they realized) was fully sufficient. *May suffice* (*arketos*) is better translated "*is* sufficient;" it was a well-known and acknowledged reality. They were well aware that they had done their full duty and more in the past service of sin. *Past* (*pareléutheis*), a perfect participle, defines that time as a closed chapter. The Textus Receptus reads "sufficient to us," but *us* (*hēmin*) lacks manuscript support and is best omitted.[14] Peter did not thus identify himself with the evils of the Gentile world.

In their pre-Christian days the recipients "wrought the desire of the Gentiles." The perfect tense *wrought* (*kateirgasthai*) defines that activity as terminated. The readers had given themselves to and carried out *the desire of the Gentiles* (*to boulēma tōn ethnōn*), the dominating intention and purpose of the pagan world. The singular categorizes those desires and intentions "as falling under a single principle contrasted with 'the will of God' just mentioned."[15] The word *desire* (*boulēma*)[16] indicates a contrast between the abiding will of God and man's fickle and uncertain desire, turned this way or that by varied lusts. *Of the Gentiles* implies that the readers "had previously been pagans, not Jews, and that they had been converted to Christianity as adults."[17]

The remainder of the verse describes how the desire of the Gentiles was worked out in practice: "and to have walked in lasciviousness, lusts, winebibbings, revellings, carousings, and abominable idolatries." *And to have walked* (*peporeumenous*) translates a deponent perfect participle in an accusative absolute construction;[18] the perfect tense shows that the course of conduct is a matter of the past for the readers. *Walked* is not the ordinary verb so translated (*peripateō*, which does not occur in 1 Peter), but *poreuomai*, which

14. Some manuscripts read "us," and others have "you" (*humin*); the shorter reading is supported by good manuscripts. See the United Bible Societies Greek text.

15. Selwyn, p. 210.

16. *To thelēma*, the reading of the Textus Receptus, appears in the majority of the later manuscripts.

17. J. N. D. Kelly, *A Commentary on the Epistles of Peter and of Jude*, p. 169.

18. The accusative participle has no expressed antecedent; it relates to an implied accusative of general reference with the infinitive "to have wrought" (*kateirgasthai*).

means "to go, proceed, travel," and figuratively, "to conduct oneself, live, walk." By the use of that verb "life is compared to a journey, but also in order to denote the eagerness with which they go on from sin to sin."[19]

The six evils enumerated form a dark picture of life in the pagan world. The list is not intended to be complete; the sins mentioned are representative of the worst evils. All the terms are in the plural to indicate the variety and frequency of those vices. Cook believed that the six sins mentioned fall into two groups, the first three being personal, the last three social sins.[20] But Lenski asserts that all six items "refer to public pagan sins," being "the pagan excesses that were connected with the practice of idolatry, the things commonly done at the celebrations in honor of heathen gods."[21] They are sins of impurity and drunkenness associated with open idolatry.

"Lasciviousness" (*aselgeiais*), "outbreaks of lasciviousness" (Alford),[22] denotes excesses of all kinds of evil. Involving a lack of personal self-restraint, the term pictures sin as an inordinate indulgence of appetites to the extent of violating a sense of public decency. The thought of moral impurity seems clearly involved.[23]

"Lusts" (*epithumiais*)[24] is likewise a comprehensive term and denotes the depraved cravings and inner vicious desires of fallen human nature that drive men to open excesses. Sensual lusts are obviously included.

"Winebibbings" (*oinophlugiais*), a term that occurs only here in the New Testament, denotes habitual drunkenness. That compound noun, composed of *oinos*, "wine," and the verb *phluō*, "to bubble up, to overflow," depicts one who is soaked to overflowing with wine.

"Revellings" (*komois*) means festive gatherings, merrymakings, revels, either private or public and religious. The term was generally used of festivities "in honour of a god, particularly Bacchus, and ending usually in the party's sallying forth from their banqueting-room to parade the streets and indulge in whatever folly or wickedness suggested itself."[25]

"Carousings" (*potois*), occurring only here in the New Testament, means "drinking parties." The picture is that of social drinking at banquets. The term in itself did not imply excess or folly, for the Septuagint used it of the moderate banquets of good men (cf. Gen. 19:3; 2 Sam. 3:20). But because of frequent occasions of excess, in New Testament times the term denoted a form of dissipation; it implies excess.

"And abominable idolatries" (*kai athemitois eidōlolatriais*) concludes the picture by pointing to the taproot of the evils portrayed (cf. Rom. 1: 18-32). Those idolatries involved the worship of many gods and took various forms in

---

19. Quoted from Calov in Fronmüller, p. 74.
20. F. C. Cook, *The First Epistle General of Peter*, p. 209.
21. Lenski, p. 185.
22. Henry Alford, *The Greek New Testament*, vol. 4 (part 1), p. 371.
23. Cf. Richard Chenevix Trench, *Synonyms of the New Testament*, pp. 56-58.
24. See under 1:14 and 2:11.
25. Robert Johnstone, *The First Epistle of Peter*, p. 312.

which devotion to the idols was expressed. That idol worship "encouraged as part of its exercise sometimes both drunkenness and sexual vice and laxity."[26] The adjective *abominable*, found elsewhere in the New Testament only in Peter's own words in Acts 10:28, means "unlawful." Since those idolatries were common and an approved part of pagan society, Peter could not have meant that they were forbidden by their laws. Though sanctioned or permitted by social laws, they were contrary to God's truth and man's innate sense of right. In classical Greek the adjective was used of things "opposed to law as laid down by instinctive convictions with regard to what is right, rather than to law as set forth in statute."[27] Going beyond the inner sense of what was proper, their idolatries led to evils that tended to make men shudder. As the only item in the list qualified by an adjective, the concluding designation underlines the nefarious nature of those idolatries. Their past association with those evils was to motivate the readers to arm themselves against such practices.

(2) The motivation from present opposition (v. 4). The reaction of their unsaved contemporaries was likewise to motivate the readers to be spiritually armed: "wherein they think it strange that ye run not with *them* into the same excess of riot, speaking evil of *you*." *Wherein* (*en hō*), as a neuter singular relative pronoun, cannot refer to the various vices just named; it looks back and summarizes the fact that the readers had abandoned their former way of life, a truth made prominent by the use of three perfect tenses in the preceding statement.

"They think it strange" (*xenizontai*) that that change had occurred. *They* are the unsaved members of the communities where the readers reside. The verb is used in the New Testament with a double sense: "to receive as a guest, to entertain a stranger" (Acts 10:23; Heb. 13:2), and then "to be surprised, be astonished, to act like a stranger" amid things new and unusual (Acts 17:20; 1 Pet. 4:12). The present indicative passive pictures those pagans as continuing to be assailed with astonishment at the change they observed in their former companions in sin; it represents the intrusion of an unfamiliar and novel element that they could not understand.

"That ye run not with them into the same excess of riot" elaborates the cause of that surprise. The phrase, in the genitive absolute, indicates just what it is that they thought so strange, *that ye run not with them* (*mē suntrechontōn humōn*), as the readers formerly did. The negative *mē* has its proper subjective force; the refusal to join them was a continual cause of surprise. *Run*, a present participle, pictures the pagan's eager pursuit of the vices mentioned (v. 3), and *sun*, "with them," underlines the Christian's withdrawal from those practices. Kelly observes that the verb "vividly conjures up the euphoric stampede of pleasure-seekers."[28] The readers' refusal to participate

26. A. R. C. Leaney, *The Letters of Peter and Jude*, p. 59.

27. Johnstone, p. 313.

28. Kelly, p. 170.

in those social and religious activities produced irritation against, misunderstanding of, and opposition to them. Best observes,

> Since heathen religious ceremonies were part and parcel of ordinary life (e.g. all civic and national activities were bound up with them) the Christians were compelled to avoid what would have seemed to their fellows a wholly innocuous co-operation and to go much further than merely separate themselves from actual heathen worship.[29]

Peter noted that the continued pagan expenditure of energy was directed toward immoral and profligate ends, "into the same excess of riot" (*eis tēn autēn tēs asōtias anachusin*). *Excess* (*anachusin*), occurring only here in the New Testament, means "a pouring out," and came to denote an abundant outpouring, "a wide stream, a flood." The readers' energies had been directed toward an overflowing of ordinary restraints. That excess was characterized by two modifiers, both in the attributive position, that depicted its essential nature: *the same* (*autēn*) identified it as a continuation of the old vices, and *of riot* (*tēs asōtias*) indicated its dissolute nature. That noun (built on the verb *sōzō*, "to save," with the negative prefix *a-*, our English *un-*) describes something devoid of a saving quality. It portrays the utter recklessness in expenditure on the part of those who have lost self-control. In Ephesians 5:18 the noun is used in connection with drunkenness, and in Luke 15:14 the adjective is used of the riotous living of the prodigal son. It declares the wastefulness and destructiveness of a life of sin.

The resultant antagonism toward Christians is tersely expressed, "speaking evil *of you*" (*blasphēmountes*). The participle is grammatically connected with the subject of the verb, "they think it strange," and records the outcome of the non-Christians' astonishment. Aware that the Christians would not rejoin them, they expressed an attitude of ill-will. *You* is not expressed in Greek; the reaction indicated is not restricted to the experience of the readers.

A few commentators, like Bigg and Beare,[30] maintain that the participle should be understood as a substantive with the force of an exclamation, "blasphemers!" They argue that had the verbal idea been intended, it would have been more natural to use a coordinated verb, "and they blaspheme" (*kai blasphēmousin*), which a few texts actually have.[31] But in the context it is more natural to understand the participle as recording the expressed reaction of the pagans and not as a comment on their character.

The verb "speak evil of" means "to speak reproachfully, to calumniate." When directed against men it means "to injure the reputation of, to defame, revile," but when directed against a divine being it means "to blaspheme," speaking intentionally in defiance of deity. The translation "speaking evil of

29. Ernest Best, *I Peter*, p. 154.
30. Charles Bigg, *A Critical and Exegetical Commentary on the Epistles of St. Peter and St. Jude*, p. 170; Beare, p. 181.
31. See Nestle-Aland, *Novum Testamentum Graece* (26th ed.).

you" limits the term to the former meaning. Thus the NEB translates, "they vilify you accordingly." If that is correct then an attack was being made on the character of the Christians personally. But since their withdrawal was related to and prompted by their new religion, the ire of their opponents would naturally also include the God whom they worshiped. Thus understood the term expressed not only hatred of the Christians but also included "the whole religion which made people the opposite of what they once had been."[32] The context favors that broader meaning; it forms a stronger bridge to what follows. Bigg observed, "The charges made by the heathen were not only false, but turned the Christian faith into impiety, the Christian virtue into vice, and involved a different and blasphemous idea of God."[33] It seems obvious that the opposition to Christianity was not politically inspired.

(3) The motivation from future judgment (vv. 5-6). The pagan blasphemy turned Peter's thought to the coming judgment. He assured his readers that their opponents would be called to account by God (v. 5) and added a much discussed statement about the judgment of the dead (v. 6).

    (a) The judgment of the blasphemers (v. 5). "Who [those blaspheming] shall give account to him that is ready to judge the living and the dead." That "sudden vehement use of" the relative pronoun (*hoi*)[34] was intended to comfort the readers who were being unjustly maligned. The sovereign God would call those vicious antagonists to account, Peter affirmed. *Shall give account* pictures a court scene and implies that when antagonists come before the divine Judge, they will find it difficult to defend their action (cf. Matt. 12:36; Acts 19:40; Heb. 13:17). It will be a reversal of the scene in 3:15.

"Him that is ready to judge" (*tō hetoimōs echonti krinai*) assumes His known identity. Peter's words in Acts 10:42 and Paul's statement in 2 Timothy 4:1 leave no reasonable doubt that the Judge is Christ Jesus. Best observes, "At 1:17; 2:23 God is the judge but it suits the context better here to take 'him' of Christ since he has been the real subject of all the statements from 3:18 onwards."[35] That is in harmony with Christ's own teaching in Matthew 25:31-46; Mark 8:38; 13:33-37; Luke 12:35-40; 21:34-36. As the Father's messianic representative, the Son has been given all judgment (John 5:22, 27; Acts 17:31). That reference to Christ as the coming Judge adds the crowning feature to the glories of the exalted Savior set forth in 3:22.

As the coming Judge, He is "ready" (*hetoimōs exhonti*), is in continued readiness as one fully qualified to exercise decisive judgment. Just as the

32. Lenski, pp. 186-87.
33. Bigg, p. 170.
34. Ibid.
35. Best, p. 154.

salvation that will consummate the hope of believers is "ready to be revealed" (1:5), so He who is the embodiment of that hope is ready to call His enemies to account when He returns in glory. "The next grand manifest divine intervention in the affairs of this world will be the appearance of the Lord to judgement."[36] Until then, believers should always be ready to give an answer concerning the hope that is in them (3:15).

"The living and the dead" (*zōntas kai nekrous*) will both be called to judgment. The two terms, used without an article, are qualitative, "such as are living and such as are dead," comprehending the two great divisions of all human beings. None will escape, whether he dies before the coming of the Judge or not. Some, like Macknight, suggest that the terms are figurative, denoting those who through faith are spiritually alive and those who are dead in their sins.[37] But such an interpretation is inconsistent with the literal meaning of the terms as they are used in connection with the judgment elsewhere (Acts 10:42; 2 Tim. 4:1; Rev. 20:12).

> *(b) The judgment of the dead* (v. 6). "For unto this end was the gospel preached even to the dead, that they might be judged indeed according to men in the flesh, but live according to God in the spirit" constitutes another Petrine comment extremely difficult to interpret. That verse "has been described as the most difficult text in the Bible."[38] Lillie notes that "perhaps a score of different interpretations" of it have been proposed.[39] It would be unprofitable to trace all the confusing and often contradictory views that have been advanced.[40]

"For" (*gar*) indicates a close connection with verse 5; possibly the intended relation is with the entire paragraph beginning with verse 1. The verse was meant to offer encouragement to the readers who were under the pressure of malicious opponents. *For* looks backward, but "unto this end" (*eis touto*) looks forward and indicates the reason for the preaching mentioned. *This* (*touto*) is appositionally expanded in the *hina* clause ("that they might be . . .") that concludes the verse.

"The gospel was preached" (*euēnggelisthē*) records a definite historical event; there is no indication of who did the preaching. The verb, which is a different term than that used in 3:19, may literally be translated, "it was evangelized," or, "gospelized." As a Christian term, it denotes the bringing or announcement of the good news in Christ. The passive voice indicates that

---

36. Johnstone, p. 319.

37. James Macknight, *A New Literal Translation from the Original Greek, of All the Apostolical Epistles*, 5:490.

38. J. Howard B. Masterman, *The First Epistle of S. Peter*, p. 143.

39. John Lillie, *Lectures on the First and Second Epistles of Peter*, p.269

40. For a history of the interpretations see William Joseph Dalton, *Christ's Proclamation to the Spirits, A Study of I Peter 3:18—4:6*, pp. 42-54.

Christ was the subject of the message and not Himself the bringer of the good news to the recipients: "even to the dead" (*kai nekrois*). The dative in the original stands prominently before the verb, with *even* (*kai*) adding emphasis; the absence of the article makes the noun qualitative: "to [such as are] dead was the gospel preached."

But how is the term *dead* to be understood? One view understands it to refer to the spiritually dead to whom the gospel is preached so that they might enter into spiritual life. That view, which "has a very long history,"[41] can appeal to Ephesians 2:1 and Colossians 2:13 for that meaning of *dead*. But Peter did not so use the term elsewhere. It requires that doubtful meaning in verse 5, and it calls for the present tense, "is being preached," rather than the aorist. That implies that the preaching has ceased. That view does not readily fit in with the warning of coming judgment in verse 5.

Others relate the preaching to the dead with the preaching of Christ in 3:19 as an event that took place during the interval between His death and resurrection. Kelly summarizes the two forms in which that view is presented:

> The verse is to be understood as a reference to Christ's Descent to Hell and His proclamation there of the good news *either* (a) to the dead generally (so many liberal theologians, attracted by the implied enlargement of the scope of salvation), *or* (b) to the souls of the OT saints (so many Roman Catholic scholars since the 16th cent.; this view has for them the dogmatic advantage of not leading to universalism). As a result of this preaching, though they have undergone the physical death which is the lot of sinful men, these souls are given the possibility of eternal life.[42]

But the assumption that the "good news" of the gospel is involved in the proclamation in 3:19 is entirely arbitrary. In 3:19 those preached to are called "spirits in prison"—either fallen angelic beings or the disembodied souls of disobedient men. There is no suggestion that those preached to were in a disembodied state. The verb used is different from that in 3:19; the verb *euanggelizomai* in the New Testament almost invariably denotes the preaching of the gospel by Christian messengers and always to a living audience. The statement does not demand that those preached to were already dead when the message was brought to them. The condensed statement can mean that when preached to, they were still alive, but they have since died. The view that those preached to were already dead involves the possibility of conversion in the world of the dead, a view inconsistent with Scriptural teaching and evangelical theology. Such a view does not suit the context, nor the picture of salvation presented in the epistle (1:3-5; 2:8; 3:10-12; 4:18; 5:8).

A widely accepted view[43] is that those described as "dead" were members

41. Dalton, p. 47.

42. Kelly, pp. 172-73.

43. Albert Barnes, *Notes on the New Testament Explanatory and Practical, James, Peter, John, and Jude*, pp. 191-92; Selwyn, pp. 214-16; Lenski, pp. 187-95; Dalton, pp. 49-54; Kelly, pp. 172-76; Moffatt, pp. 150-51; Alan M. Stibbs, *The First Epistle General of Peter*, pp. 151-52; Guy N. Woods, *A Commentary on the New Testament Epistles of Peter, John, and Jude*, p. 110; Ray Summers, *1 Peter*, pp. 166-67.

of the Christian churches addressed but had died before the writing of 1 Peter. The NIV expresses that view: "For this is the reason the gospel was preached to those who are now dead." It is in harmony with the natural meaning of the word "dead" in verse 5, though its scope here is much more restricted. The term need not refer to a violent death in martyrdom, but death by martyrdom may well have befallen some of the readers as the result of locally inspired persecutions. The death of those members, whether from natural causes or martyrdom, would naturally be a matter of spiritual perplexity and concern in the churches. But Peter assured them that the purpose in preaching the gospel to them had not failed. It brings "two results to those who believe—the blame of men and the approval of God."[44]

The true purpose of that preaching of the gospel is stated in two different ways: "that they might be judged indeed according to men in the flesh, but live according to God in the spirit." The use of the particles *men . . . de* indicates the distinctness of the two aspects. There is a clear contrast in the two verbs used: the aorist subjunctive "might be judged" (*krithōsi*) denotes a definite occurrence of judgment, and the present tense, "live" (*zōsi*), pictures the continuity of the spiritual life they had received. The two aspects are to be viewed according to a different standard: *according to* (*kata* and the accusative of the noun) indicates the standard, rule, or model of an event or thing. *According to men* (*kata anthrōpous*) indicates that the judgment that befell them was in harmony with the standards that characterize human beings. *According to God* (*kata theon*) indicates that the life they had received was a life in harmony with the nature of God, or a life in harmony with His will (Rom. 8:27). The contrast between *flesh* and *spirit* involves the same contrast as in 3:18. Christ's experience of being put to death in the flesh ended His earthly life; the judgment that befell those who were dead also ended their earthly existence. Christ was made alive in the realm of the spirit; believers too enter into a life in the realm of the spirit through union with Christ. The purpose in preaching the gospel to them was realized through their mystic union with Christ at the time of their conversion. Death did not terminate their life in Christ; they continue to live as He lives. But the fact that they had died like other men might raise the question of whether their new faith had gained them anything. In the eyes of their opponents, they seemed to have gained nothing; though they claimed to have received a new life, they died like other mortals. Peter assured them that though they had died, they would fully share in the life brought by the Savior. They live with Him now in the spiritual world, and they will share with Christ in the blissful vindication when He returns in glory. That assurance led naturally to the emphasis on Christian living in the light of the eschatological hope set forth in verses 7-11. The realization of coming judgment should be a motivating power in the lives of believers now, prompting them to appropriate the provision for victorious living available in Christ.

44. William MacDonald, *I Peter: Faith Tested, Future Triumphant*, p. 93.

2) THE NECESSARY LIFE IN VIEW OF THE END (VV. 7-11)

A fruitful Christian life, inspired by the hope of the future, is a further source of strength amid suffering for righteousness. The connecting particle *de* introduces the additional equipment needed for Christian suffering and indicates a close link with the preceding verses. Its presence is overlooked in various English versions[45] that translate it as "but."[46] The context, however, does not suggest an adversative force; it signals a new train of thought that arose from the mention of judgment in verses 5-6. Selwyn appropriately translates "moreover."[47] The Christian anticipation of Christ's return should have an impact on present Christian conduct.

In the face of persecution from without, believers, inspired by their hope of Christ's return, should band together in loving service to each other to the glory of God. Peter affirmed that the end is near (v. 7a), delineated the need for mutual ministries motivated by love (vv. 7b-11a), and pointed to the true goal of all Christian service (v. 11b).

A. THE APOSTOLIC ASSERTION CONCERNING THE END (v. 7a)

"The end of all things is at hand" summarizes the Christian anticipation concerning the future. *Of all things (pantōn),* standing emphatically forward, underlines the comprehensive nature of the end in view. The genitive *all* could be taken as masculine, "all men, all people;" in 4:17 reference is made to "the end of them that obey not the gospel." But the comprehensive pronoun is best taken as neuter, "all things," as depicting the eschatological end. *The end (to telos),* the consummation of the present course of history, implies not merely cessation of but also the goal toward which the present age moves. It is the Christian hope of Christ's return. It is unwarranted to limit that comprehensive designation to "the end of the temple, of the Levitical priesthood, and of the whole Jewish economy" in A.D. 70.[48] Neither is it to be understood as a reference to the impending death of believers in martyrdom.[49] Those views offer no proper basis for the exhortations that follow.

The verb *is at hand (ēnggiken)* is used in the New Testament of the approach of the kingdom of God in relation to the first (Matt. 3:2; 10:7; Mark 1:15; Luke 10:9, 11) as well as the second advent (Rom. 13:12; Heb. 10:25; James 5:8). The verb, meaning "to approach, to draw near," in the perfect tense (as here) views the end as impending, as having drawn near and now in a position to break in. It expresses the conviction of the early Christian church (Rom. 13:12; 1 Cor.

45. The particle is omitted in KJV, NASB, NIV, NEB, TEV, JB, Berkeley, and Kleist and Lilly.
46. It is represented by "but" in the KJV, Rotherham, Darby, 20th Cent., Weymouth, Montgomery, Goodspeed, and Williams. R. Young used "And," and Moffatt has "Now."
47. Selwyn, p. 216.
48. Macknight, 5:491. So also Jay E. Adams, *Trust and Obey,* pp. 129-30; Woods, pp. 111-12.
49. John T. Demarest, *A Translation and Exposition of the First Epistle of the Apostle Peter,* pp. 224-26.

7:29; Phil. 4:5; Heb. 10:25; James 5:8-9; Rev. 1:3; 22:20). It was in keeping with the Lord's parting instructions: "Be ye also ready: for in an hour that ye think not the Son of Man cometh" (Matt. 24:44; Luke 12:40). His anticipated return was "always near to the feelings and consciousness of the first believers. It was the great consummation on which the strongest desires of their souls were fixed, to which their thoughts and hopes were habitually turned."[50]

The delay in the expected return of Christ did create a problem for some in the early church (2 Pet. 3:4-7). Yet the passing of the centuries has not invalidated that hope. No dates for Christ's return were revealed to the apostles (Matt. 24:36). They, like we, were instructed to be ready and waiting for it. They were not conscious of anything that expressly precluded such an expectation; much that they saw encouraged it. It may also be said that the lengthy time interval must be understood in the light of God's chronology (2 Pet. 3:8-9), not our own.

The assertion that the end of the age does indeed stand near and may break in at any time well represents the view of the early church. With the Messiah's first advent the reality of the eschatological kingdom broke upon human history. With the King's rejection, the kingdom in its eschatological character was not established but awaits the time of His return. But history's encounter with that eschatological kingdom may be said to have changed the future of history. History now moves under its impending shadow. In the words of J.H. Newman:

> Up to Christ's coming in the flesh, the course of things ran straight towards that end, nearing it by every step; but now, under the Gospel, that course has (if I may so speak) altered its direction, as regards His second coming, and runs, not towards the end, but along it, and on the brink of it; and is; at all times near that great event, which, did it run towards it, it would at once run into. Christ, then, is ever at our door.[51]

As human history moves alongside the edge of the eschatological future, the line of separation at times seems razor-thin. Only God's longsuffering holds back the impending manifestation of that day (2 Pet. 3:8-9). That consciousness should have its impact on present Christian living.

B. THE URGENT DUTIES IN VIEW OF THE END (vv. 7b-11a)

"Therefore" (*oun*) grounds those duties in the consciousness of the impending end. In the New Testament that eschatological hope is frequently used to motivate Christian conduct (Matt. 24:45—25:13; Mark 13:33-37; Rom. 13:11-14; 1 Cor. 15:58; Heb. 10:25; James 5:8-9; 1 John 2:28). "The return of our Lord has always furnished the supreme motive for consistent Christian living."[52]

---

50. Nathaniel Marshman Williams, *Commentary on the Epistles of Peter*, p. 61.
51. J. H. Newman, *Parochial and Plain Sermons*, p. 241, as quoted in F. F. Bruce, *The Epistles of John*, p. 65.

Peter pointed out the proper motivation for the readers' personal lives (v. 7b) as well as their community relations (vv. 8-11a).

(1) The duties concerning their personal life (v. 7b). "Be ye therefore of sound mind, and be sober unto prayer." The aorist imperatives stress the urgent and decisive nature of the duties set forth.

The first of those two verbs, "be ye of sound mind" (*sōphronēsate*), was used of a person who was in his right mind as contrasted to one who was under the power of a demon (Mark 5:15; Luke 8:35), and then more generally of one who was reasonable, sensible, and prudent, one who retained a clear mind. The readers were urged to be self-controlled and balanced in their reactions, able to see things in their proper proportions. As Cranfield observes,

> The sound mind is equally far removed from the worldliness and unbelief of those who think to explain away the promise of Christ's coming again, and from the fanaticism and sensationalism of those who would fain predict the hour of it and the manner.[53]

The second verb, "be sober" (*nēpsate*), conveys the thought of sobriety as the opposite of intoxication. The KJV (also in 2 Tim. 4:5) translates "watch," but it is a watchfulness not related to sleepiness but to drunkenness. It is a call to remain alert and in full possession of their faculties and feelings. The eschatological context indicates that Christians should "be free from every form of mental and spiritual 'drunkenness' "[54] that results from befuddled views and feelings about the future.

The two verbs, akin in meaning, are connected by *and* (*kai*); it is a question whether only the latter or both imperatives are to be taken with *unto prayer*. The former view is represented by the ASV, quoted above, which by the use of a comma after the first verb keeps the two commands distinct. The NIV prefers to join both verbs with *unto prayer*: "Be clear minded and self-controlled so that you can pray." If the two verbs are independent of one another, two distinct duties are set forth: to maintain a personal disposition of balance and self-control, and to be fully alert in mind and attitude to pray. If both verbs are connected with *unto prayer*, the importance of that activity is emphasized. We prefer the former construction because it is more comprehensive: the readers were to maintain an inner disposition of balance and prudence as well as to maintain their prayer lives.

"Unto prayer" (*eis proseuchas*), "with a view to, in order to," or "for the purpose of prayer," implies that prayer is a normal and expected activity of the Christian life; but it is easy to become distracted in its performance. The term is general and includes prayer in all its aspects. But the original is plural,

---

52. Charles R. Erdman, *The General Epistles*, p. 78.
53. C. E. B. Cranfield, *I & II Peter and Jude*, p. 113.
54. William F. Arndt and F. Wilbur Gingrich, *A Greek-English Lexicon of the New Testament and Other Early Christian Literature*, p. 540.

"prayers" of all kinds, both private and public. What follows suggests that Christians are to maintain the practice of praying in relation to their own lives as well as in their communal relations.

✗ (2) The activities in their community relations (vv. 8-11a). The thought readily shifts to the readers' community relations as believers. The close connection between personal and brotherhood relations is underlined by the fact that verses 8-11 (consisting of a series of participles) are gramatically dependent on the imperatives of verse 7. That grammatical subordination implies that the duties now enumerated naturally flow out of the believer's personal relationship to God. Though grammatically subordinate, the words "above all things" make clear that the duties set forth are of prime importance.

Peter urged the practice of fervent mutual love (vv. 8-9) and depicted two broad areas of mutual service (vv. 10-11a).

   (a) The duty of mutual love (vv. 8-9). Peter indicated the importance of fervent mutual love (v. 8a), pointed out the way such love is manifested (v. 8b), and cited a vital example of love in action (v. 9).

      (i) The nature of mutual love (v. 8a). "Above all things be fervent in your love among yourselves." Above all things (pro pantōn), "before everything," places love at the summit as of paramount importance in Christian social relations. Peter had already mentioned love before (1:8, 22; 2:17; 3:8); he fully realized its importance. "At a never-to-be-forgotten interview, the Master thrice reminded him that the supreme qualification for ministry was love."[55]

"Your love among yourselves" emphasizes the mutual nature of the love Peter advocated (cf. 1:22). But the noun agapē characterizes that love as a love of intelligence and purpose that desires the welfare of the one loved. The use of the definite article, "the love" (hē agapē), points to the love that the readers already had experienced, and that is the central theme of the remainder of the paragraph. Its mutual character is underlined by the attributive position of among yourselves (tēn eis heautous agapēn), literally, "the into yourselves love." Instead of the reciprocal pronoun (allēlous), which would have pictured the mutual expression of love one to another, Peter's reflexive pronoun brings out the thought that Christians are all members of one body (cf. 1 Cor. 12:12). To love our neighbors as ourselves involves our own spiritual well-being.

Assuming that love in a moderate measure was already operative in the churches addressed, Peter insisted that such love should be "fervent" (ektenē), "stretched out" and up to full capacity (cf. the adverb in 1:22). The predicate adjective requires a love that is both constant and intense. The term was used to describe a horse at full gallop or to picture "the taut muscle of strenuous and

55. F. B. Meyer, "Tried by Fire," p. 161.

sustained effort, as of an athlete."[56] *Be*, representing a present participle (*echontes*), "having" or "holding," indicates that the readers were to maintain their mutual love at its highest level. Such love should be actively cultivated.

    (ii) The action of brotherly love (v. 8*b*). The causal conjunction "for" (*hoti*), or "because," introduces a reason such fervent love should be maintained among Christians: "love covers a multitude of sins." Such love has a beneficial impact on social relations because it "covers" sins. That does not mean that love condones or hushes up sins before God or men. The reference is not to sins in their Godward relation but to sins and failures in our human relations. Christian love hides those sins from its own sight, not from God's. "Love does not delight in evil" (1 Cor. 13:6 [NIV]) and endeavors to forgive and cover sin (Ps. 32:1). It refuses to deliberately expose the sins it encounters to the gaze of all; it prefers to refrain from and discourage all needless talk about them. It acts to throw a veil over those sins, like the conduct of Shem and Japheth in throwing a covering over their father's shame, in contrast to Ham's exposure of it (Gen. 9:20-23). The gracious action of true love promotes the peace and harmony of the brotherhood and is the very opposite of hatred that deliberately exposes sin in order to humiliate and injure. "Only when Christians become mean and ugly do they favor the devil by dragging each other's failings out into the public and smiting each other in the face."[57]

Love's action is necessary because believers are still weak and failing. In their close associations with each other in the brotherhood they do, regrettably, encounter a multitude of sins. *Sins* (*hamartiōn*), "the most comprehensive term for moral obliquity"[58] in the New Testament, denotes all that misses the mark and so falls short of the standard of right; it may thus include sins of weakness and moral shortcomings as well as overt acts of sin. Whenever offenses occur, love will deal with them according to the principles Jesus set forth in Matthew 18:15-17. That multitude of sins calls for a love that is fervent, willing to forgive "until seventy times seven" (Matt. 18:22). Peter did not mean that we will thereby gain forgiveness for our own sins before God. That view, favored by Moffatt, [59] seems clearly suggested in the translation of Lilly, "it wins forgiveness for many sins."[60] If the meaning is that

56. Cranfield, p. 57.
57. Lenski, p. 198.
58. W. E. Vine, *An Expository Dictionary of New Testament Words*, 4:32.
59. Moffatt, p. 153.
60. James A. Kleist and Joseph L. Lilly, *The New Testament Rendered from the Original Greek with Explanatory Notes*.

love wins a covering for one's own sins, then the middle voice would have been used.[61] Peter "is thinking of the life of the Church and not of the relations between man and God."[62] The interpretation given above better suits Peter's purpose to promote the unity and peace of the whole Christian community.

The source of that proverbial statement, which also occurs in James 5:20, is often assumed to be Proverbs 10:12: "Hatred stirreth up strifes; but love covereth all transgressions." But the Septuagint translation of the second part of Proverbs 10:12 gives a meaning very different from the Hebrew and the wording used in the New Testament. If the New Testament occurrences of the expression were drawn from Proverbs, they must be rooted in the Hebrew text or based on a variant Greek text known to both James and Peter. The expression seems to have become a detached proverb that gained independent usage in Christian circles. Selwyn suggests that since Old Testament quotations in 1 Peter are "invariably quoted from the LXX, it seems best to trace the phrase to a proverb, if not a *verbum Christi*, current in the Church."[63] Cranfield notes that "one third-century writing attributes it to our Lord."[64] Probably Peter used the familiar expression without any conscious thought of its source.

> (iii) *The example of loving hospitality* (v. 9). "Using hospitality one to another without murmuring." As indicated in the literal translation of Robert Young, Peter continued his directive without any verbal form: "hospitable to one another, without murmuring." Our English versions prefer to add some verbal form, either an imperative[65] or a participle.[66] The use of a participle is in keeping with the grammatical structure of the paragraph and more clearly indicates the close connection with the preceding verse. Peter cited a practical proof of the operation of love among Christians.

"Hospitality" (*philoxenoi*) translates a nominative plural adjective that describes one who has an affectionate concern for strangers that expresses itself in offering them food and shelter. The practice of hospitality was highly valued in the early church, and it is frequently mentioned in the New Testament (Rom. 12:13; 16:1-2; 1 Tim. 3:2; Titus 1:8; Heb. 13:2; 3 John 5-8; cf. Matt. 25:35). That fruit of brotherly love strengthened mutual ties among the churches, which were often widely scattered. Without its practice the early missionary work of the church would have been greatly retarded. When

---

61. The Textus Receptus has the future tense, but no manuscripts use the middle voice.

62. J. M. E. Ross, *The First Epistle of Peter*, p. 175.

63. Selwyn, p. 217.

64. Cranfield, p. 114.

65. KJV, RSV, NASB, NIV, NEB, TEV, JB, 20th Cent., Weymouth, Moffatt, Montgomery, Goodspeed, Williams, Berkeley, Kleist, and Lilly.

66. Rotherham and ASV.

travelers or delegates from other churches arrived, their hospitable reception was regarded as a matter of course (cf. Acts 10:5-6, 23; 16:15; 21:15-17). Hence hospitality was a necessary qualification of a local church leader (1 Tim. 3:2; Philem. 22). Whenever Christians were on journeys, they realized the value of such hospitality. It was undesirable to lodge in public inns, often the scene of drunkenness and impurity; the Christian's faith had cut him off from the pagan practices that generally prevailed there. It was highly preferable to find lodging in Christian homes, resulting in mutual fellowship and the strengthening of Christian ties. It was even more important for believers to find refuge in Christian homes whenever they were fleeing from their persecutors. Letters of introduction were used to facilitate the reception of Christian hospitality when traveling.

But Peter's use of the reciprocal pronoun (*eis allēlous*) implies that hospitality within the local group was involved. For the first two hundred years there were no separate church buildings; each local congregation would have to meet in the home of one of its members (cf. Rom. 16:5; 1 Cor. 16:19; Philem. 2). That practice would put their hospitality to a practical test.

"Without murmuring" is a frank recognition that the practice of hospitality could become costly, burdensome, and irritating. The Greek term denotes a muttering or low speaking as a sign of displeasure. It depicts a spirit that is the opposite of cheerfulness. It negates the value of the hospitality rendered and destroys the recipient's enjoyment of it. Lenski well notes that those words do not imply "that Peter's readers were grumblers and needed correction."[67] The addition makes emphatic the true character of Christian hospitality. But the words are "a reminder that hospitality can be an exasperating chore, to be shouldered cheerfully if it is to be worthwhile."[68]

(b) *The duty of mutual service* (vv. 10-11a). The thought passes from mutual love to mutual service. First, Peter presented the nature of Christian service (v. 10) and then pointed out two of its basic forms (v. 11a).

(i) *The nature of Christian service* (v. 10). The participial construction ties the picture of acceptable Christian service to what has gone before: "according as each hath received a gift, ministering it among yourselves, as good stewards of the manifold grace of God." The imagery depicts believers individually as stewards ministering to the needs of the household of God with the means that their Master has entrusted to them.

"Each" (*hekastos*), "each one," standing emphatically first, emphasizes that the duties and function of a steward have been assigned to each believer. Each member of the Body of Christ has been entrusted with at least one gift (1 Cor. 12:7; Eph. 4:7); it has no useless members.

Each Christian has his own distinctive function, "according as he received a

67. Lenski, p. 200.
68. Kelly, p. 179.

gift" (R. Young). *According as (kathōs)*, "just as," indicates that the service of each one is determined and is to be governed by the nature of the gift received. *Received (elaben)*, the aorist tense, records a definite bestowal of the gift without indicating the precise time or circumstance. Since each member has received a gift, it is clear that the gifts are not offices in the church. The term *gift (charisma)*, derived from the same root as *grace (charis)*, denotes something that has been "freely and graciously given, a favor bestowed."[69] *Gifts*, which outside the Pauline epistles occurs only here in the New Testament, denotes any capacity or endowment that can be used for the benefit of the church. The reference is not to be restricted to miraculous gifts; included is any "natural endowment or possession which is sanctified in the Christian by the Spirit."[70] Each should be employed as an expression of Christian love.

Each gift was bestowed for the purpose of "ministering it among your-selves." The reflexive pronoun *(heautous)*, as in verse 8, stresses the mutual benefit of the gifts when they are used for the benefit of the whole body. God has made the members interdependent; that which benefits others has a reflexive benefit for us. "The diversity of gifts," Masterman observes, "is therefore a means to a higher unity, the unity of many streams fed from one heaven, and feeding in their turn the river of the life of the Church."[71] The participle, "ministering" *(diakonountes)*, is used in its widest sense (cf. Mark 10:45) and denotes any beneficent service that is freely rendered to another.

All should minister in the personal consciousness of being "good stewards of the manifold grace of God." Christians are stewards *(oikonomoi)*, not owners, of the means they possess. A steward was one to whom property or wealth was entrusted to be administered according to the owner's will and direction. The entrustment was not made to him for his own enjoyment; he was responsible to use his gift for the benefit of those he served. It was a position susceptible to abuse (cf. Luke 16:1). An appointment to the office implied not only an entrustment but also trustworthiness (1 Cor. 4:2). *As good stewards* means that believers not only resemble but should actually be good stewards, blameless in every aspect, performing their duties in a noble and attractive manner.

Each believer has his share in ministering "the manifold grace of God." *The grace of God*, as a collective singular designation, comprehends all the gifts graciously bestowed, and the adjective "manifold" *(poikilēs*; cf. 1:6) displays the many-colored gifts in their infinite variety. The Lord of the church has distributed His bounty with masterly variety to enable His people successfully to encounter the manifold trials (1:6) to which they are subjected.

(ii) The forms of Christian service (v. 11a). Peter divided gifts into two functional categories: the speaking gifts and the service gifts. The

69. Arndt and Gingrich, p. 887.
70. Lenski, p. 200.
71. Masterman, p. 148.

two categories are presented in the form of two conditional sentences, but no verbal form is expressed in the conclusion, which the Greek did not feel essential. In English we feel compelled to insert some verbal form; generally an imperative, "let him,"[72] is supplied. In keeping with the structure in the paragraph, it seems preferable, with the ASV, to supply a participle.

"If any man speaketh" (*ei tis lalei*) refers to the speaking function. No limitations concerning the speaker are indicated; the one speaking is not necessarily an official but may be any individual member. The verb (which may be quite general and denote the use of the faculty of speech) is frequently used in the New Testament of teaching or preaching and so may refer either to prophesying, teaching, or exhortation. Though Peter primarily had public speaking in the assembly in view, the verb is broad enough to include speaking outside a church setting, such as ministering to the sick or even private conversation.

"*Speaking* as it were oracles of God" (*hōs logia theou*) indicates the necessary subjective feeling of the speaker as he exercises his gift. He should be conscious that what he says is God's message for the occasion. In classical Greek the term *oracle* (*logion*) denoted a response or utterance of some deity. In the Septuagint it is often used of "the Word of the Lord" (Isa. 5:24; Pss. 107:11; 119:154-69). Elsewhere in the New Testament it refers to the Old Testament Scriptures (Rom. 3:2; Acts 7:38; Heb. 5:12). Here the sense seems to be that the speaker is conscious that he is not just giving his own opinion but, under the leadership of the Spirit, is delivering God's word. That should be true of all of our words as Christians, even in what we call ordinary conversation.

"If any man ministereth" (*ei tis diakonei*) seems best understood as including all forms of Christian ministry other than speech. The individual rendering the service (*tis*, "any one") is again left entirely indefinite. It is quite unwarranted to limit the reference to the office of the deacon, as Demarest,[73] for example, does. It is the same verb used in verse 10 to include all types of Christian service; here the contrast restricts it to the realm of deeds. Those deeds, motivated by Christian love, would include the various ministeries offered in the context of the Christian brotherhood.

"*Ministering* as of the strength which God supplieth" is a timely reminder that Christian service should be rendered in a spirit of humility and divine enablement. The one serving must avoid the conceit that the strength and ability to perform the service are his own. If his service promotes the well-being of the brotherhood, he should realize that that ability is derived "of"

72. "Let him"—KJV, NASB, 20th Cent., Weymouth, Montgomery, Goodspeed, Williams, Berkeley. "Speak as"—NEB, JB. "He should"—NIV, Lilly. "He must"—Moffatt, TEV. Nothing added—Rotherham, R. Young, Darby.

73. Demarest, p. 231.

(*ex*), "out of," divine enablement (cf. John 15:4). The divine source of that strength (*ho theos*) is emphasized by the position of the words at the end of the sentence. God abundantly supplies (*chorēgei*) the needed strength to carry out His work. In classical Greek the verb was used of paying the expenses of a chorus in the performance of a drama; since the performance reflected upon the prior provision of all that was needed, the term came to denote supplying in abundance. The picture is that of a service humbly yet aggressively performed in full reliance upon God's power.

C. THE GOAL IN CHRISTIAN LIVING (v. 11*b*)

"That in all things God may be glorified through Jesus Christ" declares the true goal in all Christian living. Those words may depict the aim of the service just mentioned. But the comprehensive words *in all things* are best understood as a reference to the entire paragraph. *All* (*pasin*) can be taken as masculine, "in all the brethren" or "all stewards," but the context clearly points to the neuter, "in all things" or "in everything" in the Christian life (1 Cor. 10:31). All that Christians have and do should magnify God (*ho theos*) —emphatic by position—as the fountain of all their gifts and blessings. The true God, whom Christians know and love, should be the supreme center of their lives. Their desire should be in all that they do to give thanks to Him, to extol and ascribe honor to His name. "While his glory is unchangeable, its recognition is to be increased."[74]

"Through Jesus Christ" is a reminder that only through the reconciliation achieved in Him can God be truly glorified (1:21; 2:5; 3:18). "There is only one way to God, and our incense must be scattered on coals taken from the true altar, or it can never rise up acceptable and pleasing to Him."[75]

Peter's own grateful heart moved him to glorify God: "whose is the glory and the dominion for ever and ever. Amen." The use of the indicative *is* (*estin*) makes his words not a devout exclamation but a declaration, "to whom is the glory and the dominion." *To whom* (*hō*) may refer either to Jesus Christ or to God. In favor of the former possibility is the fact that Jesus Christ is the nearer antecedent and that in Hebrews 13:20-21; 2 Peter 3:18; and Revelation 1:5-6 the glory is ascribed to Christ. In favor of the latter is the fact that God is the subject of the sentence. Best cites three considerations in favor of God as the intended antecedent:

> (i) The reference to the glorification of God in the preceding clause links with "glory" here; (ii) The majority of NT doxologies are offered to God, and in particular the very similar doxology of 5:11 is offered to him; (iii) To speak of glorifying God "through Jesus Christ" and then to speak of glory belonging to Christ seems odd.[76]

---

74. Lenski, p. 202.
75. Meyer, p. 171.

We agree with Lenski that "we have no interest whatever in denying the ascription of divine glory to Christ; he is God, equal with the Father,"[77] but we hold that it is preferable to take *God* as the subject of the doxology.

God is magnified as one who possesses "the glory and the dominion" (*hē doxa kai to kratos*). The definite article with both nouns indicates that they are separate and distinct possessions, rightfully belonging to Him. He possesses the glory, the radiant majesty and sublimity characteristic of deity; and He exercises the dominion—might or power in action—an indication that He is the sovereign ruler over all. His might ensures His triumph over all the forces of evil on behalf of His afflicted saints.

His are the glory and the might "for ever and ever" (*eis tous aiōnas tōn aiōnōn*), literally, "unto the ages of the ages." That strengthened form of *for ever* (cf. 1:25) occurs twenty-one times in the New Testament and emphasizes the thought of eternity in the strongest way. The expression depicts eternity as "a series of ages flowing on endlessly, in each of which a number of other shorter ages are gathered up."[78]

"Amen," commonly appearing at the end of Christian prayers and doxologies, is a transliteration, alike in Greek and English, of the Hebrew word meaning "so let it be." So used, it is not a wish but a strong affirmation, placing a seal of approval upon what has just been said. Its use was common in the early Christian worship services as an expression of devout assent, as the amen in 1 Corinthians 14:16 indicates. The practice was adopted from the Jewish synagogue. The *Amen* appears at the close of doxologies in the Old Testament (cf. Neh. 8:6; Pss. 41:13; 78: 18-19; 89:52) as well as the New (e.g., Rom. 1:25; Gal. 1:5; Phil. 4:20; 1 Pet. 5:11).

Such doxologies appear in the body of the New Testament epistles as well as in early Christian letters (1 Clement has no fewer than ten doxologies). The use of a doxology is a sign of the emotional response of the writer and does not imply the end of the document. Only three New Testament epistles conclude with a doxology (Rom. 16:27; 2 Pet. 3:18; Jude 25). Thus Peter's doxology cannot be cited as the end of what was originally an independent document.

76. Best, p. 161.
77. Lenski, p. 203.
78. Johnstone, p. 351.

18

D. The Need for Steadfastness in Suffering as Christians
(4:12-19)

(12) Beloved, think it not strange concerning the fiery trial among you, which cometh upon you to prove you, as though a strange thing happened unto you: (13) but insomuch as ye are partakers of Christ's sufferings, rejoice; that at the revelation of his glory also ye may rejoice with exceeding joy. (14) If ye are reproached for the name of Christ, blessed *are ye*; because the *Spirit* of glory and the Spirit of God resteth upon you. (15) For let none of you suffer as a murderer, or a thief, or an evil-doer, or as a meddler in other men's matters: (16) but if *a man suffer* as a Christian, let him not be ashamed; but let him glorify God in this name. (17) For the time *is come* for judgment to begin at the house of God: and if *it begin* first at us, what *shall be* the end of them that obey not the gospel of God? (18) And if the righteous is scarcely saved, where shall the ungodly and sinner appear? (19) Wherefore let them also that suffer according to the will of God commit their souls in well-doing unto a faithful Creator.

That paragraph develops and reinforces the theme of Christian suffering (first touched on in 1:6-7) that is central to the third cycle of exhortations, which began with 3:13. It is not a repetition of what has already been said. Alford points out that in 3:13—4:6 the experience of suffering was treated "with reference to their inflictors: whereas this proceeds wholly on reference to a Christian's own inner hopes, and considerations within the church itself."[1] The apostle appropriately called for steadfastness on the part of his readers as they encountered persecution because they were Christians. He directed "attention more distinctly than elsewhere to the deep and varied sources of

---

1. Henry Alford, *The Greek New Testament*, vol. 4 (part 1), p. 376.

comfort which are open to the persecuted believer."[2] His use of present imperatives calls for a resolute inner attitude of steadfastness and joy to endure those experiences.

There is an intensification of tone in the paragraph; Peter brought his theme to its peak by calling his Christian readers to suffer steadfastly for their faith. The paragraph has always been the mainstay for the view that 1 Peter belongs to a time when Christians were being persecuted by the state.[3] But Van Unnik finds that in interpreting the picture of suffering in the paragraph "we have to leave out the whole thought of state action."[4] Three considerations support that conclusion: (1) the writer never speaks of the death of Christians but of their sufferings that, though very painful, were not death; (2) the accusations mentioned are slander and reproach for the Christian name, but there is no word of intervention by the state; and (3) 5:9 asserts that the same sufferings were shared by the whole brotherhood.[5] The picture of suffering is closely akin to the suffering portrayed in the preceding part of the epistle. The absence of a connecting particle at the opening of the paragraph is common in beginning a hortatory clause (cf. 2:11, 13). It serves to make Peter's appeal to the hearts of his readers more direct.

Peter introduced his appeal with the direct address "Beloved" (*agapētoi*), the second of only two occurrences of that term of affection in the epistle (cf. 2:11). Its use reminded the readers "that in all their anxieties and troubles they belong to a fellowship whose members are knit together by love."[6] The writer loved them and had heartfelt sympathy for them; but they were also the recipients of God's matchless love.

The paragraph exhorts and instructs Christians concerning the inner response they should have to suffering. Peter dealt with the inner attitude his suffering readers should have (vv. 12-13), gave them valued instruction concerning their fiery ordeal (vv. 14-16), reminded them of God's judgment in connection with their experience (vv. 17-18), and concluded with a summary exhortation to the Christian sufferer (v. 19).

1) THE ATTITUDE ENJOINED WHEN SUFFERING AS CHRISTIANS (VV. 12-13)

Of central importance for victory amid Christian suffering is the inner attitude of the sufferer himself. Peter prohibited a wrong inner reaction toward the ordeal of Christian suffering (v. 12) and encouraged an attitude of joy. Such as attitude offered assurance of the readers' exultation at the return of Christ (v. 13).

2. Robert Johnstone, *The First Epistle of Peter Revised Text*, p. 352.
3. See the Introduction.
4. W. C. Van Unnik, "The Teaching of Good Works in I Peter," p. 102.
5. Ibid.
6. J. N. D. Kelly, *A Commentary on the Epistles of Peter and of Jude*, p. 184.

A. THE ATTITUDE PROHIBITED AMID THE FIERY TRIAL (v. 12)

"Think it not strange concerning the fiery trial among you" categorically prohibits a wrong response. Peter had already used the verb that expressed that prohibition in 4:4; the thought is taken up by the adjective *strange* that immediately follows. The present imperative with the negative (*mē xenizesthe*) forbids the continued reaction, natural to the human heart, to regard the experience as something strange or alien to the Christian life. The expression does not indicate "a paralyzing shock"[7] but a continuing attitude of bewilderment and astonishment at what is happening. If unbelievers are surprised at their behavior (4:4), Christians should not be astonished if those unbelievers persecute them on that account. Jesus had predicted such experiences (John 15:20).

The reaction was prompted by "the fiery trial among you" (*tē en humin purōsei*), literally, "by the in you burning." The noun *fiery trial* (*purōsis*) denotes a process of burning; it occurs elsewhere in the New Testament only in Revelation 18:9 and 18, where it refers to the burning of Babylon. Peter used the term figuratively to denote the severity of the experience his readers were undergoing, an experience comparable to pain caused by exposure to fire. The attributive phrase, *among you* (*en humin*), "in your midst," characterizes the ordeal as one that did not directly subject all members to such burning. But the experiences of individual members made an impact on the entire Christian community. Though the external testing was limited, it constituted an internal test for all of them; with what attitude would they face that situation?

Peter did not think of that burning as a process of destruction but as the purifying fire of the refiner's furnace "which cometh upon you to prove you." A high purpose was being realized through the fiery ordeal, *to prove you* (*pros peirasmon*), "for putting you to the proof."[8] God used it as a trial or test to demonstrate what they could endure. The expression goes back to Peter's picture of the readers' sufferings in 1:6-7. Their suffering was indeed the application of the refiner's fire, intended to purify them (cf. Prov. 27:21; Ps. 66:10; Rev. 3:18). Their endurance of the trial demonstrated the genuineness of their faith and molded their character. "Only valuable metal is smelted in a furnace, and smelted to bring out its brilliance and lasting value."[9] *Cometh* translates a present participle (*ginomenē*), "befalling you," and "seems to presuppose an enduring situation rather than an unexpected crisis."[10] In the light of Jesus' words in Luke 12:49, the readers' experience was an intense manifestation of that great conflagration which Christ came to kindle in the earth."[11]

"As though a strange thing happened unto you" (*hōs xenou humin*

7. Francis Wright Beare, *The First Epistle of Peter*, p. 189.
8. Translation of Joseph Bryant Rotherham, *The Emphasized New Testament*.
9. James Moffatt, *The General Epistles, James, Peter, and Judas*, p. 156.
10. Kelly, p. 185.
11. John Lillie, *Lectures on the First and Second Epistles of Peter*, p. 287.

sumbainontos), a genitive absolute, presents the false view that prompted the readers' reaction of bewildered astonishment. Failing to understand the purifying process involved, they naturally evaluated their ordeal as a strange thing, something regarded as foreign to their acceptance of salvation in Christ. *Happened* (*sumbainontos*), a present compound participle, pictures the fiery ordeal as an undesired companion on their journey. They were at a loss to understand the situation; it seemed so contrary to the blessings promised in the gospel. As Gentile believers they had little experience of being persecuted for their faith; to them it was a strange situation, foreign to what they might have expected. But as long as they harbored that view, they would not be able to adjust to the trying experience. He who has enlisted under the banner of the crucified Christ need not be surprised if conflict, hardship, and suffering follow (cf. 2 Tim. 3:12).

B. THE ATTITUDE ENJOINED IN SUFFERING FOR CHRIST (v. 13)

"But" (*alla*) marks a sharp contrast between the false view that Peter censured and the attitude he enjoined, "but insomuch as ye are partakers of Christ's sufferings rejoice." Instead of causing them bewilderment, their sufferings as Christians should have prompted them to rejoice.

"Insomuch as" (*katho*), an adverb of degree, "in so far as, in the measure that," indicates that not all the readers had been called on to suffer as Christians to the same extent. Some must have endured its full force, others were directly affected to a lesser degree. In thus suffering "ye are partakers of Christ's sufferings" (*koinōneite tois tou Christou pathēmasin*), "ye have fellowship with the sufferings of the Christ."[12] Their sufferings had brought them into closer fellowship with Christ's sufferings, the sufferings that the Christ (*tou Christou*), the Messiah Himself, endured on earth. He endured unmerited suffering as the object of the world's hatred. As His representatives to the world, the readers were in reality experiencing the same hatred. "Their enemies would persecute Christ if He were among them, for it is really he who is the object of their hatred; and, therefore, in being persecuted themselves, they are partakers of Christ's sufferings."[13] Christians are members of the Body of which Christ is the Head; in infinite sympathy, He enters into our sufferings with us. The readers' sufferings were in keeping with their calling to be followers of the Christ who suffered (2:21).[14]

The more the readers suffered for Christ, the greater their ground for rejoicing. When Christians so perceive their sufferings, the command "rejoice

12. Translation of Robert Young, *The Holy Bible Consisting of the Old and New Covenants Translated According to the Letter and Idioms of the Original Languages.*
13. Nathaniel Marshman Williams, *Commentary on the Epistles of Peter*, p. 64.
14. Others propose interpreting *partakers of Christ's sufferings* eschatologically as a phrase that indicates their share in the messianic woes that will come on the earth just before the return of the Messiah, cf. Ernest Best, *I Peter*, pp. 162-63; A. R. C. Leaney, *The Letters of Peter and Jude*, p. 64.

ye" (*chairete*) makes sense. The present imperative calls for "not a single isolated response, but a continuous attitude and activity."[15] Peter faithfully taught the readers that which he had learned from Christ Himself (Matt. 5:11-12) and confirmed in his own experience (Acts 5:41). Faith realizes that the ground for rejoicing does not lie in the sufferings themselves but in the fellowship with Christ that they bring.

Such rejoicing also relates to the Christian's experience of the future, "that at the revelation of his glory also ye may rejoice with exceeding joy." That clause (*hina* with an aorist subjunctive) may be understood as a purpose clause; the Berkeley version translates "in order that at the revelation of His glory you may be full of joy." If that is correct then Peter meant that Christians should practice rejoicing now to assure fullness of joy in the eschatological future. It is more likely that his words refer to a contemplated result; thus the NASB translates, "so that also at the revelation of His glory, you may rejoice with exultation." If that is correct then Peter meant that present rejoicing prepares Christians to fully experience joy in that future Day. The latter view seems more likely since it explains why Christians are to rejoice when persecuted for the sake of Christ. It is in keeping with the forward position of *also* (*hina kai*), which emphasizes the relation between the two aspects of Christian rejoicing that Peter discussed. As Masterman observes, "It is through 'glorying in tribulation also' (Rom. v. 3) that the Christian is made ready for the joy that expands into fullness at the appearing of Jesus Christ."[16]

"At (*en*, 'in') the revelation of his glory" marks the time and manner of the experiential realization of that future rejoicing. Christian rejoicing will be made complete at and by the return of Christ in glory (Col. 3:4; 2 Thess. 1:10-12). Instead of the usual designation, "the revelation of Jesus Christ," Peter referred to the outward manifestation of Christ's glory at the time of His triumphant return. That manifestation will herald the contrast between His first advent in humility and suffering and His return in triumph. For Peter, the ultimate glory of believers is not their entry into the glory of heaven at death but their appearing with Christ in glory at His return.

Christians may be persecuted in the present for their faith in Christ, but at His return they will "rejoice with exceeding joy" (*charēte agalliomenoi*), "ye shall rejoice, exulting." *Rejoice*, in the aorist tense, indicates the great burst of joy that will sweep over them at Christ's return. The fullness of that joy is emphasized by the added present participle, "exulting" (cf. 1:6, 8). It adds to rejoicing "the idea of exulting, jubilating, skipping and bubbling over with shouts of delight."[17] The present tense indicates that the exultation is enduring. Whenever that eschatological hope is a living reality in the life of the believer, it inspires unswerving loyalty to the Lord and promotes a readiness to suffer for Him now.

15. Alan M. Stibbs, *The First Epistle General of Peter*, p. 159.

16. J. Howard B. Masterman, *The First Epistle of S. Peter*, p. 152.

17. R. C. H. Lenski, *The Interpretation of the Epistles of St. Peter, St. John and St. Jude*, p. 208.

2) THE INSTRUCTIONS CONCERNING THE ORDEAL OF SUFFERING (vv. 14-16)

Having lifted his readers' eyes to an inspiring hope, Peter gave them guidance about their painful present. He presented the true evaluation of their afflictions (v. 14), reminded them that *Christian* suffering excludes unworthy reasons (v. 15), and called for a response that honors God when suffering "as a Christian" (v. 16).

A. THE EVALUATION OF SUFFERING FOR CHRIST (v. 14)

"If ye are reproached for the name of Christ" pinpoints the nature of the suffering. The conditional statement does not imply doubt but assumes the reality of the situation. *Reproached* (*oneidizesthe*), in the present indicative passive, portrays unjustified reproaches and insults being hurled against the readers. It indicates that the attacks on them were verbal rather than physical. The attacks consisted of verbal abuse, slander, and defamation of character. For noble-minded, sensitive souls "there is often more bitterness [in such attacks] than in the loss of goods, or in the torments or agonies of the body."[18]

The readers had been reproached "for the name of Christ" (*en onomati Christou*), more literally, "in" or "in connection with" that name. The expression seems to be synonymous with "as a Christian" in verse 16. They had not been reproached because they called themselves Christians; nor does Peter imply that confessing to be a Christian was a punishable crime. Rather, the reproaches had been hurled at them "in connection with" the name of Christ and the revelation associated with it. Because their enemies hated that name and all that it stood for, though Christ's followers proclaim that name and exalt His authority, hatred against the readers expressed itself in assaults on them. The picture is consistent with the words of Jesus to His disciples, "Ye shall be hated of all men for my name's sake" (Matt. 10:22; Mark 13:13; Luke 21:17). That prediction found fulfillment in the early experience of the Christian church (Acts 4:17), and often since then.[19]

"Blessed *are ye*" (*makarioi*) records the apostolic verdict concerning that experience. Believers who suffer for Christ are spiritually "blessed" or "fortunate" (cf. 3:14). The absence of an expressed verb makes it a fervent exclamation. It is a joyous recognition of their spiritual prosperity. They can appropriate the words of Christ, "Blessed are ye when *men* shall reproach you, and persecute you, and say all manner of evil against you falsely, for my sake" (Matt. 5:11). Instead of hanging their heads in shame, they can lift them up with radiant faces.

"Because the *Spirit* of glory and the Spirit of God resteth upon you" confirms

---

18. John Calvin, *The Epistle of Paul the Apostle to the Hebrews and the First and Second Epistles of St Peter*, p. 308.

19. On *persecution for the name* see E. G. Hardy, *Christianity and the Roman Government*, chap. 7.

the beatitude just pronounced. "The Spirit of Glory is God's special gift to those who are called to endure for Him."[20] Compare the story of Stephen in Acts 6-7.

The double designation, "the *Spirit* of glory and the Spirit of God" (*to tēs doxēs kai to tou theou pneuma*), is beset with some textual[21] as well as grammatical uncertainty. The mode of expression is somewhat peculiar, and the designation has been differently understood. As indicated by the italics, no noun appears with the first neuter article, and the relation of the two neuter phrases is somewhat uncertain. Some, like Plumptre, propose to separate them and to translate the first "the principle or element of glory."[22] Others take the words to be "a title of Christ conceived as the Shekinah or 'visible presence' of God among men; cf. Jas. 2:1."[23] But because of the genitive modifier with each neuter article, it is more probable that the second is intended as an expansion of the first. Others keep the two together and see the presence of a hendiadys, giving the force "the glorious Spirit of God."[24] But it is most natural to take both neuter articles with *pneuma* ("Spirit")—as in the translation above—as a double characterization of the Holy Spirit.[25] The two genitives, *of glory* (*tēs doxēs*) and *of God* (*tou theou*), are placed attributively between the article and the noun *Spirit*; they point to two characteristics of the Spirit that rest on Christians. The repeated article makes each characteristic distinct. Both genitives may be understood as subjective. The Spirit *bestows* the glory, not some vague glory but *the* glory that related to suffering for Christ. God, who sent His Son, also sends the Spirit of God on those who suffer as loyal followers of His Son. It is noteworthy that in that description of the experiences of persecuted believers, all three members of the Trinity are named. The Scriptures attribute glory to each.

That Spirit now "resteth upon you" (*eph' humas anapauetai*). The forward position of *upon you* (*eph' humas*) applies that declaration explicitly to the persecuted readers. In contrast to the external storm of abuse and insult is the inner presence of the Spirit. The verb, in the present tense, pictures His presence "not coming and going, in fitful movements, or extraordinary manifestations, but dwelling with them continually."[26]

The remainder of the verse in the KJV, "on their part he is evil spoken of,

---

20. Masterman, p. 153.

21. See the United Bible Societies, *The Greek New Testament*, for the variants. A number of manuscripts, some of them early, have *kai dunameōs* ("and of power") after the word *doxēs*, "of glory." James Moffatt follows that text, "*the Spirit of* glory and power, the Spirit of *God* Himself" in his version—so also the marginal reading in RSV.

22. E. H. Plumptre, *The General Epistles of St Peter & St Jude*, p. 148. The 20th Cent. reads "the divine Glory and the Spirit of God are resting upon you."

23. Archibald M. Hunter, *The First Epistle of Peter*, p. 143.

24. Matthew Poole, *A Commentary on the Holy Bible*, 3:914—so also the versions by Goodspeed and by C. B. Williams, cf. NEB, TEV.

25. Weymouth reads "the Spirit of glory—even the Spirit of God—is resting upon you." Others read "the Spirit of glory and of God rests upon you": NASB, NIV, RSV, KJV, Young.

26. Plumptre, p. 148.

but on your part he is glorified," represents the reading of the Textus Receptus.[27] The reading has a fair measure of textual support and may have been accidentally omitted, but modern textual critics generally regard the words as an explanatory gloss. If they are accepted as genuine, they do not refer to Christ but to the Holy Spirit. They explain why the obvious presence of the Holy Spirit with believers is not acknowledged by their enemies.

B. THE EXCLUSION OF UNWORTHY CAUSES OF SUFFERING (v. 15)

"For" (gar) at the beginning of the verse indicates an important qualification to what has just been said. Peter assumed that his readers would suffer "for the name of Christ"(v. 14), but there are causes for suffering that do not qualify for that evaluation. They must suffer innocently, not as criminals. Edwards observes, "Whenever we are inclined to 'play the martyr' we might well suspect that we are not suffering at all as a Christian."[28]

"Let none of you suffer as a murderer, or a thief, or an evil-doer, or as a meddler in other men's matters." The prohibition is individual; no individual exemptions can be recognized. Whatever may have been true of the readers' past, the negative mē with the present imperative demands that no such causes for suffering should remain among them. There should be no occasion that permits their enemies to relate such evils to the name of Christ. Peter's list, which is not intended to be exhaustive, deals with clear-cut extremes. The blessedness just described demands that the readers' lives should agree with their Christian profession. It is a demand that had been stressed before (cf. 2:12, 15-16, 19-20; 3:14-17). The verb translated "suffer" (paschetō) is general and "does not define the nature of the sufferings, nor the manner, whether by legal process or otherwise, in which it is inflicted."[29] As (hōs) divides the list in the verse into two classes (the addition of "as" before each of the four terms in the KJV is unwarranted).

"As a murderer, or a thief, or an evil-doer" forms one group, and the terms are to be understood literally. A murderer, or a thief designates specific crimes, but an evil-doer (kakopoios) is a general term, "or any other kind of criminal" (NIV). The composite term denotes one who engages in the practice of morally base and evil activities. In 2:14 such evil-doers are mentioned as subject to punishment by the government, and in 2:12 their deeds are set in contrast to the good works of believers. Such specific translations as "sorcery"[30] and "thug"[31] are questionable.

---

27. For the evidence see the United Bible Society's text.
28. Clifford Walter Edwards, Christian Being and Doing. A Study-Commentary on James and I Peter, p. 150.
29. Charles Bigg, A Critical and Exegetical Commentary on the Epistles of St. Peter and St. Jude, p. 177.
30. So the NEB.
31. Suggested by Beare, p. 193.

"Or as a meddler in other men's matters" (ē hōs allotriepiskopos), by the repeated use of *as*, is placed in a category by itself. The phrase translates a composite term that occurs only here in the New Testament. The term may be Peter's own coinage. It is formed from the adjective *allotrios*, which means "belonging to another," and the noun *episkopos*, "an overseer," or "bishop" (cf. 2:25). Etymologically, the term denotes one who acts as overseer in matters that belong to another. Such formations with *allotrios* were not uncommon.[32] The intended force of the term has been variously understood. Many believe that the fourth term, like the three preceding ones, must denote some kind of punishable legal offense. Thus various translations, implying some form of criminal activity, have been proposed: "a revolutionary,"[33] "a spy,"[34] "an informer,"[35] or one "infringing the rights of others."[36] The term has been understood to refer to a political agitator engaged in proletarian activities against the establishment, a person whom the authorities must squelch. But such conjectures overlook the presence of *as* before the term, a word that differentiates it and introduces a new category. Understanding the first part of the composite term, "belonging to another," in a material sense, Calvin took it "to indicate one who covets what belongs to another."[37] Or the term may be understood to mean "the unfaithful guardian of goods committed to him."[38] Peter arranged his terms in a descending order of guilt; the term may designate an activity that was a definite social nuisance, one that irritated, aroused strong displeasure, and prompted open hostility. If that is correct then the term may refer to an unwarranted intrusion into the affairs of others. In the fourth century Epiphanius (*Ancor.* xii. 5) used the exceedingly rare term in the sense of "interfering with someone else's business."[39] Our versions use a variety of terms to present that basic concept: "a troublesome meddler" (NASB), "one prying into other men's affairs" (Rotherham), "interfering in matters which do not concern Christians" (20th Cent.), and "a busybody in other men's matters" (KJV). Such a general meaning seems most probable in the context. In accordance with the basic meaning of the term, Kelly well observes that "We can only speculate what kind of meddling the writer has in mind (excessive zeal for making converts? causing discord in family or commercial life? over-eager denunciation of pagan habits? prying curiosity?), but he plainly regards it as disreputable."[40]

---

32. See examples in Hermann W. Beyer, *allotri (o) episkopos, TDNT*, 2:621.
33. Moffatt, p. 158.
34. Helen Barrett Montgomery, *The New Testament in Modern English.*
35. JB.
36. NEB.
37. Calvin, p. 309.
38. Beyer, p. 622.
39. Kelly, p. 189.
40. Ibid.

C. THE REACTION WHEN SUFFERING "AS A CHRISTIAN" (v. 16)

"But if *a man suffer* as a Christian" (*ei de hōs Christianos*) adds a further aspect to the instruction. The conditional construction implies a present reality; Peter knew that his readers were undergoing the kind of suffering in view. *But* (*de*) implies a contrast and suggests that to suffer for the causes just indicated (v. 15) would not be to suffer as a Christian. No verb is expressed, but *suffer* is naturally added from verse 15. The use of the singular pronoun (*tis*) in verse 15, as well as the singular verbs in verse 16, implies that this is basic Christian teaching and is not merely formulated to meet the needs of the readers.[41] The use of *as* indicates that suffering as a Christian constitutes a distinct category.

Here is the third and last occurrence of the word *Christian* in the New Testament (Acts 11:26; 26:28). There seems to be an allusion to the name in James 2:7, but only here is the word used by a Christian (and then as employed by non-Christians). The name *Christian* (*Christianos*), built on the name *Christ* with the suffix -*ianos*, a Latin formation (-*ianus*), denotes a partisan or follower. Such forms were readily seized upon by the Greek and we find *Hērōdianoi*, followers of Herod, in the New Testament. Originated by non-Christians (Acts 11:26), *Christian* categorized the followers of Christ as "members of the Christ-party." His name seemed to be the one thing that held the heterogeneous mass of followers together. It differentiated them from the Jews in the public eye. Though not readily employed by the Christians themselves, the term rapidly became a current designation. It is not obvious that the name at once carried a reproachful connotation, but obviously it did develop an opprobrious significance as Christians came increasingly under attack.[42] Peter explicitly connected the name with suffering. Christians were being subjected to suffering precisely because of their loyalty to Christ. His name and cause were involved. Peter's terminology does not prove that being a Christian had become a capital offense. Such suffering as a partisan of Christ was nothing new for Christians (cf. Acts 5:41). The picture is in keeping with the warning concerning future suffering that Christ gave His followers (Mark 13:9-13).

The reaction of a believer suffering as a Christian is important for Peter; he stated it negatively and positively. Negatively, "let him not be ashamed" (*mē aischunesthō*); he should not harbor any feeling of shame as would be natural if caught in any of the evils mentioned in verse 15. If, as some believe,[43] Peter

---

41. By changing the third singular to "you" in the passage, the NIV blurs the impersonal presentation.

42. Tacitus, *Annals* xv. 44, in recording how in A.D. 64 the Christians were made Nero's scapegoats, refers to them as "a class of people loathed for their vices, who were commonly styled Christians after Christ, who was executed by the procurator Pontius Pilate when Tiberius was emperor."

43. John T. Demarest, *A Translation and Exposition of the First Epistle of the Apostle Peter*, pp. 240-41; Beare, pp. 192-93.

was preparing his readers for possible martyrdom, the prohibition hardly seems suited to such a crucial prospect, and "shame hardly seems the appropriate emotion; the word is suitable to describe a less final punishment."[44] Peter warned against a sense of false shame and moral cowardice.

"But let him glorify God in this name" states the desired positive reaction. *But* (*de*) indicates a complementary response. There is, however, a clear emotional contrast between shame and glorifying God. The present tense calls for a habitual response of glorifying God (*ton theon*), the true God whom Christians know and serve. Peter himself knew the exhilarating experience of turning suffering for Christ into an occasion of praise (Acts 5:41). To glorify God *in this name* (*en tō onomati toutō*) means more than expressing praise to God in Christ's name. Christians are to offer their praise "in connection with this name," all that Christ and His name stand for. Union with that name outwardly may involve an environment of suffering and disgrace, but inwardly it is accepted as an opportunity to praise God.

The reading in the KJV, "let him glorify God on this behalf" (*en tō merei toutō*), "in this matter," represents the Textus Receptus. Though it is the reading in the majority of the Greek manuscripts, the support for it is late. It is probably a gloss.[45] If the reading is a gloss, it shows that the Greek-speaking scribe did not understand the expression *in this name* as a reference to its use in worship. That reading means that the experience of suffering for Christ is to be accepted as the ground for exultation and the giving of glory to God.

3) THE EXERCISE OF GOD'S JUDGMENT IN SUFFERING (VV. 17-18)

The conjunction "for" (*hoti*) indicates a close connection in thought with the preceding. It explains the paradoxical exhortation not to be ashamed of suffering but to use it to glorify God. The readers were assured that God was at work amid their sufferings (v. 17a) and then comforted by a double inference from their experience (vv. 17b-18).

A. THE EXPLANATION OF THE PRESENT ORDEAL (v. 17a)

"For the time *is come* for judgment to begin at the house of God" explains the divine aspect of the readers' suffering for Christ's sake. It was the time or appropriate season for God to deal in judgment with His people. Being infinitely holy, God cannot condone sin; even His own family stands under His judgment. The readers' experience of His chastening discipline should be understood in the light of the coming judgment. It is appropriate for God's judgment *to begin* (*tou arxasthai*), commence its operation, *at the house of God* (*apo tou oikou tou theou*), His people (cf. 2:5), "as a proof of their membership in His family, and a pledge of their escape from the end of those whom the last

---

44. Best, p. 165.
45. For the evidence see Nestle-Aland, *Novum Testamentum Graece* (26th ed.).

judgment shall find disobedient to the Gospel."[46] His judgment begins *at* (*apo*)
God's house but goes beyond that to include the lost. That order in God's
judgment is clearly expressed in the Old Testament prophets (Isa. 10:12; Jer.
25:29; Ezek. 9:6), and Peter assumed that that order was known to his readers.
God acts first to remove all that is inconsistent with His holy nature in His
people.

That interpretation assumes that "judgment" (*krima*) refers to an action or
process (Acts 24:25: Heb. 6:2), rather than to the more usual idea of a judicial
verdict. Less probable is the view of Lenski who, holding to the meaning of
"verdict," understands the reference to be to the divine verdict that will be
based on the crimes men "are committing against God's house, his holy
Church."[47]

God's judgment against sin is a long process, and Peter's words need not
mean that he regarded the sufferings of his readers as the initiation of the final
day of judgment. Rather, God's dealings in disciplinary judgment with His
people in the present age are premonitory of the reality of that coming day.

B. THE INFERENCES DRAWN FROM THE EXPERIENCE (vv. 17b-18)

The connecting "and" (*de*) indicates that a further thought is involved, the
truth that God's judgment is not restricted to His household. Peter stimulated
the readers' thinking by giving them two questions to contemplate. The
conditional structure implies reality. His first question, "if *it begin* first at us,
what *shall be* the end of them that obey not the gospel of God?" (v. 17b),
implies that the judgment becomes more severe as it spreads. "If the sons are
chastised, what have the most malicious slaves to expect?" (Augustine).[48] *At us*
(*aph' hēmōn*), "from us," is structurally parallel to *the house of God*; it united
Peter with his readers as a recipient of God's judgment, resulting in their
purification and ultimate glorification. By contrast Peter asked, "what shall be
the end of them that obey not the gospel of God?" *The end* (*to telos*) points to
the final destiny of the readers' adversaries and contains what Bigg calls "a
flash of denunciation."[49] The readers were assured that though their present
sufferings as God's people were severe, they still fell far short of what awaits
the enemies of God. But Peter made no attempt to describe the implied
vengeance that will overtake "them that obey not the gospel of God." The
character of such people is described by their continuing activity; they *obey not*
(*tōn apeithountōn*), are unbelieving and willfully refuse to be persuaded by the
claims of the gospel (cf. 2:8). *The gospel of God* (*tō tou theou euanggeliō*)
indicates the depth of their guilt. *Of God*, in the attributive position, stresses
that the good news that they rejected by its very nature is God's, sent by Him

---

46. Robert Jamieson, A. R. Fausset, and David Brown, *A Commentary, Critical and Explanato-
     ry, on the Old and New Testaments*, 2:512.

47. Lenski, p. 215.

48. Quoted in G. F. C. Fronmüller, *The Epistles General of Peter*, p. 83.

49. Bigg, p. 181.

as His authoritative message of salvation to mankind. In their response to the gospel lies the stark contrast between them and the readers who accepted that message and rejoiced in God's salvation amid their sufferings (1:6-7).

The second question, "And if the righteous is scarcely saved, where shall the ungodly and sinner appear?" drives home the contrast between the Christian and his adversaries who reject Christ. The question is formulated in the words of the Septuagint translation of Proverbs 11:31, but Peter gave no indication that he was appealing to the Old Testament to support his position. It is probable that he was employing a proverbial saying as a suitable expression of his own thought.[50] If the formulation was consciously molded by Proverbs 11:31, Peter adapted the words to his own eschatological purpose.

"The righteous" (*ho dikaios*) is generic; the individual is portrayed as the representative of his class. He has been justified by faith and as such seeks to walk uprightly but is not necessarily a sinless person. As such, he is "scarcely saved" (*molis sōzetai*), "is being saved with difficulty." The expression relates to the arduous experiences of the righteous in this life and does not imply doubt as to whether he will be saved in the end. As Fausset remarks, "The 'scarcely' marks the severity of the ordeal, and the unlikelihood (in a mere human point of view) of the righteous sustaining it; but the righteousness of Christ and God's everlasting covenant make it all sure."[51] Paul instructed his converts "that through many tribulations we must enter into the kingdom of God" (Acts 14:22; cf. 2 Tim. 3:12). Clearly Peter "has none of the starry-eyed optimism of some modern Christians."[52]

If on his way to eternal glory such is the experience of the righteous, the recipient of God's grace and guidance, "where shall the ungodly and sinner appear?" *The ungodly and sinner* (*ho asebēs kai hamartōlos*) describe the individual under two aspects. Negatively, as an ungodly person he is devoid of reverence for God, impious in attitude and conduct. Positively, as a sinner he violates the standard of God's law as one who is willfully devoted to the practice of evil. The two characteristics are closely related, the second naturally following from the first. *Appear* is used as the opposite of *saved* and implies that such a person will go into perdition. The term pictures a scene like the one in Matthew 25:31-46 (cf. Ps. 1:5). Again, the solemn question is left unanswered. It is "as if faith itself feared to follow the outcast into that outer darkness."[53] Peter was not interested in picturing the sufferings of the condemned; his purpose was to help and encourage his persecuted brethren.

4) THE SUMMARY EXHORTATION TO CHRISTIAN SUFFERERS (V. 19)

The opening "wherefore" (*hōste*), together with the imperative, indicates that the verse presents Peter's summary directive to his suffering readers.

50. Ernest Best, "I Peter II 4-10—A Reconsideration," pp. 272-73, 275.
51. Jamieson, Fausset, and Brown, p. 2:512.
52. Kelly, p. 194.
53. Lillie, p. 298.

"Let them also that suffer according to the will of God commit their souls in well-doing unto a faithful Creator." The precise connection of *also* (*kai*) is open to some uncertainty. It may be related to the imperative, *let them commit*. If that is correct then Peter meant that in addition to joyfully suffering, the readers were to commit themselves to God's keeping. But the distance between the conjunction and the verb makes that interpretation improbable. Since *also* stands just before *them that suffer*, it is more natural to relate it to the subject. Lenski accepted that connection and understood Peter to mean that not all will suffer but that those who do suffer should do that further thing.[54] It seems best to agree with Selwyn that the forward position of *also* is meant to introduce "a new thought: the certainty of divine justice being exercised is a call to complete serenity of faith in God."[55]

The articular present tense participle, "them that suffer" (*hoi paschontes*), describes the characteristic experience of those addressed. Their suffering was "according to the will of God," "for the name of Christ" (v. 14), and "as a Christian" (v. 16)—a suffering now regarded from the standpoint of God's will. Behind the vicious activities of their enemies stood the wise will of God. Peter sought to assure the readers that Christian suffering "does not come at the caprice of blind chance or as the predetermination of inexorable fate but as a divine discipline."[56] Assured that their suffering was in harmony with the divine will for them, they were "not [to] quarrel with that wise and gracious will; neither let them be discouraged, or grow faint and weary in their Christian course."[57]

Peter bid those sufferers to "commit their souls in well-doing unto a faithful Creator." The order in the original (*pistō ktistē paratithesthōsan tas psuchas autōn en agathotpoiia*) is "to a faithful Creator let them be committing their souls in well-doing." Prominently named is the One to whom they were to commit themselves, *to a faithful Creator*. The character of the depository is important. Only here in the New Testament is the noun *Creator* (*ktistēs*)[58] used of God, though His creative work is frequently mentioned (Acts 4:24; Col. 1:16; Rev. 4:11; etc.). Peter's reference is not to the new creation, the new birth, but to the original creation as that which manifests God's infinite power. The epithet *faithful* highlights God's reliable character; the Creator and Preserver of His creation can be implicitly trusted. God's faithfulness as a stimulus to Christians is often mentioned in the New Testament (1 Cor. 10:13; 2 Thess. 3:3; Heb. 10:23; etc.). The omission of the definite article emphasizes the character of the divine depository.

To that God Christians should "commit their souls" (*paratithesthōsan tas psuchas autōn*), be continually entrusting themselves to His protective care.

54. Lenski, p. 217.
55. Edward Gordon Selwyn, *The First Epistle of St. Peter*, p. 226.
56. J. W. C. Wand, *The General Epistles of St. Peter and St. Jude*, p. 120.
57. Lillie, pp. 298-99.
58. In Romans 1:25 *Creator* translates the articular aorist participle, *ton ktisanta*, "the One who created."

The compound verb conveys the picture of giving over or entrusting something to the care and protection of another. It was often used of entrusting one's money or other valuables to the safekeeping of another. The term recalls Psalm 31:5 and the dying words of Jesus as recorded in Luke 23:46. As elsewhere in the epistle, *souls* means "themselves" (1:9, 22; 2:11, 25; 3:20). It is unwarranted to assume that the term is used in sharp contrast to bodies, implying the prospect of martyrdom. "Martyrdom is not envisaged," Kelly rightly observes, "for he expects them to go on living normal lives and to be energetic in practical charity."[59]

"In well-doing" (*en agathopoiia*), a compound noun occurring only here in the New Testament,[60] stands emphatically at the end. Let Christians, undeterred by hostility or suffering, go on doing that which is good and beneficial, thereby demonstrating the reality of their commitment to God. Such a performance of good deeds is a characteristic feature of the Christian life as portrayed in 1 Peter (cf. 2:15, 20; 3:6, 11, 17). Such deeds indicate the necessary balance between the inner commitment and the outward life. The scope of those actions goes far beyond the confines of the Christian brotherhood.

59. Kelly, p. 195.
60. In 2:14 a kindred form denotes the person engaged in doing good.

19

E. The Concluding Appeals to the Suffering Churches
(5:1-11)

(1) The elders therefore among you I exhort, who am a fellow-elder, and a witness of the sufferings of Christ, who am also a partaker of the glory that shall be revealed: (2) Tend the flock of God which is among you, exercising the oversight, not of constraint, but willingly, according to *the will* of God; nor yet for filthy lucre, but of a ready mind; (3) neither as lording it over the charge allotted to you, but making yourselves ensamples to the flock. (4) And when the chief Shepherd shall be manifested, ye shall receive the crown of glory that fadeth not away. (5) Likewise, ye younger, be subject unto the elder. Yea, all of you gird yourselves with humility, to serve one another: for God resisteth the proud, but giveth grace to the humble. (6) Humble yourselves therefore under the mighty hand of God, that he may exalt you in due time; (7) casting all your anxiety upon him, because he careth for you. (8) Be sober, be watchful: your adversary the devil, as a roaring lion, walketh about, seeking whom he may devour: (9) whom withstand steadfast in your faith, knowing that the same sufferings are accomplished in your brethren who are in the world. (10) And the God of all grace, who called you unto his eternal glory in Christ, after that ye have suffered a little while, shall himself perfect, establish, strengthen you. (11) To him *be* the dominion for ever and ever. Amen.

"Therefore" (*oun*) indicates a logical thought connection between the concluding hortatory section of the epistle and what has gone before. But the precise point of connection is not certain. The particle is omitted in the Textus Receptus, and the manuscripts show some diversity of readings,[1] but modern

1. For the evidence see Nestle-Aland, *Novum Testamentum Graece* (26th ed.).

textual editors agree in accepting it as original.[2] Perhaps the particle was omitted because the concluding paragraph of the epistle proper does not seem to be an obvious deduction from what had just been said, as *therefore* suggests. If it is omitted the paragraph may be viewed as an appropriate summary of the author's ethical appeals to his readers. Its use indicated a conscious connection of thought. In keeping with the inferential force of the particle, it is commonly taken to indicate a close connection with *in well-doing (en agathopoiia)*, the concluding words of the preceding paragraph. If that is correct, then we have an amplification of the ethical demands for suffering Christians.[3] Others, like Lillie, believe that the particle indicates the resumption of a subject after an interruption and looks back to the discussion in 4:8-11; "The writer now returns to finish what he had to say of the duties which his brethren owed to one another in the communion of the Church."[4] Kelly argues that either connection is too narrowly conceived; he believes that the paragraph relates to the Christian communities as a whole and "is the practical corollary of the advice and encouragement he has been trying throughout to give."[5] If that is correct then the paragraph is a summary of the ethical demands of the Christian life. Of those views the first seems the simplest and most natural.

Peter directed his appeals to the elders of the churches (vv. 1-4), offered pertinent counsel to all the members (vv. 5-9), and concluded with a warm word of encouragement to the suffering saints (vv. 10-11).

1) THE APPEAL TO THE ELDERS (VV. 1-4)

Peter named the recipients of his appeal (v. 1a), identified the person making the appeal (v. 1b), concisely designated the duty of the elders (v. 2a), underlined the motives that should govern their work (vv. 2b-3), and pointed to the reward that awaits faithful undershepherds (v. 4).

A. THE RECIPIENTS OF THE APPEAL (v. 1a)

"The elders among you I exhort" makes clear the specific group addressed. Their identity is placed prominently before the verb. But *among you*—the churches addressed—also makes clear that Peter was addressing the elders in their relation to the churches. Each of the churches had one or more elders in its midst. The context establishes that *elders (presbuterous)* is used in an official sense, but from verse 5 it is clear that the term retains an element of its

---

2. Greek text of Westcott and Hort, Souter, Nestle and Aland (24th. ed.), United Bible Societies (3rd ed.), Tasker.

3. Joh. Ed. Huther, *Critical and Exegetical Handbook to the General Epistles of Peter and Jude,* p. 228; Robert Johnstone, *The First Epistle of Peter: Revised Text, with Introduction and Commentary,* p. 378; Francis Wright Beare, *The First Epistle of Peter, The Greek Text with Introduction and Notes,* p. 197.

4. John Lillie, *Lectures on the First and Second Epistles of Peter,* p. 300.

5. J. N. D. Kelly, *A Commentary on the Epistles of Peter and of Jude,* p. 196.

original sense of age, "one older than another" (Luke 15:25). The term does not imply "advanced age but merely establishes seniority."[6] It does indicate that those leaders were not neophytes but mature members of the Christian community. The absence of the definite article characterizes them as "such as are elders."

Whenever the New Testament refers to the office, it consistently pictures a plurality of elders in the local church (Acts 14:23; 20:17-28; Phil. 1:1; 1 Thess. 5:12; James 5:14). There is no account of the institution of the office of elder in the New Testament church; when first mentioned, it already existed in the church in Jerusalem (Acts 11:30). The pattern for church leadership was obviously drawn from the Jewish synagogue. On their first missionary journey Paul and Barnabas followed that pattern in organizing their Gentile churches (Acts 14:23). In the Graeco-Roman world the term was well known as applied to leaders in civic as well as religious associations.[7] That simple terminology is consistent with the early date of the epistle. Peter was aware that in time of persecution much depended upon the prudence and fidelity of those leaders.

"I exhort" (*parakalō*), not "I command," indicates Peter's attitude toward the elders (cf. 2:11). The term does not imply the imposition of a higher authority but the method of persuasion; it appealed to the readers' sense of what was appropriate in the matter.

B. THE PERSON MAKING THE APPEAL (v. 1b)

"Who am a fellow-elder, and a witness of the sufferings of Christ, who am also a partaker of the glory that shall be revealed" is, in form, a double appositional expansion of the *I* of the verb. His intimate self-identification adds to the persuasiveness of the appeal. Aside from his name in 1:1, the writer's identity appears more forcefully here than anywhere else in the epistle. Modestly, Peter did not assert his apostolic identity. That fact has been appealed to by both opponents and proponents of Petrine authorship. Beare, who rejects apostolic authorship, sees in that self-identification "the apparatus of pseudepigraphy" and insists that it "would ill become Peter himself, but is perfectly natural in the language of another man writing in his name."[8] Polkinghorne replies, "Surely, however, a forger would most certainly have stressed apostolicity otherwise there would be little purpose in using Peter's name, so that the omission is actually favourable to Petrine authorship."[9] We agree. The self-description shows "that what Peter here urges upon elders he exemplified in his own life and office."[10]

6. E. M. Blaiklock, *First Peter, A Translation and Devotional Commentary*, p. 103.
7. James Hope Moulton and George Milligan, *The Vocabulary of the Greek Testament Illustrated from the Papyri and Other Non-Literary Sources*, p. 535; William Barclay, *The Letters of James and Peter*, p. 312.
8. Beare, p. 198.
9. G. J. Polkinghorne, *The First Letter of Peter*, p. 596.
10. R. C. H. Lenski, *The Interpretation of the Epistles of St. Peter, St. John and St. Jude*, p. 220.

"Who am a fellow-elder" (*ho sumpresbuteros*), "the fellow-elder," occurs only here in the New Testament and places the writer on a level with the elders being addressed. "He is not speaking down to them as a superior to inferiors."[11] In calling himself *elder* Peter doubtless was thinking of the commission given him by the risen Lord to shepherd His flock (John 21:15-17). The apostle John likewise called himself "the elder" (2 John 1; 3 John 1), and Papias (c. A.D. 60-130) used the term of John as well as the other apostles.[12] Though much broader, the apostolic office included the work of the elders. "What the elders were for the individual congregations, that were the apostles for the whole church."[13] Peter thus indicated that he "personally felt the responsibilities, and from experience knew the difficulties, of an elder."[14]

As fellow-elder he was also "a witness of the sufferings of Christ." *And* (*kai*) correlates his position as elder with his experience as a *witness* (*martus*). Strictly speaking, the term does not denote a spectator but one who testifies to something. Peter gave testimony concerning "the sufferings of Christ" (*tōn tou Christou pathēmatōn*), the sufferings that the Messiah Himself endured (cf. 4:13).

"Witness" may mean either an eyewitness or, more generally, one who bears testimony to what he accepts as true. If the writer was Peter the natural meaning is that he was an eyewitness of Christ's sufferings. The following description of himself as "also a partaker of the glory" points to the idea of an eyewitness experience. In the light of Acts 1:8, 22 the term implies an apostolic witness. It is in the sense of a personal eyewitness that Peter used the term in Acts 2:32; 3:15; 5:32; and 10:39. Though the thought of the Messiah suffering was once very distasteful to him (Matt. 16:22), he had seen those sufferings, and it was his task to bear witness to their reality and significance. He repeatedly did so in the epistle (1:11; 2:21; 3:18; 4:1, 13).

The gospels do not state that Peter was personally present at the crucifixion; only John is specifically said to have been there. But Peter (and other apostles) may well have been among "all his acquaintances" who observed the event from afar (Luke 23:49). It is unwarranted to limit those observers to "a number of women," as Leaney does.[15] Peter certainly did observe the agony of Christ in Gethsemane, saw Him bound and delivered into the hands of His enemies, and observed at least some of the injustices heaped on Him in the court of the High Priest. Thus understood, the term is a delicate reminder of the actual difference between himself and the elders addressed. His teaching about the sufferings of Christ was grounded in personal observation.

Those who date the epistle after the death of Peter naturally find the

---

11. Wm. C. Waltemyer, *The First Epistle of Peter*, p. 655.
12. Eusebius Pamphilus, *The Ecclesiastical History of Eusebius Pamphilus*, 3:39.
13. Huther, p. 230.
14. Johnstone, p. 379.
15. A. R. E. Leaney, *The Letters of Peter and Jude*, p. 69.

eyewitness implication unacceptable and insist that the term *witness* means "'one who testifies' . . . to what he holds to be the truth."[16] Some believe that any implication that Peter was an eyewitness is inconsistent with the fact that he placed himself on a level with the elders by calling himself a "fellow-elder." But that supposed difficulty is not compelling; having initially identified himself as "an apostle of Jesus Christ" (1:1), the term is natural because it emphasizes the validity of his testimony. If the writer meant that he, like the elders addressed, was simply proclaiming the message of Christ's sufferings, it would have been proper to call himself "a fellow-witness" to indicate his equality with them.

In the history of the Christian church the term *witness* soon developed the connotation of one who bore witness to his faith by his suffering, even unto martyrdom if necessary. But only if 1 Peter is thought to be pseudonymous can one argue that it is "certain that there is a reference here to Peter as a martyr for Christ."[17] Peter did not say that he actually shared in the sufferings of Christ, but it is true that he had already suffered for his faith and testimony. In thus suffering for his Christian witness Peter was indeed on a level with the elders addressed.

"Who am also a partaker of the glory that shall be revealed" (*ho kai tēs mellousēs apokaluptesthai doxēs koinonos*) is structurally a second appositional description of the writer. Peter identified himself in relation to the Christian hope for the future. *Also* (*kai*) indicates that the eschatological element is properly a part of the full picture. Suffering and glory were never far apart in Peter's mind. *Of the about to be revealed glory* (Gr. order) points to a glory whose unveiling is eagerly anticipated. The reference is not to the glories of heaven to be entered at death, as Barnes suggests,[18] but to the unveiling of Christ's glories at His return to earth. Having witnessed the sufferings of the Christ, Peter was assured that the revelation of the messianic glory would follow (1:11). Of that glory Peter described himself as being "a partaker" (*koinōnos*), "one who takes part in something with someone."[19] The term implies personal participation. Peter had a glimpse of that glory at the transfiguration (cf. 2 Pet. 1:16-18), but on that occasion he did not participate in it. But having experienced the living hope through the risen Christ (1:3), he knew the accompanying reality of rejoicing "with joy unspeakable and full of glory" (1:8). That inner sense of glory he shared with his readers; the transforming power of that new life connected with glory has already begun in the Christian's soul, but its open manifestation awaits the time of Christ's return.

16. Beare, p. 198.

17. Leaney, p. 69.

18. Albert Barnes, *Notes on the New Testament, Explanatory and Practical—James, Peter, John, and Jude*, p. 202.

19. William F. Arndt and F. Wilbur Gingrich, *A Greek-English Lexicon of the New Testament and Other Early Christian Literature*, p. 440.

C. THE DUTY TO SHEPHERD THE FLOCK (v. 2a)

"Tend the flock of God which is among you, exercising the oversight" concisely portrays the work of the elders under the familiar shepherd imagery. Though the Old Testament shepherd imagery is always used of the civil rulers of the nation (e.g., Ps. 78:71; Ezek. 34:2), in the New Testament the figure is applied to the spiritual leaders of the people of God. The shepherd-sheep relation expresses "the twofold functions of control and devotion."[20] The command *Tend* (*poimanate*), "shepherd ye," includes all that is involved in the work of the shepherd: guiding and guarding, feeding and folding. The aorist tense conveys a sense of urgency. It "calls upon the elders to have their official life as a unity characterized by the spirit of devotion to service."[21]

The elders were to devote themselves to "the flock of God which is among you." The singular noun *flock* (*poimnion*) depicts the unity of the Christian church. It is a diminutive form, literally, "the little flock" (cf. Luke 12:32), but the force of the diminutive cannot be pressed.[22] Its use here and in verse 3 apparently expresses endearment. Thus Rotherham translates, "Shepherd the beloved flock of God." *Of God* designates that flock "as belonging, not to the elders who tend it, but to God as His peculiar property."[23] It is a solemn challenge; how could they neglect or abuse God's flock "which is among you." *Among you* (*en humin*), placed attributively between the article and the noun, points to a close characteristic relation between the shepherds and the sheep. Calvin interpreted the expression to mean "as much as in you lies."[24] But it is more natural to give it a local force, "the flock among you"—those committed to their care. They were not to be absentee lords but actively to work with the flock around them.

"Exercising the oversight" (*episkopountes*) further characterizes the task of the elders. There is textual uncertainty concerning the authenticity of that participle.[25] It is present in the majority of the Greek manuscripts and in all the early versions, but some important manuscripts omit it. Among modern textual critics there is debate as to whether it is "an exegetical expansion (made perhaps in accordance with 2:25), or whether the shorter text is the result of deliberate excision, prompted either by stylistic considerations (namely, that after *poimanate* the word is redundant) or by ecclesiastical conviction (namely, that Peter could never have admonished presbyters [ver.

---

20. James Moffatt, *The General Epistles, James, Peter, and Judas*, pp. 162-63.
21. Johnstone, p. 382.
22. Moulton and Milligan, p. 524.
23. Huther, p. 232.
24. John Calvin, *The Epistle of Paul the Apostle to the Hebrews and the First and Second Epistles of St Peter*, p. 316.
25. For the evidence see the United Bible Society Greek text.

1] to exercise the function of bishops)."[26] Their conclusions vary.[27] Whether it is left out or included, the meaning is much the same. We accept it as most probably original; it is especially appropriate as an introduction to what follows and is fully in keeping with Peter's fondness for participles.

The participle expands on the manner in which the elders were to carry out their assignment of tending the flock. As the verbal form of the noun translated *Bishop* or *Overseer* in 2:25, it depicts the pastoral function of overseeing or caring for those under their supervision. It indicates that no official difference between elders and bishops had developed when 1 Peter was written. In the New Testament the two terms are used interchangeably of the same men (Acts 20:17-28; Titus 1:5-7). The word *elder* points to the mature age that qualified the individual for the office; the word *bishop* indicates that the duties of the office were those of spiritual oversight. Such oversight is the constant duty of the elders and the unceasing need of the flock.

D. THE MOTIVES IN SERVING AS ELDERS (vv. 2b-3)

Keenly conscious that motives are important in the service of the Lord, Peter employed three adverbial modifiers, each negatively and positively stated, to guide the work of the elders. He touched on three common vices in Christian service and their alternative virtues.

"Not of constraint, but willingly" relates to the elder's personal attitude toward his assignment. *Not of constraint* (*mē anangkastōs*), "not by compulsion," translates an adverbial form that appears only here in the New Testament. The elder should not occupy the office as a reluctant draftee, doing an irksome task because he feels that he cannot escape it. Such a feeling might arise from "a false sense of unworthiness, a reluctance for responsibility, or a desire to do no more than was morally required in the office."[28] Such feelings are unworthy of one called to sacred service. There is, however, a good sort of necessity, such as Paul mentions in 1 Corinthians 9:16, "necessity [a noun derived from the same Greek root as 'constraint'] is laid upon me; for woe is unto me, if I preach not the gospel." It was the constraint of God's sovereign will for his life that Paul willingly and wholeheartedly accepted. Such a constraint expresses itself in doing the work willingly (*hekousiōs*), deliberately, and intentionally as a matter of free will, like a volunteer who delights to do the work. Love for the Lord and His people prompts willing service.

The words "according to *the will of* God" (*kata theon*) are to be taken closely with *willingly*. Alford characterizes them as "curious, and not easily accounted for."[29] They are not in the Textus Receptus (represented by the KJV). The phrase is not found in some uncials or in some minuscule manuscripts, but it

26. Bruce M. Metzger, *A Textual Commentary on the Greek New Testament*, pp. 695-96.

27. It is *omitted* in the texts of Westcott and Hort, Nestle and Aland (24th ed.), and Tasker; included *in brackets* in the United Bible Societies text (3d ed.), Nestle and Aland (26th ed.); included *without brackets* in Souter, and the United Bible Societies text (1st ed.).

28. David H. Wheaton, *1 Peter*, p. 1247.

29. Henry Alford, *The Greek New Testament*, vol. 4 (part 1), p. 381.

does appear in various early Greek manuscripts and different versions.[30] Recent textual editors generally accept the words as authentic.[31] They were probably omitted by scribes who found difficulty in understanding their precise import. The phrase can, by expansion, be understood to mean "according to *the will of* God," or "as God would have it" (NEB). But more probably the preposition (*kata*) is to be given its familiar force of indicating a standard or model (cf. 1:15; 4:6), "according to God," that is, "just as God shepherds His flock."[32] The meaning is best illustrated "in the whole-heartedness of the Chief Shepherd himself, who could say, 'My meat is to do the will of him that sent me, and to accomplish his work.'"[33]

The second pair, "nor yet for filthy lucre, but or a ready mind," raises the matter of deriving personal gain from Christian service. *Nor yet for filthy lucre (mē aischrokerdōs)*, another adverb that occurs only here in the New Testament, means "fondness for dishonest gain," gain procured in a base and sordid way that produces shame if uncovered. That does not prohibit the elder from receiving a fair return for honest toil. Peter, like Paul, accepted the ordinance of Christ that "the laborer is worthy of his hire" (Luke 10:7; 1 Tim. 5:18). But Peter was warning against taking up the work because of a desire for material gain, "it being a shameful thing for a shepherd to feed the sheep out of the love to the fleece."[34] It is a warning against a sordid preoccupation with material advantages. It is unacceptable to enter the ministry merely because it offers a respectable and intellectually stimulating way of gaining a livelihood. That warning also includes the temptation to gain personal popularity or social influence. Where the love of gain reigns, the shepherds are prone to become mere hirelings, feeding themselves at the expense of the flock. The antidote to that evil is serving "of a ready mind" (*prothumōs*), "eagerly" or "zealously," doing so with inward delight. Eagerness to serve should precede any consideration of personal profit.

The third pair, "neither as lording it over the charge allotted to you, but making yourselves ensamples to the flock" (v. 3), concerns the elder's personal feeling toward his people. Peter used two participles, with adverbial force, to depict the wrong and the right attitudes.

The warning to the elders not to act "as lording it over" (*mēd' hōs katakurieuontes*) the people implies that they did exercise a real authority in the congregations; the subtle danger was the temptation to misuse that authority. *As* implies the assumption of a position that was not proper. The compound verb pictures the scene. The simple verb *kurieuō* means "to control,

30. See the United Bible Societies Greek text.
31. The words *kata theon* were omitted by Westcott and Hort, and Nestle and Aland (24th ed.), but they appear in the text of Souter, United Bible Societies text, Nestle-Aland (26th ed.), and Tasker.
32. A. F. Mitchell, *Hebrews and the General Epistles*, pp. 279-80.
33. C. E. B. Cranfield, *I & II Peter and Jude*, pp. 128-29.
34. Matthew Poole, *A Commentary on the Holy Bible*, 3:915.

rule, to be lord or master of." The preposition *kata*, "down," indicates intensity and depicts a heavy-handed use of authority for personal aggrandizement that manifests itself in the desire to dominate, accompanied by a haughty demand for compliance. Jesus directly condemned such an abuse of authority among His followers (Matt. 20:25-27; Mark 10:42-44). The tragic impact of such an attitude is illustrated by the account of Diotrephes in 3 John 9-10. Genuine rule in the church is an administration of Christ's lordship by His willing servants. Church leaders are designated as "those standing before" (*hoi proistamenoi*, 1 Thess. 5:12; Rom. 12:8), or "those leading or guiding" (*hoi hēgoumenoi*, Heb. 13:7, 17, 24; Acts 15:22), but not "those being lords" (*hoi kurieuontes*).

Those subjected to that abuse of authority are designated as "the charge allotted to you" (*tōn klērōn*). That noun means "a lot," and then "that which is assigned by lot," a portion or share of something. The plural, "the lots" or "the portions"[35] refers to the various congregations that in God's providential arrangement had been allotted to different groups of elders.[36] As to the size of those individual groups of believers, we have no information. The expression suggests responsibility; God had assigned the various portions of His precious possession to their personal care. The elders were not to think that they could do with their allotted portions as they pleased. That figurative reference to the local churches would have been readily understood by Peter's Gentile readers, since in classical Greek the term was used to designate an allotment of land assigned to a citizen by the civic authorities.

"But" (*alla*), by contrast, introduces the elders' true relation to their people—"making yourselves ensamples to the flock" (*tupoi ginomenoi tou poimniou*), "patterns becoming of the flock" (R. Young). Instead of domineering lords they were to be models whom their people could follow. As spiritual shepherds, they were to lead, not drive. "The life should command, and the tongue persuade" (Athanasius).[37] *Making yourselves* (*ginomenoi*) suggests conscious effort; the verb indicates a process of ever more fully becoming worthy examples. Each of them as elders "must stand out as a distinct representative of the unseen Master to whom he and his people must be conformed."[38] Though each elder works directly only with a portion of the whole flock, the singular noun, "the flock," recalls the spiritual unity of all of God's people. Their "tyrannizing could only apply to the portion over which their authority extended, but the good example would be seen and followed by the whole church."[39]

35. "There is no reference here, as has been rather absurdly supposed, to church property, or to the possessions of worldly rulers, or the province of the Roman proconsul, or to the clergy as distinct from the laity," Lillie, p. 307.

36. For that figurative usage see also Acts 26:18 and Col. 1:12. In the New Testament the term *klēros* is used of the literal casting of lots (Matt. 27:35; Mark 15:24; Luke 23:34; John 19:24; Acts 1:17, 26).

37. Quoted in G. F. C. Fronmüller, *The Epistles General of Peter*, p. 87.

38. F. C. Cook, *The First Epistle General of Peter*, p. 216.

39. Alford, p. 382.

E. THE REWARD OF THE FAITHFUL UNDERSHEPHERDS (v. 4)

"And when the chief Shepherd shall be manifested, ye shall receive the crown of glory that fadeth not away." *And* (*kai*) indicates a simple sequence. The elders' faithful fulfillment of the injunctions would be followed by the bestowal of the reward. The prospect of the future should have its impact upon their performance in the present. The difficulties of their work, as well as their consciousness of their own inadequacies and failures, would often discourage the most prudent, but "to prevent the faithful servant of Christ from being cast down, there is this one and only remedy, to turn his eyes to the coming of Christ."[40]

"When the chief Shepherd shall be manifested" (*phanerōthentos tou archipoimenos*), a genitive absolute, states the time and circumstances for the bestowal of the reward. The aorist passive participle denotes a single event, the second coming of Christ, when He "has been made manifest, has become visible" in open splendor. In 1:20 that verb was used of Christ's incarnate appearance at His first advent (cf. 1 Tim. 3:16; Heb. 9:26; 1 John 1:2). Here the reference is to His second coming (cf. Col. 3:4; 1 John 2:28; 3:2*b*). Previously, Peter had spoken of Christ's return as a "revelation" or "unveiling" (1:7, 13; 4:13); "manifested" indicates the consequences of that unveiling. Christ will be revealed in all His glory and all will see Him. The readers' reward will involve their open vindication before a Christ-rejecting world.

Christ will return as "the chief Shepherd" (*tou archipoimenos*), "the Arch-Shepherd," a designation occurring only here in the New Testament. Once thought to be Peter's own coinage, the term has been found on an Egyptian mummy label in the sense of "master-shepherd."[41] As the "Chief Shepherd," Christ is in charge of the entire flock and all the elders are undershepherds whose work will be evaluated and rewarded by Him. In relation to His work in the past He is the Good Shepherd who laid down His life for the sheep (John 10:11); in His resurrection life and present work He is the Great Shepherd, working out the divine purpose in all the sheep (Heb. 13:20). When He returns as the Chief Shepherd, Christ will consummate the work of His undershepherds with His flock.

The elders were assured that when Christ appears "ye shall receive the crown of glory that fadeth not away." *Ye* is unrestricted; it implies that the elders would faithfully perform their duties. The verb *shall receive* (*komieisthe*, cf. 1:9) conveys the thought of getting something for oneself and carrying it off as wages or a prize. In that coming day Christians will joyfully carry away as their own "the crown of glory that fadeth not away." In the New Testament the future reward of the faithful is variously pictured as "an incorruptible crown" (1 Cor. 9:25), a "crown of glory" (1 Thess. 2:19), a "crown

40. Calvin, p. 317.
41. Moulton and Milligan, p. 82.

of righteousness" (2 Tim. 4:8), or as a "crown of life" (James 1:12; Rev. 2:10). The regard assured the elders is designated "the crown of glory." The reference is not to the kingly or imperial crown (*diadēma*), the badge of sovereignty (cf. Rev. 12:3; 19:12), but to the crown (*stephanos*), the wreath or garland used on various nonimperial occasions. It was used of "the crown of victory in the games, of civic worth, of military valour, of nuptial joy, of festive gladness."[42] Such crowns were woven of various perishable materials, such as oak, olive, myrtle leaves, ivy, parsley, or of flowers such as violets or roses, and were used to celebrate on occasions of joy and victory. Questions have been raised about the exact nature of the scene pictured by *crown of glory*. It may be the festive scene at a banquet or the crowning after a struggle for victorious achievement. For Peter's readers the crowning that concluded the athletic contests would readily come to mind. That picture is in keeping with the context.

The crown to be bestowed is given a double description, "the crown of glory that fadeth not away" (*ton amarantinon tēs doxēs stephanon*). Both modifiers are placed attributively between the article and the noun as characteristics of the crown. The adjective translated "that fadeth not away" (*amarantinon*) occurs only here in the New Testament. It is a slightly different form than the adjective so translated in 1:4 (*amaranton*). The use of that variant form suggests that a slightly different meaning is intended. Instead of pointing to its quality as unfading, the suffix -*inos* seems to point to the material from which the crown is made.[43] If that is correct then the crown is described as "made of amaranth," a flower whose unfading quality was the symbol of immortality. If so, then the crown itself will never lose its beauty and attractiveness. Under either view, the crown stands in contrast to the temporal nature of the rewards achieved in this life.

The crown is further characterized as "of glory" (*tēs doxēs*); the genitive is appositional. It is the crown that consists of the heavenly glory. After His own suffering, Christ was "crowned with glory and honor" (Heb. 2:9); He will reward His faithful undershepherds by sharing with them His own unfading glory. Peter intended that prospect of a glorious future to motivate faithfulness in the present. Prophetic truth is practical!

2) THE COUNSEL TO ALL THE MEMBERS (VV. 5-9)

"Likewise" (*homoiōs*) marks the transition to a new series of exhortations (cf. 3:1, 7). Having instructed the elders, Peter wisely gave needed counsel to the members of those churches. He laid one pertinent duty on the younger members (v. 5*a*) and then appealed for humility (vv. 5*b*-7) and watchfulness (vv. 8-9) on the part of all.

42. Richard Chenevix Trench, *Synonyms of the New Testament*, p. 78.
43. A. T. Robertson and W. Hersey Davis, *A New Short Grammar of the Greek Testament*, p. 176.

A. THE APPEAL TO THE YOUNGER TO BE SUBMISSIVE (v. 5a)

"Likewise, ye younger, be subject unto the elder." The adverb, *likewise*, means "in the same manner," as though the readers' attitudes should parallel the attitude called for on the part of the leaders. The adverb indicates the transition of thought from the leaders to the members.

The command "be subject unto" has already been given for different relations (cf. 2:13, 18; 3:1, 5). The aorist imperative (cf. 2:13) urgently calls for an attitude of voluntary submission on the part of the younger. *Ye younger* (*neōteroi*), used without the definite article, "such as are younger," seems to be a designation of age. The term was commonly used of young people of both sexes. But some believe that here it means more than age and denotes "the subordinate ministers of the Church."[44] *Younger* may contrast with the elders and *likewise* may imply correspondence with the presbyters. Support for such subordinate officials has been sought in *the young men* (*hoi neōteroi*) in Acts 5:6 and 10. Wuest suggests that the reference may be to organized youth guilds in those Asian churches.[45] But nowhere in the New Testament is there evidence that such young men constituted a class of church officials. There is no indication that the younger men in Acts 5 were office-bearers; they were merely younger and more active members who voluntarily arose to perform a needed service. Still others, like Alford, think that *younger* means "the rest of the church, as opposed to the *presbyteroi*."[46] It is well known that the official elders were chosen from among the older and more mature members of the churches; but surely there were members who were as old or older than the presbyters of those congregations. It is clear that those young in age did form a natural group in the churches (1 Tim. 5:1-2; Titus 2:4-6). The term seems to refer to those who were not only younger in years but also younger in the faith and in Christian experience.

"The elders" to whom the young were to be subject is also understood in different ways. Some insist that *elders* "must be in the same sense as above, that is, in its official historical sense of presbyters in the church."[47] Lenski connects the sentence with the preceding verses and argues that it "rounds out what Peter has to say regarding the elders" and that in that demand he "shields their standing and authority."[48] That connection with the preceding verses makes the official meaning quite plausible, but it does not seem to account for Peter's use of *likewise*. Nor is it obvious why Peter would only ask the younger to show such deference to the church leaders. Were middle-aged members or those older wholly exempt from the need for such a directive?

44. Cook, p. 216; Moffatt, p. 165.

45. Kenneth S. Wuest, *First Peter in the Greek New Testament for the English Readers*, p. 126.

46. Alford, p. 383. "The 'juniors' represent the rest of the congregation," Bo Reicke, *The Epistles of James, Peter, and Jude*, p. 130.

47. Alford, p. 383.

48. Lenski, p. 225.

Others argue that *elders* (*presbuterois*) without the article most naturally conveys the basic sense of age, "to such as are older." The Berkeley translation represents that view, "the younger men should defer to those who are older." Such a transition from one meaning of the term elder to the other also occurs in 1 Timothy 5:1, 17. If that is correct then Peter's directive is a call to respect age, a common biblical theme. Peter recognized that impulsive youth should be reminded that "in patient submission, not in impetuous vigour, lies the true path of Christian conduct."[49] The young, with their eager energies, should guard against the impulse to thrust the aged into the background and insist on their own ideas or ways in the face of the more mature views of the elderly. "Deference toward the older members of a church by the young is a virtue which has never been known to grow too rank."[50]

B. THE APPEAL TO ALL FOR HUMILITY (vv. 5b-7)

"Yea, all of you gird yourselves with humility, to serve one another" (*pantes de allēlois tēn tapeinophrosunēn engkombōsasthe*). The Textus Receptus, followed by the KJV, "Yea, all *of you* be subject one to another," inserts a present participle (*hupotassomenoi*), "subjecting yourselves," after the reciprocal pronoun *allēlois*, "to one another." The textual evidence indicates that it is a scribal insertion, perhaps drawn from 2:18.[51] The presence of the participle enlarges the directive for younger Christians to submit to the elders to all the members. Without that participle the text is open to two different punctuations. It is possible to take the words *pantes de allēlois*, "yea, all of you to one another," with what precedes, "Ye younger, be subject unto the elder; yea, all of you to one another" (margin of the ASV). That punctuation is attractive, but it is not necessary. It has the disadvantage of leaving the next sentence without any particle of transition. *To one another* goes equally well with what follows. With all recent versions we prefer to place a period after *elder* and to begin a new sentence with "Yea, all of you." Those words then designate the transition in thought from the specific to the general; instead of further specific directives, Peter elaborated on the attitude needed by all of the members. Verses 5b-7 call for humility on the part of all believers. It is a virtue needed in their mutual relations (v. 5b) as well as Godward (vv. 6-7).

(1) The call for humility in mutual relations (v. 5b-c). "Yea, all of you gird yourselves with humility, to serve one another." The inclusive *all of you* (*pantes*) draws in the younger Christians with the older, the shepherds with their sheep. The mutual character of the humility enjoined is stressed by the forward position of the reciprocal dative pronoun *allēlois*, "in relation to one

---

49. Beare, p. 202.
50. Nathaniel Marshman Williams, *Commentary on the Epistles of Peter*, p. 70.
51. See Nestle-Aland, *Novum Testamentum Graece* (26th ed.).

another." Demanded in all of their dealings with each other is humility (*tēn tapeinophrosunēn*), "the humility" or "lowly-mindedness" that should characterize their personal relations. The term does not involve an attitude of self-disparagement or servility but a willingness to assume a lowly position to serve others. It is the opposite of self-exaltation, which is the very essence of sin. Such an attitude of humility is a distinctly Christian virtue. Trench notes that that very word "is itself a fruit of the Gospel; no Greek writer employed it before the Christian era, nor, apart from the influence of Christian writers, after."[52] Moulton and Milligan cite no instances of the noun in the papyri nor does it appear in the Septuagint. Josephus used it in the sense of pusillanimity.[53] "Christ and his ethics were required to make lowly-mindedness a great Christian virtue. Matth. 18, 1-3; 20, 25-28."[54]

"Gird yourselves" (*engkombōsasthe*) as an aorist imperative calls for effective action. The verb, used only here in the New Testament, means "to put or tie on" any kind of garment. Some understand the picture as that of putting on a beautiful garment, "adorn yourselves with humility as with a beautiful garment or robe."[55] But more probably the picture is that of a slave tying on the apron (*engkombōma*) to serve; the wearing of that apron distinguished the slave from the freedman. That view is in accord with the nature of the garment to be put on. The garment of humility must be put on, not as a matter of external show, but as a characteristic attitude, as a willingness to serve. That force of the term is expressed in the ASV by the words "to serve," though there is no such infinitive in the original. In all probability the term reflects Peter's recollection of the act of "Jesus in the upper room, when he tied on an actual apron and washed the disciples' feet, performing this slave's service to which none of them would stoop."[56] The presence of humility as a working virtue is appropriate to all regardless of age.

"For" (*hoti*) introduces a theological consideration in support of that ethical injunction, "for God resisteth the proud, but giveth grace to the humble" (v. 5c). Though not marked as an Old Testament quotation, Peter followed the Septuagint translation of Proverbs 3:34, except that *God* (*ho theos*) is substituted for *Lord* (*kurios*). But since those exact words also appear in James 4:6, it is possible that it was a familiar quotation in the early Christian church. In support of that is the fact that in James the saying is used in quite a different setting.

The vividness of the Greek (*ho theos huperēphanois antitassetai*) is well represented in Rotherham's literal translation, "God against the haughty arrayeth himself." *God* (*ho theos*), the very God who in mercy revealed Himself in Christ and freely forgives the penitent, is aroused to action against the

52. Trench, p. 148.
53. Flavius Josephus, *The Wars of the Jews*, IV, 9, 2.
54. Lenski, p. 227.
55. Poole, p. 915.
56. Lenski, p. 226.

proud (*huperēphanois*), who are characterized by their pride. Standing emphatically forward, the term portrays them as individuals who display an attitude of haughty superiority toward others, as those who proudly regard themselves as the standard of excellence and disdain those who fall short of the standard. As self-centered and self-sufficient, they ignore their need of God. Such an attitude God resists; He persistently sets Himself against it. The verb vividly pictures God as one who places Himself in battle array against such individuals. "God resisteth the proud" is the Septuagint interpretation of the Hebrew text, "Surely he scoffeth at the scoffers." Their scoffing is the manifestation of their arrogant self-exaltation.

By contrast, God "giveth grace to the humble" (*tapeinois de didōsin charin*), "to such as are humble he giveth grace." The quality of humility is stressed by the absence of the article as well as by the forward position of the adjective. Such lowly-minded individuals, conscious of their own unworthiness, gladly acknowledge their dependence on God and rest in His all-sufficiency. Upon such, God continually bestows His grace, His unmerited favor. God actively responds to the attitude of His saints.

(2) The call for humility under God's hand (vv. 6-7). The confirmation just advanced (v. 5c) indicates that Christian humility toward one another is inseparably tied to humility before God. The former naturally flows from the latter. *Therefore* (*oun*), because of that close connection, Peter amplified the need for humility toward God. He called on his readers to humble themselves under the sovereign hand of God (v. 6) and to trust in His care (v. 7).

(a) The duty of humility Godward (v. 6). "Humble yourselves therefore under the mighty hand of God, that he may exalt you in due time." The aorist imperative, *humble yourselves* (*tapeinōthēte*), indicates a duty that calls for immediate attention. The passive voice may be understood in the sense of the middle, "humble yourselves, become humble," or it may be taken as a true passive, "be humbled, allow yourselves to be humbled." Selwyn insists that the force of the passive be retained, "allow yourselves to be humbled, accept your humiliation."[57] Peter was not calling for passive resignation or a forced humiliation but for a voluntary acceptance of the humiliating circumstances that befell the readers under God's permissive will. They were to accept "the fiery trial" that they were experiencing (4:12) as coming to them "under the mighty hand of God." That is a familiar Old Testament expression of God's irresistible actions in human affairs, "whether in the restraining and subduing of His enemies, or in the defense and chastisement of His children, and their ultimate deliverance and exaltation."[58] Peter's readers were to submit to God's dealings with them as part of His discipline (4:12-19).

---

57. Edward Gordon Selwyn, *The First Epistle of St. Peter*, p. 235.
58. Lillie, p. 320.

Such submission is the prelude to future exaltation, "that he may exalt you in due time." *That* (*hina*), "in order that," implies that the readers' humbling would enable God to fulfill His promise of future exaltation. Peter apparently had the promise of Jesus in mind, "whosoever shall humble himself shall be exalted" (Matt. 23:12; Luke 14:11; 18:14). The Christian's hope for the future should make its impact on the present.

Peter reminded the readers that their exaltation would come "in due time" (*en kairō*), "in a propitious season, at the proper time." God would act to exalt them when, in His infinite wisdom, it was conducive to His glory and their real welfare. "Part of humility is willingness to patiently wait for things according to God's timetable."[59] Though the term is general and finds partial fulfillment in this life, its true fulfillment awaits the second coming. In the New Testament the expression *the time* (*ho kairos*) "acquires eschatological overtones, meaning 'the time of crisis,' 'the last time,' 'the time of the End' (e.g. Mt. viii. 29; Mk. xiii. 33; Lk. xxi. 8; I Cor. iv. 5)."[60] That seems to be its meaning here. A vital apprehension of that promise of coming exaltation will lead to a wholehearted willingness now to bow under God's mighty hand.

> (b) *The rest in God's care* (v. 7). Peter continued with another participial construction, "casting all your anxiety upon him, because he careth for you." A number of our modern English versions[61] translate that participle as an imperative, thereby suggesting that the verse states a separate, independent duty. That blurs the close connection of the verse with verse 6. The participle is structurally dependent on the imperative *humble yourselves* (v. 6) and indicates a correlative action of the humble-minded.

"All your anxiety" (*pasan tēn merimnan humōn*), standing emphatically before the participle, unites all the readers' individual cares and concerns, whether due to memories of the past, pressures of the present, or fears concerning the future, into one burdensome whole. None of those anxious, distracting concerns, prompting fear and worry, is excluded from the directive. Peter knew how human life is swayed by such feelings. The readers' experience of affliction and persecution naturally stimulated feelings of anxiety.

"Casting" (*epiripsantes*), "placing upon, throwing upon, handing over to," depicts a decisive, energetic act. The action of the aorist participle is concomitant with the action in the imperative *humble yourselves* in verse 6. "Holy freedom from all anxious care is essential to submission to God."[62]

---

59. Jay E. Adams, *Trust and Obey. A Practical Commentary on First Peter*, p. 150.

60. Kelly, p. 208.

61. So RSV, NEB, NIV, Weymouth, Montgomery, Moffatt, Goodspeed, Williams, Berkeley, TEV, JB, Kleist and Lilly.

62. Fronmüller, p. 90.

Christians should relieve themselves of the burden by throwing it upon Him, the One to whom they have voluntarily submitted their lives. "To be overwhelmed with anxiety is to be concerned with self rather than with Him."[63] Amid the adversities of life, Christians should trust in Him who knows what we need better than we do ourselves.

The ground for that action is "because he careth for you." To throw our cares onto God is not misplaced confidence. God's personal response to our needs is stressed by the arrangement of the pronouns in the original, "to him it is a care [impersonal verb] concerning you" (*autō melei peri humōn*). That places *to him* in close proximity to *upon him* of the preceding clause. All that creates anxiety for us, whether momentous or trivial, is a matter of concern to Him. Those few words are an apt summary of what Jesus taught His disciples concerning God's fatherly care (Matt. 6:25-34; Luke 12:4-7, 22-34). Masterman well observes, "It is the belief that God cares that marks off Christianity from all other religions, which under all varieties of form are occupied with the task of making God care, of awakening by sacrifice or prayer or act the slumbering interest of the Deity."[64] But amid the crushing burdens or the burning trials that often befall the saints, it is the cross and resurrection of Christ that remain the unshakeable demonstration of God's love and concern.

C. THE DUTY OF WATCHFULNESS (vv. 8-9)

Peter's call to spiritual alertness is made without a connecting particle, thus making it more crisp and incisive. Worry is condemned, but watchfulness is demanded. Peter issued an urgent appeal for alertness (v. 8a), painted a vivid picture of the enemy (v. 8b), urged firm resistance in faith (v. 9a), and concluded with an encouraging reminder of the sufferings of the brotherhood (v. 9b).

(1) The urgent duty of alertness (v. 8a). Two incisive aorist imperatives, "Be sober, be watchful," demand immediate action. *Be sober* is a call for the same spiritual self-possession already mentioned in 1:13 and 4:7. The Christian's life should be characterized by a consistent balance in disposition, thought, and action, and marked by self-control. *Be watchful* (*grēgorēsate*), added without a copula, goes inseparably with sobriety. It is a call to be wakefully active, morally and spiritually, and on the alert against the assaults of sin and Satan. Christians should not merely keep themselves awake but be alert, giving instant attention to approaching danger. Peter personally knew its importance, having tragically failed in the garden of Gethsemane. Casting our anxiety upon God does not absolve us of the duty of personal vigilance. "The moment slothfulness begins, that moment dangers stand thick about us."[65] In 1

---

63. Beare, p. 204.

64. J. Howard B. Masterman, *The First Epistle of S. Peter*, p. 167.

65. John T. Demarest, *A Translation and Exposition of the First Epistle of the Apostle Peter*, p. 274.

Thessalonians 5:6 those two verbs, in reverse order, are used to urge preparedness for the future. Here they alert to present danger.

(2) *The vivid portrayal of the enemy* (v. 8b). The omission of *hoti*, "because," used in the Textus Receptus,[66] adds force to the picture, "your adversary the devil, as a roaring lion, walketh about, seeking whom he may devour." Two appositional nouns identify the enemy—no common opponent. *Your adversary* properly means an opponent in a lawsuit (Zech. 3:1; Matt. 6:25; Luke 12:58), but here, and perhaps also in Luke 18:3, it has the more general meaning of an enemy. Though only here in the New Testament is the term specifically applied to the devil, it is appropriate since the devil appears before God as the accuser of the brethren (Rev. 12:10; cf. Job 1:6). The use of the definite article points to their enemy par excellence, the Christian's spiritual foe whom he cannot escape (cf. Eph. 6:11-13). The term is the equivalent of the Hebrew *Satan*, which has become the proper name of the great enemy of God and all who are His. The second term (*diabolos*), which in the Septuagint is used to translate the Hebrew term *Satan*, means "slanderer," one who knowingly and deliberately advances false charges against God and His people (cf. John 8:44). Since the term is used without an article, it is possible to take it as an adjective, "your slanderous adversary" (Rotherham); but it is better to take it as a noun, standing in apposition with *adversary*; an article is not needed since it is regarded as a proper name. In Revelation 12:9 no less than five titles are applied to that archenemy of God and man. Peter had no illusions concerning the real existence of a personal devil.

"As a roaring lion" describes his fierce and determined activity. *As* asserts the reality of his true character as a vicious beast. *Roaring* pictures him as ravenously hungry, intent on capturing prey. In Peter's day the church of Christ was already hearing his frightening roar against the saints as he sought to intimidate them so that they might become an easy prey. The figure does not indicate that official state persecution of the church was already in operation. It may be noted that the devil does not always roar; at times he comes as an angel of light (2 Cor. 11:14). Williams observes, "Smiling is as easy for the devil as roaring—and adept at both, and whichever doing, is bent on evil."[67]

"Walketh about" depicts the restless energy of the devil in his search for victims. The expression is based on Satan's own acknowledgement of his ceaseless peripatetic activities in Job 1:7. He is constantly on the prowl, "seeking whom he may devour."[68] Some manuscripts omit the pronoun that denotes the objects of his vicious search, but its presence in the majority of

66. For the textual evidence see Nestle-Aland, *Novum Testamentum Graece* (26th ed.).
67. Williams, p. 71.
68. On the manuscript variants for that phrase see the United Bible Societies Greek text; Metzger, pp. 696-97.

them strongly supports its authenticity. Depending on the accent used, it may be either the indefinite pronoun "someone" (*tina*), or the interrogative pronoun "whom" (*tina*). Either reading is possible. The NASB is representative of the former, "seeking someone to devour," and the ASV, "whom he may devour," translates it as an interrogative.[69] Mason, who represents those who accept the more vivid interrogative, thus expresses the resultant picture: "Satan is eyeing all the Christians in turn to see which he has the best chance of, not merely stalking forth vaguely to look for prey."[70] *Seeking* (*zētōn*) as a present active participle expresses Satan's persistent search, and *devour* (*katapiein*), an aorist infinitive, expresses his deadly action. The verb literally means "to drink down," like our English *gulp down*; it depicts the total destruction of the victim. Satan's aim is not merely to harass and injure; his true desire is to kill his victims by destroying their faith. Whatever human agents Satan may employ, Peter recognized him as the real instigator.

(3) The firm resistance to Satan (v. 9a). "Whom withstand steadfast in your faith" calls for effective resistance to those satanic attacks. To cower before the devil is to invite sure defeat; resistance in faith procures his flight. *Withstand* (*antistēte*), composed of *anti*, "against," and the verb *histēmi*, "to stand," presents a military metaphor; as a definite act Christians should take a solid stand in opposition to the devil as their true enemy. Scripture urges believers to flee from various evils (1 Cor. 6:18; 10:14; 1 Tim. 6:11; 2 Tim. 2:22), but nowhere are they advised to flee from the devil. That would be a futile effort. James, in giving that same command to resist the devil, adds the assuring promise, "and he will flee from you" (4:7). Ephesians 6:10-18 describes the armor we need to defeat him.

"Steadfast in your faith" (*stereoi tē pistei*) denotes the condition for victory. *Steadfast*, in a physical sense, describes something as firm, hard, solid, and compact, like a rock. In their inner attitude Christians should stand firm and unyielding like granite in resisting Satan. *In your faith* (*tē pistei*), "in the faith," or, "as regards the faith," points out the sphere or element of victory. *Faith* may be understood subjectively as denoting the Christian's personal confidence in God. Such a firm personal faith is certainly essential, but that is already indicated by the adjective *steadfast*. Here the objective sense of *the faith*, the true gospel message adhered to is essential. Victory is not assured by the personal tenacity with which we cling to our personal beliefs. Victory lies in adhering to the work of Christ on the cross, where He defeated the devil (John 12:31-33). In Christ, Satan is now a defeated foe. "Victory over Satan lies in faith, because faith unites us to Christ, the victor. By faith the devil is

69. Our versions vary: (1) "someone"—RSV, NEB, NIV, Moffatt, Berkeley, TEV, JB, Kleist and Lilly, (2) "whom"—KJV, Young, Darby, Weymouth, Montgomery, (3) omit—Rotherham, so apparently also 20th Cent., Goodspeed, and Williams, who translate "you."

70. A. J. Mason, *The First Epistle General of Peter*, p. 434.

driven to flight as is the lion by fire."[71] A counterfeit gospel will not procure that victory.

(4) The encouraging reminder concerning the brotherhood (v. 9*b*). "Knowing that the same sufferings are accomplished in your brethren who are in the world" adds a strong incentive to stand firm against the devil. It is a reminder that what the readers were experiencing was not restricted to them. *Knowing*, grammatically related to the call to withstand the devil, appeals to the Christian's sense of solidarity with other believers. The expression *the same sufferings* (*ta auta tōn pathematōn*) is exceptional because of the added genitive; it is literally "the same things of the sufferings" and points to identity in suffering. The present infinitive, "are accomplished" (*epiteleisthai*), is beset with difficulty. The form is best taken as a passive. The verb can mean "to end, to finish," but Peter could hardly mean that those sufferings were being brought to a termination for the church. It can also mean "to carry out, perform, accomplish." If that is correct then the meaning is that the sufferings of Christians are being carried out or accomplished as divinely appointed, as fulfilling a divine purpose. When that purpose is realized, the sufferings will be ended. Still others understand the verb to mean "to lay something on someone"in the sense that the sufferings are imposed on them by a hostile world. Thus Weymouth translates, "the same sufferings are imposed on your brethren." Bigg suggested that the verb means "to pay in full" and supports the translation "knowing how to pay the same tax of suffering as your brethren."[72] In support of that interpretation some argue that *knowing*, with the infinitive, cannot mean "knowing that" but must mean "knowing how." But that is not certain. In any case the expression is beset with uncertainty. It seems best to retain the translation "are being accomplished" or "are being imposed."

Those sharing such sufferings with the readers are called "your brethren who are in the world." *Brethren* is literally "the brotherhood" (*tē . . . adelphotēti*), a collective singular used only by Peter in the New Testament (cf. 2:17). It indicates more strongly than the individualizing *brethren* the oneness in nature of those subjected to such sufferings. Two modifiers, both placed attributively between the article and the noun (*tē en tō kosmō humōn adelphotēti*), further characterize that brotherhood. *In the world* may mean "everywhere," the whole Christian brotherhood scattered throughout the known world. If that is correct then the phrase is a reminder that the readers' experiences of suffering were common to believers everywhere (1 Cor. 10:13). More probably the words were intended to emphasize the truth that suffering for Christ is an inseparable part of life as long as Christians are "in the world," are living in the midst of a world that rejects Christ. Jesus told His disciples,

---

71. Gerhard, quoted in Fronmüller, p. 91.
72. Charles Bigg, *A Critical and Exegetical Commentary on the Epistles of St. Peter and St. Jude*, p. 194.

"In the world ye have tribulation: but be of good cheer; I have overcome the world" (John 16:33). The second modifier, *your*, placed just before the noun, emphasizes the reminder that the readers were aware, by virtue of a common experience, that they were a part of that brotherhood. As they shared in the brotherhood of suffering, they could look forward to the joys of the brotherhood in glory. As an encouragement to them, Peter was "quietly emphasizing the solidarity between the numerous and widely scattered little Christian communities."[73]

3) THE FINAL ENCOURAGEMENT AMID SUFFERING (VV. 10-11)

The conjunction *And* (*de*) indicates a connection with what precedes. That translation implies that those verses continue Peter's directives to the readers. But the use of *de*, which serves to introduce something new,[74] indicates that the verses add something new to the appeals that had been made. The translation *Moreover* would be preferable. Having enjoined upon the readers the Christian graces consistent with their calling, Peter committed them to the God of all grace. Verse 10 offered comforting assurance to those who were afflicted, and verse 11 is a concluding doxology.

A. THE GLORIOUS ASSURANCE TO THE SUFFERERS (v. 10)

"The God of all grace, who called you unto his eternal glory in Christ, after that ye have suffered a little while, shall himself perfect, establish, strengthen you." The assurance is grounded in the character and action of God, the true God whom Christians now love and serve.

"The God of all grace" is a title that appears only here in the New Testament (cf. 2 Cor. 1:3, "the God of all comfort"). *Of all grace* characterizes Him as the source and giver of all grace, all the undeserved favor bestowed upon us in our unworthiness. *All grace* may also point to the great variety of His gracious help for every need and occasion (cf. 4:10). Having proved Himself rich in His bestowal of grace in the past, Christians can rest assured that God will supply all their present needs.

A further characterization of God, "who called you unto his eternal glory in Christ," relates to His gracious action. His gracious character is evident from what He did, *who called you* (*ho kalesas humas*[75]); He effectively called them to His kingdom and service. The call came to them at the time they heard and accepted the message of the gospel (2 Thess. 2:13-14). In calling them God not only delivered them from their past sins but also turned their faces toward the future, calling them *unto his eternal glory* as the new goal of their lives. *His*

73. Kelly, pp. 211-12.

74. A. T. Robertson, *A Grammar of the Greek New Testament in the Light of Historical Research*, pp. 1183-85.

75. The reading "us" (*hēmas*) in the Texus Receptus is weakly supported. It marks a scribal tendency to widen the statement. See the evidence in Nestle-Aland.

eternal glory (*tēn aiōnion autou doxan*) summarily denotes all that God still has in store for His saints. The theme of coming glory has already been mentioned several times (1:7; 4:11, 13; 5:1, 4). *Eternal* (*aiōnion*) stresses the abiding nature of that coming glory as opposed to the transitory present scene; it is eternal because it belongs to the coming age that has no end. But the term denotes more than mere endlessness. "It involves conceptions of the imperishable, the untainted, the altogether satisfying, the Divine."[76]

"In Christ" can be closely related to the term just before it. If that is correct then the reference would be to the glory that is embodied in the glorified Christ (cf. John 17:24). But it is more natural to connect the phrase with *called* as an indication of the sphere or element in which the call took place—"in union with Christ" as the believer's Savior and Lord. The Christian's union with Christ assures his glorious destiny. *In* (*en*), rather than *through* (*dia*), indicates the inward union of the believer's new life (2 Cor. 5:17). The reality of that union joins present suffering with future glory and brings the former into its true perspective.

The added participial phrase, "after that ye have suffered a little while" (*oligon pathontas*), makes a closing reference to a major theme of the epistle. The participle grammatically relates to the "you" who were called unto glory and depicts the present consequences of that call (cf. 2:21; Phil. 1:29). *A little while* (*oligon*) may denote either the duration or the degree of the readers' suffering. Apparently the former is meant; yet both thoughts may be involved (cf. Rom. 8:18; 2 Cor. 4:17). The suffering *for a little while* stands in strong contrast to the eternal glory that will follow. There is no intention to disparage the reality of present suffering but to offer encouragement in its midst.

The sufferers were assured that God "shall himself perfect, establish, strengthen you." *Himself* (*autos*), placed emphatically before the verbs, emphasizes God's concern and personal activity on behalf of the readers. "It is no merely fortuitous or instrumental helps that are promised, but God's own active intervention and personal presence."[77] The verbs that follow are all in the future indicative and express firm assurance; God Himself "will perfect, establish, strengthen you."[78] Cook remarks that that piling up of verbs is "another instance of St Peter's habit of condensing a whole series of lofty thoughts in a few pregnant words."[79] The succession of verbs, without connecting links, indicates the strong feeling of assurance that surged through Peter's heart.

Perfect (*katartisei*) suggests the basic idea of fitting together, to order and arrange properly. It may be used of setting right what has previously gone wrong, to restore to a former condition, whether mending broken nets or

---

76. F. B. Meyer, *"Tried by Fire": Expositions of the First Epistle of Peter*, p. 215.

77. Selwyn, p. 240.

78. The use of the aorist optative in the Textus Receptus makes those verbs a fervent prayer-wish. For the textual evidence see the United Bible Societies Greek text.

79. Cook, p. 218.

setting broken bones (Matt. 4:21; Mark 1:19; Gal. 6:1). But it can also mean to bring to completion, to make good that which is still needed (Luke 6:40; Eph. 4:12; Heb. 13:21). It is in that latter sense that the term is used here. God will equip and outfit Christians and bring them up to the standard of usefulness for His service. He will not allow the work He has begun in them to fall short of His perfecting grace.

Establish (*stērixei*), meaning "to fix, to make firm or solid," denotes the stabilizing of something by providing a support or buttress, so that it will not totter. It is the promise that amid their sufferings, God will give Christians the fixity and immobility that will enable them to resist the temptation to deny their Lord (cf. Luke 22:31-32).

Strengthen (*sthenōsei*), a verbal form that occurs only here in the New Testament, means "to impart strength, to make strong." It promises the impartation of the needed spiritual strength to resist the devil and to endure suffering. It implies that in the readers' own unaided strength, they would fail.

A fourth verb, translated "settle" (*themeliōsei*) in the KJV, is beset with textual uncertainty. It was omitted in the two important uncials *B* and *A*, a handful of cursives, and the Vulgate version; but the majority of the witnesses support it, including 72 of the third or early fourth century. Westcott and Hort omitted it (hence its omission in the ASV), but later critical editors accept it as original.[80] Its presence in so many manuscripts is difficult to explain if it was not in the original; on the other hand, the similarity of ending of the preceding three verbs readily suggests accidental scribal omission. We accept it as authentic. As the verbal form of the noun *themelion*, meaning "foundation," it means "to lay the foundation of, to found," and so to give a firm basis. In Ephesians 3:17 it is translated "grounded." Unlike the second term, which refers to supports put around, the present term refers to the secure foundation on which something rests. The reference is thus to the solid spiritual foundation on which God will establish Christians.

The use of those four verbs is not redundant rhetoric; there is an orderly thought development. The first assured the readers that God would keep on perfecting His suffering children so that no defect would remain in them. The remaining three verbs suggest different aspects of His work. God will supply believers with the needed support so that they will not topple and fall, impart the needed strength so that they will not collapse, and set them upon an immovable foundation so that they will not be swept away.

B. THE APOSTOLIC DOXOLOGY IN CONCLUSION (v. 11)

"To him *be* the dominion for ever and ever. Amen." That is a slightly abbreviated form of the doxology in 4:11. It is addressed "to him" (*autō*), to the very God who thus acts on behalf of His people. To Him, and Him alone, all

---

80. It was omitted by Westcott and Hort and by Souter. The Textus Receptus reads it as an aorist optative. It appears as a future indicative in the texts of Nestle and Aland (24th ed.), United Bible Societies text (1st and 3d ed.), Nestle-Aland (26th ed.), and Tasker.

praise is due. The omission of a finite verb (note *be* in italics as supplied by the translators) makes it an exclamation of heartfelt adoration. It is an expression of sincere gratitude for the exhibitions of grace delineated in the preceding four verbs. Unlike 4:11, the doxology is confined to God's dominion (*to kratos*), His mighty power in action as expressed in the preceding verbs. The Christian's experience of the operation of that power can only evoke deep gratitude and praise. The expression of our praise to God will be appropriate in time and eternity. The *Amen* enabled the readers—and us—to place a personal seal upon the adoration expressed by Peter.

Part 3
Epistolary Conclusion
(5:12-14)

20

The Conclusion of the Letter
(5:12-14)

(12) By Silvanus, our faithful brother, as I account him, I have written unto you briefly, exhorting, and testifying that this is the true grace of God: stand ye fast therein. (13) She that is in Babylon, elect together with you, saluteth you; and so doth Mark my son. (14) Salute one another with a kiss of love.

Peace be unto you all that are in Christ.

Those three verses, grammatically unconnected with what has gone before, appropriately conclude the epistle. Apparently here, Peter took pen in hand to add the concluding remarks.[1] He made a summary statement concerning the letter (v. 12), added epistolary greetings (vv. 13-14a), and concluded with the benediction of peace (v. 14b).

1. THE STATEMENT CONCERNING HIS LETTER (V. 12)

Peter, in retrospect, referred to his communication through Silvanus, characterized its contents, and issued a final appeal to the readers to stand firm.

1. "If Peter dictated the present letter to Silvanus or left Silvanus to compose it, he may have added these verses on his own, but we would have expected him to indicate it," Ernest Best, *I Peter*, p. 176.

A. THE COMMUNICATION THROUGH SILVANUS (v. 12a)

"By Silvanus, our faithful brother, as I account *him*, I have written unto you briefly." That comment is beset with some difficulty concerning the intended relations of the different terms.

It is commonly accepted that the *faithful brother* is to be identified with Silas in the Acts story, Paul's co-worker on the second missionary journey.[2] That that Silas is the same man as the Silvanus of the Pauline epistles (2 Cor. 1:19; 1 Thess. 1:1; 2 Thess. 1:1) is established by a comparison of 2 Corinthians 1:19 with the Acts narrative. Peter certainly was acquainted with Silvanus during the early years of the church in Jerusalem, where Silvanus came to be esteemed as one of the "chief men among the brethren" (Acts 15:22).

"By Silvanus" (*dia Silouanou*) has been interpreted in three different ways: (1) that Silvanus was the bearer of the letter to the churches, (2) that the letter was dictated to Silvanus by Peter, (3) that Silvanus composed the letter under Peter's instructions. The first may, of course, be combined with either the second or third view. Behind the diversity lies the controversy concerning the authorship of the epistle, especially the claim that Peter could not have written the "good Greek" of this letter.[3]

In support of the position that Silvanus was the bearer of the letter is the forward position of *to you* (*humin*) in the Greek; it stands immediately after *by Silvanus*—"by Silvanus to you. . . ." That dative pronoun is most naturally taken with *I have written*. Lenski argues that by placing it prominently forward in close connection with *by Silvanus*, Peter intended to indicate that Silvanus was the bearer of the letter. "The combination of the phrase and the dative 'to you' is made even more marked," he continues, "by placing the apposition 'the faithful brother' after 'to you,'—as it were embedding the pronoun in the genitives."[4] The order implies that Peter was thinking of Silvanus as the reliable link between himself and the brethren addressed. The view that Silvanus was the bearer of the letter is supported by the fact that there is no greeting from Silvanus, but there is one from Mark (cf. Rom. 16:22). Mitchell remarks that *by Silvanus* (*dia Silouanou*) is clearly synonymous with *by them* (*dia cheiros autōn*), "by their hand" (Acts 15:23); "there is no suggestion in that case that Silvanus and Barsabbas composed the decree."[5]

Beare sought to discredit the view that Silvanus was the bearer of the letter with the assertion, "It is simply fatuous to think of a single courier conveying such a letter to all parts of the four provinces mentioned in the Address; it would take him months, or even years to accomplish such a task."[6] It is obvious

2. For a study of "Silas (Silvanus)" see D. Edmond Hiebert, *Personalities Around Paul*, pp. 88-97.
3. See the Introduction.
4. R. C. H. Lenski, *The Interpretation of the Epistles of St. Peter, St. John and St. Jude*, p. 233.
5. A. F. Mitchell, *Hebrews and the General Epistles*, p. 284. The original reads "Barnabas" instead of "Barsabbas."
6. Francis Wright Beare, *The First Epistle of Peter, The Greek Text with Introduction and Notes*, p. 209.

that an important assignment was involved, but the claim that it would take "even years to accomplish such a task" is an overstatement. We do not know how many churches would have been covered by such a mission, nor is it imperative to maintain that all of the churches in those provinces would have to have been visited. Cranfield remarks, "We need not suppose that he would necessarily visit all the churches mentioned in 1.1 himself—the letter would more probably be copied in Asia Minor, and some of the churches receive copies rather than the original document."[7] That such a mission did require an individual who was wholly dependable is obvious, but his words indicate that Peter felt Silvanus fully qualified.

It is widely accepted today that Peter used Silvanus as his amanuensis; *by Silvanus* is certainly broad enough to allow for that meaning. The employment of a scribe to record one's dictation was a common practice (cf. Rom. 16:22; 1 Cor. 16:21). Peter's use of an amanuensis seems to be important since it offers an explanation for the smooth Greek of the epistle. Professional scribes employed a system of shorthand in recording dictation and then transcribed their notes into longhand for the writer to read and approve.[8] That enabled the scribe to smooth out any irregularities in the original dictation. There is no evidence that such a procedure took place in the writing of 1 Peter, but those who have difficulty in attributing the good Greek of the epistle to Peter are attracted to the amanuensis hypothesis;[9] it offers a reasonable explanation that cannot be precluded. Thus the NIV translates "With the help of Silas." But others would go a step further. Kelly believes that Silvanus was too important a figure to allow us to think of him merely as a secretary; according to Kelly "Silvanus . . . [was] responsible for drafting the letter on the author's behalf and on his instructions."[10] That Silvanus influenced the formulation of the language is probable, but that view should not be overdrawn to make Silvanus the real author of 1 Peter. From the very beginning and throughout the letter Peter himself presented his message to his readers. The commendation given Silvanus assured the readers of the importance and trustworthiness of the one delivering the epistle to them.

"Our faithful brother" (*tou pistou adelphou*) is a pleasant testimonial on Peter's part. The definite article, *the brother*, not merely "a brother," may mean that his reliable character was known to the members of the church generally or that he was specifically known to the readers as such. The frequently adopted translation "our" seems to suggest the former view. How well the readers personally knew Silvanus is not clear. During the second missionary journey (Acts 14:40—15:6), he did have a passing contact with some of the churches addressed. He may have labored among those churches

---

7. C. E. B. Cranfield, *I & II Peter and Jude*, p. 137.

8. Bruce M. Metzger, "Stenography and Church History," in *Twentieth Century Encyclopedia of Religious Knowledge*, 2:1060-61; "The Language of the New Testament," in *The Interpreter's Bible*, 7:48, 51-52.

9. Donald Guthrie, *New Testament Introduction*, p. 780.

10. J. N. D. Kelly, *A Commentary on the Epistles of Peter and of Jude*, p. 215.

after that journey. Some, like Wand, believe that Peter's words support that understanding. He argues that the dative *to you* should be taken with *our faithful brother* and that "the sense is rather 'who has shown himself a good friend to you.'"[11] Though that interpretation is possible, it is less natural than to relate the phrase with "I have written;" it leaves the verb without an indication of the recipients.

"As I account *him*" (*hōs logizomai*) does not imply that Peter doubted his faithfulness, as the KJV translation, "as I suppose," might suggest. The verb denotes a settled persuasion or assurance arrived at after rational consideration of the evidence. The *I* of the verb is not emphatic, as though Peter meant "I think him trusty, though others do not." Peter was fully assured concerning the character and work of Silvanus. It was a justified evaluation of the man.

"I have written unto you briefly" is a backward glance over the letter. *I have written* (*egrapha*), "I wrote," is an epistolary aorist (the writer portrays himself as present at the time his readers will read the letter). In English we prefer to use either the present or the perfect tense. There is no reference to 2 Peter or to a lost letter, as some have thought. Peter believed that he had written "briefly" (*di' oligon*), "through a few *words*," when he thought of the magnitude of the theme and all that he might have said to strengthen and encourage the readers in their sufferings (cf. the synonymous expression [*dia bracheōn*] in Hebrews 13:22).

B. THE CHARACTERIZATION OF THE CONTENTS (v. 12b)

"Exhorting and testifying that this is the true grace of God" is a pithy summary of the double thrust of the epistle. *Exhorting* implies earnest and persuasive address aimed at encouraging and bracing the readers to face their trials. That hortatory tone is prominent throughout the letter. The verb may include the thought of comforting and consoling, but that does not seem to be the case here.

"And testifying" points to the second element in the epistle. *And* connects the two; they are intertwined throughout the letter. *Testifying* (*epimarturōn*), a compound form that appears only here in the New Testament,[12] emphasizes the idea of confirmation. Some have suggested that the force of the *epi*, "upon, on top of," is cumulative, that it indicates that Peter was *adding* to the teaching of their earlier teachers. But such a supplemental or corrective aim is nowhere apparent in the epistle. More probably its force is intensive, "earnestly testifying," but it may simply be directive, indicating that the testimony was aimed at confirming the truth "that this is the true grace of God." Peter bore witness to the reality that the message of salvation that the readers had received was indeed the true grace of God. *Grace* points to the objective message of salvation in Christ, and *true* confirms that message to be genuine and trustworthy.

11. J. W. C. Wand, *The General Epistles of St. Peter and St. Jude*, p. 128.
12. But Heb. 2:4 uses the double compound participle *sunepimarturountos*.

This (*tautēn*), the demonstrative pronoun, looks back to the message of salvation presented in the epistle. The message of God's grace that the readers received at conversion and were experiencing in their Christian growth was no delusion; they were to allow their sufferings to cast no shadow of uncertainty on that reality.

C. THE CALL TO STAND FIRM (v. 12c)

"Stand ye fast therein" (*eis hēn stēte*) is a summary of the hortatory message of the epistle. The expression involves a common ellipsis; the preposition *eis*, "into," implies the readers' entry into that grace, and *stand fast* called for them to stand firm. Having entered into that grace at conversion, they were to effectively maintain their stand. "Having done all, stand" (Eph. 6:13).

The Textus Receptus has the indicative, *eis hēn hestēkate*, "wherein ye stand" (KJV). If that is correct then Peter declared his approval and confidence in the readers. But the imperative is better supported,[13] is eminently in keeping with the hortatory tone of the epistle, and greatly adds to the forcefulness of the conclusion. Peter's pastoral concern lead him to pass from personal affirmation to vigorous admonition.

2) THE GREETINGS IN CONCLUSION (VV. 13-14a)

The epistle concludes with the usual greetings. Peter recorded greetings from those with him (v. 13) and asked the readers to exchange mutual greetings as believers (v. 14a).

A. THE GREETINGS TO THE READERS (v. 13)

"She that is in Babylon, elect together with *you*, saluteth you; and *so doth* Mark my son." The verb *saluteth you* (*aspazetai humas*), "sends you greetings," stands first in the sentence; it is the common formula for the expression of written greetings. Being composed of the verb *spaō*, "to draw to one's self," with the intensive prefix *a*, it expresses the thought of bridging the gap between the writer and one fondly thought of through written greetings.

"She that is in Babylon, elect together with *you*" (*hē en Babylōni suneklektē*), literally, "The one [feminine article] in Babylon, co-elect," may be understood either literally or figuratively. Those who take the words literally of a woman understand them as a reference to Peter's wife or to some prominent unnamed woman living in Babylon. Peter was a married man (Matt. 8:14), and it is known that his wife often traveled with him (1 Cor. 9:5). Tradition has it that she died as a Christian martyr. In support of the view that Peter referred to an individual woman is the fact that Mark joined in the greeting. It has even been conjectured that the word translated "elect together with you" is really the name of Peter's wife, *Suneklektē* or *Synek-*

13. For the evidence see Nestle-Aland, *Novum Testamentum Graece* (26th ed.).

lekta. The term would be rare as a personal name. But if it is a personal name here then the use of the definite article is superfluous. Further, if the reference is to Peter's wife, it would be needless to mention that she resided in Babylon. That the reference is to some otherwise unknown woman is even more unlikely. We have no information about any woman residing in Babylon who was so well known to the churches in Asia Minor that she would be personally identified without her name. Since 1 Peter is addressed to a series of churches located in different provinces (1:1), it is highly improbable that an individual woman should thus send her personal greetings to those widely scattered churches.

More probable is the view that the designation is to be understood figuratively of the local church in the city where Peter was residing when he wrote. That the designation was early understood to denote a local church is evident from the fact that Codex *Aleph*, some later manuscripts, the Vulgate, and the Peshitta version actually added the word *church*. Such a designation from a sister congregation is suggested by the fact that *church* is a feminine noun in Greek. Greetings from a sister church would be natural in a letter being sent to a series of local churches. The added place name is natural if the reference is to a local congregation. Such a figurative designation is in keeping with the biblical imagery of the church as the bride of Christ.

"In Babylon" has also been understood either literally or figuratively. Those who think of a literal city generally point to the noted city of Babylon on the Euphrates. Babylon in Egypt, a Roman military fortress located near the present city of Cairo, has also been mentioned. In support of the literal meaning scholars argue that "other geographical references in First Peter are admittedly literal,"[14] and that "there is no reason to suppose that when this epistle was written the city of Rome was currently known among Christians as Babylon."[15]

Proponents of a figurative meaning for Babylon accept it as a cryptic designation for the city of Rome. That was the earliest known view in church history; it is favored by the majority of scholars today (see the discussion in the Introduction). The meaning is intimately connected with the question of 1 Peter's place of origin. We accept that view as in harmony with church tradition concerning the later years of Peter's life.

"Elect together with *you*" (*suneklektē*), "co-elect," echoes the description of the readers as "the elect" in 1:1 (cf. 2:10). The greeting is sent from her who is "co-elect," not with Peter but with the readers, chosen with them to be members of the brotherhood of believers. It is a closing reference to the reality of the divine initiative in human salvation.

"Mark my son" can be understood literally or spiritually. That the reference is to Peter's own son is highly improbable and can be maintained only if the

14. Guy N. Woods, *A Commentary on the New Testament Epistles of Peter, John, and Jude*, p. 135.
15. Kenneth S. Wuest, *First Peter in the Greek New Testament for the English Reader*, p. 133.

preceding is a reference to Peter's wife. Tradition has amplified every known feature of Peter's life, but there is no indication that Peter had a son named Mark. The reference seems to be to John Mark, the author of our second gospel.[16] Christian tradition closely connects Peter with John Mark during the later years of his life. *Son* thus indicates a spiritual relationship. That Mark was Peter's convert is very probable, though that term (*huios*) is not used elsewhere of a spiritual father-son relationship. Paul used the term *teknon* ("child") to indicate such a spiritual relation (cf. 1 Tim. 1:2, 18). In the Septuagint as well as in the New Testament Peter's term is used in the sense of "disciple" (2 Kings 2:3, 5; Matt. 12:27; Luke 11:19). Whether or not Mark was converted under Peter, the designation "reflects the relationship of trust and affection between the older Christian leader and his younger disciple."[17]

B. THE EXCHANGE OF MUTUAL GREETINGS (v. 14a)

"Salute one another with a kiss of love" requests the readers to display their sincere brotherly love to one another. *Salute* (*aspasasthe*), in the aorist tense, may imply that after the letter was read to them they were to express their spiritual union with each other in that way. Such an expression of unity would have offered a sense of mutual strength amid their afflictions. *With a kiss of love* (*en philēmati agapēs*) denotes a kiss prompted by love as an expression of genuine affection. The attitude of the heart should evoke the external act. Paul always designated it as "a holy kiss" (Rom. 16:16; 1 Cor. 16:20; 2 Cor. 13:12; 1 Thess. 5:26). *Holy* indicates that it is to be the expression of a sanctified spiritual relationship. A kiss on the cheek was a common form of Oriental greeting among friends (cf. Luke 7:45); it was as common as shaking hands is in western culture. The practice was employed by Christians as a mutual expression of brotherly love among members of one spiritual family.

The literature of the subapostolic age reveals that by that time the kiss had become a part of public worship with liturgical significance and was widely observed during the celebration of the Lord's Supper.[18] The practice was open to misunderstanding and abuse. To eliminate various occasions for embarrassment and trouble, the early church councils issued various regulations concerning its practice. Kissing as a ritual in the western church disappeared almost completely by the end of the thirteenth century.

It should be noted that the apostles did not originate that form of greeting; the custom already prevailed. They sanctioned its use as a sincere expression of Christian love. "The obligation of brotherly love," MacDonald observes, "is a standing order for the church, though the manner of expressing it may vary in cultures and times."[19]

16. Hiebert, pp. 76-87.
17. Kelly, p. 220.
18. J. Alfred Faulkner, "Salutations," 2:442-44; R. E. Perry, "Kiss," *ZPEB*, 3:831-82.
19. William MacDonald, *I Peter: Faith Tested, Future Triumphant*, p. 109.

3. THE BENEDICTION OF PEACE (V. 14b)

The epistle concludes with the Oriental benediction of peace— "Peace be unto you all that are in Christ" (*Eipēnē humin pasin tois en Christō*), "Peace to you all, to those in Christ." Paul usually closed his epistles with *grace*,[20] but Peter used *Peace*, which he had often heard from the lips of Jesus (cf. Matt. 10:12-13; Luke 24:36; John 20:19-21, 26). He wished the readers peace in all the fullness of its meaning.

"All" emphasizes the inclusiveness of the greeting, but the added expression "that are in Christ"[21] is distinctive. The meaning is not that there were believers who were not in Christ. The phrase is an appositional expansion of "to you all" and characterizes and identifies the readers by that relationship. The kind of peace he wished them is possible only to those who by faith have been united with Christ and share His risen life, "For he is our peace" (Eph. 2:14).

The majority of the textual witnesses conclude the epistle with *Amen.*[22] It is possible that it is authentic (as in 4:11), but the fact that the scribes of a number of Greek manuscripts, as well as the Coptic and Ethiopic versions, resisted the strong liturgical temptation to add it casts doubt on its presence in the original. Modern critical editions agree in omitting it.[23] Whether it was a part of the original, all of us can add our own hearty amen as we come to the conclusion of such a practical, soul-stirring epistle.

20. 1 Cor. 16:23; 2 Cor. 13:14; Gal. 6:18; Eph. 6:23-24 (where "peace to the brethren" precedes "grace"); Phil. 4:23; Col. 4:18; 1 Thess. 5:28; 2 Thess. 3:18; 1 Tim. 6:21; 2 Tim. 4:22; Titus 3:15; Philem. 25.
21. The Textus Receptus reads "Christ Jesus." For the evidence see the United Bible Societies Greek text.
22. See United Bible Societies text; Bruce M. Metzger, *A Textual Commentary on the Greek New Testament*, p. 698.
23. So Westcott and Hort, Souter, Nestle and Aland (24th ed.), United Bible Societies, Tasker, Nestle-Aland (26th ed.).

Bibliography

THE BIBLICAL TEXT

GREEK NEW TESTAMENT

Aland, Kurt; Black, Matthew; Metzger, Bruce M.; and Wikgren, Allen. *The Greek New Testament.* American Bible Society, British and Foreign Bible Society, National Bible Society of Scotland, Netherlands Bible Society, Württemberg Bible Society, 1966. (Referred to as United Bible Society Greek text.)

Aland, Kurt; Black, Matthew; Martini, Carlo M.; Metzger, Bruce M.; and Wikgren, Allen. *The Greek New Testament.* 3d ed. United Bible Societies, 1975. (Referred to as United Bible Societies text.)

Hē Kainē Diathēkē. The New Testament. The Greek Text Underlying the English Authorized Version of 1611. Reprint. London: Trinitarian Bible Society, n.d. (A reprint of the text of F. H. Scrivener without the textual variants in his footnotes; referred to as the Textus Receptus.)

Nestle, Erwin, and Aland, Kurt. *Novum Testamentum Graece.* 24th ed. Stuttgart: Privileg. Württ. Bibelanstalt. (Referred to as Nestle-Aland, 24th ed.)

Nestle-Aland. *Novum Testamentum Graece.* Stuttgart: Deutsche Bibelstiftung, 1979. (Prints the text of the United Bible Societies text, 3d ed., but adds the manuscript evidence for many other textual variants; referred to as Nestle-Aland, 26th ed.; based on the work of Kurt and Barbara Aland.)

Scrivener, F. H., ed. *Hē Kainē Diathēkē. Novum Testament. Textus Stephanici A.D. 1550.* London: Whittaker et Soc.: Bell et Daldy, 1867. (Textus Receptus)

Souter, Alexander. *Novum Testamentum Graece.* 1910. Reprint. Oxford: Clarendon, 1962.

Tasker, R. V. G. *The Greek New Testament, Being the Text Translated in The New English Bible 1961.* Oxford: Oxford U., 1964.

Westcott, Brooke Foss, and Hort, Fenton John Anthony. *The New Testament in the Original Greek.* New York: Macmillan, 1935.

GREEK OLD TESTAMENT

The Septuagint Version of the Old Testament and Apocrypha, with an English Translation; and with Various Readings and Critical Notes. Reprint. Grand Rapids: Zondervan, 1972.

ENGLISH VERSIONS

American Standard Version, The Holy Bible, Containing the Old and New Testaments, Translated out of the Original Tongues. New York: Nelson, 1901.

Darby, J. N. *The "Holy Scriptures." A New Translation from the Original Languages.* Kingston-on-Thames, Eng.: Stow Hill Bible & Tract Depot, 1949.

Douay Version, The Holy Bible, Translated from the Latin Vulgate. Reprint. New York: P. J. Kennedy & Sons, n.d.

Goodspeed, Edgar J. *The New Testament, an American Translation.* Chicago: U. of Chicago, 1923.

The New Testament of the Jerusalem Bible. Reader's Edition. Edited by Alexander Jones. Garden City, N.Y.: Doubleday, 1966.

King James Version. *The Holy Bible Containing the Old and New Testaments.* Reprint. Cambridge: University Press, n.d.

Kleist, James A., and Lilly, Joseph L. *The New Testament Rendered from the Original Greek with Explanatory Notes.* Milwaukee: Bruce, 1956.

Moffatt, James. *The New Testament, A New Translation.* Rev. ed. Reprint. New York: George H. Doran, n.d.

Montgomery, Helen Barrett. *The New Testament in Modern English.* 1924. Reprint. Philadelphia: Judson, 1946.

New American Standard Bible. Carol Stream, Ill: Creation House, 1971.

The New Berkeley Version, The Modern Language Bible. Grand Rapids: Zondervan, 1969.

New English Bible. Oxford and Cambridge: University Press, 1970.

New International Version, The Holy Bible, Containing the Old Testament and the New Testaments. Grand Rapids: Zondervan, 1978.

The New Testament in Today's English Version. Good News for Modern Man. New York: American Bible Society, 1966.

Revised Standard Version, The Holy Bible, Containing the Old and New Testaments. Philadelphia: Holman, 1962.

Rotherham, Joseph Bryant. *The Emphasized New Testament*. Reprint. Grand Rapids: Kregel, 1959.

The Twentieth Century New Testament. A Translation into Modern English. Reprint. Chicago: Moody, n.d.

Weigle, Luther A., ed. *The New Testament Octapla*. New York: Nelson, 1962.

Weymouth, Richard Francis. *The New Testament in Modern Speech. An Idiomatic Translation into Everyday English from the Text of the Resultant Greek Testament*. Newly revised by James Alexander Robertson. 5th ed. New York: Harper & Brothers, 1929.

Williams, Charles B. *The New Testament, A Private Translation in the Language of the People*. Reprint. Chicago: Moody, n.d.

Young, Robert. *The Holy Bible Consisting of the Old and New Covenants, Translated According to the Letter and Idioms of the Original Languages*. London: Pickering & Inglis, n.d.

GRAMMARS, LEXICONS, WORD STUDIES

Arndt, William F., and Gingrich, F. Wilbur. *A Greek-English Lexicon of the New Testament and Other Early Christian Literature*. Chicago: U. of Chicago, 1957.

Barclay, William. *New Testament Words*, combining *A New Testament Wordbook* and *More New Testament Words*. London: SCM, 1964.

Blass, F., and Debrunner, A. *A Greek Grammar of the New Testament and Other Early Christian Literature*. Translated and revised by Robert W. Funk. Chicago: U. of Chicago, 1961.

Cremer, Hermann. *Biblico-Theological Lexicon of New Testament Greek*. Reprint. Translated by William Urwick. Edinburgh: T. & T. Clark, 1954.

Dana, H. E., and Mantey, Julius R. *A Manual Grammar of the Greek New Testament*. Reprint. New York: Macmillan, 1967.

Liddell, Henry George, and Scott, Robert. *A Greek-English Lexicon*. 7th ed. rev. Oxford: Clarendon, 1890.

Metzger, Bruce M. *Lexical Aids for Students of New Testament Greek*. Princeton, N.J.: Privately published, 1955.

————.*A Textual Commentary on the Greek New Testament*. London: United Bible Societies, 1971.

Moulton, James Hope. *Prolegomena*, A Grammar of New Testament Greek, vol. 1. Edinburgh: T. & T. Clark, 1908.

Moulton, James Hope, and Milligan, George. *The Vocabulary of the Greek Testament Illustrated from the Papyri and Other Non-Literary Sources*. Reprint. London: Hodder & Stoughton, 1952.

Robertson, A. T. *A Grammar of the Greek New Testament in the Light of Historical Research*. 5th ed. New York: Richard R. Smith, 1923.

Robertson, A. T., and Davis, W. Hersey. *A New Short Grammar of the Greek Testament*. 1933. Reprint. New York: Harper & Brothers, 1935.

Thayer, Joseph Henry. *A Greek-English Lexicon of the New Testament* (1889). Reprint. New York: American Book Co., n.d.

Trench, Richard Chenevix. *Synonyms of the New Testament*. Reprint. Grand Rapids: Eerdmans, 1947.

Vine, W. E. *An Expository Dictionary of New Testament Words with Their Precise Meanings for English Readers*. Reprint. Westwood, N.J.: Revell, 1966.

NEW TESTAMENT INTRODUCTIONS

Crapps, Robert W.; McKnight, Edgar V.; and Smith, David A. *Introduction to the New Testament*. New York: Ronald, 1969.

Ebright, Homer Kingsley. *The Petrine Epistles*. Cincinnati: Methodist Book Concern, 1917.

Goodspeed, Edgar J. *An Introduction to the New Testament*. Chicago: U. of Chicago, 1937.

Guthrie, Donald. *New Testament Introduction*. Rev. ed. Downers Grove, Ill: Inter-Varsity, 1970.

Klijn, A. F. J. *An Introduction to the New Testament*. Leiden: E. J. Brill, 1967.

Kümmel, Werner Georg. *Introduction to the New Testament*. Rev. ed. Translated by Howard Clark Kee. Nashville: Abingdon, 1975.

Machen, J. Gresham. *The New Testament. An Introduction to Its Literature and History*. Edited by W. John Cook. Edinburgh: Banner of Truth, 1976.

McNeile, A. H. *An Introduction to the Study of the New Testament*. Revised by C. S. C. Williams. Oxford: Clarendon, 1953.

Martin, Ralph P. *New Testament Foundations: A Guide for Christian Students*. Vol. 2. Grand Rapids: Eerdmans, 1978.

Reicke, Bo. *The New Testament Era*. Translated by David E. Green. Philadelphia: Fortress, 1968.

Rife, J. Merle. *The Nature and Origin of the New Testament*. New York: Philosophical Library, 1975.

Robinson, John A. T. *Redating the New Testament*. Philadelphia: Westminster, 1976.

Scott, Ernest Findlay. *The Literature of the New Testament*. Reprint. New York: Columbia. 1948.

Selby, Donald J. *Introduction to the New Testament. "The Word Became Flesh."* New York: Macmillan, 1971.

Streeter, Burnett Hillman. *The Primitive Church Studied with Special Reference to the Origins of the Christian Ministry. The Hewett Lectures, 1928*. London: Macmillan, 1929.

Weiss, Bernard. *A Manual of Introduction to the New Testament*. Translated by A. J. K. Davidson. New York: Funk & Wagnalls, vol. 1, 1886; vol. 2, 1889.

Zahn, Theodor. *Introduction to the New Testament*. 3d ed. Translated by J. M. Trout, W. A. Mather, L. Hodous, E. S. Worchester, and R. B. Dodge under the direction and supervision of M. W. Jacobs, assisted by C. S. Thayer. Edinburgh: T. & T. Clark, 1909.

BOOKS ON 1 PETER

Adams, Jay E. *Trust and Obey. A Practical Commentary on First Peter.* Phillipsburg, N.J.: Presbyterian and Reformed, 1978.

Alford, Henry. *The Greek Testament.* Vol. 4, part 1. London: Rivingtons; Cambridge: Deighton, Bell, 1859.

———.*The New Testament For English Readers.* Reprint. Chicago: Moody, n.d.

Ball, Charles S. *First and Second Peter.* Vol. 6, *The Wesleyan Bible Commentary.* Grand Rapids: Eerdmans, 1966.

Barclay, William. *The Letters of James and Peter. The Daily Study Bible.* 2d ed. Edinburgh: Saint Andrew, 1960.

Barnes, Albert. *Notes on the New Testament, Explanatory and Practical —James, Peter, John, and Jude.* Edited by Robert Frew. Reprint. Grand Rapids: Baker, 1951.

Beare, Francis Wright. *The First Epistle of Peter, The Greek Text with Introduction and Notes.* 3d ed. rev. and enl. Oxford: Basil Blackwell, 1970.

Bengel, John Albert. *New Testament Word Studies.* Vol. 2, *Romans —Revelation.* Reprint. A new translation by Charlton T. Lewis and Marvin R. Vincent. Grand Rapids: Kregel, 1971. (Former title: *Gnomen of the New Testament.*)

Bennett, W. H. *The General Epistles, James, Peter, John, and Jude. The Century Bible. A Modern Commentary.* London: Blackwood, Le Bas, n.d.

Best, Ernest. *I Peter. New Century Bible Based on the Revised Version.* London: Oliphants, 1971.

Bigg, Charles. *A Critical and Exegetical Commentary on the Epistles of St. Peter and St. Jude. The International Critical Commentary.* 1901. Reprint. Edinburg: T. & T. Clark, 1910.

Blaiklock, E. M. *First Peter. A Translation and Devotional Commentary.* Waco, Tex.: Word, 1977.

Blair, J. Allen. *Living Peacefully. A Devotional Study of the First Epistle of Peter.* Neptune, N.J.: Loizeaux, 1959.

Brown, John. *Expository Discourses on the First Epistle of the Apostle Peter.* Reprint. Marshallton, Del.: National Foundation for Christian Education, n.d.

Caffin, B. C. *The First Epistle General of Peter. The Pulpit Commentary.* Reprint. Grand Rapids: Eerdmans, 1950.

Calvin, John. *The Epistle of Paul the Apostle to the Hebrews and the First and Second Epistles of St. Peter. Calvin's Commentaries.* Translated by William B. Johnston. Grand Rapids: Eerdmans, 1963.

Caton, N. T. *A Commentary and an Exposition of the Epistles of James, Peter, John and Jude.* 1879. Reprint. Delight, Ark.: Gospel Light, n.d.

Clark, Gordon H. *Peter Speaks Today. A Devotional Commentary on First Peter*. Philadelphia: Presbyterian and Reformed, 1967.

Cook, F. C. *The First Epistle General of Peter*. Vol. 4, *The Holy Bible According to the Authorized Version with an Explanatory and Critical Commentary and a Revision of the Translation, by Bishops and Other Clergy of the Anglican Church. New Testament*, Edited by F. C. Cook. (Commonly known as "The Speaker's Commentary.") London: John Murray, 1881.

Cranfield, C. E. B. *I & II Peter and Jude. Torch Bible Commentaries*. London: SCM, 1960.

Dalton, William Joseph. *Christ's Proclamation to the Spirits. A Study of I Peter 3:18—4:6*. Rome: Pontifical Biblical Institute, 1965.

Demarest, John T. *A Translation and Exposition of the First Epistle of the Apostle Peter*. New York: John Moffet, 1851.

Edwards, Clifford Walter. *Christian Being and Doing. A Study-Commentary on James and I Peter*. New York: Joint Commission on Education and Cultivation Board of Missions, The Methodist Church, 1966.

Elliott, John Hall. *The Elect and the Holy. An Exegetical Examination of I Peter 2:4-10 and the Phrase basileion hierateuma*. Leiden: E. J. Brill, 1966.

Ellison, H. L. *1 and 2 Peter, 1, 2 and 3 John, Jude, Revelation*. Scripture Union Bible Study Books. Grand Rapids: Eerdmans, 1969.

English, E. Schuyler. *The Life and Letters of Saint Peter*. New York: Publication office "Our Hope," 1941.

Erdman, Charles R. *The General Epistles*. 1919. Reprint. Philadelphia: Westminster, n.d.

Evans, William. *Peter, The Epistles of "The Living Hope."* Hollywood, Calif.: Gospel Light, 1941.

Farrar, F. W. *The Early Days of Christianity*. Author's ed. 1882. New York: Cassell, n.d.

Fronmüller, G. F. C. *The Epistles General of Peter. Lange's Commentary on the Holy Scriptures*. Reprint. Translated with additions by J. Isidor Mombert. Grand Rapids: Zondervan, n.d.

Gaebelein, Arno C. *The Annotated Bible*. Reprint vol. 4 (Vol. 9 in the original with original numbering retained). Chicago: Moody, 1970.

Hart, J. H. A. *The First Epistle General of Peter*. Vol. 5, *The Expositor's Greek Testament*, vol. 5. Reprint. Edited by W. Robertson Nicoll. Grand Rapids: Eerdmans, n.d.

Hort, F. J. A. *The First Epistle of St. Peter, I. 1—II. 17. Expository and Exegetical Studies, Compendium of Works Formerly Published Separately*. Reprint. Minneapolis: Klock & Klock, 1980.

Hunter, Archibald M., and Homrighausen, Elmer G. *The First Epistle of Peter*. Vol. 12, *The Interpreter's Bible*. New York: Abingdon, 1957.

Huther, Joh., ed. *Critical and Exegetical Handbook to the General Epistles of Peter and Jude*, in *Meyer's Critical and Exegetical Commentary on the New Testament*. Edinburgh: T. & T. Clark, 1881.

Jamieson, Robert; Fausset, A. R.; and Brown, David. *New Testament*. Vol. 2, *A Commentary, Critical and Explanatory, on the Old and New Testaments*. Reprint. Hartford, Conn: S. S. Scranton, n.d.

Johnstone, Robert. *The First Epistle of Peter: Revised Text, with Introduction and Commentary*. Reprint. Minneapolis: James Family, 1978.

Jowett, J. H. *The Epistles of St. Peter*. 3d ed. London: Hodder & Stoughton, 1910.

Kelly, J. N. D. *A Commentary on the Epistles of Peter and of Jude. Harper's New Testament Commentaries*. New York: Harper & Row, 1969.

Kelly, William. *The Epistles of Peter*. 1923. Reprint. London: C. A. Hammond, n.d.

———. *The Preaching to the Spirits in Prison. I Peter III. 18-20*. Reprint. Denver: Wilson Foundation, 1970.

Leaney, A. R. C. *The Letters of Peter and Jude. The Cambridge Bible Commentary*. Cambridge: U. Press, 1967.

Lenski, R. C. H. *The Interpretation of the Epistles of St. Peter, St. John and St. Jude*. Columbus, Ohio: Lutheran Book Concern, 1938.

Lillie, John. *Lectures on the First and Second Epistles of Peter*. Reprint. Minneapolis: Klock & Klock, 1978.

Lumby, J. Rawson. *The Epistles of St. Peter*. Vol. 6, *An Exposition of the Bible*, Hartford, Conn: S. S. Scranton, 1903.

MacDonald, William. *1 Peter: Faith Tested, Future Triumphant*. Wheaton, Ill: Shaw, 1972.

Macknight, James. *A New Literal Translation from the Original Greek of All the Apostolical Epistles, with a Commentary, and Notes*. Vol. 5. Reprint. Grand Rapids: Baker, 1969.

McNab, Andrew. *The General Epistles of Peter. The New Bible Commentary*. Edited by F. Davidson. Grand Rapids: Eerdmans, 1953.

Mason, A. J. *The First Epistle General of Peter*. Vol. 8, *Ellicott's Commentary on the Whole Bible*. Reprint. Grand Rapids: Zondervan, n.d.

Masterman, J. Howard B. *The First Epistle of S. Peter (Greek Text)*. London: Macmillan, 1900.

Maycock, Edward A. *A Letter of Wise Counsel, Studies in the First Epistle of Peter*. New York: Association, 1957.

Meyer, F. B. *"Tried by Fire": Expositions of the First Epistle of Peter*. London: Morgan and Scott, n.d.

Miller, John. *Notes on James, I and II Peter; I, II and III John, Jude, Revelation*. Bradford, Eng.: Needed Truth Publishing Office, n.d.

Mitchell, A. F. *Hebrews and the General Epistles. The Westminster New Testament*. London: Andrew Melrose, 1911.

Moffatt, James. *The General Epistles, James, Peter, and Judas. The Moffatt New Testament Commentary*. Reprint. London: Hodder & Stoughton, 1947.

Morgan, G. Campbell. *Peter and the Church*. New York: Revell, 1938.

Nickolson, Roy S. *The First Epistle of Peter*. Vol. 10, *Beacon Bible Commentary*. Kansas City, Mo.: Beacon Hill, 1969.

320 First Peter

Niebor, J. *A Practical Exposition of I Peter*. Erie, Pa.: Our Daily Walk, n.d.

Oberst, Bruce. *Letters from Peter. Bible Study Textbook Series*. Joplin, Mo.: College Press, 1962.

Plumptre, E. H. *The General Epistles of St Peter & St Jude. The Cambridge Bible for Schools and Colleges*. Cambridge: University Press, 1893.

Polkinghorne, G. J. *The First Letter of Peter. A New Testament Commentary*. Edited by G. C. D. Rowley. Grand Rapids: Zondervan, 1969.

Poole, Matthew. *Matthew-Revelation*. Vol. 3, *A Commentary on the Holy Bible*. Reprint. Edinburgh: Banner of Truth, 1979.

Rees, Paul S. *Triumphant in Trouble. Studies in I Peter*. Westwood, N.J.: Revell, 1962.

Reicke, Bo. *The Disobedient Spirits and Christian Baptism. A Study of I Peter III. 19 and Its Context*. Reprint. Ann Arbor, Mich: University Microfilms International, 1979.

————. *The Epistles of James, Peter, and Jude*. The Anchor Bible. Garden City, N.Y.: Doubleday, 1964.

Ross, J. M. E. *The First Epistle of Peter. A Devotional Commentary*. Edited by C. H. Irwin. London: The Religious Tract Society, n.d.

Roth, Robert Paul. *I Peter*. Vol. 3, *The Biblical Expositor, The Living Theme of the Great Book*. Carl F. H. Henry, consulting editor. Philadelphia: Holman, 1960.

Selwyn, Edward Gordon. *The First Epistle of St. Peter. The Greek Text with Introduction, Notes and Essays*. London: Macmillan, 1949.

Stibbs, Allan M. *The First Epistle General of Peter. Tyndale New Testament Commentaries*. Introduction by Andrew F. Walls. London: Tyndale, 1959.

Summers, Ray. *I Peter*. Vol. 12, *The Broadman Bible Commentary*. Edited by Clifton J. Allen. Nashville: Broadman, 1972.

Trapp, John. *Trapp's Commentary on the New Testament*. Reprint. Evansville, Ind.: Sovereign Grace, 1958.

Vincent, Marvin R. *Word Studies in the New Testament*. Vol. 1. Reprint. Grand Rapids: Eerdmans, 1946.

Waltemyer, William C. *The First Epistle of Peter. New Testament Commentary*. Edited by Herbert C. Alleman. Rev. ed. Philadelphia: United Lutheran Church of America, 1944.

Wand, J. W. C. *The General Epistles of St. Peter and St. Jude. Westminister Commentaries*. London: Methuen, 1934.

Wesley, John; Clarke, Adam; Henry, Matthew; and others. *One Volume New Testament Commentary*. Reprint. Grand Rapids: Baker, 1972.

Westwood, Tom. *The Epistles of Peter*. Glendale, Calif: Tom Westwood, n.d.

Wheaton, David H. *1 Peter. The New Bible Commentary, Revised*. Edited by D. Guthrie and J. A. Motyer. Downers Grove, Ill: Inter-Varsity, 1970.

Whedon, D. D. *Titus-Revelation*. Vol. 5, *A Popular Commentary on the New Testament*. London: Hodder & Stoughton, 1880.

Williams, George. *The Student's Commentary on the Holy Scriptures, Analytical, Synoptical, and Synthetical.* 5th ed. London: Oliphants, 1949.

Williams, Nathaniel Marshman. *Commentary on the Epistles of Peter. An American Commentary on the New Testament.* 1888. Reprint. Philadelphia: American Baptist Publication Society, n.d.

Wolston, W. T. P. *Simon Peter: His Life and Letters.* 4th ed. London: Pickering & Inglis, 1926.

Woods, Guy N. *A Commentary on the New Testament Epistles of Peter, John, and Jude.* Nashville: Gospel Advocate, 1954.

Wuest, Kenneth S. *"First Peter." In The Greek New Testament for the English Reader.* 2d ed. Grand Rapids: Eerdmans, 1944.

Zerr, E. M. *Bible Commentary.* Reprint. Vols. 5 and 6 (in one binding). Raytown, Mo.: Reprint Publications, 1954.

OTHER BOOKS

Augustine. *The Confessions of Saint Augustine.* Translated by Edward B. Pusey. Reprint. New York: Collier, 1961.

Brown, Colin, ed. *The New International Dictionary of New Testament Theology.* 3 vols. Translation of *Theologisches Begriffslexikon zum Neuen Testament.* Grand Rapids: Zondervan, 1975, 1976, 1978.

Bruce, F. F. *The Epistles of John.* Old Tappan, N.J.: Revell, 1970.

Cross, F. L. *I Peter, A Pascal Liturgy.* London: A. R. Mowbray, 1954.

Cullmann, Oscar. *The Earliest Christian Confessions.* Translated by J. K. S. Reid. London: Lutterworth, 1949.

———. *Peter, Disciple Apostle Martyr. A Historical and Theological Study.* 2d ed. Philadelphia: Westminster, 1962.

Douglas, J. D., gen. ed. *The New International Dictionary of the Christian Church.* Grand Rapids: Zondervan, 1974.

Eusebius Pamphilus. *The Ecclesiastical History of Eusebius Pamphilus, Bishop of Caesarea, in Palestine.* Translated by C. F. Cruse. London: George Bell and Sons, 1897.

Foh, Susan T. *Women and the Word of God. A Response to Biblical Feminism.* Nutley, N.J.: Presbyterian and Reformed, 1980.

France, R. T. "Exegesis in Practice: Two Samples." In *New Testament Interpretation, Essays on Principles and Methods.* Edited by I. Howard Marshall. Grand Rapids: Eerdmans, 1977.

Fuller, David Otis, compiler and ed. *Valiant for the Truth. A Treasury of Evangelical Writings.* New York: McGraw-Hill, 1961.

Goodspeed, Edgar J. *Problems of New Testament Translation.* Chicago: U. of Chicago, 1945.

Hardy, E. G. *Christianity and the Roman Government.* Reprint. London: George Allen & Unwin, 1925.

Hiebert, D. Edmond. *The Epistle of James.* Chicago: Moody, 1979.

————. *Personalities Around Paul.* Chicago: Moody, 1973.

Hogg, C. F., and Vine, W. E. *The Epistle of Paul the Apostle to the Galatians with Notes Exegetical and Expository.* London: Pickering & Inglis, n.d.

Josephus, Flavius. *The Life and Works of Flavius Josephus.* Translated by William Whiston. Philadelphia: John C. Winston, n.d.

Marshall, I. Howard, ed. *New Testament Interpretation, Essays on Principles and Methods.* Grand Rapids: Eerdmans, 1977.

Mayor, Joseph B. *The Epistle of St. James. The Greek Text with Introduction Notes and Comments.* London: Macmillan, 1897.

Mullins, Edgar Young. *The Life in Christ.* Philadelphia: American Baptist Pub. Society, 1917.

The Oxford English Dictionary. 12 vols. Reprint. Oxford: Clarendon, 1961.

Phillips, John. *Exploring Romans.* Chicago: Moody, 1969.

Radice, Betty, trans. *Pliny, Letters and Panegyricus in Two Volumes.* Loeb Classical Library, vol. 2. Reprint. Cambridge: Harvard U., 1976.

Robertson. A. T. *The Minister and His Greek New Testament.* London: Hodder & Stoughton, 1923.

Robinson, John A. T. *The Body-A Study in Pauline Theology.* London: SCM, 1952.

Sanders, Jack T. *The New Testament Christological Hymns, Their Historical Religious Background.* Cambridge: University Press, 1971.

Sevenster, J.N. *Do You Know Greek? How Much Greek Could The First Jewish Christians Have Known?* Leiden: E. J. Brill, 1968.

Suetonius, Gaius. *The Lives of the Twelve Caesars.* Introduction by Joseph Gavorse. New York: Book League of America, 1931.

Tacitus, P. Cornelius. *The Annals and the Histories.* Translated by Alfred John Church and William Jackson Brodribb. Chicago: Encyclopaedia Britannica, 1952.

Tenney, Merrill C., ed. *The Zondervan Pictorial Bible Dictionary.* Grand Rapids: Zondervan, 1963.

Tertullian, *Disciplinary, Moral and Ascetical Works.* Translated by Rudolph Arbesmann; Sister Emily Joseph Daly; and Edwin A. Quain. *The Fathers of the Church.* Vol. 40. New York: Fathers of the Church, 1959.

Thomas, W. H. Griffith. *The Apostle Peter. Outline Studies in His Life Character, and Writings.* Grand Rapids: Eerdmans, 1946.

Unger, Merrill F. *The Baptism and Gifts of the Holy Spirit.* Chicago: Moody, 1974.

Westcott, Brooke Foss. *The Epistle to the Hebrews: The Greek Text with Notes and Essays.* 2d ed. London: Macmillan, 1892.

Westcott, Brooke Foss, and Hort, Fenton John Anthony. *The New Testament in the Original Greek*, vol. 2. London: Macmillan, 1907.

DICTIONARY AND ENCYCLOPEDIA ARTICLES

Andersen, H. G. "Enoch, Books of." In *The Zondervan Pictorial Encyclopedia of the Bible*, edited by Merrill C. Tenney, 2:309-12. Grand Rapids: Zondervan, 1975.

Beasley-Murray, G. R. "Baptism, Washing." In *The New International Dictionary of New Testament Theology*, edited by Colin Brown, 1:143-54. Grand Rapids: Zondervan, 1975.

Beyer, Hermann W. "*allotri (o) episkopos*." In *Theological Dictionary of the New Testament*, edited by Gerhard Kittel, translated by Geoffrey W. Bromiley, 2:620-22. Grand Rapids: Eerdmans, 1964.

Beyeuther, E. "Joy, Rejoice." In *The New International Dictionary of New Testament Theology*, 2:352-54.

Bietenhard, Hans. "*kurios.*" In *The New International Dictionary of New Testament Theology*, 2:510-20.

———. "*laos*, people." In *The New International Dictionary of New Testament Theology*, 2:795-800.

Blair, Hugh J. "Antinomianism." In *The New International Dictionary of the Christian Church*, edited by J. D. Douglas, p. 48. Grand Rapids: Zondervan, 1974.

Brown, Colin. "Prophet." In *The New International Dictionary of New Testament Theology*, 3:84-92.

Bultmann, Rudolf. "*agalliaomai, agalliasis.*" In *Theological Dictionary of the New Testament*, 1:19-21.

———. "*elpis, elpizō*. A. The Greek Concept of Hope." In *Theological Dictionary of the New Testament*, 2:517-21.

———. "*zōopoieō.*" In *Theological Dictionary of the New Testament*, 2:874-75.

Coenen, L. "Bishop, Presbyter, Elder." In *The New International Dictionary of New Testament Theology*, 1:188-92.

Connell J. C. "God, Names of." In *The New Bible Dictionary*, edited by J. D. Douglas, pp. 477-80. Grand Rapids: Eerdmans, 1962.

Faulkner, J. Alfred. "Salutations." In *Dictionary of the Apostolic Church*. Reprint, edited by James Hastings, 2:442-44. Edinburgh: T. & T. Clark, 1954.

Foerster, Werner. "*ktizō, ktisis, ktisma, ktistēs.*" In *Theological Dictionary of the New Testament*, 3:1000-1035.

———. "*kurios* in the New Testament." In *Theological Dictionary of the New Testament*, 3:1086-95.

Greeven, Heinrich. "*eperōtema.*" In *Theological Dictionary of the New Testament*, 2:688-89.

Günther, W.; Link, H. G.; and Brown, Colin. "Love." In *The New International Dictionary of New Testament Theology*, 2:538-51.

Hahn, H. C. "Conscience," with additions by Colin Brown. In *The New International Dictionary of New Testament Theology*, 1:348-53.

Harder, G. "Reason, Mind, Understanding." In *The New International Dictionary of New Testament Theology*, 3:122-30.

―――. "Soul." In *The New International Dictionary of New Testament Theology*, 3:676-86.

Harris, M. J. "Quiet, Rest, Silence, Sound, Voice, Noise." In *The New International Dictionary of New Testament Theology*, 3:111-14.

Harrison, Everett F. "Redeemer, Redemption." In *Baker's Dictionary of Theology*, edited by Everett F. Harrison, pp. 438-39. Grand Rapids: Baker, 1960.

Hauck, F. "*markarios, mararizō, mararismos* - The Word Group in the New Testament." In *Theological Dictionary of the New Testament*, 4:367-70.

Herren, A. Van Der. "Peter, Epistles of Saint." In *The Catholic Encyclopedia*. 11:752-55. New York: Gilmary Society, 1940.

Hiebert, D. E. "Peter." In *The Zondervan Pictorial Bible Dictionary*, pp. 640-42. Grand Rapids: Zondervan, 1963.

Hoffmann, E. "Hope, Expectation." In *The New International Dictionary of New Testament Theology*, 2:238-44.

Jeremias, Joachim. "*akrogōniaios*." In *Theological Dictionary of the New Testament*, 1:792.

Krämer, Helmut; Rendtorff, Rolf; Meyer, Rudolf; and Friedrich, Gerhard, "*prophētēs, prophētis, prophēteuō, prophēteia, prophētikos, pseudoprophētēs*." In *Theological Dictionary of the New Testament*, 6:781-861.

Link, H.-G. "Life, *bios*." In *The New International Dictionary of New Testament Theology*, 2:474-75.

Metzger, Bruce M. "The Language of the New Testament." In *The Interpreter's Bible*, edited by George Arthur Buttrick, 7:43-59. New York: Abingdon, 1951.

―――. "Stenography and Church History." In *Twentieth Century Encyclopedia of Religious Knowledge*, edited by Lefferts A. Loetscher, 2:1060-61. Grand Rapids: Baker, 1955.

Packer, J. I. "Defile." In *The New International Dictionary of New Testament Theology*. 1:447-49.

Payne, J. B., "Zion." In *The Zondervan Pictorial Encyclopedia of the Bible*, 5:1063-66. Grand Rapids: Zondervan, 1975.

Peisker, C. H. "Prophet." In *The New International Dictionary of New Testament Theology*, 3:74-84.

Perry, R. E. "Kiss." In *The Zondervan Pictorial Encyclopedia of the Bible*, 3:831-32.

Rees, Paul S. "Holiness, Holy." In *Baker's Dictionary of Theology*, pp. 269-70. Grand Rapids: Baker, 1960.

Rengstorf, Karl Heinrich. "*despotēs*." In *Theological Dictionary of the New Testament*, 2:44-49.

Rupprecht, A. "Slave, Slavery." In *The Zondervan Pictorial Encyclopedia of the Bible*, 5:453-60.

Schmidt, Karl Ludwig. *"diaspora."* In *Theological Dictionary of the New Testament*, 2:98-104.

Schmidt, Karl Ludwig. *"ethnos* in the NT." In *Theological Dictionary of the New Testament*, 2:369-72.

Schönweiss, H. *"epithumia."* In *The New International Dictionary of New Testament Theology*, 1:456-58.

Schrenk, Gottlob. *"dikaios."* In *Theological Dictionary of the New Testament*, 2:182-91.

———. *"hierateuma."* In *Theological Dictionary of the New Testament*, 3:249-51.

Stauffer, Ethelbert. *"agapaō."* In *Theological Dictionary of the New Testament*, 1:35-55.

Strathmann, H. *"marturomai, diamarturomai, promarturomai."* In *Theological Dictionary of the New Testament*, 4:510-12.

Thiselton, A. C. "Flesh." In *The New International Dictionary of New Testament Theology*, 1:671-32.

Walls, A. F. "Peter, First Epistle of." In *The New Bible Dictionary*, pp. 973-77. Grand Rapids: Eerdmans, 1962.

JOURNAL ARTICLES

Best, Ernest. "I Peter II 4-10—A Reconsideration." *Novum Testamentum* 11 (1969): 270-93.

Gundry, R. H. " 'Verba Christi' in I Peter: Their Implications Concerning the Authorship of I Peter and the Authenticity of the Gospel Tradition." *New Testament Studies* 13 (1967): 336-50.

Harrison, Everett Falconer. "Exegetical Studies in 1 Peter." *Bibliotheca Sacra* 98 (1941): 307-19, 392, 459-68.

Kaiser, Walter C. Jr. "The Eschatological Hermeneutics of 'Evangelicalism': Promise Theology." *Journal of the Evangelical Theological Society* 13 (1970): 91-99.

McKelvey, R. J. "Christ the Cornerstone." *New Testament Studies* 8 (1962): 352-59.

Moule, C. F. D. "The Nature and Purpose of I Peter." *New Testament Studies* 3 (1956): 1-11.

Snodgrass Klyne R. "I Peter II. 1-10: Its Formation and Literary Affinities." *New Testament Studies* 24 (1977): 97-106.

van Unnik, W. C. "A Classical Parallel to 1 Peter ii. 14 and 20." *New Testament Studies* 2 (1955-56): 198-202.

———. "The Teaching of Good Works in I Peter." *New Testament Studies* 1 (1954-55): 92-110.

Scripture Index

*Passages in italic represent the consecutive sections of the commentary. Subdivisions within those pages are not listed in the index.

Moody Press, a ministry of the Moody Bible Institute, is designed for education, evangelization, and edification. If we may assist you in knowing more about Christ and the Christian life, please write us without obligation: Moody Press, c/o MLM, Chicago, Illinois 60610.